COMMUNITY DEVELOPMENT

Community Development

Comparative Case Studies in India,
the Republic of Korea, Mexico and Tanzania

EDITED BY RONALD DORE AND ZOË MARS

Contributions from
Vincent S.R. Brandt, Man-gap Lee, Samuel Mushi,
V.R. Gaikwad and Ignacio Algara Cosío

CROOM HELM LONDON
UNESCO PARIS

© Unesco 1981
First published 1981 by the United Nations Educational,
Scientific and Cultural Organization,
7 Place de Fontenoy, 75700 Paris, France and
Croom Helm Ltd, 2-10 St John's Road,
London SW11, United Kingdom

British Library Cataloguing in Publication Data

Community development.
1. Community development — Case studies
I. Dore, Ronald   II. Mars, Zoë
III. Unesco
307'.09172'4   HN980

ISBN 0-7099-0806-7 Croom Helm
ISBN 92-3-101877-9 Unesco

Printed and bound in Great Britain
by Billing & Sons Limited
Guildford, London, Oxford, Worcester

CONTENTS

PREFACE

The origins of this book lay in the International Seminar on the Comparative Study of Community Development held in Seoul, in December 1973, under the sponsorship of the Korean National Commission for Unesco. Following up one of the recommendations of the seminar, the National Commission took the initiative of sponsoring a cross-cultural comparative study under the auspices of Unesco, through the Funds-in-Trust arrangement. This book is an outcome of that exercise.

The book presents four different cases of community development experience — two drawn from Asia (Republic of Korea and India), one from Africa (Tanzania), and another from Latin America (Mexico). Each of these efforts at community development has attracted considerable international attention, and each has been studied intensively. But very little effort has been made to view them in a comparative and cross-cultural perspective. The case studies included in this volume do not pretend to judge their relative superiority or success, but try to identify areas of commonality and some lessons to be learned despite the differences of culture, history and policy.

The way the project grew and implemented is itself an example of a co-operative effort — a joint venture in the best sense of the term. The participating researchers met in April 1976 for a week at the beginning of the project to define the scope of the enquiry and to formulate a common research design. Following the guidelines decided at that meeting, the researchers carried out their case studies at the micro level. Upon the completion of those studies, a meeting of experts and the researchers, held in December 1977, reviewed them and identified areas of similarity and difference. What is presented here is the revised version of the case studies in the light of the deliberations at the meeting, and an introduction written by the co-ordinator of the project, Professor Ronald Dore.

Unesco wishes to place on record its gratitude to the Korean National Commission for Unesco for entrusting this study to it, and for hosting the two meetings; the personal interest taken by the Commission's Secretary-General — Dr Kim Kyu-taik — in this project as in other activities of Unesco, deserves a special mention. Professor Dore of the Institute of Development Studies at the University of Sussex has done a remarkable job as co-ordinator and editor. We are also grateful to the authors of the four studies: Professor V.R. Gaikwad (Indian Institute of Management, Ahmerabad, India), Professor S.R. Brandt (Harvard University, Cambridge, USA), Professor Man-gap Lee (Seoul National University, Seoul, the Republic of Korea), Professor Ignacio Algara Cosío (Metropolitan University, Mexico City, Mexico) and Professor Samuel S. Mushi (University of Dar es Salaam, Tanzania).

It is our hope that this book will serve as useful reference material not only for those who are engaged in community development work, but also for social scientists interested in problems of rural development in particular, and of sociocultural change in general.

Opinions expressed in this volume are those of the authors and do not necessarily reflect the views of Unesco.

The designations employed and the presentation of the material in this publication do not imply the expression of any opinion whatsoever on the part of the Unesco Secretariat concerning the legal status of any country or territory, or of its authorities, or concerning the delimitations of the frontiers of any country or territory.

I INTRODUCTION

Ronald Dore

COMMUNITY DEVELOPMENT IN THE 1970s[1]

Community development is probably as old as recorded history — at least in the sense of attempts, through some kind of collective action, to 'improve' a (predominantly rural) community's material or spiritual life — 'improvement' being defined sometimes by new ideals preached by reforming prophets, more often by reference to other communities deemed in some sense 'more advanced'.

What is a new phenomenon of the last two or three decades is the bureaucratic institutionalization of community development. And once invented, institutionalized community development is, we can be fairly sure, here to stay as long as there are governments which subscribe overtly to developmental goals. The resources devoted to it may wax and wane as development strategies change and as the agencies in charge gain prestige and budgets on a rising tide of optimism and lose them on the ebb tide of disillusionment. The labels may change — as, in the English-speaking world of India, Anglophone Africa and the UN Agencies, the label 'community development', after the disappointment of the inflated hopes of the 1950s, gave way to new pleas for 'integrated rural development', and later for 'a basic needs strategy'. The main slogans associated with the labels may also get worn out and need replacement: the 'felt needs' of one programme giving way to 'participative planning' in another.

But much more interesting than these changes in labels and slogans, or in levels of euphoria, are the real changes, and the range of real national variation in the definitions of 'improvement' which the community development campaigns seek to bring about (for example, the relative emphasis on production or consumption; on efficiency or equity; on productivity or community togetherness) and the similar variation in the methods — of collective or individual action, of exhortation or subsidy incentives, etc. — used to achieve those ends.

The Four Cases Studies: Constraining Environments

The four attempts at deliberate improvement of rural communities which are the subject of the studies in this book have sufficient similarities in means and aims to be brought together under the generic title

13

[Phenomenography of Tanztheater ... ?] *(handwritten annotation)*

'community development'. But equally they are in many respects widely heterogeneous, and much of the heterogeneity is not the result of the adoption of different policy objectives so much as of ineluctable differences in the economic, political and social environment.

The study in the Republic of Korea concerns the pattern of change in four villages during the period of the *Saemaul Undong*, the New Community Movement. This movement, begun in 1970, can be seen as a means of helping to spread to the countryside some of the fruits of half a decade of rapid industrial growth which was already beginning to bring improved living standards to large segments of the urban population. It came, or rather, began to gather momentum, at a time when there were a number of other factors operating to induce a certain dynamism in the rural economy; the growth of urban markets for higher quality goods, new pricing policies and improved terms of trade for agriculture, the steady spread of the rural electricity network. Most important of all, perhaps, accelerating migration from rural to urban areas — and an increase in farm by-employments — bringing within sight the 'hump', the 'turning of the tide', the point at which the secondary and tertiary sectors grow fast enough to absorb more than the increase in the labour force so that the absolute numbers in agriculture begin to fall and the man/land ratio begins to improve.

Improvement efforts in such a setting clearly have a rather more supportive environment than in, for example, the situation which formed the context for the campaigns in the two villages described in the Mexican study. Although per capita income or energy consumption levels are not too different as between the Republic of Korea and Mexico, the distributional pattern and the degree of integration of the two economies seems greatly different. Mexico — partly, no doubt, because of the vastly more dispersed spatial distribution of population, partly because of its much greater ethnic and cultural heterogeneity — has followed a much more dualistic pattern of development. The rural areas of Guanajuato described by Ignacio Algara Cosío have received far less of the spread effects of the dynamic sectors of the economy than the villages studied by Man-gap Lee and Vincent Brandt in the Republic of Korea. They are less linked or oriented to urban markets, less intimately in contact with the urban centres of administration, more in need of the sorts of initial stimuli which can create acceptance of the possibility of change and breed the optimism necessary to catalyse the *will* to change. It was very much as initiators — as 'promoters' — of change that the Guanajuato government team came to these villages in 1974. One indication of the difference between the two countries is the quite widespread rural penetration of family planning practices in the one and much less penetration in the other, a difference reflected in the demographic structure. Children under 15 declined as a proportion of the population in the Republic of Korea from 43 to 37 per cent between 1960 and 1975; in Mexico the proportion remained unchanged at 47 per cent.[2]

In our other two countries, that particular index has actually increased: from 41 to 42 per cent in India; from 46 to 47 per cent in Tanzania. Both count in the World Bank's classification as Low Income Countries. India has a number of centres of highly sophisticated industrial production, one of them, in Bangalore, quite close to the two villages which are the subject of V.R. Gaikwad's study. But they represent such a small part of the economy as a whole that they have little effect in uplifting the rural areas, and have nothing like the capacity to absorb labour necessary to relieve the growing pressure of population on the land. Gaikwad strikingly records an increase in the number of landless labourers — in this basically peasant economy — from 28 million to 48 million between 1951 and 1971. In such a situation, where there is little hope of transferring substantial resources to the rural sector from other parts of the economy, it is understandable that the emphasis of rural development programmes should have been placed in recent years on raising productivity. The Farmers' Service Society whose operations are charted here represents one of the latest organizational channels for doing so, with an emphasis particularly on raising the incomes of the poorer farmers. Its scope is narrow: it does not attempt the broader programme of cultural as well as economic change envisaged by earlier generations of community development programmes proper, whose history Gaikwad describes.

Tanzania has an even more predominantly rural economy, with an even greater need for economic growth to be sustained by increases in agricultural production, but the *ujamaa* villages policy in all its various fluctuating manifestations has aimed at a much more fundamental transformation than the Indian Farmers' Service Society. One consistent theme, and at one stage the central thrust, of the policy was to transform the rural settlement pattern; to create for the first time the sort of nucleated village community which has been the norm in the other three societies for a millennium. Beyond that, attempts have been made, in both of the villages which were the object of Samuel Mushi's study, to create a wholly new pattern of production relations, establishing communal farms and seeking to build a new kind of egalitarian socialist society. Funds have been available selectively, for the support of experiments of this kind — a good deal of it from external aid rather than from any surplus generated by the secondary and tertiary sectors. In Tanzania, even more than in India and the Republic of Korea, the transfer of capital to the rural sector can be seen as justified by the complementary resources available. There is no shortage of land: population densities are still low.

Table I.1 summarizes some of these differences in constraining factors which explain something, though far from everything, of the differences in conception and strategy of the improvement efforts described in this book.

The Purpose of This Study

It will be obvious from what has been said above that it is not a purpose of this book to add to the dreary evaluative-theoretical literature yet another opinion as to whether 'community development' or 'the community development model' is or is not a 'movement designed to promote better living for the whole community through intentional, guided and target-directed change' or alternatively 'a manipulative mechanism of social control' which obscures the true nature and causes of underdevelopment.[3] If there is consensus on the nature of the 'community development model' in the minds of certain promoters thereof in international agencies, that model certainly has only a tenuous relation to what has happened in these four societies. The experiences recorded here are not to be seen as offering evidence relevant to the question whether that model — or indeed community development *tout court* — is a good or a bad thing.

Equally, it was not a part of our intention in planning this study to make a comparative evaluation with a view to awarding accolades to the country which had mounted the best community development programme. We were not engaged in some kind of community development Olympics.

Instead, it was our hope that it might be possible, proceeding in the way that all science proceeds, namely by comparison, to advance our understanding of some of the common characteristics of bureaucratically organized rural improvement programmes — to add to the slowly accumulating body of knowledge concerning what sorts of method achieve what sort of improvement goals under what sets of initial conditions. In the first place, the answers to such questions were sought within countries, in the comparison which each researcher made

Table I.1: Basic Data on the Four Countries

	Population (millions)	GNP (US$) 1976	Per capita energy consumption (kg of coal equivalents) 1975	Land area (ha.)	Primary School enrolments (% of age group) 1975	Industrial Production as % of GDP 1976	Proportion of labour force in agriculture (%) 1970	Proportion of population aged less than 15 (%) 1975
Tanzania	15.1	180	70	6.26	57	16	86	47
India	620.4	150	221	0.53	65	23	69	42
Korea, Republic of	36.0	670	1.038	0.28	109	34	51	37
Mexico	62.0	1.040	1.221	3.18	112	35	45	46

Source: IBRD, *World Development*, Report 1978.

between one village (in the Korean case two) where the development programme was generally counted a success, and one (or two) where it was not. The next step was to see if the interrelations between input and outcome observed in one national setting held good in others, or whether differences in those interrelations as between countries suggested that an important role was played by other intervening variables. The wide differences between the various programmes very much limited the scope of such inter-country comparisons, but nevertheless the programmes did all have a number of important features in common; they all required imaginative initiative, and a distributional honesty on the part of salaried officials, for instance; they all required some kind of group, if not whole-community, action for mutual benefits; they all showed a preference for egalitarian improvements over improvements that increased income disparities, and so on. The reflections on our findings which follow will concentrate on those themes, beginning with the question of community cohesion.

Community Action

The relevance of the notion of 'community' to these various programmes can best be treated under three heads:

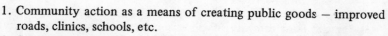

1. Community action as a means of creating public goods — improved roads, clinics, schools, etc.
2. Community action for the simultaneous production by individuals of private goods,
      either because that is more efficient than uncoordinated action,
      or because any exacerbation of inequality which might attend scattered individual initiatives is considered undesirable.
3. The promotion of greater community solidarity as an end in itself, through the institution of collective forms of production.

Only the Indian scheme, with its almost exclusively agricultural emphasis, was without any obvious activity in the first category. The one public good whose construction in recent years is recorded in detail was a tank built by the Public Works Department, in the planning and building of which neither the community as a whole, nor the 37 prospective beneficiaries as a group, played any part. Much the same was true of the other public facilities mentioned — the health centre, schools and community halls. In the programmes of all the other countries community facilities played a central role — dams and wells for drinking and irrigation water, schools, a health centre, the town square, in Mexico; bore holes, a carpentry centre, community shop and communal dairy herd in Tanzania; and an extensive programme of road widening, bridge building, installation of electricity, etc., in the Republic of Korea.

An example of the second category is latrine building, which played a part in the Tanzanian campaign, the greater efficiency of community action coming from the mutual support that a group of similarly-acting individuals can give each other, as well as from the better disease control of universal action, in the benefits of which all can share. The Korean campaigns to persuade *everyone* to switch from thatched to tiled houses, to adopt better rice cultivation techniques, probably also had some scale-economy, efficiency aspects — as certainly did the Mexican procedure, not of attempting community-wide involvement, but of starting activities such as bee keeping, rabbit keeping, pig keeping, fruit growing, etc., by the formation of groups of the like-minded within the village — rather like the block demonstration experiment for new rice-growing practices which over 30 farmers were persuaded to join in one of the Indian villages. The concern not merely for efficiency but also for equality — or for uniformity? — was certainly present in Tanzania and in the Republic of Korea, though the Mexican programme, it appears, viewed with equanimity the prospect that income gaps might grow as a result of the programme's innovations.

As for the third category, the creation of an integrated solidarity community as an objective of the programme, this was most obviously a concern of Tanzanian policy with its objective, at one point central, now apparently soft-pedalled if not abandoned, of creating communal forms of agricultural production. The ideas of equality and brotherhood on which the policy was based are very clearly expressed in the speeches of President Nyerere which Mushi quotes. The problems of establishing efficient and friction-free forms of communal farming when the sentiments of brotherhood and the generous desire to see others equal are not so strong as envious resentment of those who are more than equal — and when a common way for a Tanzanian to describe communal work is as 'working for the government' — are well brought out in Mushi's analysis.

Some of the projects undertaken in Mexico and the Republic of Korea, too, clearly sought to enhance the degree of community integration, if not to the point of establishing co-operative production. The village community centres in the Republic of Korea, the public square

·in Cieneguilla, were built for expressive, not purely for instrumental, activities; they were places where people could enjoy each other's company the better for the physical facilities provided, as well as take *collective* pride in a collective possession.

So much for the various ways the concept of 'community' entered into the aims of the various programmes. What, next, can be said about the way the different social structures of the settlements studied affected the success of these various projects?

Nothing much that is not fairly obvious *a priori*. The most elementary observation, perhaps, is that no development planner looking at a nucleated rural settlement should automatically assume that what he is looking at is a 'community'. In one of the Indian villages, Seshagirihalli, one single festival at which all ate the same food — but sitting in separate caste clusters — was the only activity which brought together all members of the village. Otherwise the three main caste groups lived in spatially separated parts of the village, used different wells — and even schools when they could — and were divided further, as is the case in many villages with sizeable clusters of landless *harijans*, by lines of class — the landed versus the landless — which largely coincided with those of caste. It was perhaps wise that the Farmers' Service Society remained, as Gaikwad stresses, entirely focused on the individual rather than seeking to catalyse community-wide action. The one activity which did require community co-operation — the school support society — was distinctly intermittent in function.

In three of the societies the settlements were all in some sense *gemeinde* in so far as nearly all their residents were born in them, but the two Tanzanian communities were very different. Both were of recent settlement, extremely diverse in ethnic origin, language and background. No traditional basis for solidarity existed, and the vicissitudes of village politics in one of the villages, Lukenge, is a striking demonstration of the fact. One prime condition for being elected headman was the willingness to reduce demands for communal labour to a minimum. As compared with Lee and Brandt's discussion of a 'predilection' for working together in villages in the Republic of Korea and of the positive sanctions of prestige attaching to giving labour and land to the community, it is noticeable that the sanctions Mushi mentions are negative ones — fines for non-performance of communal labour or for not sending children to school.

The other Tanzanian community, Kidudwe, was different from Lukenge, however. It had succeeded not only in maintaining stable leadership, but even in sustaining communal production through the

period when it was going out of fashion. Ironically the core of this cohesion lay in the sense of solidarity generated among 26 families in the
course of a prolonged dispute with officials, occasioned by their *refusal*
to enter a collective farming scheme. As the successful, hard-working
members of an earlier settlement scheme elsewhere which had at first
created individual peasant holdings, they objected to a subsequent
collectivization scheme which would have pooled operations and profits
— forcing them, as they saw it, to share the fruits of their hard work
with layabout neighbours. Paradoxically it was their shared individualism — and, presumably, the willingness to work for future rewards
— which laid the basis for their subsequent collectivism. There is,
perhaps, a general moral in the story: the chances of successful co-
operation are rather different as between self-selected, and on the other
hand heterogeneous 'mixed-ability', groups.

In Mexico, too, the difference between the two villages' performance seems clearly related to different degrees of solidarity, this time of
a traditional kind. Cieneguilla, the more active and successful village,
differed from Carbajal in having a shared Indian 'minority group'
identity, remnants of a distinct ethnic culture, and a unifying religious
organization, all creating a sufficiently strong sense of community for
there still to survive the *faena* form of communal labour which pre-
dated all modern bureaucratic forms of community development.
Additionally, too, Cieneguilla had the *external* stimulus of a long tradition of rivalry with Tierra Blanca — the community where the headquarters of Cieneguilla's municipality were located. They had previously
had to struggle against opposition from Tierra Blanca to get their school
and were eager to respond to any programme that would provide the
resources to further that competition.

The traditional elements of internal solidarity present in Cieneguilla
were found, too, in the villages in the Republic of Korea, which had a
much higher density of community organization, and much greater
cultural and economic homogeneity, than the villages in any of the
other countries. Well before the *Saemaul Undong* started, all of the
villages studied already had that physical symbol of community integration common in many East Asian villages — the village amplifier
system for instant communication to all village members. But there
again the interrelation between community solidarity and successful
programmes seems to have been demonstrated. The strongest social
bonds in the traditional Korean village — the bonds of lineage — divide
rather than unite the village community. The evidence of Lee and
Brandt's study seems to suggest (as one might expect from other con-

texts, e.g. the discussion of national unity and tribal composition in Africa) that community action is most likely to succeed when there is either one dominant lineage in a settlement, or a number of small ones; least likely when there are two or three lineages fairly equally balanced in size.

While community solidarity obviously helps to promote community-wide responses to development programmes, it does not necessarily follow that factional division prevents any kind of positive response. On the contrary, factions, if they are stable, can provide a framework for positive action and factional rivalry can be part of the stimulus. In the Mexican village of Carbajal, the rivalry between the two factions which had formerly led to competing attempts to build schools was reactivated by the dam, and it *might* be argued that the enthusiasm for the project on the part of its promoters was increased to a degree that outweighed (in productive consequences) the opposition of the Celestino faction. When factions are unstable and an uncertainty elements enters into all calculations, however, the likelihood of such a balance between factionally stimulated enthusiasm and opposition being positive becomes rather small.

So far the discussion has been about community solidarity and the possibilities of *evoking* community action. The same applies also to the likelihood of *sustaining* projects started in the course of a development programme. New habits and norms are more likely to be internalized if they are sustained by fairly intensive and supportive interaction between community members; new facilities are more likely to be maintained if there is real shared pride to back community sanctions regarding failures of maintenance. Again, what Meister calls the 'hospitality response',[4] the tendency to respond to official initiatives and undertake projects, only to let them fade away as soon as the promoters move on, is clearly more characteristic of the less united villages. See, for one example, the complete dropping of all the new cultivation techniques in the Indian village after the end of the block demonstration experiment, and not just those which involved risks incurring expenditure.

One should be careful, however, not to generalize too far from the apparent correlation between community solidarity and the success of communal efforts at improvement. Lee and Brandt suggest, first, that community solidarity in the sense of 'a consensus regarding proper moral behaviour and the harmonious settlement of disputes, a predilection for mutual assistance if there is trouble, and a strong sense of common identity in contrast to the world beyond the boundaries' is not a *sufficient* condition for the undertaking of village projects. Nor is the undertaking of village projects a *necessary* condition for rapid improvements in productivity and income which, they observe, have been achieved in other villages in the Republic of Korea by individualistic efforts with little aid from community-wide endeavours. (Gaikwad is even sharper in his judgement that where, in the area he studied, there is evidence of successful agricultural innovation, it has come about almost entirely by private initiative.) Further, Lee and Brandt remind us, some forms of successful co-operation can come not via community sentiment, but through rational individualism. It is when individuals become accustomed to working for their own calculated long-term advantage, and perceive advantages in co-operation which individual action cannot gain, that the conditions for co-operation are best fulfilled — a process which the Mexican study also illustrates.

Community and Equality

So far we have considered primarily *group* differentiation within communities in relation to solidarity and its absence. Equally important is inter-individual differentiation. Those who build on and use traditional forms of solidarity must to some degree accept traditional forms of leadership and traditional structures of inequality. The question is whether the programme seeks to modify those structures or works to reinforce them.

Formal leadership patterns can perhaps be changed more easily than most other aspects of social structure: the *Saemaul Undong*'s insistence on youthful leaders was one way of doing this, and we shall consider leadership matters in more detail presently. Differences of wealth and income, of prestige and cultural resources, however, are a different matter. In peasant communities the structure of inequality is largely determined by property ownership — differential landholdings — and that cannot easily be changed by fiat. The question whether inequalities are to be modified or reinforced applies both apropos of public goods and apropos of facilities for individual improvements.

The problem with public goods is a real one. The landless poor might be mobilized to build a feeder road 'for the good of the community as a whole' but it will not be their produce which the trucks carry over the road. All might make equal contributions to the building of the local clinic, but it will be the better-off farmers who can entertain the nurses to meals and make the most insistent claims on their attention.

The advice of the extension officer may be open to everyone, but it is the richer farmers who are best able to make use of it and whom they are more likely to call on spontaneously.[5] The co-operative may emphasize equality by exacting the same share contribution from everyone, but it is the richer farmers who disproportionately take the loans.

Clearly, the more equal in the community is the distribution of landed property, the less the problem. The view is commonly expressed that without the land reform of the late 1940s the *Saemaul Undong* would have become a very different affair in the Republic of Korea, and in several other parts of the world land redistribution seems a precondition for any kind of development which can benefit more than a favoured few. Education is also an important variable. Villagers in the Republic of Korea twenty years ago, when perhaps 15 per cent of senior house heads had been to school, were much more likely to see the more wealthy enriching themselves under the guise of acting 'for the village as a whole' than today when the literate form a large majority. Nevertheless, even in this country, the problem of community development works accentuating inequalities was a real one.

Our four countries show different reactions to this problem − or rather, let us call it 'phenomenon', for although in our egalitarian age most people would see these effects as 'problems' in two senses − a problem of increasing inequality and a problem of equity, of the unequal ratios between contributions and receipts − some would consider such effects as the cost of progress. An increase of production, the argument would run, is the key to the eventual improvement of the position of the poorest. The innovating initiatives that will change the village economy as a whole − introduce techniques that will eventually percolate to the poorer farmers − are only likely to come from the better off. (A number of studies have shown that the poorest *do* have the lowest aspirations.[6]) One does not have to go quite so far as Meister in believing that *any* erosion of traditional structures and learning of new values is a good thing[7] in order to grant the possibility that exploitation of the 'unequal balance of contributions and receipts' in kind, provided it does not make the poor worse off in absolute terms, may be a necessary step towards shared general benefits.

Implicitly, it seems, the 'cost-of-progress' view is the one taken in the Republic of Korea where there is not much concentration on those issues of equity and equality − where, generally, precise calculations of the inputs and benefits of communal works is avoided, and where, in all four villages, 'there has been some grumbling on the part of discon-

tented elements to the effect that rich and influential men usually
make sure the projects undertaken are of benefit to themselves'. So, for
the execution of road widening, river control works, etc.; the land required was expected to be 'donated' by the owners. There was no disposition to calculate prices and share burdens equally: the individual
commitment to 'the good of the community' was seen as desirable in
itself even though it was often exacted only after the most coercive
persuasion. Clearly, opportunities for the more powerful members of
the community to route paths onto other people's land were not absent
(though limited by what made physical sense). However, it is fairly
clear that there was no simple exploitation of the poor by the rich
through this mechanism. The 'community-as-a-whole' argument can cut
both ways: 'some leading men contributed more than their share of
resources and personal effort' and when piped water and electricity
were installed in Kongju B, the better-favoured villagers in the central
nucleus agreed 'after prolonged deliberation' to subsidize the charges on
the (poorer) villagers living in outlying houses.

In Mexico, too, internal distribution of benefits seems not to have
been such a preoccupying concern, for reasons partly of the objective
situation, partly to do with the nature of the PRODECOR programme.
First, objectively, the local problem was poor land and lack of water
rather than shortage of land, and differences in property ownership did
not divide the communities into employers and labourers, exploiters
and exploited. Secondly, those among the promoters who were ideologically disposed to aim for something more than 'getting some
schemes going somehow and never mind whether it was the rich or the
poor who took part' tended to think in a conceptual framework according to which 'the peasants' as a whole were collectively victims of an
oppressive national structure, itself a part of a global pattern of dependency. Stratal divisions within the peasantry did not figure largely in
their scheme of things.

In India, by contrast, an awareness of the equity problem has been
part of the 'common sense' of rural development planning for many
years. The Farmers' Service Society described by Gaikwad was one
example of a number of institutional devices deliberately introduced in
recent years to correct for power differences in the traditional society
by compensatory measures. Only small and marginal farmers and landless labourers formed the part I group of shareholders who elected five
board members, compared with two board members for the richer part
II farmers. Nevertheless, three of the five elected representatives of the
'little man' proved to be small farmers only in name and — the proof

of the pudding — the pattern of loan operations undertaken by the Society showed clearly a bias in favour of the larger farmers. The heavy guidance provided by the local commercial bank doubtless imparted to the Society an inertial preference for lending to the more efficient farmers more likely to repay their loans even in the absence of overt pressure from the richer and more powerful. But, whatever the reasons, the example seems clearly to illustrate the in-built tendencies of the local social structure to be *reinforced* by government intervention, even when that intervention benevolently seeks to *alter* power distributions.

'Seeks to alter', some would qualify, 'from above'. The conclusion widely drawn in India is that only organization of, by and for the poor can actually help the poor: 'consensual' institutions cannot do the trick. That seems to be what Gaikwad has in mind when he speaks of 'the basic need for building people's organizations in the countryside'. It is even more explicitly spelt out by the Indian Planning Commission in its 1978 *Draft Five Year Plan.*[8]

> Critical for the success of all redistributive laws, policies and programmes is that the poor be organized and made conscious of the benefits intended for them. Organized tenants have to see that the tenancy laws are implemented... Local leaders of the poor have to ensure that ... plans designed for the benefit of these ... groups are effectively administered.

The question of how official, consensus-supported action from above can work to bring this about, however, is one which the plan document does not answer.

It is interesting to speculate why it is that the consciousness of the problem is so much more explicit among planners and intellectuals in India than in the Republic of Korea or Mexico. In part the explanation may lie in the peculiar strength of egalitarianism in the British socialist traditions which have partially shaped the Indian official/intellectual ethos. It might in part be because in the absence of strong community sentiments binding the rich to poor within the villages — given a sense of human otherness between caste and outcaste almost as great as that between blacks and whites in South Africa — the distortion of institutions in favour of the rich is often a good deal more naked and one-way than in the Republic of Korea where a sense of community membership is much more real and *some* of the things done in the name of 'the community as a whole' bring disproportionate benefits not simply to the better off but to the disadvantaged.[9]

Emergent Inequality and Productivity

In the Tanzanian villages there were no existing traditional structures of inequality to be overcome. There was, however, consciousness of a different problem — that of emergent inequalities *resulting* from the differential use of the opportunities provided by government schemes. The earlier emphasis on communal production had, as one of its explicit objectives, the prevention of a situation in which inequalities could grow to the point at which one group of men become exploitative employers of — in President Nyerere's phrase 'live off the sweat of' — another group. Nevertheless, even during the period of emphasis on communal activity, differentiation proceeded steadily. Even in the more closely-knit Kidudwe, holdings within the village ranged from 30 to 3 acres, and one man had 60 acres of rice land elsewhere. The precise processes which lead to these differences are not clear, but it appears from Mushi's account that they predominantly involved individual differences in personal qualities rather than any ascribed characteristics; starting points were not so very different. Some men and women *are* endowed with more energy or more ambition than others, have a greater capacity to restrain their consumption, are cleverer at keeping accounts or manipulating markets or striking up friendships with government officials and co-operative loan officers. The declarations in 1977 that such 'progressive farmers' were to be encouraged with bank loans and other support marked a clear change in policy motivated, Mushi suggests, by the increasing concern with productivity. For too long, it was felt, output considerations had been unduly sacrificed in the pursuit of community and equality.

Mushi's evidence suggests, indeed, that there are formidable difficulties in making communal production efficient. This is understandable enough where social bonds are such that punitive sanctions are looked on as a natural way of ensuring participation in labour on communal farms, and the only acceptable system of distributing rewards is by an immediate share-out of cash whenever there is a crop sale. Mushi suggests, however, that there is no *necessary* trade-off between co-operation and productivity and that the trend to 'kulakism' does not have to be encouraged to ensure output. Perhaps so, but his evidence of the differential productivity of communal and private farms suggests that the means of making co-operation and productivity complementary have not yet been found.

In any case, while most people would accept that co-operation is a good thing and ask how much it is likely to cost in productivity, not everyone would accept the complementary view that kulakism is an evil about which the only question to be asked is how necessary an evil it has become. The moral evaluation of the kulak — which must also affect policy decisions — is more complicated. What is it that makes a first generation kulak? Is it energy, innovativeness, a sharp eye for wilt and leaf-curl, conscientiousness about weeding, careful keeping of accounts, well-calculated investment, thrifty restraint of consumption — in short, all the early capitalist virtues? Or is it the ability and willingness to browbeat and cheat dependent workers, to corrupt and curry favour with government officials and politicians? By most people's values, a kulak whose success depends on the first group of qualities ought not to be treated in the same way as one who owes his success to the second. Nor are they the same when it comes to another kind of basis for policy decision — political calculations as to whether it would be better to leave local leadership in the hands of such big farmers or alternatively in the hands of their vigilant critics — who *may*, of course, be lonely honest men struggling to combat the corrupt favouritism on which kulaks thrive, but may, alternatively, be envious men who are better at wielding the rhetoric of equality to their own advantage than at wielding a hoe. (See Mushi's account of the dispute between the lazy group and the diligent group at Kabuku which led to the founding of Kidudwe village.) In sum, for both moral and expedient assessments of the choice between what Mushi labels the liberal-incremental and the revolutionary-change models — or at least between the alternative Tanzanian policies which he puts in those categories — one needs careful analysis of the precise factors which in Tanzania are productive of class differentiation. Only then can one decide whether to laud the progress of progressive farmers or to condemn the sell-out to the kulaks.

More Help to the Poorest or Betting on the Strong

It is one thing to provide opportunities and facilities equally to all-comers and then view with equanimity the tendency for some people to respond more positively to, and derive more benefit from them than others. It is quite another to channel government assistance selectively to the richer sections of the community in the belief that the opportunities and assistance offered them will produce a higher total yield.

The question has already arisen apropos of the loans policy of the Bidadi Farmers' Service Society. The richer farmers may have got more because they could more forcefully ask for money: they may, alternatively, have been deliberately favoured in the belief that they would make the best use of it — best, here, being defined in conventional banking terms of rates of return, probability of repayment, etc. (One test would be whether this is a village where the greater tendency of the poor to use their loans for consumption and have difficulty in repayment does indeed mean that unrecoverable loans are disproportionately those made to the poor, or whether this is one of those villages where any such tendency is outweighed by the greater ability of the more powerful rich to breathe defiance and refuse to repay.[10]) The ostensible structure of the bank, however, was on the contrary designed to provide loans selectively in order to *redress* existing inequalities — even, presumably, if the cost was lower rates of return.

The same tension between the claims of efficiency and equality in the distribution of government assistance can be seen in the Republic of Korea — this time in the distribution of resources between communities rather than between individuals. Policy has oscillated. At first additional assistance was given to the most 'progressive' villages — to those which had made the best use of their ration of 335 bags of cement and were generally thought to be more advanced. Later the policy switched to one of greater benefits for the communities rated most backward.

Which of the two principles predominates, of course, will depend a great deal on the way the community development movement is perceived by central policy-makers — whether it is a welfare measure to keep the villagers happy while the industrializers get on with the *real* job of building a modern economy, or whether substantial productive contributions from agriculture are counted as an important part of, and springboard for further stages of, a comprehensive strategy of economic growth.

Participation

The rhetorical literature about community development frequently calls for programmes built on the felt needs and spontaneous initiatives of 'the people'. The wave of new interest in extensions of democratic control in universities and industrial organizations which has been apparent in the rich countries since 1968 has penetrated the resolution-making of international development conferences to the extent that popular participation is now a key element in the 'basic needs strategies' elaborated in recent years. Perhaps four different strands of thinking enter into contemporary discussions of 'participation' in rural development programmes.

1. A project that seeks to fill a need that villagers have been aware of all along has more hope of evoking their co-operation than one that does not.
2. Irrespective of whether the project coincides with long-felt needs or new persuasion-implanted needs, sharing actively in the decision to undertake it can enhance the sense of commitment to see it through.
3. Most bureaucrats and professionals (e.g. doctors in the context of community health discussions) are rogues who only too often delight in mystifying the populace in order to sustain their own privilege and power. They need to be put firmly under popular control.
4. Irrespective of whether the last is true or not, the individualistic values of independence, autonomy and refusal uncritically to accept institutional authority are, or ought to be, universal values and people should, therefore, have — or, better, seize — as much opportunity for controlling their own fate as possible.

The first two strands are typical of the early 1950s discussions of community development; the last two — not, of course, often spelt out in quite the stark form stated here — are more characteristic of the antinomian 1970s.

None of the arguments appeared to be much reflected in the strategies adopted in our four countries except in Mexico. In Tanzania, Mushi records, 'officials were largely responsible for initially suggesting — and financing — the projects', participation was left to the second-level activity of decision-making concerning the management and co-ordination of established projects — and here considerable leadership problems arose. In India, the one project which the FSS undertook was the block demonstration experiment which the manager explained to the 35 farmers involved the night before the bench-mark survey was due to begin, and got their co-operation in a single meeting; not surprisingly the offer of a guaranteed return, taking all the risks out of farming for one year at least, was too good to miss. In the Republic of Korea rather more was left to local initiative: the initial 335 bags of cement were apparently delivered to each village without a package of instructions and there was an explicit emphasis on 'transforming consciousness' towards self-help, but during the early years after the first experimental distribution of cement, there was 'forceful direction, stimulus and support from the local administration' and meetings were held 'mainly to mobilize enthusiastic participation and to organize details'; it was only later that village development councils began genuinely to take their own initiatives, partly because by then they had more experience and confidence. Only in Mexico did the programme start off with the very deliberate strategy of not taking initiatives until some sort of consensus about priorities emerged from meetings with the villagers. The problem with that strategy proved to be the boredom/attendance attrition problem. In Carbajal, at least, villagers stopped bothering to come to the meetings before the consensus had been reached.

What can one say about participation on the basis of these four case studies? Not very much since in none of our pairs of villages was there much contrast in the degree of popular participation in project selection and design. And too many other variables intervened for us to be able to draw conclusions from the intercountry comparisons. It is true that more got done and stayed done in the more directive villages in the Republic of Korea than in the more participative Mexican ones, but correlation does not necessarily indicate causation, and not the least among the relevant mediating variables is the pattern of established attitudes towards authority. Close official direction, once from *yangban* officials, now from ex-army officers on motor bikes, is a more accepted and familar phenomenon in the Republic of Korea than in Mexico where, as Algara makes plain, even the official forces of law and order may deem it prudent not to press pursuit of an outlaw murderer.

Secondly, effective participation does require skills and understanding — which can be learned and taught. Korean village development councils took more initiatives as they grew in experience and confidence. In Tanzania, one reason why Kidudwe was more effective in the 'secondary level' participation of running projects was because someone in the village had taken a book-keeping course and *knew* how to be effective.

The third point concerns the relation between participation and, not efficiency, but equality. It is an obvious enough point that the more decisions are left to the village community, the more they will reflect that community's power structure. Participation can be a recipe for rule by local bosses; bureaucrats *can* be more concerned with justice than local bully boys or magnates. None of our case studies records any such direct instance, though the reservation of a number of seats for official appointees on the Board of the Farmers' Service Society was doubtless justified precisely as a means to ensure fair play and prevent abuses of participative powers.

Fourthly, as the Mexican and the Korean cases illustrate, the factional dissension which is a common consequence of development projects may well be exacerbated by participation. Neither the Carbajal shopkeeper who wanted to take surplus water from the dam, nor the six landowners in Kongju A who put up a bitter resistance to being made to donate land for a road, were powerful enough to prevail: in each case they finally succumbed to an overwhelming majority. Less participation and stronger control by outside officials would not have altered the outcomes but might have prevented these issues reaching the levels of contentiousness that they did reach.

So far the discussion of participation has turned on the selection and execution of communal projects — roads, meeting halls, dams, etc. In those other phases of improvement programmes which concern individual family consumption practices, health, etc., it is quite clear that talk of participation in deciding programme priorities is more cosmetic than anything else. Often the central planning authorities do *not* want communities to choose in the light of their existing preferences, but to acquire new preferences first. The attack on conspicuous consumption, both traditional (weddings and funerals) and modern (electrical appliances for display rather than use) as part of the campaign in the Republic of Korea, the effort to break down caste in India, the Tanzanian hygiene campaigns and attempts to induce villagers to engage in co-operative production, are cases in point. The whole *raison d'être* of these campaigns depends on a belief on the part of the educated elite that they know better, and no amount of populist cant about participation can disguise that fact.

This last statement, I trust, can be accepted both by those who would feel that sometimes, indeed, the educated elite *do* know better (even if, as Gaikwad's study indicates, the Lingayats will accept the untouchables' hospitality and eat their biscuits only when an official is present, that at least is something) and also by those who would assume that any difference between what the people want and what the elite think they ought to want is always merely a 'contradiction between the *interests* of the community on the one hand, and those of the ruling elements in society and their "external agents" on the other' (my emphasis).[11]

Mobilization

'Mobilization' is another favourite term of the development literature. In once sense its implications are at variance with those of the demand for 'participation', conjuring up, as it does, an image of strong leaders whipping up popular enthusiasm for projects, the goals of which have been set by those leaders or their bureaucratic superiors. In that sense to say 'effective mobilization' in the context of community development campaigns at least is to say 'effective leadership' — an elusive quality whose importance the case studies demonstrate better than they help to define its nature. As between the two Mexican villages, as between Kidudwe and Lukenge in Tanzania, and as between the Ich'on pair of villages in the Republic of Korea, the difference in leadership styles and effectiveness was very clear, and it would be strange if this were not a contributory factor to the differences in performance. In part the differences in leadership style are a reflection of the different social structures of the villages: more cohesive villages *do* tend to breed more confident and dynamic leaders than communities whose leaders are required to perform a continuous balancing act between factions. In part, doubtless, the differences are the result of the accident of personality. But in part, also, there are systematic determinants which can be manipulated by bureaucratic organizers. The insistence, in the Republic of Korea, on young leaders (an insistence backed on occasion by 'strong advice' as to whom villages should elect) is a case in point.

There is a different sense of 'mobilization'. It can also mean — and this is a concern expressed in the Mexican, the Tanzanian and the Indian studies — the creation of economic-interest and political organizations capable of articulating the demands of the villagers *vis-à-vis* governmental authorities.

Within that general category, however, at least three sub-species of 'mobilization' need to be distinguished. The first is the sort of mobilization which some of the Mexican promoters had in mind — the development of an 'authentic class consciousness' in the peasants to increase their powers of organization and levels of information in order to create conditions for the 'acquisition of power by the majority' of the people, as a precondition for tackling the fundamental structural problems which are the underlying causes of backwardness. Not all the Mexican team by any means saw the PRODECOR programme primarily as an opportunity to work along these lines. But the moral authority of this approach, and particularly its appeal to young people, was such that attempts to better conditions in tacit acceptance of existing political structures were labelled, disparagingly, 'assistentialist' manifestations of the 'improvement approach'. (The appeal presumably comes in part from the association with the heroism of revolutionary movements, in part from the claim to tackle the 'fundamental', not merely epiphenomenal, problems.) Whether it was the fact that some of these 'radical promoters were most interested in theoretical criticism and spent less time on field action of any kind', or whether it was the general permeation of this approach into the team's activities which was more important is not clear, but it is not hard to guess why the programme eventually fell into disfavour with the Guanajuato government. There are occasions — if a government is explicitly revolutionary, or even if a reformist urban-based party is seeking to forestall revolution by breaking the power of a rural aristocracy — when this form of mobilizational activity oriented towards central state politics can be tolerated or even supported by state organs. But 1976 in Guanajuato was not such an occasion.

If this first sub-species of mobilization activity might be called mobilization of the underdog in the hope of one day making him top dog, the second might be called 'watchdog mobilization', the creation of village-based organizations which are capable of protecting their members' interests — for example, the sort of organization of small and marginal farmers which, as Gaikwad envisages, might ensure that genuine small farmers got all the five seats supposedly allotted to them on the FSS Board, or the sort of organization which, in Mushi's words, summarizing Nyerere's injunctions, can 'expose reactionary leaders who hide selfish motives behind the label of . . . "national interest" . . . or even extension officials who are not doing their job'. The Kidudwe founder group who successfully fought for just compensation is an actual example of such a group. The likelihood of it being a genuine objective of a community development campaign to create such organizations may be thought *a priori* to depend on the proportion of officials who see themselves as likely candidates for denunciation as corrupt reactionaries.

There is a very thin dividing line between that sort of 'watch dog' mobilization and what one might call 'hungry dog' mobilization — mobilization not to ensure justice, to control abuses of authority, to gain one's *fair* share of *universal* benefits, but to demand for one's own village a larger share of *discretionary* benefits. Mushi speaks of the village council system as 'boosting the village's capacity to bargain with the state agents of change for essential development inputs and resources'. His description of the *risala*, the prepared recitation of the village's achievements to visiting officials, ending in the demand for more funds, shows how the bargaining is done. What his discussion of the questionnaire responses further shows is that the 'demanding' habit can come to be a substitute for the effort habit. When you are likely to end up with more in your pocket if you spend your time agitating for another subsidy than if you spend it weeding your maize, who would choose to weed maize? And even if there is enough time to do both, if both the total and the marginal returns to the two activities are disproportionate, it is not surprising if farming comes to seem a mug's game and 'development' comes to be equated with 'getting money from the government'. At Kidudwe the total government subsidies for projects amounted between 1971 and 1977 to about Shs 230 per worker per year (at a cost of a labour contribution worth about Shs 95 per worker per year), not counting the 'initial massive support' at the time of the foundation of the settlement. This compares with income from agriculture of Shs 460 per worker per year in Kidudwe, Shs 164 in the region taken as a whole. (Clearly not a very high proportion of Tanzanian villages could have consistently received aid on quite this scale.)

The 'dependency syndrome' is a standard theme of the rural development literature, and rightly so, for the device of offering subsidies or cheap loans to promote socially desirable activities is a very common and useful one which governments would understandably be reluctant to do without, and it is hard to draw a clear line between providing a nutrient stimulus to − basically self-reliant − effort, and inducing a breast-fed dependency.[12] The campaign in the Republic of Korea also used special loans and subsidies on a large scale to stimulate projects, but without preventing quite a sizeable, and apparently increasing, number of projects being internally generated with little external assistance. A whole host of factors must enter into any explanation of the difference between the Republic of Korea and Tanzania in that regard, but one is the fact that in the Korean villages the villagers themselves contributed around 75 per cent of the estimated total costs whereas in the Tanzanian villages it was less than 30 per cent. This, in turn, is doubtless related to living levels. In the Republic of Korea they were such that it was reasonable to expect villagers to make cash as well as labour contributions; in Tanzania where ready cash is much scarcer (as well as accounting skills and money collectors), it becomes difficult to ask for contributions except in the form of labour. And in capital-scarce, labour-abundant societies, the labour content of most projects may seem very small by conventional accounting methods.

As between 'watch dog' and 'hungry dog' mobilization, the first is clearly desirable, the second clearly undesirable *to those who by and large accept* the legitimacy of the system the watch dogs are trying to keep efficient and clean, accept the value of self-reliance, and accept that the allocation problems which beset all state systems in this late-twentieth-century age of the developmental welfare state are not best solved by the principle of greasing the wheel that squeaks loudest or feeding the dog that barks most furiously. The distinction is not generally made in the literature on mobilization, class consciousness and popular organization, however, largely because those concerned with the topic either explicitly or in a generally romantic implicit way, do not accept the premises just listed and are in fact primarily concerned with 'underdog' type mobilization in order 'fundamentally' to change the system. And if 'underdog' mobilization is the ultimate objective then indeed both 'watch dog' and 'hungry dog' mobilization are equally to be applauded as providing a preliminary stage.(Though things are likely to go better for the society *after* the revolution if it was made by watch dogs than if it was made by hungry dogs.)

To be sure there are some, perhaps many, state systems that are so far beyond the capacity even of a legion of watch dogs to reform into efficiency and cleanliness that the only sensible thing to do is to concentrate on underdog mobilization. Marxists, of course, assume that all except socialist states are of that kind, but it is surprising how much of the writing on popular organization, by people who would in no sense accept the label anarchist, seems to assume that all states, capitalist or socialist, are inevitably of that sort.[13]

Constraining Frameworks

The preceding discussion will do as a preliminary approximation, as an introductory comment on 'mobilization' and its place in the literature, but it is not adequate for a full discussion of the extent to which the solution of local problems is dependent on, or constrained by, national structures or policies, because it assumes that underdog mobilization always aims at revolutionary changes of structures. But underdog mobilization for the *reformist* change of *policies* is also possible — from minor changes of agricultural credit or pricing policies to more major (structural?) policies like land reform. There is very little reference in these papers to specific national policies as important constraints to local development, or to specific policy changes as the objective of peasant organizations' campaigns. Instead there are references, in the Mexican and Tanzanian papers, to the common 'dependency' idea that developing countries have a choice between an open, externally oriented pattern of development and a self-contained, self-reliant national one, that the choice fundamentally determines the possibilities of rural community development, and that the self-reliant autonomous development pattern is likely to be better in that respect. This view can be held without prejudice to the issue of whether a switch to that development pattern requires as a precondition a revolutionary shift in the internal power structures, but it is usually associated with the view that (the 'compradors'/multinationals being so deeply entrenched) such a shift will prove necessary.

Exact mechanisms linking the community development projects described here to the more or less 'open' pattern of development adopted by all four countries are not easy to pin down. It is true that community development schemes directed towards cash-crop production for export have a particular vulnerability, but there were no examples of that. The difficulty of access to health services in the mountain villages covered in the Korean study are, one might think, clearly related to the fact that, in the Republic of Korea's open economy, a half of the graduates of some of the nation's major medical schools are practising in the United States. But doctors are somewhat exceptional: the people who provide nearly all the rest of the large range of skills Korean villagers are dependent on are not in an international market. In Mexico, price structures, and particularly the prices for the knitted goods which villagers produce, *might* be more favourable to them in a closed economy but that would almost certainly mean that the Mexican wearers of knitted goods would be worse off, and it would also mean there would not be those pockets of comfort in Mexican villages supported by labour migration to the United States. The case for thinking that escape from a dependency relation would make a fundamental difference to rural development problems is not an easy one to make, but that does not prevent it from being a frequent point of reference in debates on the subject, as it was in the conference which was convened for preliminary discussion of these reports.

Complementary Resources

To return to the other sense of mobilization — of community resources for community betterment, mobilization against nature or against poverty rather than against the government — it is an obvious point that communities differ enormously in the potential resources at their command. The one resource that all the villages described had in common was surplus labour (though diminishingly so in the Republic of Korea). It is easy enough to talk of 'releasing the creative energies of the people' by imaginative schemes to create employment, but the chance of doing so successfully depends on the complementary resources available. Where there is underground water to be tapped, rainfall to be trapped, turbulent rivers to be tamed, chemical or genetic knowledge which can fructify hitherto arid soils, hitherto unregarded grasses and the skill to turn them into baskets, or into paper, waste organic matter to be fed to pigs, the outline of a possible community development programme becomes clear. In the Korean villages, buoyant urban markets plus new technical knowledge made possible new more profitable use of land resources. The Tanzanian villages had access to additional land if they could also buy the equipment to exploit it. The Indian villages, by contrast, offered far fewer opportunities for releasing creative energies; small patches of grazing to support a few sheep; new ways of growing rice which, as the block demonstration experiment showed, added greatly to the risk of loss for small net increases in average income; doubtless some unused clay somewhere could be turned into bricks to make a community hall or pavements or a school. But little more. With their poor soils and lack of water, the Mexican villages were not so very obviously better off. There was a real question whether the pig farm in Cieneguilla made sense given that the feed was largely trucked in over some distance rather than produced on village fields.

It is sometimes said that there is no such thing as a natural disaster, only disasters which man-made social structures fail to cope with. One might compromise with the implied assertion and agree that some disasters are more natural than others. Likewise, poverty in some communities is more natural and intractable than in others. Some rural areas are so ill-endowed with resources that the only thing to do is to get out of them as soon as industrialization elsewhere in the economy provides alternative livelihoods and makes that possible — though certainly, in some circumstances, the alternative of rural industrialization espoused by Gaikwad makes a lot of sense.

Bureaucracy and Creative Opportunism

However well or poorly endowed with material resources a village is —

but obviously more so when it is poorly endowed — there is a need for creative imagination in seizing opportunities that might otherwise remain unperceived. There is a need, too, for 'creative opportunism' in mobilizing the motivational resources which the local culture and social structure make available as the fuel for collective effort. Both the ideology of community development and the reality of the problem of rural poverty imply the need for spontaneity, flexibility, local initiative, decentralized decision-making.Yet the very idea of a community development *programme* involves deliberate planning, budgeting, rule-bound and even-handed decision-taking in the distribution of resources; in short, bureaucracy. How can the two be reconciled? Can the bureaucracy be charismatized, or must all intimations of charisma in the village be bureaucratized?

Let us look in turn at the three links in the chain: the village leader, the relationship between him and the lowest-level bureaucrats — the village-level workers — and thirdly, the bureaucrats themselves.

Not much more can be said about village leaders on the basis of these four studies than has been said already, except to commend to the reader Lee and Brandt's close analysis of the wide variety of leadership styles, both successful and unsuccessful, within a range of not too dissimilar villages; skill in taking soundings before trying to lead a committee to a decision; a cosmopolitian acquaintance with the outside world; a respected gravity of manner; youth, age and experience; courteous willingness to listen to everybody; or a peremptory assumption that everyone will automatically accept one's advice, coming from the richest house in the dominant lineage; or not being rich or from a dominant lineage: the variety of ingredients in successful leadership defies generalized prescription and suggests that perhaps one ought not to generalize from the case of Don Pancho, the successful leader mentioned in the Mexican study, to any other Mexican situation — except perhaps to say that a leader needs to be respected, though the qualities which evoke respect can vary widely. So, perhaps, can the *need* for leaders. A comparison between the Tanzanian and the Korean questionnaire responses suggests that there was a greater degree of understanding and agreement with government policies in the latter, producing, in spite of a great deal of grumbling, a disposition to cooperate with *Saemaul Undong* policies which makes strongly persuasive leadership less necessary.

Paradoxically, apropos of need, it is where the need is greatest that the leadership is most likely to be weak or lacking. Men like Don Pancho in Cieneguilla with a good grip on their own village and useful links to the outside world are likely to have started development initiatives and got concessionary advantages from government agencies irrespective of whether there is a community development scheme or not. They also ensure that their village gets a goodly share of the resources which a new programme makes available. It is precisely the villages that lack a Don Pancho, and that are likely to be the non-receptive ones, that have the greatest need for effective leaders.

As for the link between official and village leader, what are the factors which are likely to make it most closely approximate to the ideal state of easy co-operation in the disinterested pursuit of the development programme's objectives?

There are, to begin with, certain devices which can be used deliberately to manipulate feelings of identification. The Korean device of giving village leaders the right to a postage-free postcard service was one, and doubtless the trips to training centres where they rubbed shoulders with important people also served to enhance the sense of privilege. The habit of the Ich'on D leader of dressing like an official and receiving villagers with the same manner indicates, presumably, that the policy was successful. None of the other countries tried anything similar; in Mexico (though not in India or Tanzania) it would perhaps have seemed to the young promoters of the PRODECOR campaign to be at variance with the egalitarian ideology which they brought to their work. Predominantly youthful, not career officials but members of an *ad hoc* agency, the overt and confident assumption of superior status which came more readily in the other three countries (what in post-Confucian societies is called 'the official is noble; the people, base' syndrome) perhaps did not come so easily to them, which does not alter the fact that their resources of power and money — as well perhaps as of education and class background — gave some of them clearly superior status (see Ricardo's brush with the municipal president over the plans for the village square).

Nevertheless, even where a status and power gap between official and people is accepted, the *size* of the gap is a crucial variable. The possibilities of meaningful co-operation between official and villager when there are fears that application for a loan might lead to compulsory sterilization — as Gaikwad reports there were fears among landless labourers in Bidadi — are surely not very great. The size of the gap varies depending on a number of factors: bureaucratic traditions (and here the colonial heritage of India and Tanzania is surely no advantage); overt differentials of salary and privilege (whether the official comes on bicycle or jeep, to begin with); differences in educational level; and class background, combining in some societies to make a cultural gap which it is hard to bridge. (The potential for a wide cultural gap of that kind was perhaps greatest in Mexico, and it would be interesting to know whether the more theoretical radicals of the promotion team who were reluctant to get into field work were from high-status families and had difficulty communicating with peasants.) That, among these factors, the importance of bureaucratic traditions should not be exaggerated, is suggested by Lee and Brandt's paper which records a remarkable transformation in the bureaucrat/village relation in the Republic of Korea — from one of 'humble subservience, awe, resentment, fear' to one of great 'equality and mutuality'. They attribute this, possibly, to the spread of education — the definitive narrowing of the once wide culture gap — and to the impact of what one can only call ideological 'revivalism' within the bureaucracy, and a conversion of the organization from a dominant concern with law and order administration to genuinely developmental functions.

Co-operation between official and village leaders in the pursuit of common objectives is one thing; co-operation in maintaining a cosy symbiotic exchange relationship is quite another. Village leaders are potentially — if both the norms and power distribution in the community and in the bureaucracy permit it, and all too often they do — in a 'gate-keeper' position which they can exploit to their own advantage. The official has grants and subsidies to offer, but wants guarantees of a performance that he can report to his superiors as a success, and for that he depends on the village leader's co-operation. The villagers want credit and fertilizer, or a house-rebuilding loan, or the sympathetic ear of a licensing department, and it is the village leader who has the ear and the confidence of the man who dispenses these things. Gaikwad records one village leader, R, whose exploitation of his gate-keeper role was so blatant that he actually forbade — and because of a foothold in higher-level politics was able to forbid — any direct contacts between his followers and officials.

The distinctions between official/village leader co-operation in pursuit of programme objectives, and their co-operation in mutually profitable exchange is not a sharp one, however. Don Pancho in Cieneguilla, the lordly *Saemaul* leader in Ich'on D, and the village chairman in Kidudwe, undoubtedly benefited from their pivotal position in terms of ego-satisfaction, and probably materially too. The relevant question is the balance between self-interest on the one hand and, on the other, the desire to do a good job or to benefit others, a balance which all too often gets tipped decisively towards the first.

How much it does so depends to a large degree on how far the lower level officials let it do so, on how effective they are in their job. 'Effectiveness' depends, of course, on the role in which the village-level official is cast, whether it is expected to be purely facilitative, inspirational or positively entrepreneurial. Each would require different combinations of knowledge, subject matter skills, perceptiveness, tact, conscientiousness, commitment and enthusiasm.

Knowledge and skills can be taught and tailored to the required role; perhaps, to some degree, perceptiveness and tact can also be developed by training centres. What training courses do very little about is conscientiousness, commitment and enthusiasm — which is perhaps why they are so little discussed as factors in bureaucratic efficiency (not a profitable field for the highly articulate salesmen of the training mystique), but they are, as a recent perceptive study of Kenya shows, of the greatest importance particularly for the efficiency of the field officer working on his own initiative in a village situation.[14]

What makes such a worker keen to do a good job? Organizational devices, is the standard answer of those who design public administration systems, and clearly that is an important part of the answer. To start with, tasks should not be absurdly daunting, as the task of a village-level worker in India given a bicycle and ten to fifteen villages to 'develop' clearly was. Then there is the question of how his attachments to his organization affect his morale. The village-level worker is typically at the bottom of an inverted pyramid: Ministries of Health, Agriculture, Welfare, Housing, Environment, Small Industries, Home Affairs, they all funnel their contacts with the villagers through him. It may well be hard for him to develop organizational commitments, reinforcing his goal commitments, to them all. The Mexican promoters working more often in competition with rather than as the agents of the other agencies, had the advantage that with their separate organizations — and their monthly seminar-like meetings — they were better able to develop an *esprit de corps* — though one presumably diminished by the temporary nature of the agency; there was no question of a career commitment and careers were not on offer; the thought of where they were to get their next job was bound frequently to intrude.

Selection and recruitment policies are clearly relevant. Some people have suitable personalities for promotional work and others do not. None of our studies offers much information about the backgrounds of officials though it is a safe guess that the Mexican programme which did *not* make formal educational qualifications a criterion for recruitment as a promoter was exceptional in that regard — only, perhaps, because Mexican bureaucracy in general is less bureaucratized than that of other countries where educational qualifications, being 'objective', are seen as acceptable criteria in a way that judgements of personality suitability cannot be. Where education is a criterion it is commonly also the case that those with higher levels of formal education are preferred — in spite of recent evidence from Kenya that those field officers with experience of secondary education were less likely to be keen to do a good job and to be effective than those with lower levels of schooling.[15]

The other organizational devices relevant to work motivation and effectiveness are reporting systems and incentive systems — generally, in most bureaucracies founded on a belief in original sin, with the emphasis on punitive sanctions for non-performance. The ineffectiveness of routine reporting systems and their tendency to breed ritualism and dishonesty, recrimination and hence lower morale, are widely known, but the systems are nevertheless widely persisted in. Gaikwad's account of the Ramanagaram TDB illustrates: a programme which could spend on average a mere Rs 1.8 per person per annum was nevertheless (using how much of its exiguous resources on its reporting system?) able to record that among its 140,000 population exactly 2,156 people had been converted to contraception.

The Korean example suggests, what one might have suspected anyway from much other evidence, that far more important than reporting systems in determining levels of commitment and conscientiousness is the dominant 'ethos', the prevailing ideology of the organization; the extent to which there is a *general* commitment to the organization's goals to reinforce each individual's commitment. A favourable ethos can be created simply out of group loyalty, a shared desire to see one's organization widely esteemed. It is easier to create that ethos, however, if there is commitment to the goals of the organization — if the community development programme is imbued with an ideology that the officials actually believe in. Apparently, from Lee and Brandt's account, the *Saemaul Undong* ideology, an amalgam of 'scientific rationalism, the work ethic, communal spirit, national patriotism and support from the Park government', was such an ideology. Perhaps the less clearly formulated ideology of the Mexican programme fulfilled the same role for its promoters too — certainly, it seems, for certain individuals like the murdered Dr Kleruu mentioned by Mushi, the ideology of *ujamaa* socialism had a similar quality — though again one comes back to the other link in the chain, the official-villager relation. The case of Dr Kleruu who was killed by farmers opposed to the co-operation plans he was urging on them, reminds us that the animating ideology needs not only to provide a basis for enthusiasm on the part of the officials, it also has to be a basis for a reasonable degree of rapport with the villagers. The sorts of ideology which can make promotional bureaucracies both keen and efficient and the conditions under which they do so might well repay further study.

What would also repay study, and is a little more obviously researchable, is the real cost-effectiveness of different programmes, and of the role of the bureaucrats in them. The facilitating framework of the programme seeks to promote development in the village by feeding to it two kinds of resources: physical resources on the one hand, and guidance, information and inspiration provided by animators or extension agents or promoters on the other. For the same budget, one can have less of one and more of the other. And everywhere there seems to be a tendency for budgeting funds to gravitate towards the latter — staff costs — rather than the former. Anyone who has seen an official committee designing a 'programme' or even a rural development seminar with many official participants discussing one, will have noted the loving attention which is given to details of staffing, transport, training, hierarchies and co-ordinating committees.[16] Such matters are more often debated with enthusiasm and expertise than are details of farmers' cultivation practices and how they might be changed. So much so that one may be forgiven for suspecting that in the budgeting of programmes, staff needs have first priority and direct material provision of resources takes what is left over. The Ramanagaram TDB budget quoted in the Indian study devoted 5 per cent of its expenditure to the housing of project staff and 1.5 per cent to housing the rural poor. That may not be typical, and for none of the programmes discussed — a lot of their staff costs being embedded in general administration budgets — was it possible to make an accurate assessment of the balance between material and staff costs. But the evidence of the relative costliness of staff, and of their frequent ineffectiveness, is sufficiently strong to suggest a simple rule: never provide information and guidance (embodied in bureaucratic personnel) if the provision of useful material resources is a feasible alternative. (The rule is likely to have the greater force, the greater the gap between bureaucratic salaries and farmers' living levels.) The device in the Republic of Korea of starting its community development campaign by delivering 335 sacks of cement and some steel reinforcing rods to each village is a rare and pertinent example.

Several topics have been mentioned which would repay further study, but this introduction, will not conclude with the usual platitudinous call for 'further research'. A good deal of research has already been done; and the lessons drawn by each of the authors from their case studies are reasonably well known. The reason why that knowledge has little effect on policy, however, is not so much because of ignorance as because of selfishness. Too many people have an interest in continuing to act in ways that waste resources and squander opportunities for genuine development because it is in their interests to do so — and I have in mind not only villagers who seek to enrich themselves at the expense of other villagers but also, and especially, officials who are content with ritual target fulfilment provided only that they can conform to the expectations of superiors whose own concern, in their turn, is to feed the hypocrisies and illusions of their political masters.

It is not so much research as honesty of purpose that is in short supply in the community development field.

Notes

1. The editor acknowledges his debt to all those who participated in the Seoul Symposium which considered the preliminary report of these studies. Many of the ideas in this Introduction found their first expression in the discussions of the Symposium. He would also like to express his indebtedness to Ethel Royston for cheerfully and efficiently undertaking much laborious typing and retyping.

2. IBRD, *World Bank Report* (1978), p. 102.

3. For such exercises, see Alpheus Manghezi, *Class Elite and Community in African Development* (Uppsala, Scandinavian Institute of African Studies, 1977), pp. 39-68, and all the polyanna theorists — du Sautoy, de Schlippe, etc. — whom he is at pains to attack.

4. Albert Meister, 'Characteristics of community development and rural animation in Africa', *Community Development* (Rome), no. 27-28 (Summer 1972), p. 105.

5. See the studies by Polly Hill (*Studies in Rural Capitalism in West Africa*, Cambridge, 1970) and S.J. Eldersveld *et al.* (*The Citizen and the Public Administrator in a Developing Country*, Scott, Foresman & Coy, Illinois, 1968) quoted in Manghezi, *Class Elite and Community*, p. 55.

6. See R.N. Haldipur, 'Community development and Panchayati Raj', in India, Indian Council of Social Science Research, *A Survey of Research: Sociology and Social Anthropology*, vol. 2 (1974), p. 46. For a discussion of the ability of co-operatives to embrace the poor in nineteenth-century Britain and contemporary Africa and Latin America, see UNRISD, *Rural Co-operatives as Agents of Change: a Research Report and a Debate* (Rural Institutions and Planned Change, vol. 8), UNRISD Report no. 74.3 (Geneva, 1975), pp. 71-5.

7. See Meister, 'Characteristics of community development', p. 100.

8. Page 15, para. 1. 98.

9. For a review of the tenuous and variable relations between objective conditions of inequality and the emergence of egalitarianism see Barrington

Moore's recent book *Injustice: The Social Bases of Obedience and Revolt* (London, Macmillan, 1978).

10. For a discussion of the evidence for big farmers being more likely to default on loan repayments, see M. Lipton, 'Agricultural finance and rural credit in poor countries', *World Development*, vol. 4, no. 7 (July 1976), p. 546.

11. A. Manghezi, *Class Elite and Community*, p. 58.

12. For a discussion of the patron state apropos of dependency, see UNRISD, *Rural Co-operatives*, pp. 94-6.

13. For a general expression of the view (in relation to the futility of community development) that there are no local or personal problems which are not, fundamentally, an expression of national or social ones, see Manghezi, *Class Elite and Community*, pp. 39-68.

14. David K. Leonard, *Reaching the Peasant Farmer: Organization Theory and Practice in Kenya* (University of Chicago Press, 1977), especially Chapter 6 on motivation.

15. David K. Leonard, ibid., Chapter 6.

16. See M.P. Moore on 'programmitis', 'The bureaucratic perception of policy options', *IDS Bulletin*, vol. 8, no. 2 (September 1976).

II COMMUNITY DEVELOPMENT IN THE REPUBLIC OF KOREA

Vincent S.R. Brandt and Man-gap Lee

1 THE NATIONAL SETTING FOR KOREAN RURAL DEVELOPMENT

Geographic Features

Korea consists of a peninsula extending about 450 miles south from the northeast Asian mainland. In addition there are some 3,500 adjoining islands, most of which are small and rocky. The latitude is about the same as that of Syria, Spain, North Carolina or southern California, and the area of the whole peninsula, about 220,000 square kilometres, can be compared with the British Isles, Romania or New Zealand. Most of the country is mountainous; only 20 per cent of the land area is flat enough for cultivation. The northern and eastern sectors are almost entirely mountainous, while the western and southern sectors contain most of the rice-growing areas. Major rivers run from east to west or from north to south. Because of the irregularity of both the western and southern sea-coasts there are many harbours, but the difference between high and low tide on the west coast is so great that navigation there is difficult.

Korea has a monsoon climate intermediate between the continental climate of China and the marine climate of Japan. Four seasons are clearly discriminated, and the winter is fairly cold. Therefore barley as a winter crop can be cultivated only in the central and southern parts of Korea. Nevertheless Korea has a long growing season with 50 to 60 per cent of total precipitation concentrated in June, July and August. The timing and amount of rainfall, which is uncertain, is a crucial factor in determining good or poor harvests.

History

A relatively homogeneous native culture prevails throughout the peninsula, and Korean, an Altaic language, is spoken everywhere. Nevertheless the influence of China, which borders on Korea in the north, has been profound throughout its history. As a self-governing, centralized, bureaucratic-agrarian kingdom, Korea also modelled most of its political institutions on those of China.

After the liberation from Japan in August 1945, Korea was divided along the 38th parallel by the military authorities of the Soviet Union and the United States, which occupied the northern and southern portions of the peninsula respectively. Subsequently two governments were established; the Republic of Korea in the south in 1948 and in 1949 the Democratic People's Republic of Korea in the north.

— In 1950 the Korean War broke out. It lasted for three years. As a result most of the modern urban-industrial facilities were destroyed, and millions of people lost their lives. A great deal of geographic and social mobility also took place during this period.

Administration

When the military government took over in 1961, it made only a few changes in the system of local administration inherited from the previous regime. The elected local councils were dismantled, and other local officials who had been elected were appointed by higher authority.

The administrative structure of the country is outlined in Figure II. 1.

Figure II. 1

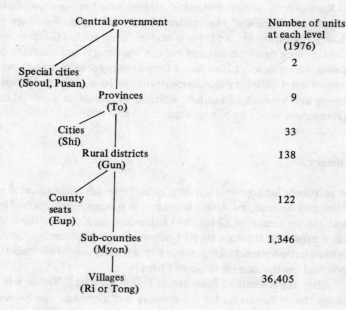

	Number of units at each level (1976)
Central government	
Special cities (Seoul, Pusan)	2
Provinces (To)	9
Cities (Shi)	33
Rural districts (Gun)	138
County seats (Eup)	122
Sub-counties (Myon)	1,346
Villages (Ri or Tong)	36,405

In rural areas the basic unit is the village, which is either a single natural community or (more frequently) comprises a number of separate hamlets and neighbourhoods depending on settlement patterns. Often a *ri* is divided into two neighbouring sections (as in the case of the sample villages described in this report) that correspond more closely to sociological and geographic communities. The national average of about 27 *ri* in each *myon* and 10 *myon* in each *gun*, conceals considerable regional variation. As of 1975 there was an average of 74 households and 389 persons per village (*ri* or *tong*). Except for sparsely settled mountain communities on the islands, most villages are within 10 km of the *myon* office.

The sub-county or *myon* office is staffed by full-time government officials, most of whom are recruited locally. Each *ri* or *ri* section has a headman, who is appointed from among village residents by the *myon* chief for a two-year period, usually after consultation with influential local farmers. The position is in a sense honorary, since the village head or *ri* chief is paid only a token salary by the government; but the burden of work is heavy. The village head is responsible for compiling a large variety of statistics, supervising tax collections, and mobilizing village labour for various projects — mostly work on *myon* roads. He must constantly travel back and forth between his village and the *myon* office relaying a steady stream of orders, exhortations, public health directives, and agricultural advice. He tries to represent the interests of his fellow villagers to the authorities. In addition, he is charged with the general responsibility of promoting loyalty to the regime, social harmony, and general community development. Although each village household (except for the very poor) is expected to contribute a small amount of rice annually to recompense the village head for his efforts, perhaps making his total remuneration $300 to $400 a year, only well-to-do farmers can usually afford to occupy this position.

Population

The population of the Republic of Korea in 1975 was about 35 million living in an area of 98,757 square km. The population density is 354 persons per square km, which makes the country one of the most densely populated areas in the world — particularly considering the fact that only 20 per cent of the land area is cultivable. The population of the Democratic People's Republic of Korea has been estimated at about 15 million.

This high population density in the south is the result both of natural increases and the fact that a great many refugees moved south. In 1960, the natural increase rate was estimated at about 2.8 per cent. As a result of population control policies the rate of population increase had declined to about 1.7 per cent in 1974.

Recent years have also seen rapid urbanization. In 1935, ten years before the liberation, 93 per cent of the population lived in rural areas (places with a population of less than 20,000). By 1975 only about half of the population lived in rural towns and villages. In 1945 72.5 per cent of all households in the Republic of Korea were engaged in farming, but by 1974 the percentage had decreased to 40.2 per cent, and there has even been an absolute decline in the total farm population: from 15 million to 13.5 million between 1967 and 1974.

Rapid population growth is related to development in many ways: the pressure of population on the land is so great in the Republic of Korea that the average farmer has only about two acres. One result of the massive rural-urban migration is that 20 per cent of the country's entire population (or about 7 million people) now live in a single primate city, Seoul. Other cities have also grown rapidly, and consequently through the country formerly underemployed agricultural labour has been made available for industry in large numbers. Where rapid population growth exists with limited resources, there is the likelihood that the benefits of economic development will be unfairly distributed or spread very thin.

Economic Growth

Immediately after the liberation from Japanese rule in 1945, the Korean economy was in a state of total chaos, both because of the abrupt severing of ties with Japan accompanied by the departure of Japanese managers and technicians, and because of the separation of the peninsula into Soviet and American spheres of influence. In addition there were communist guerrillas operating in the south. And finally there was the outbreak of the Korean War in 1950, during which nearly all modern industrial facilities were destroyed.

During the latter half of the 1950s some reconstruction was carried out, and a start was made at drawing up a comprehensive plan for economic development. Such development efforts were interrupted by the fall of the Rhee government in 1960 as a result of corruption and maladministration. Subsequently there was a period of almost a year of

political and economic disorder and instability until the military *coup
d'état* in 1961. The first five-year economic development plan was
implemented by the new military government in 1962.

Growth rates have risen since then, to an average of 9.4 per cent p.a.
between 1962 and 1975, compared with 4.4 per cent in the years 1953-
61. Per capita income reckoned in 1961 at $83, one of the lowest in
Asia, was around $700 in 1976. Exports have increased dramatically,
the balance of payments has moved steadily away from the large
deficits of the early 1960s and the domestic savings ratio has steadily
risen from close to zero to 17 per cent of GNP.

Tables II.1-II.2 give an indication of the structural transformation of
the economy in these years.

Table II.1: Sectoral Shares in the Economy, 1962-76 (%)

	GNP by sector				Labour force by sector			
	Primary industry	Mining & manufacturing	Other	Total	Primary industry	Mining & manufacturing	Other	Total
1962	40.3	13.3	46.4	100.0				
1966	38.9	15.9	45.2	100.0	57.9	10.8	31.3	100.0
1971	26.5	24.4	49.1	100.0	48.4	14.2	37.4	100.0
1976	20.4	36.0	43.6	100.0	44.6	21.9	33.5	100.0

Source: Bank of Korea, *Economic Statistics Yearbook* (1975, 1977).

The percentage contribution of agriculture to GNP has fallen by one
half over the period — with a much smaller decline in agriculture's proportion of the labour force. Whereas agriculture is estimated to have
contributed 50 per cent of the increase in national income between
1954 and 1961, it contributed only 8 per cent of the increase in
1962-74, compared with 40 per cent for mining and manufacturing. On
the other hand, the priority given to agriculture in the three successive
five-year plans has somewhat increased according to an analysis by the
Korea Development Institute. 'Increase of agricultural productivity'
occupies fourth place in its listing of objectives for the First Plan.
'Increase of farm household income' moves up to second place for the
second, while 'self-sufficiency in food, increase of income of farmers
and fishermen, and improvement of their living conditions' is put in
second place in the 1972-6 plan.[1]

The *Saemaul Undong* has been a major means of working towards
this objective.

Agriculture in Korea before 1962

Most farmers in Korea were poor and illiterate until quite recently. In 1937 under the Japanese occupation only 19 per cent of a total of 2,810,000 farm households (both North and South Korea) owned all their own land. Another 26 per cent were combined owner-tenants, while over 55 per cent were pure tenants. The average size of these landholdings was less than 1.5 hectares. By 1949 the average landholding in the Republic of Korea, where population density is higher than in the north, was 0.87 hectares; only 45 per cent of all paddy fields were irrigated.

The land reform enacted in 1949 and implemented the following year improved the farmers' social and political situation considerably, but because of the very small individual landholdings, population pressure, the lack of advanced agricultural technology, and the import of cheap foreign grain, extreme poverty was still widespread. Although the number of tenant farmers had been reduced from over 50 per cent of all rural households to only about 10 or 20 per cent, average farm income by the late 1950s was only about one-half that of urban workers.

In 1958, 87 per cent of the income of rural households came from farming, and of this 78 per cent derived from the sale of crops. Rice was the most important income source (43.4 per cent), with vegetables next (9.5 per cent). If the statistics are considered for persons engaged in fishing and forestry or those living in regions where rice cannot be grown, the concentration of most farmers on rice and vegetables is even more striking. Non-crop income accounted for only 1.7 per cent of the total.

During this period (1955-62) population growth remained a major cause of rural poverty. Even though the rural population was declining as a percentage of the total, it continued to increase in absolute terms. The population per household also increased from 5.9 in 1954 to 6.2 in 1958. At the same time, however, there was enough increase in the total land under cultivation to raise the area per household from 0.88 hectares in 1954 to 0.92 hectares in 1958.

Although the great majority of farmers were cultivating their own land or operating as owner-tenants, nevertheless some 10 to 15 per cent of adult males had no land of their own. Most of these were agricultural labourers who were unemployed or underemployed for much of the year; even owner-farmers were not able to keep busy during the slack season.

If we compare the Republic of Korea with Japan and the United States in 1958, we can see that farm productivity was extremely low (Table II.2).[2]

Table II.2: Comparative Agricultural Productivity, 1958

	Production per unit of land area	Working hours	Productivity per 100 hours (1 *suk* equals 4.9 bushels)
Korea, Republic of	1.70	180	0.94 *suk*
Japan	2.34	183	1.28 *suk*
America	1.18	4	29.50 *suk*

The lack of modern agricultural technology at this period was related to the low level of rural education. According to a 1958 survey, only 36 per cent of household heads had attended school, although some of the others had learned the Korean alphabet in special classes for adults.

Rural Development

In 1962 at the start of the First Five Year Plan the military government carried out a number of administrative changes affecting rural development. The office of sub-county chief was made appointive instead of elective, and the lines of authority from the Home Ministry down to local levels through the provincial and county administrative offices were tightened. In 1963, although a civil government was re-established and national assemblymen were again elected from rural districts, the local councils, which had previously been elected, were abolished, so that there was virtually no popular participation in the highly centralized administration of rural areas.

Two important measures designed to aid farmers and promote agriculture were carried out at this time. The Agricultural Co-operatives Federation and the Agricultural Bank were merged in an effort to improve the hitherto inefficient and corrupt administration of fertilizer distribution, grain collection, and agricultural credit. In addition a law was enacted to prohibit the lending of money at usurious interest rates to farmers and fishermen. The law was extremely unpopular in rural areas, however, and proved to be largely unenforceable.

A more important change, however, was the government's new attitude towards economic development, as reflected in the five-year plans. The First Five Year Plan provided for the increased production of fertilizer and pesticides, the promotion of commercial cash crops and animal husbandry, a rigorous family planning programme, and the rearrangement of farm land. In spite of these measures agricultural productivity and incomes grew rather slowly during the 1960s, and, with the rapid development of the urban industrial sector, the increasing gap between rural and urban production and living standards received more critical attention.

Significant positive changes outside the five-year plans were taking place in both the economic and cultural aspects of rural society during the 1960s. First, there was the establishment of village radio amplifiers in the late 1950s and 1960s in order to develop communication in rural areas. Then with the mass production of cheap transistor radios after 1964, it became possible for a great many farm families to receive broadcasts directly in their homes. Secondly, as part of the National Reconstruction Movement (NRM) established by the military government in the early 1960s, NRM workers residing in villages undertook a number of development activities, including the promotion of family planning and various kinds of cultural programmes. Third, there was a rapid improvement in educational facilities. The 1958 survey cited previously showed that over 64 per cent of household heads had never been to school. By 1969 this percentage had been reduced to 43 per cent. In other words, more than half the members of any village council would have received by 1969 a primary school education.

Other changes were taking place in the countryside that were closely related to the five-year plans. First, was the rapid urbanization already recorded. In some areas, farmers now complain of a labour shortage, and women and girls spend much more time working outdoors than in the past.

Another important change was the increase in agricultural productivity, particularly in the area of commercialized agriculture — the production of cash crops for the growing urban markets. A greatly expanded agricultural extension service administered by the Office of Rural Development promoted the use of improved seed varieties, a more effective use of fertilizer and pesticides, better farming skills, and the use of various kinds of small machine. Although grain production remained relatively stagnant, much greater amounts of vegetables, livestock, silkworms and fruit were produced during the 1960s. Since 1972 grain yields also have increased sharply. Rice production, which in 1958 had been 235.6 kg per ten acres, was 285 kg in 1965 and 429 kg in 1976, thanks in part to the introduction since 1972 of new 'miracle' rice seed varieties. In recent years rice yields have improved to the point where the country is now self-sufficient, and domestic rationing ended in 1976.

The third change associated with government planning has been the improvement in farmers' living standards as a result of the improved land population ratio, greater farm productivity, and higher prices for agricultural products. We stated earlier that farm income in 1959 was only half that of urban labour. By 1974, the average annual income of farmers was roughly on a par with that of workers in the cities. Much of the improvement has occurred quite recently as a result of higher rice yields and higher, subsidized rice prices. Average farm income in 1974 was some 40 per cent higher than the previous year.

Notes

1. KDI, *Korea's Economy: Past and Present* (May 1975), p. 25.
2. The Agricultural Bank, *Agricultural Year Book* (1959), p. 77.

2 THE HISTORY OF COMMUNITY DEVELOPMENT

In the Republic of Korea numerous attempts to promote rural development have been made by the government as well as by civil and religious agencies. Some projects were designed to develop the rural economy through increased agricultural production, while others tried to eliminate what were regarded as backward, irrational or unsanitary practices. Efforts were made to promote organization and co-operation. Educational policies have fostered more scientific attitudes, persuading farmers to carry out wedding and funeral ceremonies or ancestor worship rituals with less extravagance. In other cases efforts were made to reform the social system.[1]

Community development (CD) programmes proper were first instituted in 1958, when the Central Committee of Community Development was established under the Ministry of Reconstruction. Initially pilot villages were selected in four provinces, to which trained development leaders were sent. Village residents were encouraged to draw up their own development plans, which were carried out through voluntary, co-operative participation. Where local resources were inadequate, the government supplied half the cost of technical services and supplies using counterpart funds for US aid. Most of the villagers'contribution was in labour.

By late 1961, the number of demonstration villages had increased to 818 in 86 counties, and there were 368 paid CD specialists at work. It is impossible to evaluate the success of this particular developmental effort, however, because of the social, economic and political instability that prevailed during the period. The Syngman Rhee government collapsed in 1960, and in May 1961 Chang Myon's Democratic Party government was overthrown in a military *coup*.

In March 1962 all village development programmes were transferred to the Office of Rural Development, where they were integrated with the agricultural extension service. As a result there was an interruption of CD efforts in the sense of co-operative, self-help village projects based on local initiative. However, the movement for National Reconstruction established in 1961 to modernize people's attitudes and ways of thinking did have some of the objectives of the community development movement. So did the Federation of Agricultural Co-operatives after its merger with the Agricultural Bank in 1961. These comprehensive co-operatives — not really co-operatives in the generally accepted sense of the term but rather branches of a centrally directed bureaucratic organization — included extension functions as well as marketing, input supply, credit, storage and processing functions.

It was not until 1970 that the government initiated a new kind of CD programme. In April 1970 at a meeting of provincial governors President Park proposed a national movement, the *Saemaul Undong* (New Community Movement), to improve the quality of life in villages. In July of the following year, also at a meeting of provincial governors, he discussed the need to raise farmers' income and develop their desire for modernization. In the following month he adopted as the New Community Movement's slogan, 'diligence, self-reliance, and co-operation'.

President Park assigned primary responsibility for administering the New Community Movement (NCM) to the Ministry for Home Affairs, and officials were appointed to deal with provincial development, urban development, rural development and home improvement. At the same time, a national meeting of mayors and county chiefs was held to discuss and evaluate the new programme.

During the first year of operation (1970-1) 335 sacks of cement were supplied to each of 33,267 villages, so that the residents could improve their local environments. They were urged by officials to use the cement during the slack season (winter) to widen and improve local roads and bridges, or to construct small irrigation and flood control projects, meeting halls, public laundry facilities, storage tanks for compost, etc. The choice of projects and means of carrying them out were to be left to the farmers, although in actual fact local officials exerted a great deal of influence on village decision-making.

On the basis of its evaluation of the results of village improvement efforts during the first year of operation, the government further developed the organization, ideology and operating procedures of the New Community Movement (NCM) in 1972. In March of 1972 a central committee of the NCM was established, made up of the vice-ministers of ministries concerned. In July an elaborate school and study centre for NCM leaders was built in Suwon. During 1972 the policy was to provide 500 sacks of cement and 1 ton of steel reinforcing rods to each of the 16,600 villages that were judged to have made the best use of the supplies furnished during the previous year. By this means it was hoped that a spirit of constructive competition would be established, and that the other, less successful villages would be stimulated to emulate those that received additional help. Each of the 'developing' 16,600 villages was again encouraged through frequent and intensive contacts with officials of local administrative agencies to carry out further road, bridge-building, and flood-control projects as well as the construction of water supply systems. The cost of supplies furnished in 1971 was about $8,000,000, while $6,000,000 was invested in 1972.

In December 1972 an intensive propaganda campaign was launched, emphasizing that the NCM had the highest priority in terms of national policy. There was further consolidation and intensification of the movement in 1973. Presidential prizes and decorations were awarded to the most successful village leaders. At the National Conference of Educators in March 1973 the President again stressed the importance of modernizing and rationalizing Korean society by means of the New Community Movement. A special NCM bureau was set up in the National Agricultural Co-operative Federation and in the Office of Rural Development. Sections dealing with NCM affairs were established in city, provincial and county governments.

A system was established in 1973 under which all villages were classed into one of three categories on the basis of degree of self-reliance and development: (1) *'basic'* (undeveloped) villages (18,415); (2) *'self-reliant'* (developing) villages (13,943); and (3) *independent* (developed) villages (2,307). The amount of funds invested by the government increased from $6 million (1972) to $42 million in 1973 and $60 million in 1974. Since experience had shown local leadership to be a crucial factor in successful village development, NCM leaders were elected in each village to organize and direct an increasingly large variety of projects. The contribution of farmers in 1974 was valued at $204 million, making a total investment in that year of $264 million.[2]

As the momentum of rural CD efforts increased, the movement was extended to the urban sectors of society, taking on the attributes of a 'nation-building ideology', NCM organizations were established in schools, factories and urban neighbourhoods. President Park envisaged the adoption of the *Saemaul* ideology (in particular, the principles of self-help, diligence and co-operation) by the entire nation as a means of increasing productivity and strengthening the state against the threat of North Korean communism. Accordingly, at the National *Saemaul* Training Institute, members of the urban elites were enrolled together with village leaders, sharing the same spartan life, uniforms and rigorous schedule of ideological indoctrination. It was hoped that in this way divisions based on class, status and the differences between rural and urban backgrounds could be subordinated to a sense of joint participation in national development.

In spite of the severe stagflation resulting from the abrupt rise in oil prices during 1974, government expenditure on NCM increased by more than 40 per cent over 1973. At his New Year's press conference in 1975, the President defined the NCM as a national spiritual revolution for a better life. He added that the NCM goal for 1981 (the last year of the Fourth Five Year Plan) was an average annual farm household income of 1,400,000 won, or about $2,800. Also in 1975 a special official was appointed in each county with the rank of vice-county chief, to promote and co-ordinate New Community activities. Additional emphasis was placed on increasing farm income and wages, on NCM education and on NCM activities in urban areas.

In general terms, NCM rural projects during the initial three years of operation (1971-3) dealt mainly with such environmental improvements as replacing thatched roofs with tile, metal or composition, the widening of roads and bridges, and improved water supply, both for irrigation and for household use. Emphasis during the next three years (1974-6) has been more on increasing village economic self-sufficiency, and accordingly there has been a slightly greater emphasis on raising income levels and agricultural productivity, but it is to a closer examination of those objectives that we now turn.

Notes

1. Yun Byung-gil, *The Historical Aspects and a Comparative Study of Cases in the Community Development Movement of Korea* (Report of the third National Policy Seminar, Graduate School of Public Administration, Seoul National University, 1972).

2. Ministry of Home Affairs, *Saemaul Movement* (1974), pp. 52-3.

3 OBJECTIVES

Since the New Community Movement was initially conceived and implemented as a national programme to be carried out in every village according to a central master plan, the general objectives have been fairly uniform throughout the country. In its most succinct and frequently reiterated form, the goal of the New Community Movement is to 'transform the consciousness' of Korean farmers so that they can bring about the modernization of rural society through their own efforts. The philosophical and ideological emphasis has been overwhelmingly on changing farmers' attitudes and customs so as to promote 'diligence, co-operation and self-help'. Thus the centralized planning and direction of the movement has been balanced by an insistence that villagers should accept primary responsibility for choosing and carrying out local development projects. During the first few years (1970-3) when the movement's momentum was being generated largely by administrative initiative and pressures from outside the villages, similar projects emphasizing improvements to the village environment predominated everywhere. Subsequently, as village development councils acquired more experience, know-how and confidence in their ability to take effective action, New Community projects have increasingly reflected the particular desires, needs and ecological constraints or potential of different communities.

Economic Transfers

Although a major objective of the movement has been to redress the imbalance between rural and urban incomes and living standards, economic transfers from the industrial to the rural sector have until quite recently been relatively minor. The total amounts invested by the government in cement, reinforcing rods and loans for replacing thatched roofs have been quite small; most of the input has come from farmers' labour and other village resources. Since an additional special bureaucracy was not recruited for the New Community Movement, administrative expenditures have also been kept to a minimum.

Much more substantial investments have been made in agricultural development since 1961 (and particularly after 1971) by the government through the Office of Rural Development (extension service) and the National Agricultural Co-operative Federation (rural credit). But while the work of these agencies has been co-ordinated with the NCM, it is not, strictly speaking, part of the movement itself. Another major investment by the government has been in subsidies to maintain relatively high rice prices for the farmer. These substantial expenditures — for extension work, rural credit and price subsidies — have served to foster an environment of relative prosperity in rural areas within which the New Community Movement has been able to thrive. To the extent that they represent an essential ingredient in its success, they can be regarded as in fact a transfer from the industrial sector. Nevertheless, self-sufficient rural development continues to be a basic principle of the New Community Movement. The local leaders receive no pay, and as villages reach the coveted 'independent' status, they can expect less outside help. In each county there are some larger, publicly financed projects in such areas as irrigation, flood control, electrification or road-building, but in such cases contributions by villagers of labour, land and other resources are also proportionately greater.

Political Links

Another major objective of the New Community Movement has been to improve the morale and self-confidence of the farming and fishing population. Official statements stress that involvement in successful village self-help projects will promote the farmers' love of community and that as a result his national patriotic feelings will also be intensified. Each villager is continuously urged to contribute his best efforts, both in order to improve his own living standards and to strengthen the country. The spirit of the New Community Movement is frequently referred to as a 'driving force for nation building'. Local officials give lectures on such matters in every village at least once a month. Thus the NCM has tried to expand national consciousness by involving farmers and fishermen from even the most remote communities in a nationwide effort. The rural population has been called on to work harder and produce more, not just for their own welfare but to make the nation strong and contribute to the process of development.

Official pronouncements — in the press, at the New Community Leaders' School in Suwon, and in the villages — do not fail to attribute the progress of the last five or six years in general and the improvements in the farmer's environment associated with the NCM in particular, to the leadership of President Park Chung Hee. It is not possible to determine precisely whether the movement was originally launched with the objective of promoting greater grass-roots political support for the President, but it has in fact achieved that result among a substantial portion of the rural population.

Economic Change

Many of the projects have focused primarily on raising agricultural productivity and farm income. In each village the mix is somewhat different, depending on the felt needs of the community, local resources, and the ecological potential for developmental efforts. During the initial phase of the movement diversified projects having an immediate and important effect on daily life were emphasized in order to maximize the movement's psychological impact, reinforcing the farmer's confidence in his own ability — through hard work and co-operation — to bring about positive changes.

During the planning and initial implementation of the movement the assumption was made that rural economic stagnation in the Republic of Korea was due to the farmer's traditional attitudes: his conservative resistance to change, his fondness for costly ritual and ceremony, his laziness in winter accompanied by a predilection for drink and gambling, and the priority that he gave to kinship over community solidarity. The strategy adopted by the NCM planners was therefore designed to jolt the rural population out of such habits and through the inculcation of a spirit of 'diligence' co-operation and self-help' bring about a cultural transformation leading to modernization. The extent to which these assumptions were correct, and the question of how much NCM self-help projects have actually contributed to raising rural incomes will be discussed later.

While NCM pronouncements often cite increased agricultural production and a rise in the personal incomes of farmers as major objectives, more emphasis is placed on changing the villagers' mentality and improving the quality of village life, both by establishing co-operative, harmonious relationships, and through building a more convenient environment. There has been a slight shift since about 1974 in the kinds of projects favoured, however, both by the authorities and by village development councils. Particularly in the case of the more developed villages somewhat greater emphasis is now being placed on projects primarily designed to augment agricultural production. The Office of

Rural Development (ORD) and the National Agricultural Co-operative Federation (NACF) are the agencies directly concerned with promoting agricultural development and rural economic growth through outside inputs, while the NCM is more concerned with persuading farmers to build a new kind of community themselves.

Political Change

As a result of the first two years of operations, NCM administrators were convinced that effective local leadership was a crucial factor in the success of village self-help efforts. Accordingly, younger activists have usually been supported by *myon* officials for leadership roles. Although the principle has been maintained that villagers should elect their own NCM leaders, the election frequently resembles more traditional ways of reading a consensus. The opinions of the most influential local residents, which are likely to be well co-ordinated in advance, will usually determine the election's outcome. Official pressures are also taken into consideration in view of the importance of maintaining good relationships with the local bureaucracy.

The problem of ensuring that local community leaders are loyal to the central authority does not really exist in the Republic of Korea; administrative control of political affairs in rural areas is so tight that there is little possibility of anyone exercising effective leadership who is opposed to the existing government.

Korean villages have a long tradition of self-government. While most major decisions were made informally in the past by a small group of influential men, meetings open to all adult males were also held periodically at which anyone could freely express his ideas. The result was a form of consensus politics controlled and directed by a small elite. The NCM has utilized this tradition, not to propagate general political skills, but specifically in an attempt to involve the entire population emotionally as well as physically in selecting, planning and carrying out development projects.

Cultural/Educational Exchange

The transmission to villagers of 'modern' values has from the beginning been a major objective of the movement. Korea's urban elite saw themselves as having adopted enlightened modern attitudes, while country folk were thought to be still enmeshed in conservative ways that obstructed progress. As a result during the early stages of the movement many rural customs and practices were denounced, and efforts were made to eliminate them. More recently, however, New Community education has recognized greater merit in traditional village institutions, so that the emphasis has been more on fostering rational scientific thought than on the wholesale rejection of the past.

Social Relational Change

Koreans are extremely proud of the quality of their family life. In fact, the traditional ethical emphasis on family and lineage cohesion has been so great that one of the objectives of the NCM has been to reduce what reformers have regarded as an exaggerated concern with kinship duties and loyalties. Accordingly, regulations providing for simplified family rituals have been enacted, and there has been a good deal of attention given in NCM propaganda to the importance of subordinating family and kinship goals to the interests of the entire community.

Building a strong sense of community and fostering co-operation within villages has been a primary goal of the NCM from the beginning. So far, during the first six years of its existence, the movement has placed more emphasis on collective effort and disciplined restraint than on individual freedom or the fulfilment of personal ambition.

Consumption

Farmers are constantly also being told through official channels that diligent community effort will increase their individual wealth and raise living standards. Higher rural standards of consumption have been a central objective of the New Community Movement from its inception. 'Let us lead a better life' has been a slogan frequently used by President Park. Many of the self-help projects have been aimed at providing better housing, a more sanitary and convenient water supply, village electrification, and the encouragement of diversified cash-crop agriculture to increase farm income.

Family planning has been promoted through an elaborate, intensive, and relatively successful programme in rural Korea for almost fifteen years, and so has not been a major concern of the NCM. Nor has health care, which at the village level has had a low priority in the Republic of

Korea until very recently. As living standards improve, farmers have been increasingly anxious to obtain better medical treatment, but the shortage of doctors and nurses in the countryside makes it necessary for most villagers to visit clinics in town or cities.

NCM policies have tried to eliminate what the central government authorities regard as wasteful and immoral expenditures. In addition to regulations limiting the scope of ritual and ceremonial expenditures, local officials provide periodic 'instruction' (sermons might be a better term) as part of the general effort directed at eliminating 'immoral' behaviour in the villages, both through outside pressure from local officials, and by mobilizing community opinion against drunkenness, gambling and delinquency among young people.

It will be apparent that the New Community Movement operates on two levels: (1) as a comprehensive national ideology designed to promote productive modernization and covering every aspect of behaviour; and (2) as the organizational context for specific self-help projects planned and carried out by villagers with official help and encouragement. Thus, efforts by the Office of Rural Development (agricultural extension services) to develop new rice varieties are supposed to be infused with the *Saemaul* spirit, even though the extension service is quite separate organizationally from the NCM. On the other hand, an irrigation project carried out in winter to make village paddy fields more suitable for the new seeds developed by the ORD provides an example of a typical NCM activity. The Park government is trying to promote both rural economic growth and CD within a larger context of the psychological mobilization of the entire country for national objectives, and official rhetoric is usually couched in these terms. It is important, therefore, in analysing and interpreting the results of NCM efforts to be specific about the level of activity under consideration.

4 INSTRUMENTS OF THE NEW COMMUNITY MOVEMENT

Administrative Structure

Although many governmental agencies are involved in various aspects of the NCM, the main supervisory responsibility has been assigned to the Ministry of Home Affairs, which also controls local administration and the police. At the highest level, however, it is the Office of the President (the Blue House) that establishes the movement's basic principles and has the ultimate authority with regard to both planning and execution.

Every month at the Cabinet Council a detailed report is made to the President on New Community matters, and he gives instructions to all the ministries and other agencies concerned. The Ministry of Home Affairs co-ordinates planning and implementation through a monthly meeting called the Central Conference. This conference is attended by the Minister of Home Affairs and the Vice-Ministers of the Economic Planning Board, Education, Agriculture and Fisheries, Commerce and Industry, Construction, Health and Social Welfare, Communications, Culture and Public Information, and Science and Technology. In addition there are the Second Minister without Portfolio (economic affairs), the Directors of the Offices of Forestry, Procurement and Rural Development, and the Vice-Presidents of the National Agricultural Co-operatives Federation and the Fishery Co-operatives. Less formal meetings at this same level take place on a weekly basis among the officials concerned to deal with immediate problems.

In the special cities (Seoul and Pusan) and the provinces, the city or provincial government draws up and executes, in accordance with the general directives of the central government, NCM plans that also take into consideration particular local conditions. In 1973 a special branch of the provincial and local governments was established to deal with NCM affairs. A monthly provincial conference is held to discuss and co-ordinate plans as well as to solve problems as they arise. The governor, vice-governor and the chief provincial officials dealing with education, rural development (extension service), agricultural co-operatives, the army reserves and militia, the communications media, construction, electric power generation, etc., attend the provincial conference.

Detailed planning and execution is carried out through the county (*gun*) offices where the position of vice county head has been established specifically to deal with NCM affairs. A monthly conference is attended by influential local officials in charge of the police, educational institutions, rural guidance (extension), co-operatives, etc.

So also at the sub-county (*myon*) level, which is the lowest level of administration employing full-time government officials, frequent meetings are held by the sub-county chief and other local officials to consider how to promote projects in the villages of their district, while village leaders frequently gather at, or come individually to, the *myon* office, to receive directions, report on their activities, and co-ordinate efforts.

Relatively few additional bureaucratic personnel have been recruited specifically to work on NCM affairs, although the bureaucracy as a whole has continued to expand rather rapidly. Existing personnel have usually been reassigned to full-time supervisory functions dealing with the NCM, while other officials, as part of their contribution to the movement, have been expected to work more intensively and longer hours in order to cope with the additional workload. All officials who have passed the national civil service examination for the third grade (the ranks equivalent to that of vice county head) are required to put in a nine months' apprenticeship working on NCM matters berore taking up their regular functions.

Educational programmes have played an important part in the NCM. The central *Saemaul* Leaders Training Institute, at Suwon, has already been mentioned. Similar schools have been established in provincial cities, towns and rural county seats. According to the government's statistics, in 1974 some three and a half million persons received *Saemaul* education in 150 schools throughout the country. This kind of instruction, which is relatively brief and is held during the agricultural off-season, attempts to inculcate the principles of self-help, co-operation, diligence, integrity, frugality and 'scientific thinking' in the rural population. There is great stress on the importance of active co-operation under the direction of *Saemaul* leaders (who receive more intensive, specialized leadership training), in order to achieve both social and economic development. Also, the effort to build prosperous rural communities is carefully related to such issues as national unity, patriotism and support for the Park government.

Another important stimulus promoting the NCM are the decorations and prizes conferred on outstanding leaders or villages by President Park. A national meeting of 4,000 individuals selected for their superior achievements in the movement was first held in 1973. In 1975 the national NCM rally was nearly twice as big and 214 leaders were singled out for special awards. Also, special assistance grants were awarded to 2,500 villages at this same meeting. These ceremonies, which recognize the superior performance of bureaucrats as well as farmers, seem to have had a considerable impact, not only on those who attended, but on society as a whole. It receives the most extensive television coverage.

Village Leadership

Each village (*ri*) has two NCM leaders, one for men and one for women. They (particularly the male leader) are responsible for the planning and execution of village projects. The development committee, an organization that existed before the New Community Movement, comprises the NCM leaders, the village head, the neighbourhood chiefs, and other influential residents of the village. The village head, who is responsible for general administration, and the NCM leader are expected to work closely together in promoting village development. Often the NCM leader is a former village head and vice versa.

The role of the (appointed) village head, the *ri* chief, was described earlier. In the nature of his position it is virtually impossible for him to exercise effective leadership without the support of the more influential men in his community, i.e. those with wealth, education, experience and moral authority.

The New Community leader, who is chosen by his fellow villagers, must also be a respected and popular man in order to promote NCM activities effectively, and he must co-operate closely with the village head. The government has established the following criteria for village NCM leaders, and a certain amount of informal pressure is usually applied by the sub-county office in order to influence the eventual choice. He should: be a native of the village, if possible; demonstrate will and interest in development; be a graduate of an agricultural school; possess the qualities of understanding, judgement, patience, sympathy, co-operation and endurance; be creative but respect the opinions of others; demonstrate a spirit of service and self-sacrifice; be industrious, sincere and healthy; and finally, should have a firm economic base.

The NCM leader is not paid, but he receives a number of special benefits and privileges: he may ask questions and propose ideas concerning development to higher-level organizations using a special NCM postcard; he has preferential access to rural credit; while on NCM business he can purchase train and ship tickets at a discount; his children receive preference in the distribution of scholarship funds; and he acquires the status of an official.

While the development council meets more or less regularly throughout the year to discuss problems and progress (in fact it makes most of the substantive decisions), there are also meetings of all village household heads for the elections of NCM leaders and the approval of major projects. The general meeting would also be responsible for the acquisition and management of NCM common village properties and facilities. A law has been enacted enabling villages to register as corporate bodies, so that they may acquire and manage collective property.

Categories of Villages

The categorization of villages mentioned earlier perhaps needs explanation. It was based on organization, communal facilities and development performance and was designed to stimulate competition. The lowest category, 'basic' or undeveloped (*kich'o*) was applied to villages that lacked both material resources and effective leadership, and where only meagre attempts had been made to organize co-operative effort for development projects. Therefore both educational indoctrination and financial help was regarded as necessary to get things moving.

Progress in the next category, 'self-helping' or developing (*chajo*) villages, was thought to be held back mainly by lack of financial resources, leadership and organization problems having been overcome. And finally independent or developed (*charip*) villages are those where extensive self-help projects have been carried out, income is rising, and expanding resources developed within the village are being put to further productive use.

Some official criteria — based on actual accomplishments — for inclusion in the three categories are listed in Table II.3.

The emphasis on degrees of self-reliance in the nomenclature reflects one aspect of the movement's theoretical orientation. It was believed that as a result of successful developmental accomplishments farmers' attitudes would change and communities would become increasingly capable of making further progress on their own without additional outside help.

Of the 34,665 rural villages in the Republic of Korea in 1973, 18,415 (53 per cent) were 'basic', 13,943 (41 per cent) were 'self-helping', and only 2,307 (6 per cent) were 'independent'. The planned goal was that

Table II.3: Criteria for Village Categorization

Completed projects	Basic village (*kich'o*)	Self-helping village (*chajo*)	Independent village (*charip*)
Village roads	improved main road within village	improved branch roads within village	–
Farm roads	improved access road to village from highway	improved access roads to fields	–
Stream bank control	stream in village controlled	stream between villages controlled	large or small stream outside village controlled
Irrigation of rice fields	80%	85%	90%
Agricultural mechanization	–	power driven insecticide equipment	power tillers and power threshers
Co-operative work	co-operative work teams	co-operative projects for production	co-operative projects for production
Village capital fund	$600 per village	$1,000 per village	$2,000 per village
Savings	$20 per household	$30 per household	$40 per household

by 1975 the percentages in each category should shift to 11 per cent, 60 per cent and 29 per cent respectively, and that all villages would be 'independent' by 1981. Average annual farm household income was to increase from W430,000 ($860) in 1972 to W1,400,000 ($2,800) in 1981. So far the plan has been realized so successfully that there is some suspicion that the promotion of villages to higher categories may be a matter of bureaucratic manipulation rather than a reflection of reality. There has also been considerable criticism both by farmers themselves and by outside observers of the somewhat arbitrary initial classification procedures. Nevertheless, the system does, in fact, appear to have stimulated competitive efforts by farmers.

Local Decision-making and Implementation of Projects

Proposals for local projects are formulated by the village development committee and then approved or rejected by the general meeting of all household heads. At this time decisions are also approved concerning the total projected input of village labour and resources as well as the amount of assistance to be requested from the local authorities.

Annual requests for outside support must be submitted by villages to the sub-county (*myon*) office before 10 September. The *myon* office makes adjustments and assigns priorities to the various projects. Then a combined plan and funding request is submitted to the county (*gun*) office before 20 September. Similarly, county proposals are formulated after deliberation by the local council, and these are presented to the provincial governments by 30 September. After discussion and approval provincial plans are forwarded to the Ministry of Home Affairs by 10 October.

At the interministerial NCM Central Conference decisions are made regarding the total funding available for projects. Then after further examination by the Economic Planning Board the overall NCM budget is submitted to the National Assembly for formal approval.

The government provides support for local projects in accordance with this national NCM budget. Materials such as cement and reinforcing rods are made available to local areas by the provincial governors, utilizing the services of the Office of Procurement. Other materials such as polyethylene, wood or roofing are purchased by the county officials for distribution to villages. Sub-county officials inform the village NCM leaders of the impending arrival of materials, which are stored in the village after the amounts are confirmed. There is joint responsibility for the safe-keeping of these materials among sub-county officials and village leaders.

Financing

Budget allocations for the NCM have increased substantially from $8 million in 1971 (0.7 per cent of the national budget) to $360 million in 1976 (9 per cent of the national budget). Table II.4 shows the kinds of project undertaken by the different ministries in 1973 and 1976, with the budgeted amounts (1976) and percentages of the total (1973 and 1976) for each general category.

Among the various agencies involved in the NCM the Ministry of Home Affairs spent the most in 1976, with 25 per cent of the total. Next comes the National Agricultural Co-operatives Federation (23 per cent), the Ministry of Health and Social Affairs (14 per cent), the Ministry of Commerce and Industry (12.8 per cent), and the Ministry

Table II.4: NCM Projects 1973 and 1976

Ministry	Type of project	1976 Amounts (million of won)	1976 % of total	1973 % of total
Home Affairs	18 kinds of basic development project	43,493	25.1	48.4
Finance	Saemaul training for bankers	75	–	–
Education	4 kinds of project dealing with Saemaul education	567	0.3	1.7
Agriculture and Fisheries	18 kinds of project for increasing income	19,457	11.2	23.9
Commerce	5 kinds of project such as electrification	22,244	12.8	10.5
Health and Social Affairs	7 kinds of project such as water supply systems	23,535	13.6	5.5
Construction	2 kinds of project such as rural housing	3,943	2.3	4.7
Transportation	3 kinds of project such as NCM at seaports	51	–	–
Communications	2 kinds of project such as village public address systems	3,974	2.3	1.5
Culture and Public Information	8 kinds of project such as Saemaul broadcasting	505	0.3	0.3
General Affairs	Saemaul training for govt. officials	480	0.3	–
Science and Technology	4 kinds of project (technological services)	244	0.1	–
Office of Forestry	7 kinds of reforestation project	5,128	3.0	2.3
Office of Labour	3 kinds of project such as training of labour leaders	101	0.1	–
Office of Rural Development	6 kinds of project for rural income increase	1,002	0.6	1.2
Office of Fisheries	10 kinds of project dealing with the distribution of marine products	1,926	1.1	–
Office of Railways	2 kinds of project; improvement of environment in vicinity of railways	200	0.1	–
Seoul City Govt.	3 kinds of project; environmental improvement	5,812	3.3	–
National Agricultural Co-operatives Federation	17 kinds of project; increases in farm production	39,709	22.9	–
Fishery Co-operatives	10 kinds of project; increasing income in fishing villages	1,131	0.7	–
totals		173,577	100.0	100.0

of Agriculture and Fisheries (11.2 per cent). These agencies account for 86 per cent of the total funds invested in the movement, 95 per cent of which were used for rural development.

An additional source of funding apart from the national budget is the presidential grants. Starting in 1972 with $270,000 distributed to 20 villages, these grants increased to $23,400,000 for 8,672 villages in 1976. It is believed that the system of special grants for outstanding performance plays an important role in promoting developmental zeal at the village level.

Government investment, or outside support, is only a small part of the value of total investment, most of which comes from village labour and other resources. During the period 1971 to 1974 the value of all inputs was estimated at W277.4 billion, or $554 million, of which the government's budgetary support contributed only 22 per cent. In 1976 government funds accounted for only 16 per cent of the total accounted expenditure; the contribution of materials and money by villagers was 36 per cent and the remaining 48 per cent comprises the value of local labour contributions. Table II.5 illustrates this trend in terms of NCM investments.

Table II.5: Distribution of NCM Funds

		1971	1972	1973	1974
Total investment (billion won)		12.2	31.3	98.4	132.8 (122.3)
Government investment (billion won)		4.1	3.3	21.5	30.8 (29.3)
Percentage of investment (rural) (area)	ENVIRONMENTAL improvement	100.0%	97.3%	81.0%	52.7%
	increases in income and productivity	–	2.7%	19.0%	44.7%
	spirit-enhancing activities	–	–	–	2.6%
	total	100	100	100	100

Source: Ministry of Agriculture and Forestry, *Yearbook of the Ministry of Agriculture and Forestry 1976*, p. 86.

5 THE VILLAGES

General Characteristics

In accordance with the comparative guidelines laid down for the project as a whole, we selected — after a good deal of searching and a number of false starts — two matched pairs of villages in different regions of the Republic of Korea. The first pair is in Kongju *Gun*, a largely mountainous county some four hours south of Seoul by train and bus or, more directly, two and a half hours by express bus. (In the remainder of this report and in the tables these communities will be referred to as Kongju A and Kongju B.) The two villages are a ten- or fifteen-minute walk apart along the same stream in a deep valley. There is no bus service, and it takes slightly less than an hour to walk to the county seat. The residents of the upper village have built a road with great effort over the mountain that rises behind their houses. It is passable in dry weather for jeeps, small trucks, motorcycles and bicycles. A road from the lower village continues down the valley, crossing the stream many times before it joins a national highway. It, too, is just a jeep track, and it is not passable when the water is high. The upper village, Kongju A, was finally promoted from the lowest NCM category — 'basic' to 'self-reliant' — in 1976, while the lower village, Kongju B, achieved the highest classification of developed in 1974.

The second pair of villages is located about an hour southeast of Seoul in Ich'on *Gun*, a relatively flat, well-watered country that has been famous traditionally for producing the best quality rice. Transportation is good with a regular bus service every hour during the day to the sub-county office and the county seat. (These villages will be referred to in this report as Ich'on C and Ich'on D.) The less successful village, Ich'on C, was only recently promoted to 'self-reliant' from 'basic'; the other, Ich'on D, has been an outstanding example of a progressive community since before the beginning of the *Saemaul* movement in 1971.

The maps and the tables below provide more detailed data concerning the two sets of villages.

The most striking difference between the two sets of villages is that the average amount of arable land per capita in the mountain area (Kongju) is much less than in the plain. Also, there are far more rich farmers and somewhat fewer poor farmers (by ownership of land) in

Figure II.2: Kongju A and B Villages

HEIGHTS IN METERS

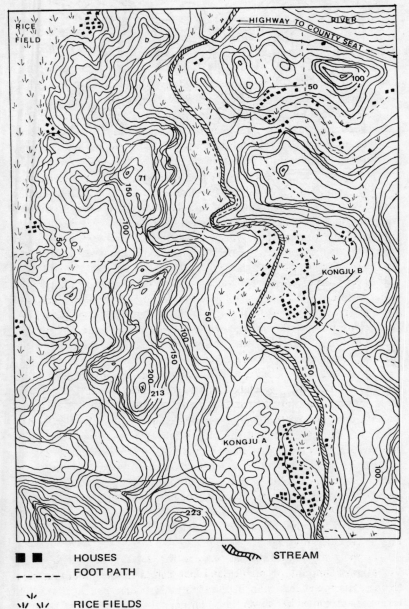

■ ■ HOUSES
- - - - - FOOT PATH

🌾 🌾 RICE FIELDS

Figure II.3: Ich'on C and D Villages

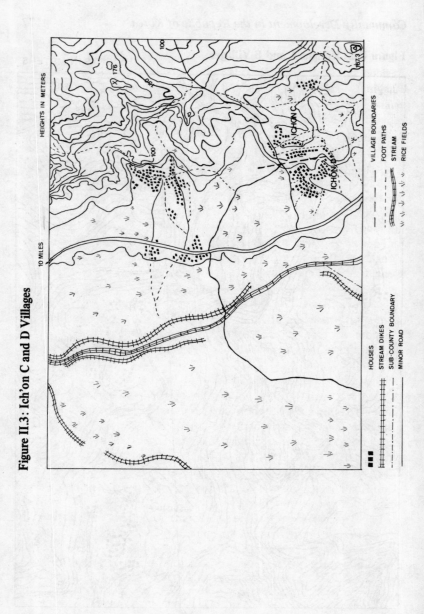

HEIGHTS IN METERS

10 MILES

100

176

ICH'ON C

ICH'ON D

167.3

HOUSES

STREAM DIKES

SUB-COUNTY BOUNDARY

MINOR ROAD

VILLAGE BOUNDARIES

FOOT PATHS

STREAM

RICE FIELDS

Ich'on C and D (plain) than in the mountain villages, Kongju A and B. Residents of both mountain villages had less agricultural equipment and machinery and intended to buy less in the near future than the wealthier farmers in the two Ich'on villages. Also, there are more farmers in these latter communities who own all the land they cultivate.

With regard to most other features, however, the contrast between villages within each pair is greater than or as great as that between pairs. In Ich'on D, the more successful village nearer Seoul, a great majority of the households are in the middle and wealthy categories, and there are relatively few really poor farmers. In Ich'on C, however, there are many rich and poor households with far fewer middle-level households. Although Kongju A and B have fairly equal land distribution with a preponderance of households in the poor or lower middle categories, Kongju A has the highest proportion of tenancy while its neighbour, Kongju B, has the lowest tenancy rate of all four villages. Ich'on C employs by far the most landless agricultural labourers, and our survey showed it also has the highest percentage of households with an annual income of less than W500,000 per year of all four villages. Differences in land and wealth, there, were relatively slight between the two mountain villages, while the contrast was much greater between the wealthier communities in the plain.

The educational picture is rather complex because of the existence in rural Korea of three different kinds of instruction: a conventional school system; a traditional system of locally funded schools giving elementary instruction in Chinese characters and the Confucian classics; and government-sponsored adult education programmes for the illiterate. Our data show that the richest and most advanced village, Ich'on D, has a far higher number of high school (mostly agricultural high school) graduates, but that the percentages for the other categories are roughly similar among all four villages.

Two kinds of structural division, class and lineage, are characteristic of rural areas. In our sample the two mountain villages have a lower class background, while the other pair of communities share upper class traditions. Three different patterns of lineage composition, a variable that appears to be critical for development, are illustrated in our sample. The less successful villages of each pair have an approximately equal distribution of population and wealth among three major lineages. The more successful mountain village has many small lineages, no one of which is predominant, while the more successful village in the plain has a single dominant lineage.

In terms of settlement patterns the more compact of the mountain

Table II.6: Data on Sample Villages

	Kongju A	Kongju B	Ich'on C	Ich'on D
Number of households	60	41 41	60	76
Household size (avg.)	5.1	6.1	5.5	5.2
Avg. size of landholding	.75 ha.	.77 ha.	1.1 ha.	1.3 ha.
Distribution of landholdings (in p'yong; 3,000 p'yong = 1 hectare) %				
less than 1,000	15.7	20	5.3	1.7
1,000 – 2,000	29.4	17.5	18.4	6.8
2,000 – 3,000	27.5	30.0	23.7	28.8
3,000 – 4,000	17.6	20.0	21.1	10.2
4,000 – 5,000	3.7	10.0	15.8	11.9
more than 5,000	6.0	2.5	15.8	40.8
Stratification by type of holding (%)				
owner and owner-farmer	30	51	67	65
mostly owner (some rented land)	25	38	10	11
mostly tenant (some owned land)	20	2	2	8
tenant	11	3	4	3
labourer, no land	4	0	14	6
other	10	5	2	8
settlement pattern	compact	dispersed	dispersed	compact
topography	mountain	mountain	plain	plain
structural features	three commoner lineages of approx. equal size & wealth	many small commoner lineages none predominant	three yangban[a] lineages of appr. equal size & wealth	one yangban[a] lineage of overwhelming (70%) dominance

Facilities				
electricity	*			*
piped water	under construction			under construction
warehouse	*		*	*
telephone	*	*		*
clinic	*			*
laundry				*
factory	*			*
barber shop			*	*
village hall	*		*	*
sewage system				*
rice mill	*		*	*

Education				
– illiterate	4%	14%	10%	17%
– can read simple Korean	27%	17%	10%	12%
– some knowledge of Chinese characters	5%	2%	5%	9%
– dropped out of elementary school	8%	2%	0%	0%
– elementary school completed	47%	48%	55%	32%
– junior high completed	7%	12%	14%	14%
– high school completed	2%	5%	4%	14%
– some college education	0%	0%	2%	2%

aYangban refers to the hereditary upper class of pre-modern Korea.

villages has developed less rapidly, while the reverse is true on the plain.

Village Organizations

In addition to the village chief, the *Saemaul* leader, and the development committee, there are other organizations, both formal and informal, in the villages. The degree of effective organizational activity in each case depends on the villagers' perceived needs, the energy of leadership in each organization, and something else that might be called a local predilection (or lack thereof) for engaging in collective activities across kinship and neighbourhood boundaries.

Among our four villages, Ich'on D is by far the most highly organized. The ability of the village leadership to mobilize continuing energetic participation in organized activities appears to have contributed greatly to the village's success under the NCM. The formal organizations in Ich'on D, which are all designed to promote community development, are generally typical of the other four villages as well: 4-H Club, Children and Mothers Club, Village Development Fund, *Saemaul* Fund, Roof Improvement Fund, and Forestry Fund. The village head and the development committee participate to some extent in the management of these 'public' organizations.

Ich'on D is exceptional, not only in the extent to which its residents are active in most of these organizations, but also because there are two private institutions based outside the village that have engaged in developmental activities there. A Protestant church was established on the edge of the village in 1949, and as a result a college-educated clergyman concerned with the welfare of the villagers has been in almost continuous residence. This progressive influence has also presumably been available to Ich'on C, however, which contributes about half of the members of the congregation.

A registered nurse operates a small health clinic in Ich'on D in one corner of the town meeting hall. A national organization obtained financial support some years ago from the Federal Republic of Germany with the objective of making medical services available in rural areas. The clinic is now self-supporting on the basis of the very small fees for medicine and services charged by the nurse.[1]

All of the villages have private collective funds to assist members in paying heavy wedding and funeral expenses. Ich'on D is the only one of the four, however, that has a travel fund. Each member saves a certain amount of rice annually to finance the costs of group travel. In the spring of 1976 about twenty middle-aged couples travelled together by chartered bus, and in the autumn there was another excursion of elderly men.

Although Kongju B is not as outstanding an example of a *charip* or 'independent' village as Ich'on D, there are real and substantial differences that separate it from its *chajo* ('self-helping') neighbour, Kongju A. From the standpoint of leadership, mobilization of co-operative labour, and effective (as opposed to 'statistical') completion of NCM projects, Kongju B's performance is better, despite the somewhat contradictory indications of the official *Saemaul* accounting presented in Chapter 6. More importantly for the long run the greater community solidarity of Kongju B on the one hand and the more competent individual farming practices of its inhabitants on the other are resulting in higher incomes and the gradual acquisition of more land at the expense of Kongju A.

The rural economy, both on the production and distribution side, is now increasingly tied in with organizations and institutions outside the village. Villagers are much more dependent on the local administrative (sub-county) office, the agricultural co-operative branch, the extension service, the tax office, the health clinic, and local markets (usually at the county seat) than in the past. It appears that the number of visits by village residents to such organizations increases with social and economic development. A 1969 survey showed that only about 10 per cent of village household heads (in an area somewhat comparable to Ich'on) visited the sub-county office more than five times a year. The equivalent percentages for visits to the extension service and the co-operative in 1969 were 5.5 per cent and 1.7 per cent respectively. In all four villages residents today have far more frequent contacts with these same institutions. For example, the percentages of household heads who visited the sub-county office more than five times a year was as follows:

Kongju A village	54.6[2]
Kongju B village	54.8
Ich'on C village	63.3
Ich'on D village	58.5

An important reason for closer contacts with outside organizations, particularly those providing services to the farmer, is their rapid expansion in recent years. Before 1960 there was only one extension service office in each county, usually staffed by three or four workers. Now each sub-county has a branch with three full-time workers. The county extension office at Ich'on has, to serve perhaps 20,000 farm households, eighteen regular employees and another five supplementary workers. Equipment included a jeep, seven motorcycles, fifteen bicycles, film and slide projectors, an amplifier, two rotary tillers, a power sprayer, a water pump and a portable generator. The villagers' livelihood is also much more closely tied in today with the operation of local agricultural co-operatives, which distribute fertilizer, control the supply of rural credit, and purchase and store rice, among other functions. But most farmers are still quite critical of the way co-operatives function.

Of the four villages only residents in Ich'on D visited a health clinic fairly frequently (52.3 per cent of Ich'on D residents said they visited a clinic more than five times annually). This is probably because of the existence of a small clinic right in the village. In the other communities most people only go to a health clinic (usually at the county seat) in cases of severe illness or injury.

The schools, which are administered nationally by the Ministry of Education, constitute another external organization that exerts considerable indirect influence on the villagers' lives. In each of our villages, however, children had to travel to other communities for their schooling, and although the importance of the *Saemaul* movement is emphasized by teachers, they do not play an active role in the actual operation of development efforts. The training course for *Saemaul* leaders is given at a nearby high school in both counties.

Notes

1. While the clinic is convenient for minor illnesses, it is needed much less in D village than in many other rural areas, e.g. Kongju A and B villages, where access to the nearest doctor or hospital is much more difficult. Residents of C village also use the clinic.

2. Kongju A and B villages are much further away from the sub-county office than are Ich'on C and D.

6 EXECUTION OF THE DEVELOPMENT PROGRAMME

By 1971 the desire for change and considerable knowledge about the possibilities of development programmes were extremely widespread in rural Korea. In every village some form of technological innovation together with social structural and attitudinal changes had occurred in the course of developmental efforts by the Japanese, the US military occupation, the United Nations, AID, the Korean government, and private relief organizations. Limitations on land, capital and access to markets rather than conservative beliefs were the principal constraints during the 1950s and 1960s. Farmers with capital, competence and good land near urban areas or main roads began to make substantial profits during the 1960s, and others, while less fortunate, were eager to imitate them.

The history of community development accomplishments in Ich'on D village (the most successful of our four communities) goes back well before the beginning of the *Saemaul* movement in 1971. The Church World Service Organization sponsored development projects in Ich'on D during the period 1968-70, providing financial and other kinds of assistance. Presumably, this village was chosen as a pilot area, because the inhabitants had already demonstrated a capacity for effective co-operative effort. Under the strong and competent leadership of one highly respected and successful farmer, Ich'on D had already undertaken a number of self-help projects in the early 1960s. Farmers in this village foreshadowed the NCM by raising money collectively to improve village roads and replace thatched roofs with tile or composition. A roof improvement plan with co-operative financing was adopted, by which ten households were able to change their roofs each year. The village had also set up a loud speaker and amplifier, so that residents could be kept informed and co-operative work groups easily mobilized.

Women in this village had shown unusual initiative in carrying out sanitary improvements to their kitchens and toilet facilities in accordance with advice from the local agricultural extension agents. In addition, by restricting their family rice consumption, they were able to save enough money to set up a kind of credit union with regular monthly meetings. Such co-operative efforts among village women are remarkable in a *Yangban* village where conservative prejudice against female activities outside the home is particularly strong. These projects were expanded and others initiated under the guidance of a professional development worker sent by the Church World Service. The village also undertook a project to utilize the energy of methane gas generated in toilets. In 1970 when the government began to implement the New Community Movement, it chose Ich'on D as one of the experimental pilot areas.

Both of the Kongju villages, which were relatively isolated because of poor roads, had made efforts in the 1960s to improve their access to the main highways. Because of the mountainous terrain, however, they were only partially successful, and transportation still remains a major problem in this area.

During the first year of intensive *Saemaul* activities (1971), emphasis was placed throughout the country on environmental improvement, but many other kinds of development projects were also undertaken. These are shown in Tables II.7-II.9, which were compiled from local government sources. These official data are somewhat misleading, however, because they show that Kongju A and Ich'on C were just as active as their neighbouring villages, whereas in fact this was not the case. It seems evident that what counts is not so much the number of projects as the quality of participation, the effectiveness of leadership, the efficiency of organization, and the quality of performance – the difference for example, between a solidly built embankment to control floods and a few token rocks piled to impress outsiders. Since 1974, however, Kongju A has become somewhat more active. Villagers attribute this in part to the special aid and encouragement furnished by local officials as part of the government's programme to upgrade 'undeveloped' villages. Kongju A was promoted to the 'developing' (*chajo*) category in 1976. In the winter of 1976-7, Kongju A village residents were engaged in installing a series of piped water systems somewhat similar to that installed by Kongju B in 1974.

Kongju B village was awarded a special presidential grant of $2,000 as a result of its outstanding performance in 1973. With this money it was decided to complete the electrification of the village (completed in November 1974) and buy a machine for making straw bags. A national assemblyman, whose mother's tomb is located in the village, donated some $600 towards the construction of a village meeting hall. His son, who is in the diplomatic service, raised an equal amount from Koreans living abroad, while labour was supplied by the villagers.

Although Kongju B received its presidential prize and was promoted to the highest category of 'developed' village at a relatively early date,

Table II.7: Projects for Environmental Improvement

Kind of project	unit	Kongju A						Kongju B						Ich'on C						Ich'on D					
		71	72	73	74	75	total	71	72	73	74	75	total	71	72	73	74	75	total	71	72	73	74	75	total
widening village paths	metre			500	600	700	1,800			300	500	800	1,600	50					50	200	1,690				1,890
improving fences around houses	metre			280	100	350	730				340	380	720			80			80	600	240				840
laying out and improving sewers	metre			200	100		300										120	180	300	240	340	100			680
access road to village	metre		100	400	200		700				280		280					300	300		700				700
stream embankment	metre	500					500																		
replacement of thatched roofs	house	8	8	9	8	7	40	5	8	9	8	7	37		4	3	6	10	23	41	37	30			108
repair of old houses	house											3	3			1	1	1	3	2	1				3
construction of simple piped water system	house										23		23	60					60						
electrification	house				53		53			37	4		41	76					76	76					76
methane gas project	house																								
improvement of post and telegraph service	house																					10			10

Table II.8: Projects for Increasing Income

Kind of project	unit	Kongju A						Kongju B						Ich'on C						Ich'on D				
		71	72	73	74	75	total	71	72	73	74	75	total	71	72	73	74	75	total	72	73	74	75	total
access roads to fields	metres	900	600				1,500	200	300	500			1,000		100	100	200		400	100	100	200	200	600
bridge construction (small)	metres			7	15		22									9			9	already constructed				
improvement of wells	no.			1	1		2				1	1	2						2	already adequate				
construction of village meeting hall	no.			1			1				1		1						1	already possessed one				
village store	no.			1			1													already had a store				
construction of new wells	no.		3	1			4			1	2		3						5	not needed				
communal laundry	no.		2	1			3			1	2		3							already constructed				
cooperative cultivation	hectares	5	5	8	10	10	38	8	10	10	10	15	53							joint planting of 300 chestnut trees				
cooperative efforts to eradicate noxious insects	hectares	10	10	15	18	20	73	8	15	15	10	20	68											
cultivation of tree seedlings	nos. of seedlings				5,000		10,500				15,000		15,000		7,000				7,000	7,000				7,000
village afforestation	nos. of seedlings				5,000		19,500																	
rice polishing facility	no.																		1	1				1

Table II.9: Other Saemaul Projects

Kind of project	unit	Kongju A						Kongju B						Ich'on C						Ich'on D					
		total	71	72	73	74	75	total	71	72	73	74	75	total	71	72	73	74	75	total	71	72	73	74	75
Projects to encourage a developmental mentality																									
village credit union	1000 won	55				20	35							100					100	2,400	100	490	400	550	860
village savings association	1000 won							100					100	790	60	130	200	200	200	2,390	200	360	510	610	710
women's savings association	1000 won																								
Other kinds of savings funds	1000 won	411			411			582			582			100			30	70		1,234	210	300	350	300	74
Other miscellaneous projects																									
stone stream embankment	metres	300		100	50	50	100	300					300	30					30	30					30
changing drainage pipe	metres	3			3			6			6			2	1	1									
village library	metres													1						1					

it has been disappointed by the lack of outside support since then. Originally the government had announced that villages would be rewarded in accordance with their accomplishments. Then in 1975 the policy changed, and official aid was no longer given to the most successful villages. Instead, it was channelled almost entirely to less developed communities in order to enable them to catch up. The resulting discouragement and slackening of developmental momentum in many areas has forced the authorities to reconsider, and the system of providing incentives for outstanding performance is gradually being resumed. The leaders of Kongju B insist that even without any outside aid they are continuing to carry out a wide variety of developmental projects with their own resources. Nevertheless, they point out that much greater progress could have been achieved if they had received as much help as Kongju A during the last two years.

Ich'on C, the least successful of the pair of Ich'on county villages, has become more active since 1975, continuing its work on roads, fences, roofs and a sewage system. In spite of these efforts there is a considerable and possibly a growing gap between Ich'on C and its neighbour Ich'on D, which, as one of the nation's outstanding villages, is undertaking increasingly ambitious projects.

Compared to the relatively poor, mountain communities in Kongju county there are many farmers in the Ich'on villages who possess substantial landholdings and considerable private wealth. Ich'on D has so far been more successful than Ich'on C in utilizing this resource for developmental purposes. Ich'on D received a presidential grant in 1976 and is currently investing the money in a household water supply system.

The Role of Officials

An important part of the change process that has accompanied the NCM has been the shift in local officials' perceptions of their roles. Intense pressure has been exerted on local administrators by the central government to ensure the achievement of NCM goals. The result is that the transition of the local bureaucracy from a *status quo* and control-oriented institution to an action-oriented instrument of developmental change, which was taking place slowly in the 1960s, has been greatly speeded up. It is at this level that the insistent ideological indoctrination of NCM seems to have had its greatest effect. The work load of local officials is now much heavier than before, and they are preoccupied with encouraging, cajoling or bullying farmers into greater co-operative self-help efforts, rather than, as in the past, enforcing bureaucratic regulations and promoting their own interests. Financial control and inspection by Seoul of local accounting has become much stricter, so that opportunities for personal enrichment are relatively meagre. Most local officials now spend half or more of their time away from their desks talking to villagers and guiding or inspecting projects. Also, they are required to give monthly 'pep talks' in each village in order to promote the *Saemaul* spirit. The result is that the county and sub-county offices are busier and less preoccupied with routine clerical tasks than in the past. Also, the new and dominant concerns — ideological indoctrination and practical problem-solving —seem to have been accompanied everywhere by an improvement in bureaucratic morale.

Along with this change in function and perspective there has been a more subtle shift in official attitudes towards the rural population. Since energetic participation by farmers is necessary for compliance with the movement's insistent directives from Seoul, their status relative to that of officials appears to have improved considerably. While there is no question of the superior authority and prestige of, for example, the sub-county head, his traditional attitude of arrogant condescension towards villagers is giving way, particularly among younger officials, to a relationship based more on interdependence and mutuality. Well-to-do farmers are now likely to have as much or more property and income as the higher ranking local officials. Also, their sons have usually graduated from high school, so that the great economic and educational gap that used to exist between farmers and officials has been significantly reduced.

Division of Benefits

A good deal of discussion and friction is almost invariably generated at the village level over the apportionment of effort and benefits for each co-operative project undertaken. In fact, the ease or difficulty with which such problems are resolved is one measure of the extent of community solidarity and the effectiveness of local leadership. Because of the great complexity of these problems, and the variation that exists in different villages, generalization is difficult; nevertheless some patterns are discernible.

There is some tendency for the richest and poorest residents in each village to evade their responsibilities for the contribution of labour and other resources. Landless or nearly landless villagers live by selling their labour, and since their livelihood is close to the subsistence level, they are reluctant to work on projects that bring them no immediate tangible return. They often point out that the road- and bridge-building or the irrigation and flood control projects are increasing the productivity and value of the more prosperous farmers' land, and that this is being accomplished thanks in part to the free labour contributed by the poor. Also, poor farmers are less likely to see the need for cement fences and tile roofs, which they regard as luxuries requiring a substantial expenditure of their extremely scarce resources. The co-operative self-help projects undertaken under the aegis of the NCM are usually scheduled for the winter months in order to avoid the busy farming season and utilize underemployed farm labour. But if there is any opportunity for poor farmers to work for money during the slack season, they will not participate willingly in NCM projects.

While the richest farmers are usually among the first to make improvements to their own houses, they are less likely to feel any urgent need for developmental efforts on behalf of the whole village, particularly if the *Saemaul* projects require the contribution of labour that is needed to exploit fully their own productive facilities. Wealthy farmers will, of course, participate wholeheartedly in road building or irrigation projects that benefit their own landholdings, and there has been some grumbling on the part of discontented elements in all four villages to the effect that rich and influential men usually make sure the projects undertaken are of benefit to themselves.

While local elites do not always perceive their interests as congruent with those of the village as a whole, there are other cases in which leading men of the village have contributed more than their share, both in terms of resources and personal efforts.

According to Confucian ethics persons of high rank have a responsibility to promote the collective welfare, and the positive sanctions for such behaviour in terms of local prestige are considerable. Particularly in Ich'on D one man of wealth, energy and integrity is universally respected for his determined efforts to promote development, even before the initiation of the NCM. He then led the movement in its early stages, and although he is now too old (according to government regulation) to hold the office of *Saemaul* leader, his voice still has great weight in village councils.

Even though most of the support and labour input for *Saemaul* projects usually comes from the middle-level farmers, this does not mean that severe problems concerning the distribution of benefits do not arise for this group as well. Prolonged argument and stubborn resist-ance by owners who were required to donate small portions of their land for road-widening and straightening projects has occurred in all four villages. In some cases there is still bad feeling as a result of the strong collective pressures utilized to compel individual acquiescence. Where disputes of this kind have reinforced existing lineage divisions or personal rivalries among influential men, cohesive community spirit and action have been impaired. To some extent this is what occurred in Kongju A and Ich'on C, the two less successful villages of our sample. In Kongju B, the potential for such conflict was as great or greater than in Kongju A because of the existence of six stubborn individuals who adamantly refused to give up land required to complete the widening and straightening of the village's main access road. In spite of numerous meetings where the village consensus in favour of building the road was clearly expressed and personal pleas were made by the village head and the *Saemaul* leader, the six landowners maintained that the sacrifice they were asked to make far outweighed any potential benefits to be derived from the new road. In Kongju A, this kind of dispute exacerbated existing divisions within the village and made co-operative efforts more difficult to carry out, while in Kongju B, the aggrieved individuals were isolated and forced to acquiesce, however unwillingly, as a result of the formation of a fairly solid village consensus.

Two other kinds of project in which the division of benefits often becomes an issue are electrification and piped water supply, particul-arly if there is a dispersed settlement pattern. The unit cost for out-lying houses is much greater than for those in larger clusters, and where, as is frequently the case, the outlyers are poor, a problem of equitable distribution of costs and benefits arises. Kongju B typifies this kind of settlement pattern, and the problem presented a challenge to local decision-making in that the provision of electricity and piped water for only a part of the village was perceived by villagers as a threat to community cohesion and morale. As a result of prolonged deliberation the higher installation costs for the outlying households were eventu-ally subsidized in part by the village as a whole.

The Decision-making Process

During the first or experimental year of the NCM (1970-1), firm guide-lines for the role of local administrative agencies had not yet been established, and as a result there was a good deal of variation in the amount of guidance and direction that was exercised from one county to another. Although more or less forceful suggestions as to the kinds of project that might best be undertaken were made to village leaders, actual decision-making concerning the use of the cement furnished by the government was usually left to the village councils. The response of villages varied greatly, ranging all the way from distribution of an equal share of the cement to each household (often for re-sale) to highly organized co-operative projects in accordance with NCM objectives. As a result of this initial experience the central authorities concluded that successful community development required strong and effective village leadership in a context of forceful direction, stimulus and support from the local administration. Consequently, during the next year bureaucratic pressures on villages to carry out development projects in conformity with a predetermined plan were increased. The principles of local community initiative and decision-making were widely proclaimed, and local officials encouraged farmers to hold frequent meetings with regard to the planning and carrying out of *Saemaul* projects.

In actual fact, however, the meetings were held mainly to mobilize enthusiastic participation in the movement and to organize the actual details of co-operative self-help projects. Most decisions concerning the number and type of projects to be undertaken were made by officials outside the villages. Subsequently, as the movement gained momentum there has been a somewhat greater delegation of authority to village councils, particularly in the case of the more rapidly developing communities. There is still close co-ordination between villages and local officials in the annual planning of *Saemaul* projects, but bureaucratic control has become more flexible, taking into consideration both special ecological factors and the particular desires of villagers. During the early years of the movement farmers often complained that they were obliged to undertake projects that were not well suited to the particular situation in their village. Because of the dependence of most villages on outside resources for the successful completion of their most important projects, local officials have usually had an effective veto power over village decision-making. Sometimes, as in the case of both Kongju A and B, the desired projects (in this case connecting roads to national highways) are regarded as too ambitious, and no help is forthcoming.

In general local initiative is encouraged, provided most of the materials and labour can be furnished by the villagers themselves. Nevertheless, there is close supervision and, ultimately, control over every aspect of *Saemaul* activities. Both the Ministry of Home Affairs and the President's office keep a close watch on movement activities, and there is never any question where authority lies. Decisions are made in Seoul concerning the kinds of project that will be encouraged, the funds that will be made available, and the responsibilities of various ministries for solving problems as they develop. Emphasis on this latter function – the co-ordination of efforts by a large number of government agencies in order to get quick results – has been a distinctive feature of the movement from its beginning.

In our sample, Ich'on D, which has been given national attention (including a presidential prize) for its superior performance, receives relatively little direction from the sub-county and county officials, most of whose efforts are now directed at improving developmental efforts in less successful villages.

Analysis of Inputs

Government figures showing the *Saemaul* project expenditures in our four villages during the period from 1971 through 1975 are contained in Tables II.10 and II.11.[1] These data can be summarized as follows:

Table II.10: Sources of Expenditure (in thousand won)

	Kongju						Ich'on	
	A		B		C		D	
Total projected amount	19,083	%	16,562	%	22,740	%	15,122	%
Actual total	15,226	100	12,643	100	8,856	100	13,622	100
Government support	747	4.9	1,770	12.8	1,694	19.1	1,024	7.5
Loans	2,720	17.9	1,810	14.3	1,825	20.6	1,840	13.5
Villagers' contribution (mostly labour)	11,779	77.2	9,163	72.5	5,337	60.3	10,758	79.0
No. of projects	19		15		15		15	

The inhabitants of Kongju A undertook 19 projects at a total expenditure of W15,226,000 ($30,452), or an average of W253,767 per household over the five-year period. Of the total 4.9 per cent was provided as grants, while 17.9 per cent was loaned to villagers, mainly by the government-controlled National Agricultural Co-operatives Federation. The remaining W11,759,000 (77.2 per cent) was furnished by village residents, mainly in the form of labour. Similar data for the other villages can be readily obtained from the table.

Table II.11: Expenditures for *Saemaul* Projects 1971-5. Kongju County: Villages A and B (500 won = $1.00 (1976); unit: 1,000 won)

Kind of project	Kongju A					Kongju B				
	projected total	actual total	govern-ment assistance (grants)	loans (govt. backed)	village contribu-tion	projected total	actual total	govern-ment assistance	loans	village contribu-tion
roads within village	1,089	1,089			1,089	1,450	1,450			1,450
improving fences and walls	1,930	850			850	586	586			586
sewers	396	396	43		353	342	128			128
access road to village	386	386			386					
stream embankment	493	493			493					
replacement of roofs	4,075	2,800	200	600	2,000	4,010	2,310	110	330	1,870
piped water system	1,680	1,680			1,680	2,900	1,700	1,000		700
electrification	3,445	3,445		2,120	1,325	2,565	2,405		1,480	925
access roads to fields	1,530	1,210			1,210	1,260	1,260			1,260
small bridges	912	566	208		358	30	30			30
pump installation	40	40			40					
village meeting hall	410	410	74		336	713	713	353		360
village store	280	280			280	320				
communal well	156	156	48		108	170	170	42		128
communal laundry	62	62	26		36	25	25	15		10
cultivation of tree seedlings	665	285			285	500	500			500
village afforestation	835	385			385					
field drainage	633	633	148		485	715	390	150		240
stone embankment						856	856			856
burying drainage pipe	60	60			60	120	120			120
totals	19,083	15,226	747	2,720	11,779	16,562	12,643	1,770	1,810	9,163
average expenditure per household	254	254	12	45	196	357	357	33	44	224
percentage of total	100	100	5	18	77	100	100	13	14	73

It is obvious that by far the largest input was local labour. Most of the government support consisted of cement and reinforcing rods. Loans were made mostly for electrification and roof replacement. Villagers also contributed some materials and relatively small amounts of cash. For example, when electricity was installed in Kongju B, a great many meetings were held (some villagers estimated as many as thirty) to persuade people to put up money. All but four households, who later joined at reduced rates, each paid W26,000 ($52.00) and obtained loans of $80.00 from the Korea Electric Company.

The average amount invested for all four villages over the five-year period is W12,586,750 ($25,172). Of this, 9.6 per cent was government grants, 16.3 per cent loans, and 73.5 per cent self-support. Comparable figures for the nation as a whole show that the average invested per village was W16,337,000 ($32,674). Of this only 56.3 per cent was supplied by villagers, while the government furnished the remaining 45.3 per cent as grants or loans. The reason for the large discrepancy between the average for our four villages and the entire nation is probably because the national figures include funds budgeted for *Saemaul* education and the mobilization of the urban unemployed on public works projects.

The pattern for the other two villages was similar with, again, roof replacement and access roads being the chief items where the projected expenditure was a good deal greater than that actually incurred. Additional items appearing in the Ich'on inventory were: methane gas utilization, a public lavatory, a barbershop and a rice mill (all in D only), and the repair of old houses and a village library in both (the last a modest W10,000 in each). Expenditures per household were about 60 per cent of the level in the Kongju village.

The least successful village of our sample, Ich'on C, is distinctive in three respects: first, it received the greatest amount of government grants and loans: secondly, it had the smallest local contribution per household; and finally, there was the greatest difference between plans and actual accomplishments. The most prosperous village, Ich'on D, had the highest proportion of local contributions as a percentage of total investment, and it also came the closest to fulfilling planned goals. The amount of labour contribution per household was considerably greater in the relatively poor Kongju villages than in those of Ich'on county.

It is apparent that there is wide variation among villages, both in the amount of outside help received per household and in the contributions of local residents.

Contributions of Villagers

The contributions of local residents can be divided into four types: labour, cash, materials, and some combination of the three. The most usual combination is of labour and cash — for example, in the cases of roof replacement, electrification and water supply systems. Labour and materials are contributed together when private land is 'donated' in order to permit the construction of wider roads, a meeting hall, or other community facility.

We have used a simple and rather crude basis for comparing individual participation in *Saemaul* projects among the four villages. For example, if 23 persons participated in roof replacement, 30 in road construction, and 10 in well repair, we have simply added the numbers together to obtain total participation (in this example, 65) without attempting to weigh the results for duration of labour or amount of monetary contribution (see Table II.12). The high rate of individual participation of Ich'on D residents is obvious from these figures.

Table II.12: Participation in Projects

	Kongju				Ich'on			
	A	%	B	%	C	%	D	%
Total participation	802		424		563		1140	
Average participation per household	14.6		10.1		11.5		22	
Labour alone	626	77	260	61	350	62	766	67
Money alone	54	7	56	15	79	14	125	11
Labour and money or materials	114	14	80	19	86	15	170	15
Materials alone	18	2	28	7	48	9	75	7

There were nine projects in Ich'on D in which 90 per cent or more of the residents participated, while in the other villages there were only four or five. Similarly, 60 per cent or more of Ich'on D residents participated in sixteen projects compared to eight or nine in the other villages.

In the poorest village, Kongju A, the percentage of labour contribution is highest, while that of money contributions is lowest. Ich'on C had the highest percentage of contributions of money and materials without labour.

In general the most popular projects in all four villages were as follows:

1. access roads to the village;
2. access roads to the fields;
3. roof replacement;
4. electrification;
5. stream control;
6. credit and savings systems.

Particular geographic and sociocultural factors determine the desirability of other projects. For example, the two Kongju villages are particularly concerned with improved access to the main highways. Also, their mountain stream creates a problem during the flood season. Because of the availability of good springs, they have been able to construct simplified systems for piping water to each house. The Ich'on villages have no serious transportation problem or environmental challenge, but installing a piped water system is much more difficult.

Note

1. Officials familiar with the way these figures are compiled admit that there may be substantial errors of as much as 20-30 per cent in some cases.

7 EVALUATION OF EFFECTS

With regard to the evaluation of results of the NCM we have relied more on the opinions of the villagers (who did realize we were trying to evaluate the NCM) and local officials, than on statistical data concerning the actual development projects. The data, which have been largely presented in the previous chapter, are useful as an indication of the kinds of activities engaged in and the approximate scope of village efforts, but they do not appear to be accurate in an 'accounting' sense. In many cases they have undoubtedly been inflated through a kind of informal collaboration between lower-level officials and village leaders.

Villagers' Evaluations

It is evident that there has been a significant improvement in the economic situation of most Korean farmers during the six-year period (1971-6) of the NCM. We asked all the household heads in each village the following question: How does your general living standard and financial situation compare to that in 1971? This question was phrased in exactly the same way as it had been on surveys made by the Korean author in 1959 and 1969 in a village not far from Ich'on. It is noteworthy that about 80 per cent of the respondents in all four villages answered that conditions were better in 1976 than in 1971. In the 1958 survey, on the other hand, only 51 per cent of the household heads said their situation had improved since just before liberation in 1945, even though the status of most of them had changed from that of tenants to independent farmers as a result of the land reform of 1949-50. In 1969 51 per cent of the respondents said their condition had improved since the first (1959) survey. Table II.13 summarizes these findings.

It is also remarkable that about 40 per cent of the 1976 respondents in each village said their situation had improved 'greatly' since 1971, whereas the percentages who gave this answer in 1958 and 1969 were 5.3 per cent and 9.8 per cent respectively.[1]

Replies to the open-ended question, 'If your economic condition has improved, what do you consider to be the reason?', were also revealing. Most frequently credit was given to the greater yields of the

Community Development in the Republic of Korea 101

Table II.13: Improvement in Living Standards

Evaluation	1959 survey %	1969 survey %	A village %	B village %	C village %	D village %
Improved greatly	5.3	9.8	40.0	45.2	55.1	43.1
Improved a little	35.4	41.2	38.2	42.9	24.5	38.5
No change	29.5	27.1	16.4	9.5	8.2	10.8
A little worse	12.8	12.7	3.6	0.0	2.0	4.6
Much worse	15.2	7.5	0.0	0.0	6.1	3.1
Don't know and no response	1.8	1.7	1.8	2.4	4.1	0.0
Total	100.0	100.0	100.0	100.0	100.0	100.0

Note: 1. In the 1959 survey the respondents were asked to compare their present (1959) living situation with that just before the liberation in 1945.

2. In the 1969 survey the respondents were asked to compare their living situation in 1969 with that in 1959.

3. The respondents in the four villages (A, B, C, D) were asked to compare their present (1967) living situation with that in 1971.

new rice seeds. Only half as many respondents attributed the improvement to the NCM, while others recognized the importance of the expansion of cash-crop agriculture and higher subsidized rice prices in raising farm income. Farmers in the Kongju villages, where there is less rice surplus and access to town markets is more difficult, were somewhat more inclined to credit the NCM with improving their condition. In Kongju B particularly the NCM was regarded as slightly more important than the development of new rice seed. In the Ich'on villages, on the other hand, the NCM as a cause of rural development came out a poor fourth behind rice seeds, commercial farming and higher rice prices. In Ich'on C only one household head listed the NCM as the main cause of improved conditions, while in Ich'on D, which is regarded nationwide as one of the most successful *Saemaul* villages, only 18 per cent of the respondents gave it priority (see Table II.14).

Another survey question sought the respondent's views concerning the relative importance of the NCM's contribution or potential contribution in the following areas: (1) higher incomes; (2) the improved convenience of village facilities; (3) co-operation; (4) confidence in a better life in the future; (5) the reform of behaviour; and (6) trust in the government. In interpreting the responses we assigned three points for 'contributes greatly', two points for 'some contribution', one point for 'slight contribution', 0 points for 'neither contributes nor obstructs'

Community Development in the Republic of Korea 106

Table II.14: Reasons for the Improvement in Living Standards

	Kongju A		Kongju B		Ich'on C		Ich'on D		Total
	1st choice	2nd choice	1st choice	2nd choice	1st choice	2nd choice	1st choice	2nd choice	
Development of new rice seed	20	5	14	6	21	2	30	4	102
Saemaul movement	13	3	18	5	1	–	10	2	52
Development of farming technique	2	2	1	–	–	–	–	4	10
Individual effort	4	3	–	1	1	1	–	1	8
Electrification	1	–	–	–	–	–	–	1	2
New cash crops	–	4	2	5	7	8	3	9	38
New ways of thinking	–	1	–	1	–	3	–	1	6
Rise of rice price	–	–	–	1	–	3	–	7	12
More manpower	–	–	–	–	7	1	–	–	8
Govt. support	–	–	–	–	1	–	–	1	2
Other	5	–	3	1	2	1	6	5	23
Total	45	18	38	20	40	18	49	35	263

Note: 1. This item was an open-ended question, and therefore the categories were not structured in advance.
2. This question was given only to those who said that their living situation was improved compared with that in 1971.

and minus one point for 'harmful'. Among the six kinds of possible answers income increases obtained the lowest score. This was true in the overall score for all four villages and for each separate village as well. Improved convenience was given the highest score, while behavioural reform, co-operation, confidence in a better life, and trust in the government followed in that order.[2] Nevertheless, if all the responses to our various questions concerning the evaluation of the NCM are taken into consideration, it is evident that the opinion of the overwhelming majority of people in these villages is favourable. It should be emphasized that the NCM has also been effective in ameliorating the deeply rooted distrust of the government on the part of the rural population. Farmers have been oppressed and exploited by the bureaucracy throughout much of Korean history, including the period since liberation in 1945. Officials have been haughty, authoritarian and greedy, issuing unreasonable orders and extracting agricultural produce and *corvée* labour on numerous occasions without compensation. A rural saying compared government policies and projects allegedly undertaken for the farmers' welfare to a dragon. They had a glittering beginning (the dragon's head) but faded away to nothing (the tail of a snake). Accordingly, most villagers were sceptical at the beginning of the NCM. Only in Ich'on D, which already had a record of successful development, was there a predominantly optimistic view of the NCM right from the start.

The villagers were also asked, 'To what extent to you think each of the NCM projects was beneficial to you personally?', and the answers were scored and ranked. Table II.15 summarizes the findings.

The most 'beneficial' projects in the Kongju villages were: electrification, access roads to fields, the village meeting hall, bridges, dikes, drainage and the change of roofs. In the Ich'on area the most beneficial projects were listed as: the village meeting hall, sewage system, access roads to fields, electrification, a mutual credit system, and access roads to the villages. The most highly appreciated projects in all four villages were electrification, access roads to the fields, the village meeting halls, and access roads to the village.

In response to a slightly different question, 'which projects do you regard as most successful?', the ranking of replies for each village is as shown in Table II.16.

In this case the answers probably reflect the degree to which villages conformed to official expectations and the extent to which projects were pushed through to completion. The variations reflect particular circumstances in the different villages. For example, for Kongju (A and

Table II.15: Answers to the Question: 'To what extent was each of the following projects beneficial to you?'

		Kongju A rank	Kongju B rank	Ich'on C rank	Ich'on D rank
1.	Road entering into village	3	6	2	9
2.	Road to fields	2	3	1	7
3.	Roof improvement	9	2	10	11
4.	Fence improvement	20	12	34	19
5.	Improvement of old house	22	16	28	26
6.	Water supply	21	10	37	36
7.	Well for common use	18	24	21	33
8.	Water pump	17	17	7	21
9.	Washing place	11	23	14	6
10.	Warehouse	10	—	16	10
11.	Common working place	30	—	25	24
12.	Place to sell goods in common	15	—	19	14
13.	Barber shop	16	—	23	2
14.	Common cooking place	—	—	24	8
15.	Village hall	4	4	4	1
16.	Electrification	1	1	6	3
17.	Maintenance of brook	12	9	11	17
18.	Sewage system	26	25	3	4
19.	Small bridge	5	5	13	—
20.	Small river	24	19	15	12
21.	Small pond for irrigation	32	—	33	22
22.	Collective cultivation	—	28	26	30
23.	Control of insects	29	15	12	18
24.	Growing seedlings	27	14	31	34
25.	Afforestation	13	11	17	25
26.	Conservation of soil	14	13	29	32
27.	Under-drain	7	8	35	35
28.	Stone dike	6	7	27	13
29.	Burying earthenware pipe	23	26	9	16
30.	Rice mill	—	—	18	15
31.	Methane gas	—	27	22	31
32.	Communication facility	8	—	8	23
33.	Credit Union	28	18	5	5
34.	Other systems for saving money	19	20	20	20
35.	Village library	31	22	30	28
36.	Playground	—	—	36	27
37.	Inspection tour	25	21	32	29

Table II.16: Ranking of Projects for Success

A	B	C	D
Roads to fields	roof change	sewage	roof change
Electricity	electricity	roof change	sewage
Warehouse	roads to fields	roads to fields	roads to fields
Village hall	water supply		warehouse
			village hall

B) the installation of electricity was entirely associated with the NCM, while in Ich'on (C and D) private electrification projects were already underway before 1971. In Kongju A the warehouse had been completed just before our survey, so that this accomplishment was still fresh in everyone's mind. The piped water supply system in Kongju B was a source of great pride because it had seemed to be an unimaginable luxury for a mountain village. Actually, because of the steep slopes and the location of good springs, it had been relatively easy to carry out. Better access roads to the fields have made the farmers' work much easier, particularly because of the proliferation in recent years of rubber-tyred ox-drawn carts. Where previously seeds, fertilizer, compost, tools and agricultural produce all had to be carried back and forth over narrow trails on the farmer's back, he now can take much larger loads without effort. The top rank given to the village hall by Ich'on D is significant in view of the fact that this hall is in constant use and plays such an important role in the development process.

At the beginning of the *Saemaul* movement the government placed great emphasis on the replacement of thatched roofs; as a result local officials frequently used tactics that bordered on coercion in persuading farmers, particularly in villages that were visible from the main highways. Although low-interest loans were made available to cover part of the costs of roof replacement, poorer farmers has to go deeper into debt in order to pay the entire amount. There were other widely criticized abuses associated with the programme such as the sudden windfall profits of manufacturers and merchandizers of tile, composition and metal roofing. The result was considerable initial resentment and resistance to the roof change programme. On the other hand, although critics have denounced the roof replacements as a superficial way of giving an impression of progress that would please high officials, in actual fact there are excellent economic reasons for replacing the thatch. Villagers fully recognize the advantages of the new roofs as shown in the answers to our survey questions. Not only are they spared the cost and labour of adding fresh thatch each year, but the additional rice straw made available for compost, fuel, fodder, rope and bag-making constitutes an important agricultural by-product. In fact it is estimated that the cost of putting on a new permanent roof is only about three times the annual maintenance cost for thatch. Finally, farmers are proud of the appearance of their new roofs, even though foreign tourists may regret the disappearance of the more picturesque thatch. Thatch has always been a symbol of relative poverty in Korean villages, where in the past the few wealthy farmers usually had tiled roofs.

As part of our effort to evaluate change associated with the *Saemaul* movement we asked villagers to compare their progress with that of other communities. In each of our matched pairs, they appear to have used the neighbouring village as a standard for comparison, although not specifically requested to do so. Respondents in the two 'developed' villages (Kongju B and Ich'on D) generally believed their own communities to be 'more successful' or 'successful to a considerable extent', while answers in the two other villages were more negative as shown in Table II.17.

Table II.17: Responses to the Question: 'Is Your Village More or Less Successful than Other Villages?'

Response	Kongju		Ich'on	
	A%	B%	C%	D%
far more successful	5.5	22.0	0.0	60.0
somewhat more successful	33.0	36.5	4.0	31.0
about the same	18.0	12.0	6.5	7.5
somewhat less successful	38.0	26.0	31.0	0.0
far less successful	0.0	0.0	57.0	0.0
no response	5.5	3.5	2.0	1.5

This pattern is possibly less important, however, than the contrast between the two pairs. In the Kongju villages the percentages of those who thought their own village was successful or unsuccessful are quite similar, while in Ich'on the opposite is the case. Almost 90 per cent of Ich'on D residents regarded their village as successful, while about the same percentage in Ich'on C labelled their performance as unsuccessful.

In a further effort to get at the reasons for faster development in two of the villages, we asked about failures and the reasons for failure under the NCM. We had some difficulty in interpreting the answers, however, because many respondents confused the question, citing their unfulfilled expectations or failure to meet government goals rather than the village's inability to complete a project once it had been undertaken. For example, the strong collective and still unrealized desire of the two mountain villages for better roads shows up in their responses to this question; for Ich'on C the emphasis is on completing the replacement of all thatched roofs and for Ich'on D the installation of piped water. Where the answers were related to actual unsuccessful projects, villagers cited lack of co-operation as the most frequent reason for failure. In interpreting such data, however, it is important to consider not only why co-operation is more prevalent and effective in one village than another, but also how it varies in the same village with different kinds of projects. Where participants can readily imagine immediate and desirable benefits from a project, it is much easier for a leader to obtain co-operative effort, even though there may be some underlying causes of friction. But if there is any question about the fairness of the eventual distribution of benefits, or if there is considerable doubt regarding the final success of the enterprise, participation will be much harder to organize. For example, community construction projects such as roads, bridges, stream embankments and public buildings are popular and usually inspire both co-operative effort and local pride. But villagers are less likely to be able to imagine significant personal gains from afforestation, group efforts to exterminate insects, or the planting of seedlings for sale.

Dissatisfactions and Complaints

During the interviews, and particularly the informal interviews, some serious objections were expressed to the way in which projects had been carried out. Several of our informants complained that the government, in its efforts to carry out a uniform national plan, had not sufficiently considered the particular conditions that exist in any given village. Often, promised financial aid was not provided when it was required, and projects were initiated during the wrong season. Local officials in subsequent interviews admitted that problems such as these existed. Other complaints arose from the nature of the projects undertaken. For example, the 'donation' of land for village roads without adequate compensation has been a source of friction everywhere. Even after agreements have been reached and the road is completed, the affected landowners usually remain profoundly dissatisfied.

In every village poor farmers complain that collective labour projects usually mean sacrifice on their part and benefits for those who own more land.They understand the importance of co-operative effort in order to improve conditions for the entire village, but the immediate imperative for them is to obtain a return for their labour in order to survive. As a result there is often an undercurrent of friction, with the poor farmers claiming that the *Saemaul* projects only help the rich, and other villagers criticizing the poor for their failure to co-operate more enthusiastically. There are also complaints about the unequal distribution of benefits, particularly with regard to the installation of electricity and piped water.

Local administrative officials, while recognizing the partial validity of such complaints, sometimes criticize the farmers for having become spoiled as a result of all the government attention and assistance. They complain that the ideal of co-operative self-help is fading, and that most people are only concerned with immediate material incentives. Farmers try to take advantage of the government's *Saemaul* policy, they claim, in order to make unreasonable demands or protests to the local administrators, who feel vulnerable because they are under close scrutiny by higher bureaucratic echelons.

An educated person who lives in one of the villages but does not farm said that the NCM has achieved marvellous results in a concrete, practical sense, but that it lacks the sound spiritual foundation that is necessary if the movement is to continue to bear fruit. The similarity of such criticism to that of some of the local officials is striking. In both cases the complaint is that farmers do not adhere wholeheartedly to the particular value systems that are being introduced from outside. The villager is criticized on the basis of the change agent's own ideological standards, and there seems to be surprise and disappointment that farmers should try to maximize their own self-interest instead of adopting the new ideals.

Personal animosity and jealousy provide another source of complaints. In two of the villages we heard a considerable amount of unfavourable gossip concerning present and former leaders. In both cases villagers asserted that development efforts had been impeded, in one instance by incompetent, weak leadership, and in the other because village funds had been habitually misused to entertain outsiders.

Even in the most successfully 'developed' village not everyone was content. One person complained about the constant noise pollution from the loudspeaker. Others objected to the domination of *Saemaul* activities (as well as everything else) by a single kinship group. There is also some strain in each village between the older and younger generations. The responsibility for leadership of the NCM has been entrusted to younger activisits, but Korean cultural tradition heavily emphasized the authority and prestige of older men.

Finally, the tendency of a dominant lineage or neighbourhood to monopolize decision-making for its own advantage was cited by a number of informants as an 'unfair' aspect of the NCM. Particularly in Ich'on D where 70 per cent of the population and 90 per cent of the wealth belongs to one lineage, members of other kin groups revealed considerable dissatisfaction.In Ich'on C and Kongju B the dispersed settlement pattern resulted in a situation where small outlying clusters of houses felt that their interests had not been sufficiently represented.

The New Community Movement and Social Change

It is relatively easy to distinguish differences in the degree of co-operation and willingness to participate in group efforts among our four villages. Chapter 9 discusses this issue in more detail. It is much less easy, however, to estimate the degree of fundamental change in attitudes, work habits, and social relationships in any given community as a result of the NCM activities. Undoubtedly there has been much more co-operative effort on community development projects everywhere during the last six years than if there were no *Saemaul* movement.

But as we have indicated elsewhere, much of this may be due to bureaucratic pressure rather than to enlightened perceptions or changed habits. Where rational, individual self-interest and co-operative work for village development are clearly and tangibly congruent, then we can expect a continuation of joint efforts. The political machinery for deciding on development plans, mobilizing labour, and supervising the actual work is in existence at the village level, and people have acquired a good deal of experience in making it work. In the short run, at least, the evidence suggests that farmers are in fact encouraged by the completion of successful projects and tend to collaborate more readily on more ambitious undertakings as a result. The question is, as farmers' wealth and living standards rise, and as they become more closely tied to national markets both as agricultural entrepreneurs and as consumers, will there be an erosion of community solidarity and co-operation? There is also plenty of evidence to support such a prediction for the longer term.

With regard to changes in values and attitudes it should be kept in mind that because of the extraordinary history of the Republic of Korea during the last 75 years, the modernization or social mobilization of the typical farmer was well advanced by 1970. Agricultural stagnation in our opinion was due more to economic constraints in the 1960s than to a conservative mentality.

Korean farmers for the most part have demonstrated that they will aggressively seize real opportunities when they are available. Evaluation of the *Saemaul* movement in terms of concrete results is made more difficult, because much of the increase in productivity and income that has occurred since 1971 can be attributed to other factors. A more detailed description of this process is contained in the following section.

Other Sources of Developmental Change

Before going on to try to pinpoint the variables associated with different outcomes of the *Saemaul* movement in different villages, it is necessary to describe the rapid pace of economic and social change in rural society due to other factors. *Saemaul* policies, activities and results must be evaluated within the broader context of national rural development. In particular, the relatively favourable social and economic environment within which the movement has taken place has had a profound effect on the community development campaign. Accordingly, determining which particular 'outcomes' in any given village situation are attributable to the NCM is a complex task requiring as much qualitative evaluation as quantitative measurement.

During the late 1960s, as the industrialization and urbanization process in the Republic of Korea rapidly gained momentum, the rural-urban gap widened in terms of most quantifiable data. In fact, as we have pointed out previously, this was one of the reasons why the programme was launched. Nevertheless, a quiet sociocultural revolution of sorts was also going on in rural Korea during the same period that helped prepare the ground for more tangible forms of development later on. The educational level of the rural population was rapidly increasing, as more schools were built, and ambitious farmers were able to send their children to middle and high school. The young men who adopted new attitudes and goals as a result of their experience in military service – both during the Korean War and subsequently – began to assume influential roles as heads of households and local opinion leaders. Mass communications, most notably the domestic production of cheap transistor radios and improved transportation systems, enabled farmers to participate in, or at least observe, the modernizing sector of

Korean society to a much greater degree than ever before. The result was that traditional humility and resignation began to give way to strong aspirations for a better life combined with the realization that new ideas, technologies and customs would have to be adopted.

Very large-scale rural-urban migration during the 1960s and early 1970s was a structural factor that had an important effect on village society. While most migrants were poor and landless (or nearly landless), many others came from relatively well-to-do, upper-class rural families. In both cases, there was the same desire to escape rural stagnation and find improved economic and educational opportunities in the city. Also, many non-conformists and young trouble-makers who tended to be involved in village conflicts left during this period. The effect was to increase the proportion of middle-level farmers in most villages, creating more homogeneous local communities both in terms of wealth and the potential for co-operative effort.

The industrialization and urbanization process was having other profound effects on rural life. Aggressive and competent farmers were increasingly able to take advantage of the growing urban demand for fruits, vegetables and other farm products to engage in commercial agriculture on a larger and more profitable scale. Their example stimulated others, so that the small farmer, who had been predominantly subsistence oriented, began to think increasingly in terms of raising cash crops.

Also, during this same period the foundations were being laid for more effective governmental support of agriculture through expansion of the Office of Rural Development (extension services) and the Agricultural Co-operatives Federation (rural credit). These efforts have been steadily intensified, and one result has been the introduction of new seed varieties and new methods of cultivation throughout the country. By the late 1960s most farmers were able to obtain adequate or nearly adequate supplies of fertilizer and pesticides. Since 1971 there has been a major breakthrough in rice production as the result of the introduction by the Office of Rural Development of new, Korean varieties of 'miracle' rice strains. Yields have increased rapidly, and the many problems of adaptation to local conditions and tastes are gradually being solved. At the same time, higher, subsidized rice prices are guaranteed to farmers by the government.

Relative rural prosperity today must be attributed primarily to such basic economic factors rather than to the effects of the *Saemaul Undong*. The expansion of urban markets for agricultural products, the increasing effectiveness of government services (particularly the introduction of high yield rice strains) and higher rice prices have greatly improved the farmers' terms of trade during the last five years.

Most farmers in the four villages that we studied believe the movement has been a success, and they can point to fundamental improvements in their village environments, their living standards, and their life chances as evidence. Also, there has been an enormous outpouring of governmental propaganda proclaiming the movement's achievements, and this has had a cumulative effect, helping to convince not only the rural population but also city dwellers, members of the bureaucracy involved in administering the movement, and personnel staffing the mass media.

The cynical outsider can assert that in terms of improved agricultural productivity and higher farm incomes the NCM 'success' is largely an artificial one, since the most fundamental positive changes in the rural economy are the result of other governmental policies extraneous to the movement itself. But from a somewhat different perspective such cynicism is not really justified. After all, the fundamental objective of the movement has from the beginning been the psychological and ideological mobilization of the farm population. Also, at the level of national ideology the movement has been proclaimed in such broad terms as to encompass and inspire all aspects of the developmental process.

A great deal of careful planning, combined with a flexible approach to problem-solving has characterized the NCM at all levels. Pressures for quick results from the top of the highly centralized governmental structure have been intense, so that the movement has been pursued at all levels with unflagging bureaucratic zeal. While some differences in administrative style can be observed from one county or sub-county office to another, supervision by higher echelons is close and continuous, and in general the administration of the movement has been quite uniform. The ideological component has perhaps been most strongly expressed and has had a particularly salutary effect in transforming personnel of the local bureaucracy into developmental activists, most of whom now devote a large part of their working hours to exhorting and encouraging farmers to greater co-operative effort. Inevitably there have been excesses and abuses as part of such a massive administrative undertaking. Three or four years ago there were frequent complaints that labour and resources were being wasted on NCM projects that were not adapted to local needs and conditions, and many *Saemaul* leaders were criticized for pressuring their fellow villagers into fulfilling official norms without enough concern for individual interests. But in the villages we studied in 1976 the old attitudes towards authority, which had combined humble subservience, awe, resentment and fear, seemed to have shifted considerably; farmers still recognize that they are dependent on outside help, but their relationships with the local bureaucracy are increasingly characterized by equality and mutuality. Although there was a good deal of official interference in local decision-making during the early stages of the movement, villages now are encouraged to draw up their own *Saemaul* development plans in accordance with local community needs, aspirations and resources. The governmental role has become less one of control and more one of providing advice and support.

Notes

1. Although the Ich'on villages are near the place where the previous surveys were carried out, the Kongju villages are far away in an entirely different kind of topographical setting.

2. In terms of order of priority the villagers estimate of the beneficial effects of the NCM differs from that of *Saemaul* leaders as revealed through a 1974 survey. In a study of 150 village *Saemaul* leaders it was found that 38 per cent cited 'promotion of co-operative spirit', 30 per cent 'increase in income', and 23 per cent 'improved convenience' as the major achievements of the NCM. Park Tong-Seu, 'Roles, selection and leadership techniques of *Saemaul* leader', *Korean Journal of Public Administration*, vol. XII, no. 2 (1974), pp. 76-7.

8 EXPLANATIONS

Why did the campaign have different outcomes in different villages? Depending on the observer's perspective, the primary explanatory factor can be sought either in the various features of the campaign itself or in the differing characteristics of the villages. In fact, of course, the complexity is enormous, as village institutions, thought, behaviour and individual personalities encounter a whole range of outside influences. The researcher at the village level, at least in the Korean context, tends to perceive the campaign as a relatively fixed, well-defined influence from outside, and he is therefore likely to concentrate his efforts on finding local explanations for the various kinds of community responses that take place. At least that has been our experience.

The villagers themselves emphasized three main elements that they thought were most closely related to their success or failure: cooperation, leadership and outside support. The existing mix of cooperative potential and leadership was different in each village at the beginning of the NCM, and the response to outside initiatives during the last six years has also been extremely varied. Poorer villages such as those in Kongju are more dependent on outside help than the Ich'on villages where there is a relatively favourable land/population radio. Many villages have been the scene of previous development efforts over the past 30 years by foreign organizations or missionaries, as well as by agencies of the Korean government. In our sample the most enterprising and successful village, Ich'on D, did in fact receive both advice and material assistance from a church group for several years prior to the implementation of the *Saemaul* movement. But this same village is also the one where energetic local leadership was mobilizing people to undertake development projects ten years or more before the beginning of the current national effort.

Characteristics of the Movement

We will begin by discussing outcomes in terms of some particular features of the movement.

1. *Uniformity and Bureaucratic Rationalization*

The *Saemaul Undong* has been administered in a generally uniform manner. Because of the highly centralized, 'top-down' structure of the administration and the very close supervision exercised over local agencies by higher echelons, the general package of material aid, advice and pressure for results that is delivered to each village varies within relatively narrow limits. There have been several significant changes in the programme through time, as problems were encountered and adjustments made; but the changes have been uniformly applicable throughout the country.

The major area in which official inputs have varied is that of rewards to villages for superior performance. In the earlier stages of the movement the amount of outside aid furnished each year depended on the village's category in a hierarchy of developmental stages (see Chapter 4 for a description). In addition, the President has awarded numerous special prizes. In our sample the relatively successful villages, Kongju B and Ich'on D, were promoted to the highest category, 'developed' (*charip*), fairly early in the course of the movement. In addition they have both received presidential prizes.

Another aspect of the situation that may be unique to the country is the relative homogeneity of village culture and social structure. There are no significant ethnic or linguistic differences in rural areas, and everyone shares a common moral and religious tradition. Finally, as a result of a thoroughgoing land reform in 1949-50 there is a relatively egalitarian distribution of land and wealth.

Because of the uniformity of administration very similar kinds of project have been undertaken in villages that varied greatly in terms of location, resources, lineage composition, topography and climate. Initially this meant that some villages moved ahead much more rapidly because of a variety of favourable factors as, for example, in Ich'on D, where developmental momentum had already been established, forceful leadership was available, the location was convenient, and *Saemaul* projects were well adapted to the village's needs and capacities. Because of their early accomplishments such villages received still more outside aid and were able to carry out further co-operative projects. Thus the policy of promoting competition and offering incentives probably increased the differentiation among villages during the first couple of years of the movement. Subsequently, and especially since 1974, governmental efforts have been concentrated more on bringing up the level of backward villages, and as a result the most undeveloped village of our sample, Kongju A, has recently received a disproportionate share of aid and encouragement. In some 'developed' (*charip*) villages the diminution of material incentives has meant a slackening of co-operative effort and the loss of some development momentum. This does not appear to have been the case in our two *charip* villages, Kongju B and Ich'on D, however.

The government's insistence on stimulating community self-help efforts everywhere and the more recent move to speed up the pace of development in backward villages is having an important effect. In previous developmental efforts (both public and private) there has usually been a tendency to concentrate on pilot villages that were easily accessible, where competent educated leaders were available, and where there was already a reputation for sober hard work. The result was to accentuate the differences between progressive, industrious communities and conservative, apathetic ones. The growing opportunities for profits in cash crops that have become available in recent years have reinforced this tendency, as the progressive and more centrally located villages responded more effectively to market incentives. In this sense, therefore, it is not a question of attributing different outcomes to the effect of the *Saemaul Undong*. Rather, the increasing differences among villages, particularly with regard to farm income and productivity, that seemed to be an inevitable part of the development process are being somewhat mitigated by the effects of the movement.

Another similar result of the movement's highly centralized direction and uniform format deserves mention. The scope of activities and the concentration of supervisory responsibility under the Ministry of Home Affairs has forced its local administrative branches (the county and sub-county offices) to adopt standard, routine procedures in order to cope with the workload. Home Ministry representatives also have the authority to compel local representatives of other ministries to co-ordinate their *Saemaul* activities. The result has been a more rational and equitable distribution of governmental assistance than in the past, when informal personal contacts and the possibility of deals profitable to local officials frequently affected the distribution of whatever help and advice was available.

The effects of the government's policy of stimulating competition have had slightly different outcomes in our two matched pairs. Between the Kongju villages there seems to be considerable rivalry, although Kongju B currently is still generally acknowledged to be more successful. Kongju A residents talk about catching up, and in fact they have accomplished a good deal since 1975. In the Ich'on pair, however, the superiority of Ich'on D is so obvious that farmers in Ich'on C do not see any possibility of imitating their neighbours' performance, and they acquiesce in their lower status within the movement.

2. *Concrete and Diffuse Objectives*

Saemaul Undong planning was shaped by the disappointing results of piecemeal governmental programmes to promote rural development in the 1960s. Efforts to stimulate agricultural production by expanding extension services, promoting community solidarity, and increasing rice prices were all relatively ineffective. It was therefore determined that a major impact would have to be made on the farmer's consciousness by concrete demonstrations of the effectiveness of co-operative self-help. Thus, there was insistence from the start on maximizing joint labour participation in projects that would provide a constant tangible reminder of the benefits obtained through the NCM. Different villages reacted to this initiative in various ways. In some communities the village environmental improvement projects were criticized as costly and superficial because of poverty, conservative inertia or resentment at outside interference. This seems to have been the case in Ich'on C, particularly, but to some extent in Kongju A as well. In Ich'on D the emphasis on changing roofs and improving the appearance of houses has inspired an extravagant (by Korean rural standards), village-wide investment in housing construction which certainly reflects the greater resources at the disposal of many farmers, but also appears to have status implications. In other words, it has become important to keep up with the Joneses (or in this case, the Hongs). Even the poorer houses are neat, and the yard fences have nearly all been rebuilt in approved geometric, concrete style. In the neighbouring village, Ich'on C, the contrast is dramatic. A few well-off farmers live in ostentatious dwellings, but most of the village is housed — even though many roofs have been changed — pretty much as it always has been in the past. The same contrast on a lesser scale is visible between Kongju A and Kongju B.

In addition to this concrete aspect — manifested primarily in an environmental improvements — the campaign has had an important abstract ideological dimension that has already been discussed at some length in Chapter 3 under *objectives*. The effort to promote and integrate in one ideological campaign scientific rationalism, the work ethic, communal spirit, national patriotism and support for the Park government is difficult to evaluate. It seems evident, however, that in spite of intensive efforts at indoctrination this aspect of the campaign is far less important to villagers than concrete changes in their environment and living standards. Rather it is the local purveyors of the message who appear to have been most influenced by it.

On the other hand, there is no question but that most residents in all four villages (except for members of some of the poorer households) do in fact have a favourable attitude towards governmental objectives and give the administration credit for doing a good job. Also, there does seem to be some indication that residents of the villages that have responded most effectively to the pressures and incentives of the NCM (Kongju B and Ich'on D) have in fact assimilated the *Saemaul* ideology to a greater extent than those in the other two, in being more positively accepting of the movement's standards, its collectivity orientation, etc., as will be illustrated below.

3. *Consonance with Pre-existing Attitudes and Values*

We asserted above that there was a considerable degree of cultural homogeneity in Korean villages. One aspect of such homogeneity is a widespread consensus regarding traditional values. A rustic version of Confucian social ethics still provides the ideal standard for a good deal of village behaviour. There is also a widespread and deeply rooted tradition of co-operation and communalism, although its expression varies with the particular history and ecology of each village. Where lineage ideology and *yangban* or upper class tradition is particularly strong, communal solidarity is usually less pronounced. During the 1950s and 1960s substantial modification and erosion of these traditional beliefs and norms took place as part of the modernization process, and as a result a considerable generation gap exists in most villages.

The *Saemaul Undong* strongly reinforces such Confucian values as respect for authority, diligence and personal probity. Its emphasis on co-operative work and the development of a communal ideology supports an aspect of the Korean tradition that was being challenged by individualistic currents of thought and patterns of behaviour. The movement's campaign against extravagant kinship ritual and ceremony has come into conflict with deeply rooted village customs, but it has often been accepted with approval by younger villagers despite the initial outrage of their parents. The *Saemaul* emphasis on correct behaviour and hard work on the part of young people, however, has had the strong backing of most of the adult rural population.

Each of our four villages has reacted somewhat differently to the *Saemaul* movement's insistence that co-operative labour on development projects should occupy most of the farmers' time during the agricultural off season rather than drinking, gambling and talking in informal men's groups. Until very recently the serving of wine was an important part of most social occasions. The effectiveness of the *Saemaul* campaign against drink has varied sharply in the four target villages, with the two least successful, Kongju A and Ich'on C, showing a greater tendency to retain the drinking habits of the past. In Ich'on D, the most progressive village, there is a strongly puritanical atmosphere with no wine shops in the village. Whether the actual consumption of alcohol has decreased or not is difficult to determine. The point is, however, that most drinking is now done in private or outside the village. In Kongju A there are six places where one can buy wine, and they were well patronized, while in Kongju B there were only two. Informants in Kongju B told us that their village had previously been similar to Kongju A, but that customs had changed as a result of the NCM. In Ich'on C drinking still seemed to be an important accompaniment to most social situations.

The delegation of authority to younger leaders, which conflicts directly with custom, was already taking place before the NCM began, as villages tried to cope with their changing environment. Today leaders in all four villages are in their thirties or forties, but the extent of their activism and the success with which they were able to mobilize productive effort in groups varied considerably. (Leadership will be discussed in more detail later.)

It should be emphasized again, however, that in spite of the campaign to promote co-operative and communal effort as internalized social norms, individual goals and ambitions are now stronger everywhere relative to collective values than in the past. The government may have had some success in its attempts to make kinship considerations subordinate to community objectives, although the variation among villages in this regard makes generalization difficult. Certainly the persistence of kinship loyalties and cohesion as an obstacle to development is well demonstrated in our two less successful villages, Kongju A and Ich'on C.

4. *Links with the Local Bureaucracy*

The development of more effective linkages between the village on the one hand and the national bureaucracy and economy on the other has been one of the most important contributions of the NCM. Such linkages provide avenues for the flow of technology, resources, advice and controls in one direction and the distribution of agricultural products in the other. There is some flow of information from the villages that is fed back into the administrative decision-making process, but it is probably minimal.

Closer ties with local administrative agencies have resulted in different kinds of reactions in our four villages. The leaders of Kongju A tend to stress their hardships and difficulties, pleading for additional outside help at every opportunity. In Kongju B the pattern is less dependent and more one of trying to fulfil official expectations and demonstrate that the village is worthy of recognition. In Ich'on C there is a more traditional stance, combining efforts to placate and obtain favours from officials with a certain 'standoffishness' that resists too much interference in village affairs. In Ich'on D the two village leaders play the role of full-time local bureaucrats, even to the point of imitating their clothes and manner, as well as their commitment to rural and national development. As a result, *Saemaul* goals and activism penetrate village life from early morning until late at night.

In every case there is far more interaction between villagers (particularly village leaders) and local government officials than in the past. On the one hand officials are more concerned with, and more active in influencing, village affairs. On the other, villagers, after six years' NCM experience, now recognize the importance of outside support for the success of both community and private ventures.

Another kind of linkage (horizontal) that has been fostered by *Saemaul* bureaucratic pressures, and that has already been referred to, is the greater co-ordination of developmental activities among different government agencies.

Characteristics of the Villages

In the following section we shall discuss those characteristics of our four villages that seemed to us to be most closely related to the degree of progress achieved under the NCM:

1. *Lineage Composition*

From other Korean rural studies we had tentatively hypothesized that in villages where *yangban* (former hereditary upper class) kinship groups were dominant, the resulting conservatism and authoritarian insistence on status superiority would impede village-wide co-operative efforts to intiate change. The situation in Ich'on C, where there are three rival lineages, supported this hypothesis. The antagonism and distrust that exists between members of different lineages makes joint activities on a village-wide basis difficult. If a leader is from one lineage, members of the others are reluctant to recognize his authority. In Ich'on C there is one man of recognized stature and competence who is said to have the respect of all lineages. But he is unwilling to take on the leader's role, because he believes that jealousy and hostility are inevitable.

The neighbouring village, Ich'on D, which also has a *yangban* background, is one of the most successful in the nation. Here there is a single dominant lineage that comprises 70 per cent of the total population. Under forceful leadership, members of this kinship group have been able to work together effectively, not only to complete a large variety of typical NCM environmental projects, but also to increase agricultural productivity and incomes. Members of this lineage, unlike many others, do not seem to be overly concerned with the past glories of their ancestors, and there is little expenditure of time and resources on formal ritual. Apparently their status was not particularly high in the past; under the Japanese most of them were tenants. Since liberation in 1945, farmers of Ich'on D have gradually acquired more and more land from their neighbours in Ich'on C, although the latter used to be better off.

In the Kongju villages, which have a commoner background, the least successful, Kongju A, has a lineage situation similar to that in Ich'on C. Three rival lineages compete for status, wealth and power, and co-operation has been difficult. In Kongju B, however, there are no dominant lineages, and it appears that this situation has made it easier for one man to obtain the confidence and support of people from other kin groups.

2. *Wealth and Land Distribution*

In each of our matched pairs the least successful village has more poor farmers. Also, in each case the more successful village has reportedly been acquiring land at the expense of its neighbours for many years, suggesting that 'success' as defined by the NCM may be due to other, underlying factors of a long-term nature.

Land distribution is a case in point. It showed a marked difference between the proportions of owner-farmers and landless labourers in the two Kongju villages. The differences are, in fact, sharper than those figures suggested, since the owner-tenants of Kongju A rent a larger portion of their acreage, on average, than those in Kongju B. The difference in ownership distribution in the Ich'on village is less marked, but Ich'on D's advantage was increased by renting in larger amounts of land to make average operating units of 1.7 ha. of which 1.3 was owned, compares with 1.1 ha. average for both ownership and operational units in Ich'on C.

3. *Settlement Patterns*

The problem of a dispersed settlement pattern in one village of each of our two pairs has already been discussed in Chapter 5. The different kinds of outcome — positive in the case of Kongju B and negative in the case of Ich'on C — indicate that while dispersal does make concerted action more difficult, frequent communication and strong feelings of mutuality can overcome the disadvantage. There are many other villages in Korea where houses are much further apart than in any of our sample communities, and if several small, widely dispersed hamlets are congruent with different kinship groupings, the problem is compounded. Where such structural obstacles to collective action exist, the need for strong leadership, effective local organization for bringing about concerted action, and outside support becomes particularly great.

4. *Leadership*

As indicated previously, where there are rival kinship groups of approximately equal size and wealth, as in our Kongju A and Ich'on C villages, the leader faces difficult problems. In both villages the residents blame their poor performance on inadequate leaders, and there is gossip about malfeasance in office. It has been impossible for us to determine whether such accusations are justified, or whether they merely reflect the jealousy and animosity of different kin groups. In any case, our observation of patterns of interaction in the village has revealed some obvious differences in leadership style. In Kongju A the *Saemaul* leader, and to some extent the village head as well, spent a good deal of time in small, relatively congenial groups, attempting to bring influential farmers around to their points of view. When the development council met, however, there was a great deal of wrangling, and the leader tried everything — entreaty, mediation and bullying — in order to reach some sort of consensus. The result seems to be a not very successful version of the familiar two-stage process, in which an effort is made informally ahead of time to reach agreements that will be ratified at the larger formal meeting. The current *Saemaul* leader is determined to exercise strong leadership, but he seems to be frequently involved in efforts at mediation in order to try to cope with the antagonisms that his forceful action has provoked.

Although the style of leadership in Kongju B and Ich'on D is quite different, these two relatively successful communities shared a significant characteristic. Meetings of the development council took place frequently in a businesslike atmosphere. Opposing opinions were forcefully expressed, but the group in each case comprised men who were used to working together and coming up with practical solutions. Discussions were largely technical, and when decisions were reached, there was confidence that they would have the support of the entire community. In other words, the machinery for consultation and decision-making was not only effective but in constant use.

In Kongju B the village head, while not particularly forceful, is well liked and has a high reputation for conscientious service to the community. He was unfailingly courteous and took great pains with the many farmers who visited his office during the day. He also worked closely with the somewhat more dynamic *Saemaul* leader, who had been his classmate in primary school.

In Ich'on D the two energetic, hard-driving leaders, who appeared to adopt a style patterned after that of full-time local officials at the sub-county or county level, maintained a rather brusque, almost peremptory manner in their official dealings with other villagers, most of whom were their relatives. While there was some grumbling about this commanding style, particularly on the part of older villagers who were not members of the dominant lineage, their proven competence made their actions acceptable. The most prestigious (and richest) person in the village is a former village head and *Saemaul* leader who is now about sixty years old. The early developmental surge of the village several years before the inception of the NCM was largely due to his leadership, and his opinions are still extremely influential.

The *Saemaul Undong* adminstrators recognize the crucial importance of effective village leadership, and there are continuing governmental efforts to provide additional training and incentives. Although village *Saemaul* leaders are formally elected, sub-county officials have sometimes exercised considerable influence on their choice. Villagers tend to resent such interference in the selection process, particularly where local development programmes run into difficulty.

5. *The Role of Women*

Because of the important role of women in developmental activities we asked specifically for the villagers' opinion on this point. It turned out that the contribution of women was valued much more highly in the Ich'on villages, where most of the population were descended from *yangban* (upper-class ancestors), than in Kongju where commoner ancestors predominated. In Korean tradition the subordination of women and strict prohibitions against their undertaking any kind of activity outside the home have in the past been most characteristic of *yangban* households, so our findings were contrary to what might have been expected on the basis of class background alone.

The decisive element here seemed to be the more modernized outlook of the villages nearer Seoul due to higher levels of education, the greater influence of mass communications, and participation in national markets. By contrast, the Kongju villages are somewhat isolated and therefore more conservative. Also, because of the relative shortage of land, many men in the mountain villages do not have enough work to keep them occupied and as a result female labour in the fields is not crucial. In the more productive agricultural areas nearer Seoul there is usually a labour shortage, with women spending much more time in the fields than even just a few years ago.

Nevertheless, even in the Kongju villages women do contribute considerable labour to the NCM projects. If a male is sick or unable to participate in co-operative activities for some other reason, his wife or a female member of the household may replace him. Women are likely to be diligent workers, and they are often employed in the more menial tasks such as road-building, carrying pebbles, or assisting in the construction of a building such as the meeting hall. Also, the participation of women in co-operative activities is often welcomed because it promotes an aura of cheerfulness in which joking and singing lighten the burden of hard work. There are separate women's projects such as the rice saving movement in which each housewife is encouraged to set aside a small amount of rice each day, both to reduce domestic consumption and as a means of saving. In the Ich'on villages, particularly Ich'on D, women are quite active with their own projects, which include management of a credit union, the manufacture of rice sacks, noodle-making, the management of co-operative kitchens during the busiest farm seasons, keeping the village streets clean, and the promotion of various sanitation measures.

9 COMMUNITY DEVELOPMENT AND THE NOTION OF COMMUNITY

The inculcation of a sense of community at the village level through co-operative projects designed to improve living conditions and increase agricultural productivity has from the start been a major objective of the *Saemaul* movement. There was recognition by the planners that the degree of community solidarity varied from one village to another, but it was generally assumed, in accordance with conventional CD doctrine, that a lack of communal spirit in most villages was one cause of stagnation in agricultural development. The *Saemaul* administrators also started with the conviction that most traditional rural customs, attitudes and values were not conducive to rapid development and should be eliminated or reformed. The original objective was to create a new kind of dynamic, rational and collective village unit as the basis for a more productive agricultural sector of society.

In fact, there are many deeply rooted communal aspects of social organization in Korean villages. The ideal of subordinating individual self-interest to the welfare of larger groups is an important ethical principle in the cultural tradition. There are a great many communities where neighbourhood and natural village cohesion is strong, with well-developed patterns of mutual assistance and collective effort. But in many other communities the kinship group, i.e. the family, and, to a lesser extent, the lineage segment, has had priority over such territorial groupings as the neighbourhood, hamlet or village. Even where communal feeling is particularly strong, kinship ties have greater formal legitimacy. The problem from the governmental planners' point of view, then, was not only that selfish individuals might obstruct collective efforts, but that it was regarded as necessary to shift the main focus of cohesion and group effort from a kinship to a territorial base. The *Saemaul Undong* was organized therefore in order to increase community solidarity while undermining lineage loyalty, which was regarded as a conservative factor obstructing progress.

In each village the particular balance or tension between kinship solidarity and community solidarity depends on such factors as lineage composition, division of wealth, leadership, settlement patterns and traditional class status. Kinship solidarity tends to be hierarchical and authoritarian in nature while community solidarity is more egalitarian.

125

Where there is one dominant lineage, as in Ich'on D, characterized by progressive, energetic leadership, kinship solidarity can play a crucial role in development. In a sense kinship solidarity in Ich'on D is coterminous with community solidarity because of the dependence and intimidation of the farmers who are not members of the dominant lineage. We have already described at some length how kinship solidarity can impede developmental efforts when there are two or more lineages of approximately equal size and influence as in Kongju A and Ich'on C.

Community solidarity is more intangible in nature. When asked what factor was most important in the success or failure of NCM projects, villagers generally replied that co-operation is most crucial. It is difficult to determine, however, whether this answer is the result of ideological indoctrination or of a rational effort to weigh several different factors. Responses to other questions that were designed to reveal the degree of co-operative spirit and extent of joint participation showed that Kongju B and Ich'on D were in fact more collectivity oriented than the two less successful villages. In Kongju B the answers to our open-ended questions showed a widespread concern with co-operation. Respondents did not complain that they were asked to contribute too much labour for SMU projects. Rather, complaints focused on the fact that not everyone contributed his fair share, and this was seen as a threat to community solidarity. In Kongja A, however, there were numerous objections to the constant mobilization for co-operative labour. 'Co-operation' for many of the poorer residents of Kongju A had a negative connotation, associated with the pressures on them to contribute unpaid labour.

In our two matched pairs of villages the government's contention appears at first to be self-evident; that the greater degree of collective spirit and co-operative effort in the two successful, 'developed' villages has resulted in a neater village appearance, better roads and bridges, more pride and self-confidence, higher productivity, and better working relationships for decision-making on a day-to-day basis. But the problem is not so simple. How do we account for the fact that in some villages people work together more harmoniously and productively; In our most successful sample village the basis of solidarity is kinship cohesion. And as we noted previously, farmers in the two more successful villages have been improving their economic situation at the expense of their neighbour over a much longer time period than that of the *Saemaul Undong*, and most of this improvement has been due to individual initiative. Thus, other factors in addition to solidarity (or at least the *Saemaul* version of solidarity) are presumably responsible. Indeed, one might even postulate that the causal connection between co-operation and progress may sometimes operate in the other direction; and that on occasion it is the more prosperous, more rational, investment- and market-oriented farmers who perceive most clearly the advantages of co-operation on projects that are beyond the resources of any single individual. Thus, a new kind of collectivism can be seen as emerging from wealthier, more progressive communities where the *Saemaul Undong* has served as an effective catalyst.

There seem to be endless complexities in getting at the meaning of the term solidarity. Traditionally in most Korean villages there were many occasions during the year — of a ritual, ceremonial, economic, social welfare and recreational nature — when people joined together in co-operative, group activities. Such occasions were usually genuine expressions of village solidarity during which reciprocity and interdependence were freely expressed with little calculation of individual contribution or profit. Participation by everyone in accordance with ancient customs that were sanctioned by non-economic values, was the most important consideration. Today, however, *Saemaul Undong* local administrators are emphasizing improved living standards as the main incentive for participation in co-operative projects. A good deal of criticism has, in fact, been directed at the *Saemaul Undong* because of its lack of 'spiritual' content at the local level.

On the other hand, there are many other villages where solidarity in the more traditional *gemeinschaft* sense is still strong, even though it has not been expressed in an enthusiastic commitment to *Saemaul* goals. A consensus regarding proper moral behaviour and the harmonious settlement of disputes, a predilection for mutual assistance if there is trouble, and a strong sense of common identity in contrast to the world beyond village boundaries do not necessarily entail a predilection for village-wide public works projects. There are still other villages well known to the authors where progress in economic terms (productivity and income) has been relatively rapid on the basis of determined efforts by individuals or groups of relatives rather than as a result of community-wide efforts. Co-operative labour among kin is a well-established custom in Korea, and where, as in many villages, related households live close together, the system works quite effectively. Given today's higher rice yields and the burgeoning opportunities for profitable commercial agriculture, competent farmers with adequate land can usually make a good living, whether they roll up a successful *Saemaul* record or not. Today it is in the villages that have major irrigation and flood control problems, or where access to fields or the main road is particularly difficult, that outside help and the promotion of large-scale co-operative effort is most necessary. The Kongju mountain villages are examples of this type.

Another aspect of community solidarity is its relationship to the enforcement of group norms through social censure. During the 1950s and 1960s the traditional consensus regarding norms and behaviour was increasingly challenged in rural areas as young people absorbed new ideas and imitated new models from outside their communities. Consequently a degree of social disorganization occurred in many villages. The *Saemaul Undong* has helped to reimpose recognized standards, some of which, like diligence, co-operation and discipline, reinforce patterns of behaviour traditionally sanctioned by Confucian ethics. The movement has also tried to reduce the prevalence of drinking, gambling and extravagant ceremonial expenditures in rural society. In both Kongju B and Ich'on D there does seem to have been a greater receptivity to *Saemaul* values, and a resulting puritanization of village behaviour. Small community gossip and in the case of young people direct censure are effective sanctions, and violators are isolated and shamed. In many cases it is the younger, activist leaders and women who have played crucial roles in bringing about the new conformity to stricter behavioural standards. But such collective pressure for the adoption of more strict codes of behaviour is by no means universal. In other cases influential opinion leaders resist change and outside interference, and as in most other countries a fondness for strong drink is not given up easily.

The kind of solidarity that leads to success according to NCM criteria means the capacity of village residents to work together day after day without immediate tangible reward on projects that will benefit the entire village. It comprises not only the desire to change the environment and improve living conditions, but also an activist orientation — a confidence that group effort will in fact produce the desired results. At one end of the scale such solidarity can be jeopardized when farmers are doing well on their own and see no need or personal advantage to be derived from co-operative projects. At the other end, conservative, subsistence-oriented attitudes combined with the lack of self-confidence and distrust of all outside interference make it extremely difficult in some communities to generate enthusiasm for contributions of unpaid voluntary labour.

The kind of achievement-oriented solidarity under consideration here requires a certain unity of outlook and purpose, or at least a willingness to subordinate immediate private or small group interests to longer-range common goals. In this regard we recognize that in spite of our efforts at analysis the essence of solidarity — its most intangible component — remains elusive. Perhaps this quality, which is closely related to the kind of interpersonal relationships that prevail in the small community, can best be approximated by the term morale. In our sample villages the four characteristics associated with solidary relationships that seem to be most closely correlated with effective, sustained, co-operative effort are the lack of strong rivalry among lineages, effective leadership, relative equality of land distribution, and the existence of a progressive, responsible village elite.

As described earlier, lineage rivalry operates in Kongju A and Ich'on C to make the decision-making process more difficult and more acrimonious. Decisions are likely to be made as a result of outside pressure or as a compromise between conflicting views rather than as a reflection of widespread participation. In Ich'on C when the members of one lineage began to exert preponderant influence in the development council, the representatives of the other two lineages joined forces against them. In Kongju A where there had previously been serious internal political problems, some improvement has occurred. The current leader has the advantage of being associated with a rapid increase in government aid. This support from the local administration has enabled him to take a harder line in dealing with recalcitrant villagers, and he had forced agreement more than once by threatening to resign.

In any case, local-level bureaucrats recognize that leaders can only function well if they have the confidence and respect of most villagers, but no easy solution to the problem of lineage rivalries seems to be available.

We have shown in the previous chapter how inequality of wealth and land distribution undermines solidarity, since both the poorest and wealthiest farmers usually feel they have little interest in contributing labour to NCM projects.

Finally, some attention should be given to the dynamic aspects of village solidarity. Although our research in the Kongju and Ich'on villages did not cover a long enough period to enable us to gauge change in the mood or attitudes of our informants, it seems evident that marked shifts do take place. Periods of great enthusiasm and intensive effort are sometimes followed by disillusionment and a reluctance to co-operate. Initial cynicism and resistance to the mobilization of co-operative labour can give way gradually to a recognition of the long-term benefits of group efforts. But there is always the problem of sustaining developmental momentum once it has been established. It seems to us that today in the Republic of Korea this is as much a function of adequate material incentives, effective village organizations, institutional linkages with local agencies, and the development of increasingly rational patterns of thought and behaviour as it is of community solidarity.

10 LESSONS TO BE LEARNED

External Factors

The community development effort in the Republic of Korea has been characterized by extensive governmental material and organizational contributions, and it has taken place within a generally favourable economic environment. The response of different villages to external stimuli has, of course, varied, and assistance from outside is in many cases not enough by itself to bring about sudden, startling improvements. Nevertheless, the economic situation of nearly all Korean farmers is gradually improving, and the NCM must be given some of the credit.

In a rapidly modernizing nation such as the Republic of Korea, inexorable cultural and economic forces are shaping farmers' attitudes in new directions, and developmental programmes must be flexible and pragmatic. The somewhat doctrinaire ideological orientation of the *Saemaul Undong* has been increasingly tempered by trial and error efforts to find ways of getting quick results. Where farmers are increasingly individualistic and concerned with the acquisition of consumer goods, attempts to revive pre-modern communalism as a kind of moral order are unlikely to have much sustained success. In general, continuing co-operation in carrying out village projects is only possible if each participant is reasonably confident that he will receive direct, concrete and fairly immediate benefits as a result.

On the other hand, the ideological dimension of the *Saemaul* movement, which comprises both the introduction of new ways of thinking and the revitalization of old beliefs, has evoked a considerable response in many communities. It seems obvious to us, however, that the acceptability of the *Saemaul* message depends directly on the improved economic conditions that have accompanied it.

The farmer's terms of trade, that is, the relationship of the prices paid for farm produce to the cost of necessary manufactured goods, must not be so disadvantageous as to condemn the average landholder to subsistence agriculture. In other words, the national economy must provide incentives for increased productivity in the form of higher real incomes. Otherwise community development consists merely in finding more benign ways for villagers to take in each others' washing, and no sustained developmental momentum will be generated.

Another essential condition for village development in the country

131

that has little to do with village values or solidarity is the establishment of local administrative organizations to provide essential services for farmers and ties between villages and the larger regional or national society. The *Saemaul* campaign has been waged in the local co-operatives, rural guidance offices (agricultural extension), and in local administration more feverishly than in the villages and with even greater continuity. As we have indicated elsewhere in this report, increased supplies of rural credit, more readily available technological advice, and improved facilities for the storage, transportation and marketing of agricultural products have been the most important factors in rural development.

The fact that the NCM has been organized from the start on a national scale and imposed on rural areas under the personal direction and with the full backing of the country's highest officials distinguishes it sharply from previous rural development efforts. Of still greater importance is the continuing pressure from the highest administrative levels for tangible results, a pressure that has been maintained and in some ways even intensified over a period of six years. The decision to give supervisory authority for administering the movement to the Ministry of Home Affairs has been of great importance in resolving problems of bureaucratic rivalry, competition and obstructionism.

All of these external factors, which might be regarded as making up a kind of ecology of village development should also be considered from the standpoint of timing. For example, the electrification project that succeeded in Kongju county in 1976 probably would have failed ten years earlier, in spite of the fact that farmers were just as eager to have electricity then and were willing to work just as hard for it. Rapid industrialization has brought about sharp increases in the availability of technical expertise, all kinds of manufactured material, and other government resources.

In the Korean case, then, the indications are that industrialization and urbanization paved the way for rural development, both because of the creation of new markets for agricultural goods and because much larger sums could be allocated to the agricultural sector in governmental budgets.

Factors within the Village Community

The importance of timing is also apparent at the village level. Mass communications and frequent trips to town and cities during the past ten or fifteen years have revolutionized villagers' conceptions of appropriate living standards. Local markets are full of domestic, mass-produced consumer goods of every description; farmers and their wives are now cash- rather than subsistence-oriented. During the past five or six years there have been in most villages a series of small successes, both in NCM activities and in private agriculture. One result has been a development of know-how and self-confidence among individuals and groups that is leading to further advances both in productivity and the determination of individuals to improve their life chances.

At the level of the small agricultural community, our research has indicated that certain aspects of village social organization are related to developmental success:

1. An obvious but none the less crucial factor is that sharp structural (usually kinship) divisions within the village complicate the problems of leadership and make sustained, concerted action more difficult to achieve.
2. In villages where there is particularly unequal land distribution with a relatively large proportion of both very poor and well-off farmers, widespread participation in the CD programme is harder to organize.
3. Effective village leadership is crucial. Actually, every village has two formal leaders, both of whom are deeply involved in local development projects. It is absolutely essential that they work well together. In the small face-to-face community, leaders must possess two kinds of characteristics: forceful direction and competence; and the ability to command respect and trust within the village.
4. The task of village leaders is greatly facilitated if the most respected, wealthy and influential residents give their active support and assume responsible roles in the movement. Sometimes there may be just one or two important men whose enthusiastic participation is crucial. In other communities these informal leaders (*yuji*) may number as many as ten or twelve and constitute the real power in village politics. In the latter case there is a danger that traditional procedures for reaching a consensus by avoiding controversy will result in stagnation. Success in NCM activities is closely associated with the development of effective and frequently used mechanisms for consultation and decision-making.
5. There is a crucial but intangible quality comprising such factors as solidarity, morale, a sense of mutual obligation, social censure, territorial loyalty, and in the Korean term, *insim* (human heartedness), that varies a great deal from place to place. This phenomenon, which

has both traditional and modern components, helps determine the extent and intensity of participation in co-operative community projects. While obviously related to the four structural characteristics mentioned above, it is, as we discovered in the previous chapter, extremely difficult to pin down.

6. We have already emphasized that despite considerable cultural uniformity, villages in Korea differ quite markedly in terms of conformity to standards of propriety, the extent of adoption of technological innovations, and the capacity for collective action. In those communities where hard working, thrifty, innovative farmers are preponderant and set the sub-cultural tone, steady economic development can be expected regardless of the degree of participation in joint community activities. Where such a village also engages enthusiastically in the *Saemaul Undong*, then as in Ich'on D exceptional progress is possible.

   The modernization of attitudes and behaviour, which permits farmers to take advantage of the opportunities provided by a developing economy and the services offered by an increasingly ubiquitous administrative bureaucracy, is also important. Where extremely unfavourable local conditions exist, either because of geographic isolation, poor resources, or especially conservative leadership, then the *Saemaul Undong* can play a crucial role in speeding up the process.

7. Although *Saemaul* ideology and policy overwhelmingly emphasize the successful completion of co-operative community projects as its main goal, the revitalization of internal village organs for consultation and decision-making as well as the formation of closer ties between village leaders and local officials may be indirect benefits of greater long-run usefulness.

8. A final lesson that we and the Korean authorities are learning is that successful rural economic development makes it very hard to maintain the kind of communal tension that is at the core of *Saemaul* ideology.

A spirit of individual agricultural entrepreneurship is becoming increasingly pervasive. Commercial farming is in many ways more demanding than the agricultural practices of the past, requiring rational planning and careful budgeting in order to finance investments in new agricultural technology. Thus the leisurely patterns of the past, which were based on relatively simple agricultural techniques known to all and utilizing intensive inputs of underemployed labour, are no longer viable. The contrast in terms of development, then, is not so much between solitary communities and collections of hostile, suspicious, individual peasants, as it is between conservative, easy-going farming practices and hard-driving, market-oriented, materialistic ambition. From a certain kind of nostalgic perspective a great deal is being lost, perhaps. The generosity, hospitality, mutuality and slow, serene rhythms of traditional rural life are steadily giving way, as villages are more closely integrated with the national society and economy. On the other hand, there is no question but that the overwhelming majority of farmers is pleased with the way things are going and looks forward to greater material abundance, whatever the cost in terms of the dislocation of former life-styles. The upper middle-level farmer increasingly sits around his television set at night rather than exchanging views and gossip with his neighbours at some time-honoured meeting place. He is more likely to calculate his costs and benefits carefully before deciding to contribute labour or resources to a village project. He is less dependent on his neighbours and more closely tied to outside sources of credit, agricultural raw materials, and technical advice than ever before. His aspirations are increasingly linked with individual profits and the purchase of consumer goods. The *Saemaul* movement has accomplished many of its purposes, and most farmers think favourably of it. But we doubt that rural society in the Republic of Korea is more collective or community-oriented than it was six or seven years ago.

One of the themes running through this report is the tension between a CD doctrine that puts major emphasis on co-operation and self-help (what might be called the effort to transform rural villages into diligent, harmonious social units) and the way in which rural development has largely taken place, i.e. through structural reforms in the provision of services to farmers and improved access to expanding markets. The response of villagers to these new opportunities has been partly based on individual initiative and partly on co-operative group action, the particular mix varying from one village to another. While *Saemaul* ideology has reinforced the utopian and communalistic traditions that are still strong in rural Korea, the movement's implementation has in fact been closely meshed with a hard-headed, economist's approach to development. The criticism of ideologues who regret that their vision of community is being tarnished by the forces of materialistic individualism and new technologies has been widespread in contemporary Korean society. The entire process of industrialization and its accompanying social change is often denounced by discontented intellectuals.

As we indicated in Chapter 9, powerful communal traditions still persist. But the forces of change are pervasive. Planning emphasis is now being directed more towards regional co-operation among villages, sub-counties and counties, and while efforts continue to promote collective psychological mobilization, there is widespread recognition that farmers are motivated predominantly by more impersonal, material incentives. But no doubt the tension will continue.

III COMMUNITY DEVELOPMENT IN TANZANIA

Samuel S. Mushi

1 THE NATIONAL SETTING FOR TANZANIA'S COMMUNITY DEVELOPMENT

Tanzania includes two formerly separate, independent nation-states, namely Tanganyika (the mainland) and Zanzibar (the islands). The two countries united on 26 April 1964 to form the United Republic of Tanzania. This study is concerned with community development on the mainland part of the Republic.

The Land and Its People

With a total area of 360,000 square miles, Tanzania (mainland) is one of the largest countries in Africa. However, about 30 to 40 per cent of this immense land mass is arid or semi-arid. Some 60 to 70 per cent of the land is arable, with varying degrees of soil fertility and rainfall. In comparison with many landlocked African countries, Tanzania has good communications with the outside world, being bordered by navigable lakes in the south, west and northwest, and by the Indian Ocean in the east. Its long coastline with several natural harbours is an appreciable asset. Its geographical position accounts for the historical experience with various colonial rulers — the Arabs, Portuguese, Germans and British — as well as trade links with the outside world even before the establishment of formal colonial administration.

The arable parts of the country have tremendous potential for agriculture and forestry, particularly because of the presence of large rivers which can be harnessed for both irrigation and hydro-electric power. Already the government has begun to utilize this potential in several regions (e.g. Nyumba ya Mungu Dam in Kilimanjaro, Kidatu and Rubada in Morogoro). The existing potential for hydroelectric power is capable of supplying electricity to every village in Tanzania and leaving a surplus for 'export' to neighbouring countries.

Tanzania has over 120 tribal or linguistic groups. The tribal configuration has several interesting characteristics which affected the style of politics during the first decade of independence. First, in comparison with other African countries (e.g. Nigeria, Kenya, etc.), Tanzania's tribes are many but small, with population sizes ranging from several thousands (e.g. the Zanaki) to several millions (the Sukuma).

Second, with the possible exception of the Chagga, the Haya and the Nyakyusa, none of the tribes was historically strong enough politically or economically to pose the threat of secession. Third, however, there was at the time of independence such a big gap between the development levels of these various tribes and regions that the government found it necessary to adopt a deliberate policy to correct the inherited development imbalance. For. disc

This development imbalance is largely due to the varying influence of the Christian missionaries and colonial policy. Western education was introduced early in areas where there was early missionary activity such as Kilimanjaro, Bukoba, Tukuyu. These areas have remained the main source of high-level manpower in all fields despite the government's decade-old effort to redress the balance in educational opportunities. Colonial policy compounded the problem further. Both German and British administrations were interested in developing certain key cash crops (e.g. sisal, cotton, coffee) that were in great demand at home. Thus only in the areas that could grow such crops was there any effort to create the necessary infrastructure (roads, schools, health facilities, etc.). Indeed, the pattern of colonial roads and railways bears witness to this; starting either at an administrative town or an estate or plantation, they ended at the sea port, with no feeder roads to open up the rest of the country. Further, as a matter of deliberate policy, colonial administrations set aside some areas of the country to act as 'labour reserves' providing a regular supply of cheap migrant labour to the foreign estates and plantations. Kigoma Region (the Waha tribe in particular) is probably the best example of regional or tribal underdevelopment resulting from this colonial policy.

Fourth, unlike Kenya, Rhodesia and even Zambia, Tanzania had a very small white settler population (several hundreds) and a relatively small Asian and Arab population (several thousands out of a total population of about ten million in 1961 or about sixteen million in 1977). However, this small foreign element had the advantage of education, business and farming skills *vis-à-vis* the local people at the time of independence. But this relative advantage did not lead to political claims because of the smallness of the foreign groups and the history of the country as a United Nations Trustee Territory.

Finally, the country is multi-religious. The configuration of religions and denominations in Tanzania corresponds roughly to the pattern of colonial penetration. Thus the majority of the people on the coast and along the Arab slave trade routes are Muslims, and the majority of those in the cash-crop growing areas whose climate was favourable to white missionaries and settlers are Christians of various denominations. Traditional religions are to be found in the remote areas which experienced the least colonial penetration.

These land and population characteristics have strongly influenced the Tanzanian style of politics and development policy since independence. First, between 1961 (independence) and 1967 (Arusha Declaration), the central leadership was preoccupied with finding ways to integrate the 120 tribal groups into a unitary political system. Hence the formation of a single Workers' Union (NUTA in 1964), a single party system (TANU in 1965) and affiliation of all important national institutions and co-operative groups with the single party. However, this effort was not accompanied by the kind of intense inter-ethnic struggles experienced elsewhere in Africa mainly because of the weaknesses of the tribal and racial groups.

Second, development policy has continued to emphasize the correction or development imbalance between tribes, regions and urban and rural areas. Hence the introduction of a 'quota system' in the selection of secondary school entrants, and emphasis on rural development projects particularly since the Arusha Declaration. Of course there are other reasons as well for the emphasis on rural development as far as Tanzania is concerned. We shall discuss these reasons later.

Third, the colonial inheritance has also had an influence at the ideological level. Colonial development policy created a very weak class structure; indeed, an immature class structure at the time of independence. This situation led to the adoption of a 'unique' brand of socialist ideology, namely *ujamaa*, emphasizing class *collaboration* rather than class *struggle*. The main problems resulting from this conception of socialism (*ujamaa*) will be pointed out in various chapters of this study.

The Political and Administrative System

The Tanzanian central leadership recognized very early after independence the need to re-shape the political and administrative apparatus inherited from colonial rule. Indeed, the achievements in this area during the first decade of independence (1961-72) were probably greater than those in the economic sphere. The objective was to evolve a political and administrative system that was indigenous (rather than an imitation of the Westminster model), capable of unifying various interests, tribes and communities in the country, and development-oriented (rather than just concentrating on 'law and order'). Much that has been achieved in this field is a result of the central leadership's imagination and willinⴲness to experiment with new forms of societal organization. We shall only outline the main changes and features which shed some light on the political and administrative context in which Tanzania's community development (CD) effort has taken place.

First, Tanzania opted for the one-party system which was established by law in July 1965 following President Nyerere's imaginative treatise on 'Democracy and the Party System' published in 1961.[1] This meant also affiliating all the important national institutions, including the workers' and peasants' organizations, with the single party. The objective here was to minimize factional politics and to foster national unity. Through this arrangement, it has also been possible to develop and sustain (now for over a decade) a central unifying ideology based on the concept of *ujamaa* (or familyhood). What is even more important is that, contrary to the criticism heard in the sixties, Tanzania's one-party system has been able to retain the essentials of democracy, particularly democratic elections, both for party functionaries and the National Assembly. For example, in the three parliamentary elections that have been held under the system (1965, 1970 and 1975), over two-thirds of incumbent MPs, including well-established political figures such as ministers, were replaced by popular vote, a higher casualty rate than in many older two-party democracies of the West. Of course there are still issues which are being debated within Tanzania, such as there being a single presidential candidate selected by the party machinery.[2]

Second, the traditional authorities (chiefs, etc.) were abolished or subjected to the new party and government organization (1962).

Third, the political and administrative structures were brought closer to each other to minimize conflict between the two. For example, from 1963 onwards, politico-administrative posts were created in the districts and regions in the name of Area and Regional Commissioners (now Secretaries) to serve as both party and administrative bosses in their respective areas. Again, bureaucrats have been appointed to party posts while party functionaries have been allocated posts in the government bureaucracy. This has been possible because of three factors: first, the civil service has been politicized and the old assurance of 'tenure' and 'permanence' has been eroded; it is just as easy (or difficult) to remove a civil servant from his office as to remove a party functionary or a minister; secondly, the party now pays its functionaries salaries and other emoluments comparable to those in the public service, and thirdly, the legal supremacy bestowed on the party in 1975 has further increased the attraction of political roles. The merger of the two parties (TANU on the mainland and Afro-Shirazi on the islands) to form Chama cha Mapinduzi (CCM) in February 1977 also increased this attraction, for it introduced a pension scheme for party and other political functionaries.

Fourth, measures have been taken since independence to decentralize the decision-making power to the grass-roots level in an effort to promote local initiatives and 'development from below'. On the government side this took the form of development committees. On the party side, the cell system (a cell = 10 households) was introduced in 1964 as the basic unit of mobilization. On the people's side, co-operatives and self-help groups were encouraged and created from 1962 onwards as part of the 'participatory strategy' of the old Community Development Movement. This strategy will be explored in some detail in Chapter 2. The decentralization of the decision-making power evolved gradually from 1962 to 1972 when a major administrative decentralization was undertaken. The main features of this administrative reform will be discussed in Chapter 4 which examines the implementation machinery.

Finally, with the nationalization measures brought about by the Arusha Declaration in 1967, a large parastatal sector has emerged, manned by its own state bureaucracy. Its strategic importance will become clear in the following section.

Structure of the Economy and Development Strategy

The Tanzanian case shows how difficult it is to change the structure of a colonial or neo-colonial economy. Despite the leadership's intentions, the structure of the economy has not changed fundamentally from that inherited at independence. The most conspicuous change has been in the tertiary sector (services) which has received overwhelming emphasis in terms of budgetary and manpower allocations. The slow change in the structure of the economy can be seen from the following figures.[3]

In 1961 (independence), the primary (export) sector (agriculture, forestry and mining) accounted for 45 per cent of all incomes generated locally. This was in keeping with the colonial investment pattern which emphasized the extractive sector to meet industrial needs in the metropolis. Agriculture was the main source of foreign earnings, accounting for about 80 per cent of all export earnings in 1961. For the next fourteen years the situation remained virtually unchanged, for in 1975 agriculture still accounted for over 70 per cent of total export earnings and about 40 per cent of the GDP.

The inherited secondary sector (manufacturing) was virtually negligible in size and concentrated on such consumer items as beer, cigarettes, etc. It represented about 3.7 per cent of the GDP in 1961 and 5.3 per cent in 1964. Although between 1964 and 1972 it was the fastest growing sector of the economy, it accounted for only about 10 to 11 per cent of the GDP with average growth rate of 9.8 per cent (in real terms) per annum during the period. However, between 1972 and 1975 the sector experienced a declining growth, nearing zero growth rate by 1975 (i.e. 0.3 per cent). Three main factors account for this decline. First, there was a widespread underutilization of capacity in the factories mainly due to lack of essential inputs and incentives under the stringent leadership code of behaviour. Second, the famine of 1973-5 led to the importation of more consumer goods (food) than producer goods and also more emphasis on the production of food than industrial goods. Third, following the Arusha Declaration (1967), industry and directly productive activities were de-emphasized in favour of socioeconomic infrastructure. In particular, the party ruled in 1971 that emphasis should be on the provision of rural water supply, health and educational facilities. Thus by 1975 the tertiary sector (services and associated administrative costs) amounted to about 71 per cent of the total development budget in the regions.

As can be seen from Table III.1, the primary sector (mainly agriculture) has remained dominant. The dominance of agriculture in the Tanzanian economy emphasizes the importance of rural development and the need for viable community development programmes. Furthermore, about 95 per cent of the population live in the rural areas and 90 per cent depend on farming for their livelihood. The fact that about 50 per cent of the population are either too young (under 15) or too old (over 55) to work, and that the population growth rate is approaching 3 per cent per annum poses the need for increasing productivity in the rural areas — particularly the agricultural sector which is the mainstay of the economy. Between 1970 and 1973, the agricultural growth rate (2.7 per cent) was below the population growth rate (2.8 per cent). The droughts and worldwide inflation of 1974-5 made the situation worse; for the GDP grew at 2.2 per cent in 1974, but by 4.6 per cent in 1975/6 as a result of the heavy 'life-or-death-farming' campaigns.

Whereas in the rural areas the economy is largely in the hands of small peasant holders (with the exception of a few large state farms),

Table III.1: Composition of GDP by Main Sectors, 1968, 1971 and 1974

Year	Primary sector Million shs	%	Secondary sector Million shs	%	Tertiary sector Million shs	%
1968	3,126	42.5	1.040	14.1	3,186	43.3
1971	3,607	39.6	1,524	16.7	3,982	43.7
1974	5,497	39.2	2,285	16.3	6,257	44.6

Source: 'Hali ya Uchumi wa Taifa katika mwaka', 1974/5.

the major means of production, most of which are located in the modern urban sector, are controlled directly or indirectly by the state. By 1966, Tanzania had seen the inadequacy of the inherited economic and financial structure. The enunciation of the rather vague ideology of 'African Socialism' in the early sixties was not accompanied by the requisite institutional changes.[4] In practice it meant a mixed economy with heavy reliance on external sources of investment capital and skilled manpower. Moreover, between 1963 and 1966, efforts to attract foreign investment and manpower to implement the First Five Year Development Plan (July 1964 to June 1969) were generally unsuccessful. Instead, there was flight of capital from the country through foreign planters, traders and industrialists. Whereas the First Plan had relied on foreign sources to the tune of 78 per cent of the total projected central government investment, only 35 per cent was secured. British direct investment, for example, fluctuated between 7 million and £9 million a year during the pre-Arusha period (1961-7) compared with £45.50 million for Kenya. In fact, this failure of external finance was the main catalyst for the process of nationalization initiated following the Arusha Declaration; and, in a sense the Arusha Declaration was itself a result of 'economic necessity', an attempt to find alternative strategies to boost internal resources. Hence the declaration's emphasis on self-reliance as a development strategy.

Nationalization was accepted as the only alternative in the effort to control the economy and to direct the country's future development. The major means of production and distribution which were nationalized in 1967 included the following: land, forests, mineral resources, water, oil and electricity, communications, transport, banks, insurance, import and export trade, wholesale business, the steel, machine-tool, arms, motor-car, cement and fertilizer factories, the tile industry, any other big industry on which a large section of the population depend for their living, or which supplies essential components for other industries and large plantations, especially those which produce essential raw materials.[5]

Despite these sweeping nationalization measures, the economy still remained 'mixed'. The Second Five Year Plan, which was launched in July 1969,[6] reserved certain strategic industries (chiefly banking, insurance, petroleum and armaments) for wholly nationalized enterprise, a second group of basic industries for firms in which the government holds a majority interest, a third for partnership ventures in which either a government or co-operative organization has an interest, not necessarily a controlling one, and an open list, mostly of industries involving small- or medium-sized operations which are not restricted in ownership form.

Nationalization in Tanzania was conceived as a mechanism for the control of surplus as well as a means of promoting socialist development. Thus an argument is marshalled in the Second Plan that: 'Considerable benefits will accrue in the long run from the expansion of public ownership because: (a) it will be possible to create a genuine Tanzania industrial know-how faster than under conditions of unrestricted private enterprise; (b) it will be possible to pursue a more effective industrial strategy than possible under private enterprise; (c) the profits made in industry will be reinvested in Tanzania.'[7]

Tanzania's brief experience with the nationalized economy has posed the need to make a distinction between a state-controlled economy, a socialist economy and a self-reliant economy. Nationalization, though a necessary starting-point for a country like Tanzania, does not automatically lead to socialism or self-reliance. We shall point out the main constraints that the experience has revealed.

First, nationalization in Tanzania has to a large extent resolved the contradiction between foreign and local control of the economy in favour of the latter. This was achieved by a simple act of legislation. Socialism, however, in most definitions, goes beyond these legal relations of production, and involves more complex changes in the social relations of production. In the urban, modern sector of the economy a new parastatal bureaucracy has grown up, and its management style has rendered ineffective the workers' self-management programme. In the rural sector, the mode of interaction between the peasants/villagers and the agents of the public service has stifled the objective of popular participation in decision-making, and also led to a conception of *ujamaa* villages as merely 'bloc farms' rather than socialist communities.[8] We shall return to this issue when we discuss the village case studies.

Second, control of the economy through nationalization and the parastatal system has not been able to block all the avenues of foreign exploitation. This is largely due to Tanzania's technological dependency: dependency on foreign consultants, expertise in various industrial fields, patents, machinery and even 'marketing intelligence'. Thus exploitation has continued to occur through high consultancy fees, over-invoicing and high prices of imported goods. Efforts to diversify the sources of technology have not been too successful as a solution to technological dependency. The differences in models and levels of sophistication have often led to confusion and problems both in the transfer of skills to local technicians and in stocking spare parts.

Third, given the low resource-base of Tanzania's nationalized economy, it is little wonder that self-reliance has come to mean in practice sending more external aid to prepare the grounds for 'eventual' self-reliant development along the socialist path. Foreign aid has increased tremendously in the post-Arusha period, from less than Shs 100 million (about 24 per cent of the total development expenditure in 1967/8) to nearly two billion, and about 62 per cent in 1975/6, the bulk of it from the traditional Western sources. Between 1969/70 and 1975/6, aid from the socialist world amounted to Shs 645 million, or about 21 per cent of the total, but this was mainly due to the big Chinese loan for construction of the Tanzania-Zambia Railway. In the two years 1974 and 1975/6 after the completion of the railway, aid from the socialist camp dropped drastically to some 4 per cent of the total.

Fourth, dependency on Western financial aid has logically meant also dependency on Western supply of technical manpower in the form of technical assistance teams, consultants, etc. Thus Western consultancy personnel and technical assistance teams have increased more than three-fold during the post-Arusha period, apparently to correspond with the level of Western financial aid. This dependency can be seen in both the urban modern sector and the rural sector. For example, out of 21 regions which have prepared the Regional Integrated Development Programmes (RIDEP), 18 of them had been assisted by technical assistance teams from the West or from such Western-dominated multilateral organizations as the World Bank. It is therefore difficult to see how a socialist, self-reliant economy can emerge from these circumstances.

The current economic development policy consists of four main strategies. The first strategy outlined in the Third Plan entails a shift from low to high emphasis on directly productive activities with a view to creating an industrial structure which optimizes both the satisfaction of domestic demand and the use of domestic resources, with the basic industries given priority. These include textiles, leather and sisal industries, food-processing industries, metal-based industries, industries producing glass, cement, fertilizers and petroleum products, chemical-based industries, paper and wood-products industries.

The second strategy is to encourage low-cost small-scale industries in both urban and rural areas. These cottage industries are supposed to be initiated, controlled and financed by the villagers themselves with very little government input. To this effect, a Small Industries Development Organization (SIDO) has been created to spearhead development in this direction. The third strategy is to mobilize the people in the context of *ujamaa* villages to produce more grains and cash crops under the supervision of the reconstituted party (CCM) and decentralized administration. Popular participation in decision-making, in plan formulation and execution at the village level is the main feature of this strategy.

Finally, from mid-1977, the central leadership of the party made a conspicuous shift to emphasis on individual rather than on a collective effort as a strategy (probably a 'temporary' one) of achieving higher levels of productivity. Thus, for example, more emphasis is now placed on 'bloc farming' than on 'communal farming' in the *ujamaa* villages; and individuals are being encouraged to establish small- and medium-sized industrial, commercial and farming enterprises. This is clearly a shift from what was happening during the first decade of the Arusha Declaration (1967/77) when private entrepreneurs were denied credit in favour of co-operatives, *ujamaa* villages and other collectives. The reasons for this shift will become clear when we discuss the performance of the *ujamaa* village programme as a model of community development.

The above approaches are geared to the achievement of both long-term and short-term objectives. The long-term objectives are: to steer development in a socialist direction; to reduce the country's financial and technical dependency on external supplies; and to correct the rural-urban and interregional earning and consumption imbalance. The short-term objectives are: to raise the level of employment both in urban and rural areas, and to increase the productivity of the industrial and agricultural sectors through a tighter mobilization of locally available resources — human, material and technical. How these objectives have been tackled in the different phases of the community development programme will be discussed in some detail in Chapters 2 and 3 and also in Chapters 5-7, which examine the achievements of the two villages chosen as case studies.

Notes

1. J.K. Nyerere, *Democracy and the Party System* (Government Printer, Dar es Salaam, 1963).

2. For a detailed analysis of the party and the electoral system, see The Election Study Committee, *Socialism and Participation: Tanzania's 1970 National Elections* (Tanzania Publishing House, Dar es Salaam, 1974).

3. The figures given in this section have been collected from a number of sources. See particularly *Economic Surveys* (or now called 'Hali ya Uchumi wa Taifa') from 1960 to 1976 (Government Printer, Dar es Salaam); S.S. Mushi, 'Indigenization of the economy in an underdeveloped country: The Tanzanian experience', paper for the Universities of East Africa Social Science Conference, Dar es Salaam, December 1976; A. Coulson, 'Financial Aspects of Decentralization', Decentralization Research paper no. 75.6, University of Dar es Salaam, 1975.

4. J.K. Nyerere, *Ujamaa – The Basis of African Socialism* (Government Printer, Dar es Salaam, 1962).

5. TANU, *The Arusha Declaration and TANU's Policy on Socialism and Self-Reliance* (Government Printer, Dar es Salaam, 1967), see the Appendix.

6. United Republic of Tanzania, *Tanzania Second Five-Year Plan for Economic and Social Development Vol. 1* (Government Printer, Dar es Salaam, 1969), p. 59.

7. Ibid., p. 59.

8. For a more detailed discussion of this point, see S.S. Mushi, 'Popular participation and rural development planning in Tanzania' (paper presented at a CAFRAD Seminar on Integrated Urban and Rural Development, Tangier, November 1977).

2 THE ORIGINS, PURPOSES AND PHASES OF TANZANIA'S COMMUNITY DEVELOPMENT PROGRAMME

As can be seen from Table III.2, Tanzania's CD programme has undergone many changes since the colonial days, and several phases can be identified. There is a danger, however, of distinguishing phases merely in terms of quantitative change or by minor change in strategies, mobilizational slogans or even changes in regime or individuals in power. Such an approach would be incapable of raising fundamental questions relating to the purposes of the CD effort and the relative impact of the resulting social change on individuals, groups and communities.

It is for this reason that the distinction must be based on a theoretical understanding of the goals and processes of CD under different ideologies and models. This understanding can draw from the abundant theoretical literature and empirical studies of rural development programmes of countries with differing ideological orientations. For no development programme can be said to be entirely 'ideology-free' in so far as it is geared to achieve certain *valued* results or to benefit certain groups in a particular way. We shall therefore start with a brief discussion of the main models of CD found in the literature; and then we shall discuss the various phases of Tanzania's CD programme, indicating when and why it shifted from one model to another.

Models of Community Development

It is possible to distinguish three comparatively significant models of CD in the literature. These can be tentatively and approximately called:

the liberal-incremental model
the revolutionary-change model
the guided-evolutionary model.

The first is rooted in the basic values of Western liberal democracy. The main agents of change and development are private individual entrepreneurs, such as progressive farmers, the so-called 'kulaks', and others who have ready access to state resources, and can afford to experiment

Table III.1: Evolution of Tanzania's Community Development Ideology: Institutional Changes, Mobilizational Slogans and Programmes for Rural Development, 1920-77

Periods of major change	Ideology (expressed or manifest)	Dominant mobilizational slogans	Main rural development programmes	Administrative structure	The political system
1920-45	Imperialism and exploitation	Native welfare & civilization	Plantations settlers and key cash crops for overseas markets	Colonial bureaucracy and indirect rule	Unrepresentative central Gov't, & traditional systems
1945-61	Added: Local capitalism	Added: Progressive farmer and 'multi-racialism'	Added: Yeoman-type progressive farmer & agricultural rules	Added: Party elective local Gov't. & nat'l legislature	Added: Multi-party system & 'multi-racialism'
1961-3	Undefined (independence honeymoon) ('Uhuru na Kazi')	Self-help and co-operative	Self-help schemes and social services	Bureaucratic and centralized	Dominant-party system & 'non-racialism'
1963-5	Mixed economy ('African socialism')	Added: Nation-building concept	Transformation & improvement approaches	Added: Development committees & politicization of bureaucracy	One party de facto; traditional rulers out; union with Zanzibar
1965-7	Defining a socialist ideology (Arusha declaration)	Nation-building	Improvement approach and amending or winding up settlement schemes	Further politicization of the bureaucracy	Mass one-party de jure; cell system
1967-9	Ujamaa & self-reliance	Self-reliance (nationalization)	Ujamaa villages	Further politicization; Regional Development Fund decentralized	Ideological party supreme; re-defined membership; purged leaders
1969-71	Ujamaa and self-reliance	Self-reliance	Added emphasis: rural education, water and health	Proposals for civil service reform (partial decentralization)	Added: Office and factory party branches
1971-3	Added: Workers' participation; Mwongozo	Workers' participation: Mwongozo; self-reliance	Added emphasis: Rural productivity ('Politics in agriculture' policy); village operations	Administrative decentralization	Party role enlarged; leaders re-examined; disciplinary committee set up et up
1973-5	Added: Workers' participation Mwongozo	Added: Adult literacy UPE, 'Life-or-death' farming; 'operation Kilimo'	'Operation Tanzania', full rural collectivization target, 1976; 'Life-or-death' farming	Decentralization continues; capital shift to Dodoma begins	Party role enlarged; leaders re-examined; disciplinary committee set up
1975-7	Added: Workers' participation; Mwongozo with a few steps backwards; change of strategies	Workers' participation; Mwongozo; self-reliance with emphasis on higher productivity by collectives and individuals	'Operation Tanzania'; full rural collectivization target, 1976; 'Life-or-death' farming	Proposals for further decentralization to ward and village levels	Merger of TANU and Afro-Shirazi parties; birth of CCM, New Union Constitution

Source: Worked out from reading, analysis of documents and personal experience.

with innovation, unlike the poorer peasants who have a strong preference for traditional methods of doing things, partly because of insecurity.[1]

For those who advocate this model, progress is measured by two
criteria: economic growth — with little concern for the distribution of
the proceeds of growth — and stability of the polity and of the class
structure on which it rests.[2] Leadership is expected to fall to key individuals and interested groups within the community, for whom the programmes are made particularly attractive.[3] This strategy may be buttressed by three mechanisms. First, there may be a strong bureaucracy
to provide the necessary inputs to dynamic individuals and influential
groups and, of course, to enforce law and order. Second, patron-client
mechanism may be established (varying from country to country) to
provide a link between central authorities or bureaus and the localities. Third, there may also be mechanisms to ensure a 'trickle-down'
of some resources to the most desperate sections of the rural masses
so as to contain the worst effects of the rising expectations which may
have destabilizing consequences.[4]

The revolutionary change model, by contrast, is rooted in other
socialist theories of societal change; and sees a fundamental revolutionary change of the pre-existing sociopolitical and socioeconomic
system, not just change *within* the system, as necessary for development. The state and a vanguard or cadre-based party are the main
agents of change and mobilization — of mixed indoctrination and coercion — whether in the Russian 'democratic centralist' or the Chinese
'mass line' manner.[5] Emphasis is on groups and collectivities — particularly the least privileged in the community — not individuals in isolation. Redistribution of income is considered as important as total economic growth, and also redistribution of power — its transfer from the
former exploiting to the exploited classes.[6] Even where appeal to tradition is used at some stage (as was the case in China at the early stages of
the revolution) to legitimize rapid changes, there is usually a sharp
break with traditional norms within a short period.

Finally, the guided-evolutionary model is an 'unstable' model,
lying somewhere between the other two. It depends largely on central
mobilization of individuals and collectivities through direct state action,
but it is essentially a 'mixed economy' model, relying on a mixture of
group and individual incentives and action of coercion and pervasion
(often buttressed by appeals to tradition) and seeking a balance
between material and normative goals, and a redistribution of wealth,
consonant with political stability and continued economic growth.[7]

Planning, an essential feature of this model, seeks to achieve a balance between bureaucratic action and mass or popular action. Thus, like the liberal-incremental model, the guided-evolutionary model cannot avoid 'compromises' and 'reconciliation' of competitive interests.[8]

We intend to analyse the various phases of Tanzania's CD programme in the context of these three broad models. It will be seen that at one stage the programme was being implemented under clearly liberal-incremental assumptions; at another stage there was a break with the liberal model and an assertion of the revolutionary-change model. We shall show that the current stage is rather confusing, having revolutionary assumptions at the ideological and policy level but clearly moving closer to the liberal model at the policy execution level. Reasons for this ambivalence and apparent contradiction will be attempted in the final summing up of the case studies.

The History and Phases of Tanzania's Community Development

Tanzania's CD programme can be divided into three phases; namely (1) the colonial phase, 1920 to 1961; (2) the pre-Arusha phase, 1961 to 1967; and (3) the post-Arusha phase, 1967 to 1977, itself subdivided into the *ujamaa* villages phases, 1961-73, and the development villages phase, 1974 onwards. Each of these phases is distinguished by either a major ideological shift or significant changes in mobilizational strategies; and therefore this section should be read with close reference to the historical summary presented in Table III. 2. In this section, we shall discuss phases one and two; and in Chapter 3 we will examine the specific objectives of the post-Arusha phase, with examples taken from Morogoro district.

The Colonial Phase: 1920-61

Until the end of the Second World War, colonial development policy in Tanzania was mainly a response to the needs of the domestic markets in the metropolis. The concern of the Germans, when they invaded Tanganyika in the 1880s, was to develop it 'into a wide and very important field for German enterprises',[9] and this was continued by the British when they effectively took over power from the Germans in 1920. The 'home needs' objective was the dominant one.

Thus the initial emphasis was on the settler plantation economy, producing such cash crops as coffee, sisal and tea; the only other important cash crop being cotton which was produced by African small-holders. This concentration on a few export-oriented cash crops meant that development resources (e.g. technical information, extension services, social infrastructure, etc.), went to the areas which could produce them, the remaining areas being left entirely underdeveloped, producing only enough for their own consumption.

Furthermore, there was neither a clear rural development policy nor planning during the interwar period. The mode of planning that was adopted after the war had nothing to do with mobilization of the rural masses. The Planning Commission (set up in 1946 to formulate a ten-year development plan) admitted that the plan was no more than 'a series of objectives with an approximation of their costs'. The amount allocated to implement these plan objectives was meagre and much of it went to the urban areas or to the promotion of cash crops for export — for the purpose, as the Colonial Development Act of 1929 put it, 'of aiding developing agriculture and industry in the colony or territory *and thereby promoting commerce with, or industry in, the United Kingdom*'[10] (emphasis added). Colonial development was thus seen as a by-product of metropolitan needs. Between 1948 and 1958/9, Tanganyika received only a total of £10 million from the British Treasury as a result of such Acts, and much of it was invested in export-oriented activities.[11]

British development policy for Tanganyika about 1950 to 1961 when the country gained independence was a response to two additional factors. First, the war had created a shortage of essential supplies such as oil-seeds and meat; hence the hasty introduction of various production schemes in the rural areas, such as the abortive groundnut scheme. Second, the era of nationalism had started and political pressures were being exerted on the colonial regime to do something for the rural communities.

The rural development programmes introduced between 1950 and 1961, however, had an impact on a very small section of the rural population. There were two sets of programmes. One, now referred to as the 'progressive farmer model', created settlement schemes for 'progressive' farmers who were supplied with the necessary inputs such as credit and extension services. The second was a reclamation programme to improve the farming practices of the subsistence farmers through the enforcement of such agricultural rules as ridging, terracing, etc. In practice, priority was given to the progressive farmers, and the creation of a yeoman-type 'buffer class' in rural Tanzania. As D.W. Malcolm, Principal Assistant Secretary, Department of Agriculture and Natural Resources, wrote in 1952:

I want to see the emergence from our hitherto undifferentiated African Society of a substantial number of rich men. The 'wealthy coffee growers' [of Mbinga], if they have reached the same level as those of Kilimanjaro, will be getting a cash income of about £25 per year. That is not what I mean by riches; I would like to see men in a sufficiently strong financial position to be able to send their sons overseas for education; to afford motor cars, good houses and the like, and I believe that the emergence of such relatively wealthy individuals in the community will provide a stabilizing factor of immense importance to the future of this country.[12]

In summary, then, we can say that the colonial phase of CD in Tanzania had three main objectives. The first objective was to facilitate production of key cash crops required in overseas factories. The second objective was to create a strong rural middle class which would stabilize the rural communities and the colonial system as a whole. The third objective was to effect some improvements in welfare within the rural subsistence sector.

This was very much a third-order objective, however. For example, there were hardly any dispensaries, let alone hospitals or health centres, in the rural areas. Population grew slowly: between 1947 and 1957 at less than 2 per cent p.a. whereas between 1957 and 1967 the rate was about 2.5 per cent and between 1967 and 1977 about 3 per cent, mainly reflecting the changed post-independence emphasis on health facilities. There was little provision, either, for related social services such as rural water supply and education which have received large budgetary allocations during the post-independence period.

The colonial CD programme was based on the assumptions of the liberal-incremental model. It was assumed that there would be a 'trickle-down' effect from the efforts of the progressive farmers and plantation settlers from which the broad masses would benefit. But the fact that the model functioned in a colonial context further limited the impact of the trickle-down effect, for the greatest part of the surplus was exported rather than reinvested in the home country. For this reason, agricultural productivity improved only slowly. For example, between 1945 and 1960, cotton yields went from 53 kg per acre only to 59 kg, a slow rate of improvement compared with more productive agricultural systems. This was largely due to the fact that credit and extension facilities were rarely extended to the smaller farmers.

Moreover, as a matter of policy, all financial institutions were required to invest at least two-thirds of their savings deposits outside the country. Thus, while deposits in Tanzania rose from Shs 36 million at the end of 1938 to Shs 359 million at the end of 1948, local lending by the banks (mostly to urban Asians who themselves invested their profits outside the country) rose from Shs 31 million to only 36 million. Again, by directing a significant proportion of their loans and advances to the export-import trade and plantation agriculture, the colonial administration reinforced the enclave character of the economy which has remained till today.[13]

The last is one example of the way in which the rural development programme's effects were distorted by general features of colonial economic policy. There were other features of that policy which had similar effects and have also had an enduring legacy.

First, as a matter of deliberate policy, certain regions, especially the central and western belts, were encouraged (often forced into contracts) to supply labour to the plantations and estates outside their own homelands. In some cases, as Gulliver recounted in the case of the Ngoni and Ndendeule, the process of labour migration led to temporary depopulation of the youths who would have contributed to the development of their areas.[14] Until now some regions, such as Kigoma, have not fully recovered from this 'labour-reserve' policy which created a habit of migration in search of labour. The policy had lasting socio-psychological consequences as well, for example, the desertion of wives and children for the long-term absentees and the low status the former labour-reserve communities have continued to have.

Second, the neglect of the subsistence sector is partly responsible for the increasing dependence of the villages on the state. Famine was a regular feature in many rural villages in the colonial phase because of the precarious balance between output and consumption. In each case of famine, the villages looked to the government for relief; and the government, rather than revolutionize the economy, set up relief centres, a response which increased village dependence on it rather than solving the problem of subsistence and famine.

Finally, colonial rural development approaches fostered a deeply-rooted 'anti-government' feeling amongst the peasantry, and a tendency that has continued till now to consider the political party as a weapon to defend themselves against bureaucratic encroachment. This attitude resulted from the inconsistent use of compulsion to enforce ill-defined agricultural rules, often administered by ill-trained extension officials (Instructors). The peasants' distrust and fear created during this phase has created problems in the post-colonial phases when the government tried to balance developmental persuasion and compulsion within a democratic, participatory framework, as the Morogoro case will show.

The Pre-Arusha Phase, 1961-7

At independence (1961), the nationalist government inherited a number of rural development schemes and tenant-farming settlements, most of which had been established in the mid-fifties by the British administration in response to nationalist criticism. The schemes were an attempt to accelerate progressive farming among selected individuals under bureaucratically controlled conditions. The leaders were eager to effect more dramatic transformation in the rural areas and to spread the fruits of development to the communities which had not been affected by the colonial development programmes. To achieve these two objectives, two programmes of rural development were adopted in 1963/4, usually referred to as the 'transformation approach' and the 'improvement approach'.

The 'transformation' was the creation of new village settlements with modern farming systems financed by the state. 'Improvement' meant trying to apply the concept of 'community development' which had been put into practice in some Asian countries such as India, relying on mass education, exhortation and persuasion to induce change-oriented attitudes. Change was expected to be gradual but to reach far more communities than the settlement programme which concentrated on a few selected progressive farmers.

Both approaches had elements of continuity with the colonially bequeathed liberal-incremental model, in that both sought (the first immediately, the second eventually) to create communities of progressive farmers. Indeed, President Nyerere's early formulation of *ujamaa* as the basis for 'African socialism' (1962) was ideologically as Western as it was traditional and idealistic. The analysis of the performance of the two programmes given below will show that, in fact, there was no ideological departure at all.

Performance of the Transformation Approach. The main features of the capital-intensive village settlements (recommended by a World Bank mission) were to be as follows. Each settlement would bring together 250 families. Title to land would be held by individuals but farm planning, mechanical cultivation and general services would be organized on co-operative lines and initially directed by a manager. The farming systems would embrace one or two cash crops and livestock together with some subsistence food production. Further, the settlers would be provided with piped water, education and health facilities.

The First Plan proposed to launch over 60 such model villages between 1964 and 1969, each costing about £150,000, and the exercise would continue till the whole countryside was filled with such villages.

The planners believed that the experience would 'allow considerable acceleration of the process of modernizing Tanganyikan rural production and raising the income levels of farmers . . . to about £150 per annum (per family), as compared with present-day cash income in the traditional environment of £25'.[15] By mid-1965, 23 settlements were already in operation. However, the programme was facing serious problems and the government was considering ways of modifying it. The problems resulted from organizational conflicts, increasing village dependence on meagre government resources, and low settler productivity. As these problems provided some lessons for the post-Arusha phases it is worth elaborating them briefly.

First, organizationally, the resettlement machinery consisted of a Comission and an Agency, the latter being the executive arm of the former. Since the Commission consisted of five ministers representing different ministerial priorities and emphases, interministerial rivalries developed, making it difficult for the Agency to take quick decisions. The ministerial hierarchies at the centre were replicated at the regional, district and sub-district levels, each departmental staff in the field emphasizing the priorities of his own ministry. Further, the presence of a government manager at the settlement level made the settlers feel that they were hired labourers. Because of these conflicts and delays in the recruitment of settlers, the Commission was abolished in 1966 and its work was taken over by the Settlement Division of the Ministry of Lands, Settlement and Water Development. The government further decided to replace bureaucracy with democratic participation at the settlement levels: 'The settlers will be encouraged to identify themselves more closely with the schemes by actually participating in making the decisions on how the settlement should be run, with the Divisional Staff filling the role of advisers rather than managers.'[16]

The second problem was that the transformation model increased the inherited village dependence on state subventions. Supplied with a free socioeconomic infrastructure, an initial monthly allowance of Shs 30 per settler, and loans with generous repayment period of 25 years, the settlers exerted little effort as they expected the government subventions to continue. In most settlements, the loans were consumed rather than used for productive purposes. Indeed, an inverse relationship was observed between the level of assistance given to a settlement and settler productivity:

It was found that on the schemes where the settler was given an axe and *jembe* [hoe] and told to clear the bush and build his house himself, the response was praiseworthy, whereas on the pilot schemes where capital was used to make the lot of the settler easier, the response was disappointing.[17]

The third, and related, problem was low productivity on the settlements. This was partly because most settlements failed to attract people who had 'a feeling for agriculture as a profession'; or a 'receptivity to new ideas and methods', and a 'capacity for hard work',[18] such as, according to the regulations, were to have been chosen. In many areas, the settlements were seen simply as a method of handling or forestalling the political consequences of the growing rural and urban unemployment. In others, recruitment was based on 'good political record'. In a few extreme cases, the settlements were seen as a place to send 'trouble-makers'.

Furthermore, there was great uncertainty as to the ideological status of the settlements. Although the schemes had been conceived in capitalist (and commercial) terms by the World Bank, they had a 'capitalist-socialist' mode of production. Thus, for example, land was individually held while most operations were communal; again, while the settlement managers appealed to the settlers' profit motive, the politicians preached the 'equality' and 'classlessness' of the traditional African society which President Nyere had stressed in his 1962 treatise. Either way, the necessary productivity was not forthcoming and the effective ending of the transformation approach was announced by the Second Vice-President, Rashidi Kawawa, on 4 April 1966.

Settler-farmers on pilot schemes in general show far less enthusiasm, and are less hard-working, than 'settlers' in 'spontaneous' and un-assisted schemes. They are also full of complaints and expect the Government to give them everything . . . In future, it has been decided that, instead of establishing highly capitalized schemes and moving people to them, emphasis will be on modernizing existing traditional villages, by injecting capital in order to raise the standard of living of the villagers.[19]

This was a reversion to the improvement approach which, during these years, had been carried on with diminished funds and enthusiasm.

The Three Year Plan (1961/2-1963/4) described the approach through CD as an attempt to 'arouse and mobilize the dormant human resource of the nation so as to improve the economic, social and cultural life, and to co-ordinate the efforts of the people themselves with those of central and local government and voluntary agencies'.[20] The plan allocated £229,195 for CD work, including CD training centres, visual aids workshops, field staff, self-help schemes, community centres, film units and social development teams.[21]

'Self-help' and 'co-operatives' became the mobilizational slogans of the improvement approach, and community development action was to be 'by adult education, exhortation and example, to enlighten both men and women on possibilities of attaining a different, higher and more satisfying standard of living'.[22] In order to introduce the element of democracy in local decision-making, which was lacking in the colonial period, development committees were created in 1962 at village, district and regional levels. Although at the end of the First Plan (1969) the improvement approach through CD action, widespread extension services, self-help projects, and co-operatives, had more 'successes' attributed to it than the transformation approach, it had revealed a number of weaknesses.

First, the co-operative movement was becoming a burden on the peasants rather than an instrument for their improvement. Enthusiasm for rapid change had led to the mushrooming of what some bureaucrats have termed 'political co-operatives', organized from the top 'without genuine local demand or even understanding'. Training of personnel had not kept pace with the rate of growth of the movement; corruption had increased; the proliferation of societies, unions and marketing boards was creating a new form of 'middleman'; progressive farmers were benefiting most; the movement was becoming undemocratic; and the peasants were losing faith in their leaders, as a Presidential Committee of Enquiry showed in 1966.[23]

Second, it was difficult to co-ordinate and to plan the various self-help activities of the rural communities due to the departmentalized administrative structure at the local level. Each extension official looked to his departmental head in Dar es Salaam both for directives an and for promotion; and the committee structure was unable to induce the intended 'team spirit' under the circumstances.

The third, and related, problem was that the role of the CD field staff was not well defined. As a result, there were often not sufficient focus on any particular programme or programmes, as CD workers were given a wide-ranging area of responsibility which dissipated their energies and produced little in the way of real development. The fact that there were many other non-government agencies doing the same work complicated the situation even further.

Fourth, the village-level personnel were often young and inexperienced, and subject to very frequent transfers. The lack of continuity led to many unfinished self-help projects, with corresponding loss in local enthusiasm.

The final problem was the failure of the techniques of using demonstration farms and demonstration plots. First, attempts were made to use farms of community 'opinion leaders' and traditional leaders for demonstration purposes — in accordance with the stress laid by rural sociologists on the importance of informal channels of communication and the role of influential persons, who could be expected to make their communities adopt innovation. The approach failed to produce any tangible results in the areas where it was applied. In some tradition-bound communities, the people did not want to 'compete' with their leaders; in others, the opinion leaders minimized campaigns in fear of such competition.[24]

Second, in many cash-crop areas, demonstration plots and much of the available extension service and credit were concentrated on the farms of 'progressive farmers' with the standard argument already cited. Often, however, the poorer peasants either paid little attention to the demonstration plots or associated success with the wealth of the owners. After all, the farms of the progressive farmers had always been better kept and, moreover, the extension staff had always preferred to deal with the progressive farmers, a bias which has continued even in the post-Arusha era, according to two recent studies.[25]

Third, in other areas the farms of Agricultural Instructors (usually local men residing within the community) were converted into demonstration plots. One negative consequence of this was that some instructors used this as a way of becoming progressive farmers themselves, concentrating more on their farms than on 'demonstration' work. In Morogoro District, for example, many of the demonstration plots in the fifties belonged to Agricultural Instructors, and some interviewees attributed failure of demonstration to this fact.

Finally, in a few areas, demonstration results disproved the experts, having produced an output inferior to that attained using traditional methods. This was partly due to the fact that the demonstration work was often entrusted to the little-qualified instructors who could not use the modern inputs in accordance with soil and climatic requirements of their areas. In some cases, for example, tractors were used where the traditional hoe would have done less damage to the humus content. In other cases, as in the Uluguru Mountains of Morogoro, new systems of ridging and terracing failed to achieve higher yields — and when they were enforced authoritatively on all peasants (for a tendency to rely on command rather than persuasion was a further weakness of the scheme) positive hostility to the development programme was often the result.

Notes

1. For elaboration of this point, see S.S. Mushi '*Ujamaa*: Modernization by traditionalization', *TAALULI*, vol. I, no. 2 (March 1971), pp. 20-4.

2. This was, for example, a key consideration in the colonial rural development programmes in most African countries. It is still an important consideration in the countries which have opted for the liberal model, such as Kenya and the Ivory Coast. For the Kenyan case, see Colin Leys, *Underdevelopment in Kenya* (Heinemann, London, 1975); for the Ivory Coast case, see Christian P. Photholm, *Four African Political Systems* (Prentice-Hall, Englewood Cliffs, N.J., 1970).

3. Kenya's Special Rural Development Programme is a good example.

4. For a useful summary of 'trickle-down' theories see P.L. Raikes (Differentiation and progressive farmer policies', BRULUP Seminar Paper (University of Dar es Salaam, 1972), pp. 13-15.

5. For a useful discussion of the Chinese sub-model, see the relevant sections in Franz Schurmann, *Ideology and Organization in Communist China* (University of California Press, Berkeley, 1968). For the Soviet sub-model, see David Lane, *The End of Inequality? Stratification Under State Socialism* (C. Nicholls and Company Ltd, Manchester, 1971).

6. This is in keeping with the classical Marxist-Leninist theory of 'Dictatorship of the Proletariat'. Lenin, for example, would advise the workers and peasants to concentrate more on the effort to snatch political power from the former exploiting classes than on narrow, short-term economic gains. He thought the latter preoccupation would end up in mere reform rather than revolution.

7. See, for instance, the arguments given by Nyerere on the question of equality and redistribution of wealth in his various writings on socialism in Tanzania, particularly in the volume on *Freedom and Socialism* (Oxford Press, Dar es Salaam, 1968).

8. For elaboration of this point, see S.S. Mushi 'Revolution by evolution: the Tanzanian road to socialism' (PhD thesis, Yale University, 1974) especially Chs. 5 and 6.

9. Carl Peter, quoted in R.F. Eberlie, 'The German achievement in East Africa', *Tanganyika Notes and Records*, vol. LV (September 1960), p. 195.

10. Barbu Miculescu, *Colonial Planning: A Comparative Study* (George Allen & Unwin, London, 1958), p. 57.

11. Antony H. Rweyemamu, 'Nation-building and planning processes in Tanzania' (PhD thesis, Syracuse University, 1966), p. 45.

12. Quoted in John Illife 'Agricultural change in modern Tanganyika: an outline history' (paper for the 1970 Universities of East Africa Social Science Conference, University of Dar es Salaam, 27-30 December 1970), p. 27.

13. For elaboration, see J.F. Rweyemamu, *Underdevelopment and Industrialization in Tanzania* (Oxford University Press, Nairobi, 1973), pp. 27-35.

14. P.H. Gulliver, *Labour Migration in Rural Economy* (East African Literature Bureau, Nairobi, 1955).

15. The First Plan, vol. 1, p. 33.

16. A.M. Babu, Minister of Lands, Settlement and Water Development, 'Development since the Declaration', *The Standard* (Tanzania), 8 December 1967.

17. Ibid.

18. Summarized from a longer list given in John R. Nellis, *A Theory of Ideology: The Tanzanian Example* (Oxford University Press, Nairobi, 1971), Ch. 6.

19. Ministry of Information and Tourism, *Press Release*, IT/1, 302 (Dar es Salaam), pp. 3-4.

20. Three Year Plan, pp. 94-5.

21. Ibid., pp. 92-5.

22. First Plan, vol. I, p. 17.

23. *Report of the Presidential Special Committee of Enquiry into Co-operative Movement and Marketing Boards* (Government Printer, Dar es Salaam, 1966).

24. P.L. Raikes, 'Differentiation and progressive farmer policies', pp. 5-13.

25. R.V. Saylor, 'An opinion survey of Bwana Shambas in Tanzania' (ERB Paper, University of Dar es Salaam, 1970); H.V.E. Thoden Van Velzen, 'Staff, kulak and peasant', in L.R. Cliffe, J.S. Coleman and M.R. Doorbos (eds.), *Political Penetration in East Africa* (Oxford University Press, Nairobi, 1974).

3 THE OBJECTIVES OF THE POST-ARUSHA PHASE

The broad objectives of the *'ujamaa* approach' to CD are contained in the Arusha Declaration of February 1967 and in a number of other policy statements issued by the central leaders since 1967. It is important to make distinctions between: the broad objectives of the *ujamaa* ideology of strategy at the national level; the particular manifestation, interpretation and implementation of these objectives in a regional context (in our case, Morogoro District); and the 'tactical' reordering of these objectives in the light of experience and circumstantial factors.

The broad objectives and goals of *ujamaa* represent what Schurmann has termed 'pure ideology', and the broad national, as well as the specific regional, strategies represent the 'practical ideology' side of the equation. At the level of ideology, therefore, contradictions and discrepancies may take two forms, namely pure v. practical ideology at the national and/or local level, and national v. local objectives and needs. In examining these issues, we shall divide the post-Arusha period into two phases, namely the *'ujamaa* villages' phase and the 'development villages' phase, most examples coming from Morogoro District.

The Impetus for Ideological Shift

The broad objectives embodied in the Arusha Declaration were partly a response to the main contradictions of the two approaches described above. First, there were contradictions at the ideological level. Mwalimu Nyerere had published his treatise on *ujamaa* in 1962, commending the reactivation of the norms of equality and social justice attributed to traditional African communities. This ideological position contrasted sharply with the capitalist and acquisitive orientation of rural development programmes (reinforced by the 'liberal' norms of the many foreigners who still remained in the civil service. Second, there was a contradiction between the effort to promote local initiative through the participatory committee structure from the village to the regional level and the 'centrist' ideology of the bureaucrats.

Third, there was a discrepancy between the rising material expectations of the masses and the actual material outputs of the two programmes. The fact of capital intensity in the 'transformation approach' was itself a contradiction, since there was labour surplus in both urban and rural areas. And even the 'improvement approach' which was designed to spread the fruits of development more widely was also beginning to work in favour of the more privileged groups, enhancing rather than reducing the urban-rural, interregional and interpersonal inequalities.

Finally, there was a contradiction between the goal of 'self-reliance' emphasized by the central leaders of the party from 1965, and the growing dependency syndrome: the villages depending heavily on government subsidies and government depending heavily on foreign aid and investment much of which, as we have seen, failed to come. Thus, even though the Arusha Declaration was proclaimed as a reassertion of 'political principles', it was in reality a response to a difficult economic situation and unpleasant experiences with community and national development programmes.[1]

The Objectives and Strategies of the Ujamaa Policy

The lessons learned from these experiences were clearly reflected in the Arusha Declaration which emphasized socialism and self-reliance as the only 'rational choice' for Tanzania's development. The criterion for seeking, accepting and utilizing foreign resources was defined, a stringent leadership code of behaviour was enforced to limit the acquisitiveness of the leaders, a new educational programme was recommended to emphasize the norms of socialism and self-reliance, and a new policy for developing the rural communities (*Ujamaa Vijijini*) was issued. The Declaration, therefore, appeared to mark the beginning of the end of the liberal-incremental model, although not in any dramatic way.

The Tanzanian socialist revolution was to be a 'revolution by evolution', drawing in an eclectic way from the communalist tradition of the rural communities, the liberal tradition of the West, and the experience of the East.

We shall become a socialist, self-reliant society through our growth. We cannot afford the destruction of the economic instruments we now have nor a reduction in our present output. The steps by which we move forward must take account of these things. Our change will, therefore, be effected almost entirely by the emphasis of our new development and by the gradual conversion of existing institutions into others more in accordance with our philosophy.[2]

The *'ujamaa* approach' to CD was defined in the President's policy document titled 'Socialism and Rural Development' (1967), and has subsequently been elaborated upon by various leaders in the light of experience. According to the original document, the rural communities would be organized into *ujamaa* villages, collectivities in which the members would practice 'face-to-face' democracy – electing their own village government, planning their own development (with the necessary government assistance), and working together for the benefit of all.

The implementation strategies suggested were closer to the 'liberal' model than the 'revolutionary' model. Emphasis was on 'voluntariness'; the peasants would be educated (by government and party leaders) until they themselves saw the benefits of living and working in *ujamaa* villages; coercion as a mobilizational tool was strictly forbidden. Popular participation in decision-making was to be a dominant feature of the *ujamaa* approach; but there should be a mechanism to enforce the disciplined acceptance of jointly-taken decisions at the village level. 'We must have both freedom and discipline. For freedom without discipline is anarchy; discipline without freedom is tyranny.'[3]

The new *ujamaa* approach was largely a reaction to the problems experienced with earlier policies, notably the two progressive farmer and village schemes approaches. It had six interrelated economic and sociopolitical objectives:[4] (1) realizing economies of scale; (2) increasing labour productivity; (3) improving innovativeness; (4) securing equality; (5) raising rural welfare; and (6) enhancing village self-reliance and self-determination. We shall consider each in turn.

Economies of Scale

Ujamaa villages would afford economies of scale through low spending per unit of production in large communal enterprises. For example, large-scale poultry or maize production could result in relatively lower labour requirements (per bin or per ton) for operations such as feeding, planting, maintenance, harvesting, storage and processing. It would also make mechanization more economical. Economies of scale could also be achieved in produce marketing and purchasing of inputs. Moreover, in larger communities, public funds would be spent more efficiently for public services such as agricultural extension, education, health schemes, water supply and the basic economic infrastructure.

Experience has shown, however, that actual 'economies of scale' are small except when it is a matter of full utilization of expensive equipment, and the justification for mechanization is doubtful in the current economic and technological conditions of Tanzania characterized by shortage of capital, local industrialization and technical skills, on the one hand, and abundance of land and labour on the other. Tractorization has, indeed, universally been preferred to the less costly intermediate technologies, including animal and human-powered equipment — a 'hangover' bequeathed by the village settlement phase — but it may only compound the problem of unemployment and underemployment while incurring sizeable costs in foreign exchange — which can be ill afforded.

Labour Productivity

The belief that labour productivity would be improved was based on two assumptions. The first concerning economies of scale has already been discussed. The second was that people will work *better* and *harder* in groups than as individuals. This is likely to be true only under several conditions: first, if the community is organized in such a way that it affords better training and communication of technical skills than the individual could afford alone; second, if there are well-defined (and binding) sanctions against non-compliance; and, thirdly, if those concerned believe that they stand to gain from the particular community activity. That is, exertion will depend on the existing incentives.

These conditions have not always existed. For example, some villages have not received adequate extension services; others have no well-established sanctions, or where they exist they have not been enforced in any systematic way; in a few extreme cases (particularly during the 1969-73 period), the villagers thought that they were working for the government rather than for their own development. The outcome of these inadequacies has been low labour productivity, as examples given later will show.

Improving Innovativeness

The *ujamaa* communities would be subjected to a new and non-traditional form of organization which makes communication and acceptance of new skills and information easier. Although traditional 'solidarity groups' would be utilized (partly for programme legitimation purposes), the ultimate aim would be to break through the traditional inertia or the 'cake of custom'. Moreover, large-scale communal production would enable the *ujamaa* communities to 'act like big farmers'; and would therefore have adequate economic security to be able to set aside some of their pooled resources and to take the risk of innovation, which would be beyond the means of the poor small-holder.

The argument about innovativeness is correct as far as it goes. But there is also the danger of 'over-innovating' or, more correctly, 'mis-innovating', and 'over-adopting' by simply and immaturely replacing one set of production tools with another more complex and more costly one. The best example is the mania for tractorization to which we have already referred. De Vries and Hansel have stated this danger very well from their experiences with the Tanzanian Agricultural Extension Service: 'in many *ujamaa* villages we see signs of increasing over-adoption of innovations such as tractor ploughing, fertilizer application or using feed concentrates that may not pay under the existing cost-price conditions.'[5] There is no point, they suggest, in raising the yield of maize from five to ten bags per acre if the tractor ploughing or fertilizers or insecticides required can not be paid for with the extra five bags.[6] 'Over-adoption' results sometimes from villagers' fears of being thought 'not modern' if they reject innovations, sometimes from officials offering free farm inputs through grants or soft loans as an incentive to farm *ujamaa* villages at least in name.

Securing Equality

The preceding CD approaches, as we have already pointed out, led to wide gaps in the distribution of incomes and development resources. All these approaches were biased towards the progressive farmers and the developed cash-crop areas.

However, it proved to be very difficult to correct the interregional development imbalance during the first decade of the Arusha Declaration (1967-77), for several reasons. First, the government bureaucracy was reluctant to pursue equity at the cost of a temporary lowering of social productivity. Thus very little reorientation has occurred. Second, the parastatal bodies operating in the regions (such as the crop authorities) have continued to apply the usual technico-economic tests when allocating industries and projects to the regions; and obviously the more developed regions with well-developed infrastructure have been selected. Thirdly, even where the regions have allocated 'equal' or nearly 'equal' amounts (as was at one time the case with the Regional Development Fund), it was found that the poorer areas had very little capacity to spend the funds because of poor infrastructure, whereas the more developed ones would 'overspend' and request supplementary funds.

The area of equity is the one that shows a clear contradiction between policy pronouncements and the hard facts of practice. Yet one
must also pose the question as to what kind or level of interregional
equality should be sought. The experience of the older socialist states
has shown that complete equality could lead to economic and technological stagnation, quite apart from its being unachievable.[7]

Raising Rural Welfare

Another inheritance from the colonial and pre-Arusha approaches was
the big gap between village and town life. Thus one aspect of the objective of raising rural welfare is to narrow this gap. Even after a decade-
long effort to do this, all indicators still show that the rural communities are in a disadvantaged position *vis-à-vis* the urban dwellers; less
education (in 1974, 40 per cent of all *ujamaa* villages had no schooling
facilities); lower adult literacy level (50 per cent v. 80 per cent in the
towns); worse health facilities (all consultant hospitals are in towns);
less per capita income (Shs 400 v. Shs 1,000), etc.

Correction of the rural-urban gap is not merely a question of the
'equity principle'; it is also an economic principle in at least two senses.
First, improvement of rural welfare *vis-à-vis* the towns limits further
rural-urban migration, may strengthen the 'back-to-the-land' campaigns
for the urban unemployed and therefore lead to a more productive
labour force in the rural areas. Second, improvement of rural welfare
also leads to a wider internal market which is not only necessary for
economic growth but also creates a symmetry between the structures
of production and consumption. Furthermore, the *ujamaa* approach
seeks to promote rural welfare by minimizing the avenues of exploitation: of village communities by the urban elites (and metropolitan
firms), on the one hand, and villager by villager, on the other.

Self-reliance and Self-determination

'It is not possible', said the President, 'to accept socialism without self-
reliance, or vice-versa',[8] and self-reliance, implying also self-determination, is intended to characterize all levels of the nation: 'If all the
families in a village are self-reliant, then the village as a whole is self-
reliant; if all the villages in a district are self-reliant, then the district is
self-reliant; if all districts in a region are self-reliant, then that region is
self-reliant, and *therefore* if all the regions are self-reliant, the whole
nation is self-reliant.' How far a peripheral country like Tanzania can
dispense with trade and technology imports, and how its economy
would have to be restructured to do so remain, however, unanswered

questions.

The illustrative examples of performance of the post-Arusha, '*ujamaa* villages' phase given in the section below do not take account of these fundamental questions. We have simply taken the policy at its face value.

Performance of the Ujamaa Villages Phase, 1967-73

Although a few 'socialist' villages had existed even before the Arusha Declaration, such as those under the Ruvuma Development Association, the era of '*ujamaa* villages' started around 1969 when most villages were formed or old village settlements were reconstituted in accordance with the party *Ujamaa Vijijini* policy paper of 1967.

The chief requirements for a *ujamaa* village were, first, a nucleated settlement — which usually required the 'villagization' of scattered homesteads — and secondly, some degree of collective farming either replacing, or combining with, individual exploitation of land. Such villages were to be brought about by voluntary commitment, on the liberal model. Coercion as a mobilizational tool was strictly forbidden, subsidies were offered which made it advantageous for communities to adopt the label '*ujamaa* village' even if they did not conform to the prescription of the policy.

The achievements of this phase were unsatisfactory in terms of the rate of villagization and the promotion of communal solidarity, productivity and self-reliance.

Since the *ujamaa* programme depended largely on voluntariness, the rate of movement to villages could not be dramatic. The change from 809 villages in 1970 to 5,556 villages in 1973 is probably a laudable achievement under the persuasive strategy. The rate of villagization between 1969 and 1973 (and the number of people living in the villages) is shown in Table III. 3. The rate depended partly on the mobilizational vigour of the local party organization and, in particular, the Regional and Area Commissioners. Thus, for example, it was chiefly as a result of Dr Wilbert Kleruu's personal energies and motivation that Mtwara and Iringa were able to bring into villages 64 per cent and 36 per cent of their total populations, respectively, within that period. This dynamic leader was assassinated in 1971 by a 'kulak' whose farming interests in Ismani (Iringa) were being threatened.

Further, the response was low in the more developed cash crop areas. Hence the association of the policy with poverty-stricken areas reduced

Table III.3: The Rate of Villagization, 1969-73

Year	1969/70	1970/71	1971/72	1972/73
Number of villages (cumulative)	809	1,956	4,484	5,556
Population in villages	531,200	1,545,240	1,980,862	2,028,164

Source: Prime Minister's Office.

its general respectability.

Although these villages were called *'ujamaa'* villages, the production relations had strong individualistic elements, especially in the production of food crops. For example, of the seven most established *ujamaa* villages in Morogoro District in 1971, none could be said to have evolved socialist relations or production. The preference for individual/private farms can be seen in Table III.4 where communal and private farms are compared in size, as is the proportion of the total cultivated land which was planted, weeded and harvested. Although the private acreage may well be underreported (to give the impression of commitment to *ujamaa*), even as the figures stand, in each village (except the two which did not have private farms) more land was under individual than communal cultivation; more of the private farms cultivated were weeded and harvested (100 per cent) than of the communal farms (62 per cent); and about 87 per cent of the private farms were used for food crops, with Bwakira Chini and Kauzeni producing almost all their food crops on individual farms (compare Tables III.4 and III.5, though most of these villages also received food subsidies from the government between 1969 and 1973). The emphasis on individual farming in these villages suggests that the traditional spirit of co operation which existed under situations of subsistence and insecurity cannot now be considered the pillar of socialist reconstruction.

The actual areas of communally operated land varied from 0.5 to 2 acres per worker with an even greater variance in the acreage per inhabitant owing to wide disparities in the dependency ratio (between 30 per cent and 70 per cent of the population).

Low productivity was partly a result of low discipline in implementing plans for communal production which had been agreed upon jointly by the villagers and officials. The contents of Table III.5 (which should be compared with Table III.4) reveal this indiscipline which apart from leading to non-fulfilment of plans, caused losses in public resources. Several observations arise from Table III.5.

Table III.4: Comparison of Communal and Private Farms in Seven Selected *Ujamaa* Villages in Morogoro District, 1970/1 Season

Village	Communal farm (acres)		Private farms — food & cash (acres)			
	Total cultivated	% Planted and weeded	Total cultivated	% Planted and weeded	Food	Cash
1. Lukenge	94	50	DK	DK	DK	DK
2. Sesenga	23	42	None	–	–	–
3. Mkata	201	50	140	100	85	55
4. Bwakira Chini	108	68	109	100	109	–
5. Kikundi	30	88	49	100	39	10
6. Kauzeni	89	61	148	100	148	–
7. Kizinga	41	100	None	–	–	–

Source: Compiled from a table given in File D.3/24/Vol. IV, '*Ujamaa* villages general', a report of Co-ordinator of Agriculture (August 1971), Morogoro District Office.

Table III.5: Production Plans and Levels of Fulfilment for Communal Farms in Seven Selected *Ujamaa* Villages in Morogoro District, 1970/1 Season

	Planned (acres)		Cultivated (acres)		Planted (acres)		Weeded (acres)		% Plan fulfilment	
	Food	Cash	Food	Cash	Food	Cash	Food	Cash	Food	Cash
1. Lukenge	48	80	24	70	24	40	22	25	46	31
2. Sesenga	53.5	140	13	10	13	6	7	2.5	13	1.8
3. Mkata	251	600	139	62	140	58	62	35	25	6
4. B/Chini	153	125	8.5	100	4	70	4	70	2.8	56
5. Kikundi	30	50	29.5	–6	29.5	53	29.5	–	98	–
6. Kauzeni	529	50	36	53	36	53	4	51	0.8	100
7. Kizinga	–	–	31.5	9	31.5	9	31.5	9	100	100

Source: Morogoro District Office (ibid.).

First, apart from further revealing the humble start on the road to village self-reliance, the low level of plan fulfilment is also a reflection on the planning inexperience of both the peasants and the experts who approved (in many cases, recommended) the targets. The enthusiasm of both led to overambitious targets which could not be fulfilled. Higher levels of plan fulfilment were achieved where the targets were more realistic.

Second, there was greater compliance with food-crop targets than with cash-crop targets. This must be considered a perfectly rational choice on the part of the peasants who have been used to subsistence economy and have experienced famine in the past. Whenever cash crops conflicted with the production of the basic food crops, the latter were given preference, the official plan not withstanding. Even such villages as Bwakira Chini and Kauzeni, which produced a negligible amount of food on the communal farm, used their private farms exclusively for food crops.

Third, the village plans led to wastage of government funds and manpower at various stages. All cultivation costs, seeds and fertilizers, were provided free, being funded largely by the Regional Development Fund (RDF). As can be clearly seen in Table III.5, in each case (except Kizinga which depended on its own resources) more acreage was cultivated than was planted, and more was planted than was weeded, each stage entailing a loss to the nation. In a few cases not shown in the table, not all that was weeded was finally harvested; the peasants having expected the government to send in members of the National Service or TANU Youth League to assist in harvesting, for this practice was widespread in Morogoro.

What the Morogoro data suggests is that in practice, as opposed to political rhetoric, there was still bureaucratic paternalism and lavish subsidies which suppressed the goal of popular initiative and self-reliance. We shall now turn briefly to the 'development village' phase, 1974 to 1977.

The Development Village Phase, 1974-7

Villagization took a new turn in 1973. At its 16th Biannual Conference, the party (TANU) resolved that living in villages was a concern for all the regions, and not just for the underprivileged ones. The President followed with a firm declaration that everyone must live in a village by the end of 1976. As a result, through a combination of persuasion and coercion, by mid-1977, about 85 per cent of the population had moved into some 8,000 villages. It is expected that when the programme is completed (now estimated around mid-1978) over 14 million people will be settled in about 10,000 villages.

Apart from these 'quantitative' changes, however, there appear to be 'qualitative' policy changes as well. The main ones are the following. First, the emphasis on total villagization has led to a deliberate de-emphasis on socialist relations of production in the villages. For example, most newly established villages are now called 'development villages', with more emphasis on 'bloc' and individual farming than on the communal *shamba* emphasized in the earlier phase. In fact, many formerly genuinely socialist (*ujamaa*) villages have now decided to make a 'step backwards' to become development villages.

Second, the policy now recognizes at least three types of village, namely traditional, development and *ujamaa* villages. Each of these can be registered under the Villages and *Ujamaa* Villages Act of 1975; each can form its government (Village Council) and expect to get assistance from the central government; the '*wajamaa*' are no longer universally getting the preferential treatment they used to get in the earlier phase. Current emphasis is on productivity and having a viable programme of action at the village level.

Third, since mid-1977, the central leaders have publicly declared their intention to encourage and support — materially and morally — private local individuals who are engaged in activities which promote the welfare of their communities or the nation as a whole. The activities may be in commerce, farming or small and medium industries. The banks have been instructed to give credit facilities to such individuals.

It is not entirely clear whether these changes represent an ideological shift back to the pre-Arusha liberal orientation, or simply a change in strategy. Disappointment with the performance of both nationalized modern sector and communal farming operations, and also the droughts and world inflation of recent years have played a part in bringing about the shift. But the influence of large-scale Western aid, consultancy firms and technical assistance teams also cannot be discounted. For example, World Bank teams have not taken cognizance of communal farming wherever they have formulated integrated development plans (e.g. Kigoma, Mara, etc.). They have only been concerned with *rational* allocation and utilization of resources to achieve optimal results in terms of measurable inputs and outputs.[9]

Notes

1. For elaboration of this argument, see S.S. Mushi, 'Revolution by evolution: the Tanzanian road to Socialism' (PhD thesis, Yale University, 1974), Ch. 2.

2. J.K. Nyerere, *The Arusha Declaration Teach-in* (The Information Services, Dar es Salaam, 1967), p. 11.

3. J.K. Nyerere, 'Freedom and Development', *The Standard* (Tanzania), 18 October 1968.

4. These objectives are discussed in greater detail in H. Hansel, J. de Vries and P.C. Ndedya (eds.), *Agricultural Extension in Ujamaa Village Development* (Ukulima wa Kisasa Printers, Ministry of Agriculture, Dar es Salaam, 1976), pp. 28-34.

5. Ibid., pp. 31-2.

6. A problem with the World Bank Maize Programme. Even if subsidies for fertilizer purchase make it profitable for the farmer or collective, it may still not make sense nationally. For an interesting analysis of this important issue, see Yashpal Tandon, 'The food question in East Africa: a partial case study of Tanzania', also Okello Oculli, 'Malnutrition and food policy in Africa', both papers for the Third Biannual Conference of the African Association of Political Science (Rabat, Morocco, 23-26 September 1977).

7. B. Galeski, *Basic Concepts of Rural Sociology* (Manchester University Press, Manchester, 1972), p. 100.

8. J.K. Nyerere, *The Arusha Declaration Teach-in*, p. 4.

9. For elaboration, see S.S. Mushi, 'Popular participation and rural development planning in Tanzania', pp. 82-4.

4 THE INSTRUMENTS OF THE *UJAMAA* PROGRAMME

The *ujamaa* programme is provided with adequate formal implementation machinery. First, there is the formal administrative machinery which reaches the villages via the elaborate extension service. Second, there is the party machinery extending to the village and cell level. Third, there is the elaborate planning and development of a committee structure. Fourth, there is the village government itself. Fifth, there are the crop authorities and other national and local organizations (such as Mtibwa Estate in the case of our case studies) which provide production inputs and marketing facilities.

In this chapter, we shall be concerned only with the formal structure of these bodies and their official role.

Government Administration and Extension

The major decentralization reform of July 1972 was intended to make the villages more productive, more innovative and more involved in decision-making and plan formulation and execution.[1]

Administrative decentralization meant also a massive movement of staff from Dar es Salaam to the regions between 1972 and 1975 and to the wards and villages between 1976 and 1977 when various cadres of technicians were shifted from the regional and district headquarters to live and work with the peasants in the wards and villages. By December 1977 about 8,000 such technicians had already been sent to the villages; and more are being trained in various agricultural, technical and ideological institutions.

The key ministry responsible for the development of the villages is the Prime Minister's Office, itself a creature of the decentralization reform. The PMO is supposed to be the spokesman for the regions; responsible for issuing planning guidelines to the regions, districts and villages as well as for ensuring that the regions are well staffed. This super-ministry is currently located centrally in Dodoma, the new capital of Tanzania, from where it can easily reach the regions via its *Ujamaa* and Co-operatives Directorate. It receives and processes quarterly and annual reports from the regions and provides the feedback and remedial

177

action.

The Ministry of Manpower Development is another key ministry in relation to manpower training, allocation, transfers, up-grading, etc., although some of its functions in this field are decentralized to the regions and districts where Manpower Development Managers work under District and Regional Directors. The other development ministries have also decentralized their experts to the regions and extension field staff to the district and ward levels. (The mainland is divided into twenty regions, subdivided into districts which are further divided into several wards. Each ward contains four to seven villages, and for some administrative purposes wards are grouped into divisions.) The ministries include Agriculture, Water, Works, Natural Resources, Health, Education, Commerce, etc. Each has a regional and district functional manager who supervises the field staff in his area of specialization, but works directly under the District Development Direction (DDD) or Regional Development Direction (RDD) rather than referring every little matter to his ministerial boss in Dar es Salaam. At the regional and district levels, the Regional and Area Secretaries (formerly Commissioners) are the overall administrative and party leaders of their respective areas, the Regional Secretary being the equivalent of a minister, and the Development Director his principal secretary. About 40 per cent of central government development budget was to be allocated to the regions to be spent on regional projects other than those undertaken by the central government or national institutions. This is in addition to a Regional Development Fund (RDF) of several millions which is allocated on a per capita basis to the regions, whilst the unspent balance can be accumulated from year to year.

The Party Structure and Role

In addition to the formal government bureaucracy, there is a parallel party structure. At the district and regional level it is headed by popularly elected chairmen, and a secretary, who is also the Regional or District Commissioner. These two people work through an Executive Committee at each level, which in the context of the Party Supremacy Act of 1975, is supreme in so far as policy is concerned. The structure is replicated at the ward and village level (whose party officials are also salaried and, from mid-1978, pensionable), and goes even further to the cell level where every ten households have an elected party leader.

The formal role of the party at the village level includes educating the people on the goals and purposes of various government policies; making the people committed to the objective of *ujamaa* and hard work; assisting the people in securing essential resources from the government bureaucracy, and performing general mobilization and animation work to promote compliance with centrally initiated projects and programmes as well as raising the level of local initiative. The party also acts as an avenue for popular participation, particularly at the cell and branch levels. The cell is the basic unit of mobilization, communication and, of course, administration of sanctions against non-compliance with community-approved targets.

The party also plays an important role in the planning process. At every stage of the planning process, a party organ scrutinizes the priorities listed in the plan drafts to ensure conformity with the central unifying ideology, leaving technical details to the experts. How well this task is done has depended on a number of factors, including the calibre of the party functionaries at each level.

The Planning and Development Committee Structure

Under the decentralized structure, an elaborate committee system was introduced through which the planning exercise takes place. Which body talks to which in this structure is shown in Figure III.1.

The composition of these planning and decision-making bodies is such that it combines expertise and popular representation. At the village level, the planning committee is popularly elected by the Village Assembly which consists of all the members. At the ward level, the WDC consists of elected ward councillors and a few experts from the government extension service, including the Branch Party Secretary who is Secretary of the Committee. At the district level, the DDPC has more experts than people's representatives, for it is essentially a planning committee, an executive arm of the DDC which has more representative elements and is chaired by the elected District Party Chairman with the area Commissioner (now Secretary) acting as the Secretary of the Council. The DMT and the RMT (at regional level) are entirely composed of civil servants, the experts under the DDD and RDD (through the Planning Officers), respectively. There is no elective body at the regional level, the RDC being a body of experts and appointed or indirectly elected party functionaries under the chairmanship of the Regional Secretary or Commissioner.

The planning process has several bottlenecks which affect perform-

Figure III.1: The Planning Process from Village to the National Assembly

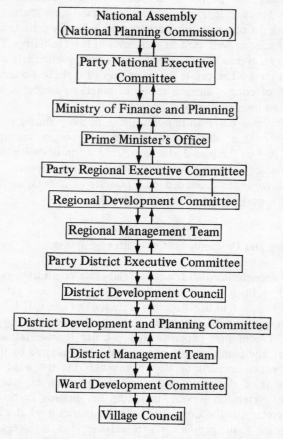

ance at the village community level. We shall mention only the main ones here.

First, it takes the full planning cycle (from about October to June) before the level of financing is known. Thus planning is done without full knowledge of funding. This leads to a mere listing of projects at the village level rather than a careful analysis of needs and priorities in the light of available resources, both locally and nationally. Second, since the allocation battle is ultimately fought in the Treasury, all the levels — village to region — tend to exaggerate their requirements so that they can end up with what they actually want after all the 'cutting' has been done. This, again, limits the value of planning. Third, in the areas where the village organization is not strong enough or the villagers are not 'politically conscious', the lengthy and complicated planning framework tends to eliminate popular participation in favour of the technocrats.[2] We shall return to these and related constraints in the chapters on programme execution and evaluation.

The Village Government and Organization

The Tanzanian central leadership has realized from experience with previous approaches to CD that the success of CD programmes depends, to a very large degree, on the quality of organization and leadership at the village level.

Hence, there have been programmes for training both village leaders and village members. Three types of training have been emphasized: ideological, technical and managerial. Ideological training for the leadership has been given at the Kivukoni College and its five zonal colleges; as well as in the form of leadership seminars, workshops, etc., organized by the regional and district party organization. In some cases, the village leaders have been encouraged and helped to visit other villages (in the more advanced regions) to see progress and learn from it. Technical training involves learning of such skills as carpentry, masonry, craftsmanship, the use of ox-ploughs, etc., in the district training centres and various agricultural institutes. Members for such courses are selected by the villagers themselves. Managerial skills for the village leaders and members include such subjects as book-keeping, management, etc., which are offered in a number of institutions in the country, but especially the Co-operative College at Moshi. The Prime Minister's Office also has an important division/section dealing with Village Management Training (VMT). Because of the recent massive collectivization, however, training has lagged behind the demand.

A second measure to strengthen village-level organization was the Village and *Ujamaa* Villages Act of June 1975, which defines the village as an economic as well as political and administrative unit. The Act provides for two types of villages: registered villages which will, when developed, act as multi-purpose co-operatives; and *ujamaa* villages which will have all their activities run on a socialist basis. The multi-purpose co-operatives will facilitate mainly the provision of agricultural services, including inputs such as fertilizers and seeds, credit and technical advise, exploiting the economies of scale; while the *ujamaa* villages will have the area of co-operation to include communal production, distribution and the ownership of the means of production.

Organizationally, according to the Act, each village will have a Village Assembly to be composed of all adult inhabitants and act as the policy-making body; and a Village Council, which is its executive body elected by the Village Assembly. Each Village Council has five committees as shown in Figure III.2 with additional sub-committees as necessary. Potentially, at least, this organizational base can boost the village's capacity to bargain with the state agents of change for essential development inputs and resources.

Figure III.2: Village Organizational Structure as per Villages and *Ujamaa* **Villages Act, 1975**

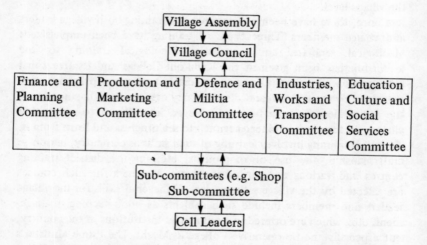

A third measure to strengthen the villages is the recent decentralization of personnel from the regional and district centres to the ward and village levels. There are also plans to create a Ward Development Directorate on the same pattern as the district and regional directorates. The Ward Directorate will be responsible for co-ordinating the technical services and other inputs required by the villages. Since ordinarily a ward consists of from four to seven villages, the provision of the essential resources and supervision of the community effort is likely to be more effective than it is at present.

Crop Authorities and Other Organizations

There are also various crop authorities, public corporations and local organizations which provide production and marketing facilities to the villages. All the major crops — coffee, cotton, tobacco, pyrethrum, sisal, cashew, etc. — are looked after by an 'authority' which engages in three main tasks, namely production, marketing and research. There is also a Livestock Marketing Authority and Ranching Corporation concerned with animal husbandry and marketing of meat and other dairy products. Although these are controlled directly from their headquarters, they have their own extension service in the regions and districts; and they usually work in consultation with the district and regional directorates in their dealings with the village producers. With the abolition of the old co-operative societies and unions in mid-1976, the marketing function was taken over by the crop authorities temporarily, pending the maturity of the villages which will eventually handle the marketing of their own produce.

With regard to the promotion of village industries and crafts, a Small Industries Development Organization (SIDO) was set up in the early seventies. Already SIDO has organized its own extension network and has established a famous training school at Tabora (among other places). Its important role in promoting rural industrialization has been realized and emphasized by the government, and the organization has received large budgetary and manpower allocations to extend its services to the village level.

Further, state farms have been introduced for 'certain agricultural products for which growth is required and which benefit from mechanization and/or large-scale irrigation, from organized innovation, and from centralised management of large-scale operation' to quote the Second Plan.[3] They are intended also to serve for cadre training and as models for *ujamaa* villages as well as to boost national production.

The plan envisaged over 250,000 acres of new state farms during the plan period (1969-74/5): wheat (ten farms), rice (four farms), vine (one), dairy (two), ranches (nine), oilseeds (one) and coconuts (two farms). About three-quarters of those planned have already been established, though not all are operating successfully.

Finally, there are other local organizations and firms which have been given the responsibility of supervising and servicing the villages in their areas. An example in the Mtibwa Sugar Estate (and Factory) in Turiani Division, Morogoro District whose special relationship with the sugar-growing villages in the area will be described in the case studies which follow.

Notes

1. See J.K. Nyerere, *Decentralization* (Government Printer, Dar es Salaam, 1972).
2. For elaboration, see S.S. Mushi, 'Popular participation and planning for rural development in Tanzania', esp. part III.
3. The Second Plan, vol. 1, pp. 30-1.

5 THE VILLAGES: KIDUDWE AND LUKENGE

Rationale for the Choice

Kidudwe and Lukenge villages were selected for three main reasons. First, I had studied these villages during their formative years (1972-3), and therefore I would have the opportunity to see change over time. Second, the two villages started with a common intention of producing sugar cane, an important cash crop for Tanzania. Third, the two villages were close to the Mtibwa Sugar Estate (and Factory) which was supposed to guide them to maturity (i.e. in cane-growing). The interaction between developing *ujamaa* communities and an estate that was just being transformed from a private, capitalist institution into state property seemed to offer an opportunity to analyse the inner dynamics of *ujamaa* transformation and the forces opposed to it. The two villages offered, therefore, a fruitful field for my preferred method of analysis — one which moves back and forth between the macro and the micro. They promised to help our understanding both of the politics of *ujamaa* in a small selected area and of the implications for the national objective of socioeconomic transformation.

The General Characteristics of the Villages

Both villages are located in Turiani Division of Morogoro District. They are about four miles apart, Lukenge lying to the south-west of Mtibwa sugar factory and Kidudwe to the south-east; they both border the Mtibwa sugar estate, as shown in Figure III.3. However, the villages are in different wards; Lukenge being in Sungaji ward, about thirteen miles from the ward and divisional headquarters and Kidudwe in Diyongoya ward, about six and eleven miles from the ward and divisional headquarters respectively. On average, they are both about 75 miles from Morogoro town, the district and regional headquarters. Both villages started as '*ujamaa* villages' (see their history in Chapter 6), but Lukenge has reverted to a 'development village' while Kidudwe has continued to remain an '*ujamaa* village'.

In the general Kidudwe area, there is another village created during the 'Operation Tanzania' collectivization period (1974-7), usually called Kidudwe development village or, simply, Kidudwe II, to distinguish it

Figure III.3: The Location of Kidudwe and Lukenge Villages *vis-à-vis* Mtibwa Sugar Factory and Estate

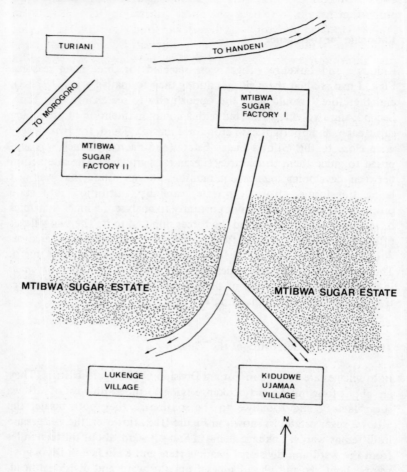

from Kidudwe *ujamaa* village. When we need to refer to both villages we shall do so as Kidudwe I and Kidudwe II; in any other context, however, Kidudwe means the *ujamaa* village. In the following pages, we shall give the general features of the two villages, which will be elaborated upon in Chapters 6 and 7.

The Land and Type of Agriculture

Turiani Division is a very rich agricultural area, although a very small proportion has, in fact, been put under cultivation. Its rich soils can support virtually any crop — both cash and food — and, taking the past decade as a whole, the rains have been very satisfactory, except in the past three years when the rains have failed, leading to famine in Lukenge and many other villages in the area.

There is no land constraint at present. The land claimed by each of the two villages, which has not been accurately surveyed, is estimated to be in the region of 50,000 acres, and there is room for expansion beyond these vague limits. However, there are two big constraints on further expansion, namely the huge uncleared forests and vermin, mainly tsetse fly, and the wildebeest. So far the villagers have been using only the areas which were initially cleared with government assistance (less than 30 per cent of the area claimed); and every 'message' that is read to a visiting government official (or a researcher) contains a request for assistance to clear the forest and to fight the vermin which destroy crops and animals.

Both villages grow sugar cane as the main cash crop. The other main crops (mainly for food) include maize, paddy and millet. Both keep dairy cattle (ten head in each case), poultry, sheep and goats; but they have had varying success — particularly with the sugar cane — for reasons we shall explore later. While the cattle are communally owned, the sheep and goats are individually owned in each case.

Table III.6: Livestock Ownership (Goats and Sheep) at Kidudwe and Lukenge, mid-1977

Village	Households with less than 10	Households with more than 10	Total	Percentage of total household %
Kidudwe	18	12	30	28
Lukenge	37	10	47	20

Population and Sociocultural Features

Several tribes and religions are represented in each village. By mid-1977, Lukenge had 230 families, or households, while Kidudwe had 106. Lukenge's population draws on some 17 tribes from various parts of Tanzania. Their relative strength is depicted in Table III.7. The Pangwa and Zigua are by far the strongest, jointly constituting half the village population. As we shall see later, this numerical strength has also been transformed into political power in the struggle for the leadership of the village.

Table III.7: Relative Strength of the Tribes in Lukenge Village, mid-1977

Over 60 families	Up to 10 families	Less than 10 families
Pangwa and Zigua	Sandawi, Bena, Mbunga, Kaguru and Gogo	Nyakusa, Kwere, Fipa, Rundi, Hehe, Luguru, Shambala, Makua, Yao, and Kutu.

Source: Lukenge Village Office.

Kidudwe's population represents over 20 tribes from many parts of mainland Tanzania and also has a few people originating from outside Tanzania. The tribal and religious heterogeneity of Kidudwe is depicted in Table III.8 which analyses a large section of the labour force. In terms of religious affiliations, the Christians (Catholics and Protestants combined) are dominant, for they constitute about 62 per cent of the population as against the Moslems who constitute about 33 per cent and Pagans about 5 per cent. In tribal terms, the Pare are at the top, with about 36 per cent of the total, followed by the 'native' tribes (Zigua and Nguu) who constitute 16 per cent. As we shall see later, however, these sociocultural factors are not the only ones determining 'group solidarity' or even the pattern of village politics. For apart from education and related 'class' factors, there are other historical factors which have divided the population along other dimensions.

Population composition in the two villages has several interesting features which should be noted briefly here, for they have a bearing on the performance of the villages which we shall discuss later.

First, the huge Lukenge population is a post-operation phenomenon; whereas there were only 45 families at the end of 1973, they had grown to 230 in mid-1977. No such change occurred in Kidudwe which resisted the 'infiltration' of 'non-*wajamaa*'. Second, Lukenge has a relatively low child population, partly because most of the new entrants were bachelors and partly because fewer men have more than one wife (10 per cent v. Kidudwe's 22 per cent), and also many people have left their first or second wives in their areas of origin. Thus whereas at Kidudwe the settlers have actually established a 'home', Lukenge seems to be a 'calling port' for many of the young bachelors. Third,

Table III.8: Tribal and Religious Configuration of a Section of Kidudwe's Labour Force of mid-1977

Tribe	District of Origin	Catholic	Protestant	Muslim	Pagan	Total
1. Pare	Same	7	33	19	0	59
2. Zigua & Nguu	Native	–	–	27	–	27
3. Pangwa & Bena	Njombe & Rudewa	13	3	–	1	17
4. Kaguru	Kilosa	2	5	2	2	11
5. Gogo	Dodoma	7	1	–	3	11
6. Chagga	Moshi	7	3	–	–	10
7. Ngoni	Songea	5	–	–	1	6
8. Sandawe	Kondoa	5	–	–	–	5
9. Fipa	Sumbawanga	4	–	–	–	4
10. Shambla	Lushoto	1	1	1	–	3
11. Nyiramba	Iramba	–	1	1	–	2
12. Kwere	Bagamoyo	–	–	1	–	1
13. Nyakyusa	Tukuyu	1	–	–	–	1
14. Nyaturu	Singida	–	–	1	–	1
15. Sukuma	Geita/Mwanza	1	–	–	–	1
16. Kuria	N. Mara	–	1	–	–	1
17. Mbunga	Kilombero	–	–	1	–	1
18. Rundi	(Burundi)	1	–	–	–	1
19. Kamba	(Kenya)	–	–	1	–	1
20. Maragoli	(Kenya)	1	–	–	–	1

Source: Kidudwe Village Office.

Table III.9: Population Composition in Kidudwe and Lukenge Villages, mid-1977

Village	Families/ households	Men	Women	Child-ren	Old & dis-abled	Total popu-lation	Labour force	B/A %
Kidudwe	106	106	89	365	None	560	195	35
Lukenge	230	230	280	442	6	958	510	44

Source: Kidudwe and Lukenge Village Offices.

most of these young men supply labour to Mtibwa Estate rather than to the village community, whereas Kidudwe has been able to resist this. The average number of children per household at Lukenge is 1.9 as compared to 3.5 at Kidudwe where the population is more settled. The term 'household' is used interchangeably with the term 'family', both meaning at least an adult person with a house/hut at the village, whether or not he or she is married, and with or without children.

Education and Other Social Services

Tanzania has placed a strong emphasis on adult literacy and an important aspect of its CD approach is the campaign for 'functional literacy'.
This goes beyond the older concern merely with reading and writing,
to include the basic skills required in each area as well as an element of
political education. The President has called the new approach 'education for liberation', an important element in the policy of 'education
for self-reliance'. In 1973 the party leadership passed a resolution to the
effect that full adult literacy should be achieved by the end of 1975,
and intense campaigns were organized in the villages. The literacy levels
achieved in the two villages are given in Table III.10. The big difference
between Kidudwe 1 and Lukenge will be explained along with other
differences in Chapter 8.

**Table III.10: Levels of Adult Literacy in Kidudwe I, Kidudwe II and
Lukenge Villages, mid-1977**

Village	Total adult population	Literate	Illiterate	Per cent literacy	Variation from national average
Kidudwe I	195	160	35	82	+21%
Kidudwe II	990	614	323	62	+ 1%
Lukenge	510	332	178	65	+ 4%

Source: Kidudwe and Lukenge primary school records.

There is a similar difference in the response to the drive for universal
primary education which in 1974 the party resolved to achieve by the
end of 1977 instead of the 1989 target contained in the Second Plan.
Kidudwe Primary School (which admits pupils from the two Kidudwe
villages) has built extra classrooms (on a self-help basis with the government providing building materials) and now has double streams in Standards 1 and 2. Most classes have more than 45 pupils which is the maximum recommended by the ministry. At Lukenge, on the other hand,
class sizes are below the required level. This is partly because there are
fewer children at Lukenge, but also because of differences in attendance.

There were by the end of 1976 about 20 children of school age
(between 6 and 12) who were not in school, and about 156 at Kidudwe
II, whereas there was none at Kidudwe *ujamaa* village. According to
the head teacher of Kidudwe Primary School, parents of this village
'lobby' to have their children admitted at an earlier age than that pre-

scribed by the Ministry of National Education (i.e. 7 years). They have also requested the school to provide kindergarten facilities. The situation is entirely different at Lukenge. According to the head teacher of Lukenge Primary School, many parents are reluctant to send their children to school. It took heavy campaigns, including sending some parents to court (where they were fined), to achieve the present level of admission. Again, the parents did not take advantage of the kindergarten facilities made available by the school although the teachers are freer than at Kidudwe where they are overburdened.

Both villages have been provided with the other basic social services, although most of these services are not adequate. Most inadequate are the health facilities; for in each case there is only a first aid box at the village, with clinic service (a mobile one) being provided once a week. For the more serious cases, the villagers have to travel between 9 and 12 miles to find a proper dispensary or hospital. In both villages, every household is required to have a pit latrine; but whereas there is universal compliance at Kidudwe, about 20 per cent of the new entrants at Lukenge had not complied by mid-1977, although campaigns were continuing. With regard to water supply, Kidudwe has two boreholes (with hand-operated machine) within half a mile of the village centre; and Lukenge gets fresh water from a nearby river and has one borehole. Both villages are linked to Mtibwa Sugar Factory by a three-mile road; but whereas Lukenge gets a bus service to Turiani (where there are market facilities) only twice a week, Kidudwe has a bus service (reaching the school) daily, mornings and afternoons.

The basic services available at each village are summarized in Table III.11. Each village has an office and sufficient storage facilities; but each has to travel several miles to the flour mill. In each case the original settlers have houses with corrugated iron roofing; 17 at Lukenge (built with government assistance) and 26 at Kidudwe (built with the villagers' own resources). The rest of the houses are thatched with grass in the traditional way. The differences in housing do arouse envy among the new entrants.

Table III.11: Availability and Proximity to Basic Social Services at Kidudwe and Lukenge Villages, mid-1977

Services available	Villages	
	Kidudwe	Lukenge
School	10 minutes' walk from village centre, Std. 1-8	At village centre
Dispensary/ Clinic	First aid box; hospital 9-12 miles away; clinic service on Thursdays	First aid box; hospital 10-12 miles away; clinic service once a week
Water	Two boreholes, ½ mile from village centre	Fresh water plus one borehole
Roads	3½-mile road from Mtibwa to the village	3-mile road from Mtibwa to the village
Transport	Bus service to school twice daily, morning and afternoon	Bus service to Turiani twice a week, only in dry season
Shop	One communal shop, no private shops	One communal shop, no private shops
Storage	Adequate storage facilities	Adequate storage facilities
Market	At Turiani, 10 miles away	At Turiani, 12 miles away
Flour mill	None at the village; a private one at Kidudwe II	None at the village; available several miles away
Office	One room available for office	One room available for office
Housing	26 with corrugated iron roofing; the rest with traditional thatch	17 with corrugated iron roofing; the rest with traditional thatch
Latrines	A must, and every household has complied	A must, but 20 per cent of the new entrants have not yet complied.

Source: Kidudwe and Lukenge villages.

6 THE EXECUTION OF VILLAGE PROJECTS

The previous chapter has already suggested that Kidudwe has done better than Lukenge in both qualitative and quantitative terms. The present chapter will explain some of the historical background to this difference.

Development of the Villages, 1969-77

Lukenge started as an *ujamaa* village on 23 March 1969 with 17 families. The creation of the village was largely a government initiative. The government had two aims. First, it wanted to accommodate the 17 families in a flood-free area, that is, some distance away from the river which had flooded in 1968 causing great damage to the residents. Second, the government wanted to create *ujamaa* villages which would supply sugar cane to the nearby sugar factory to supplement that of the Mtibwa Estate and eventually to replace the contributions of the private (capitalist) outgrowers who had been supplying the factory since the mid-sixties. Lukenge would be the first of such villages in Turiani Division and others would be formed in the course of time.

The government offered the 17 families lavish incentives to agree to live and work together for the benefit of all of them. The incentives included free construction of access roads, free clearing of the forests and building plots, free house (with corrugated iron roofing) for each family, free tractorized cultivation during the initial years, a school and some medical facilities, free animals (10 head of cattle), and promises of much more. From 1969 to 1973, there were regular visits by officials from the regional, district and divisional headquarters, for there were only about 21 promising *ujamaa* villages in the whole district. The original members estimate that there were about three visits by officials from different levels each week between 1969 and the end of 1972.

Because of the above incentives and regular visits by party and government officials during the *ujamaa* phase (1969-73), Lukenge did relatively well, being selected as the 'best village' in the district in 1970. The relatively good performance of Lukenge during this period is shown by three indicators: the growing population due to new entrants, the rising production level and the 'equitable' distribution of the proceeds. The number of families had increased to 45 by 1973 with a labour force of 87 (Table III.12). The dramatic rise from 45 to 230 families by 1977 was entirely due to 'Operation Tanzania' which had elements of compulsion rather than the principle of voluntariness and persuasion followed in the earlier phase.

Table III.12: Population Changes at Lukenge Village, 1969-77

Year	Families	Men	Women	Children	Old and disabled	Total	Labour force
Mid-1969	17	17	6	24	1	48	23
" 1970	23	23	11	n.a.	n.a.	n.a.	34
" 1971	27	27	16	49	3	95	43
" 1972	43	43	14	100	3	160	59
" 1973	45	45	42	103	3	193	87
" 1974	n.a.	n.a.	n.a.	n.a.	3	n.a.	190
" 1975	135	135	93	n.a.	4	n.a.	228
" 1976	142	142	135	n.a.	5	n.a.	272
" 1977	230	230	280	442	6	958	510

Source: Lukenge Village Office.

As in many other new villages, Lukenge was encouraged to produce both food and cash crops. The village started with paddy and sugarcane as the main crops. In 1970/1 it produced 262 bags of rice worth nearly Shs 16,000 and in 1973/4 it produced 133 bags of rice and 200 tons of sugarcane worth nearly Shs 92,000. Considering the generally low productivity of most villages, this was no mean achievement. As we shall see when we analyse the inputs, however, the actual contribution by the villagers themselves was not as big as the political leadership claimed.

Apart from its production record, however, Lukenge was 'praised' during the pre-operation period because it appeared to be steering the *ujamaa* way. Sugarcane production was entirely communal, and so was over 50 per cent of food crop production. Again, the communal production was distributed more or less equally during the first two years since all the families had participated and much of the input had come from the government. For example, in the 1970/1 season the village distributed Shs 3,000 earned from the sale of 50 bags (out of the total of 262 produced) of rice: the highest received Shs 139 while the lowest got Shs 98. The situation was to change radically with the influx of new entrants, from 1974 to 1977, as we shall see later. We shall now turn briefly to Kidudwe.

The origin of Kidudwe *ujamaa* village is quite different from that of Lukenge; for it started with 'negative' incentives. The village was founded on 18 August 1971 by 26 families which had been expelled from Kabuku Settlement Scheme in Handeni District. Founded in 1965, Kabuku was one of the few fairly successful schemes of the transformation approach we discussed earlier, and its main crop was sisal. Each of the 250 families at Kabuku was assigned about ten acres of sisal. The settlement was known to have two types of family, those who worked hard and made a profit from their farms and the lazy ones who made no profit. All the 26 families which were finally expelled claim to have belonged to the hard-working group.

With the Arusha Declaration in 1967, emphasis changed from 'settlements' which emphasized individual production within a block farming system to *ujamaa* villages emphasizing communal production. At Kabuku settlement, as would be expected, the change was hailed by the members of the lazy group whereas it was abhorred by the more industrious members. Thus when in 1969 the district political leadership directed the settlement to transform itself into an *ujamaa* village, the 26 families resisted, arguing that their effort would be exploited by the lazy members because communal production would entail a sharing of the proceeds. The debate went on for several months and some of the objecting members were locked up briefly; but no agreement was reached. According to the original migrants, the 26 families were then expelled from Kabuku and deposited in a go-down (grain store building) at a place called Kanga in Morogoro District. A few months later the Morogoro authorities moved them to Kidudwe area to establish an *ujamaa* village. The population they found in the area was gradually absorbed into the new village organization, and the population grew, as shown in Table III.13.

Table III.13: Population Changes at Kidudwe *Ujamaa* Village, 1971-7

Year	Families	Men	Women	Children	Total	Labour force
1971/2	26	26	32	184	242	58
1972/3	37	37	32	206	275	69
1973/4	43	43	41	212	296	84
1974/5	55	55	46	242	343	101
1975/6	90	90	66	359	515	156
1976/7	106	106	89	365	560	195

Source: Kidudwe Village Office.

The history of Kidudwe, then, reveals several differences from that of Lukenge. First, it was founded by disappointed and frustrated families who had been expelled from a settlement scheme. In contrast, the 17 families at Lukenge came mostly from traditional environments. Second, the 26 families of Kidudwe were from the beginning tied by a bond of 'struggle' with the authorities, starting from Kabuku where they saw themselves as being 'oppressed' by the authorities. They continued to struggle for compensation for their property at Kabuku, and in mid-1977 were still pressing for some Shs 40,000 per family to be paid in a lump sum. The government was offering less than a fifth of that amount in instalments — which were being paid in spite of disagreement on the final figure. Third, apart from the cost of clearing the forest (some Shs 35,000) and the basic social services, the initial government assistance to Kidudwe was not as lavish as that extended to Lukenge. For example, the 26 houses with corrugated iron roofing were built with the early compensation instalments. In other words, Kidudwe learnt to be self-reliant earlier than Lukenge, and this was later reflected in the performance, as we shall see.

The Role of Government and Party Officials

The role of government and party officials in mobilizing the villages to a higher performance fluctuated considerably between 1969 and 1977, according to the view of the villagers themselves. At Lukenge, in particular, the contrast between the 1969-73 period and the post-1973 period was seen as sharp. Not only was there less attention and assistance but also an element of compulsion in getting new entrants into the village. Kidudwe, by contrast, has been more favoured since 1974, since it is the only village in Turiani which retained its *ujamaa* production relations in the operation period, and encouragement it was thought, might induce other villages to go *ujamaa*. For example in 1974 the Ministry of Agriculture provided it with 100 chicks and another 100 in 1975. They were also offered 10 cows and a bull in 1975 to strengthen the dairy project. The village has also been promised a sugar-processing machine to make brown sugar which it can sell to Mtibwa Sugar Factory instead of selling the cane.

However, the local leaders (Ward and Divisional Secretaries) have not been on good terms with Kidudwe. Two examples were cited by the villagers. First, they complained that the local leadership engineered matters so that branch party leadership was wholly picked from

Kidudwe II which is non-*ujamaa*. The two villages shared the branch because Kidudwe I had less than 250 families, the minimum required for a party branch. Voting forms were not distributed to Kidudwe I for the CCM party elections (May 1977) and therefore the village did not participate in the elections. When the matter was reported to the district, the Area Secretary (i.e. District Commissioner) directed that Kidudwe *ujamaa* village should form its own branch even though it had less than 250 families. Second, they complained that the local leader did not visit their village regularly or forward their problems to the district and regional authorities. This was partially admitted by the Ward Secretary who explained in an interview that:

> Kidudwe Ujamaa Village is well ahead of the other villages in this ward; it has more educated people than the others, and it understands *ujamaa* more than the rest. So we have to concentrate effort on the other less developed villages.[1]

However, members of Kidudwe *ujamaa* village had their own interpretation. They believed that the ward leaders hated them for being 'foreigners' (over 80 per cent coming from outside the division and district, see Table III.8). Second, they believed that they envied their relative success in sugarcane production and the attention paid to them by the district and regional leadership. It is quite possible that there may be something in these claims. For the Ward Secretary is a very 'traditional' man, having been the traditional leader, *Mfumwa Mkuu*, for Sungaji Ward before the abolition of traditional authorities in 1962. Furthermore, Kidudwe villagers have been by-passing him and dealing with district authorities directly, a thing which has irritated him and the other ward officials.

Lukenge, on the other hand, having lost the attention it used to receive from the district, has in part regained it largely because of the intense village leadership crisis that has existed there since 1974. We shall look at this leadership crisis and the effects on programme execution in a later section.

The Role of Mtibwa Sugar Estate

As we mentioned earlier, the two villages were expected to specialize in sugarcane as their main cash crop, and Mtibwa Sugar Estate was expected to guide these villages to maturity. The Estate would provide the villages with the basic techniques, advise on and organize timely cutting of the cane and provide transport facilities to the factory. As it turned out, however, the Estate became a competitor rather than a promoter of the villages. To understand why this was so, it is useful to outline briefly the history of Mtibwa Estate.

Mtibwa Sugar Estate originally belonged to a Greek farmer. The Estate was later sold to Messrs Thakabhai and Manubhai of Kenya, and later (1967) resold to the Madhvani Group of Companies which had a monopoly of the sugar industry in Uganda. Trouble developed between this group and the peasant outgrowers who had been supplying cane to the factory since the early sixties. The company wanted to discourage the peasants from growing sugarcane and instead to expand the Estate's own production, but the peasant outgrowers were defended by the local political leaders and their complaints against the company reached as far as the Ministry of Agriculture in Dar es Salaam. Then, when the *ujamaa* era started, the government wanted *ujamaa* villages to replace the individual peasants as outgrowers and wanted them to produce about half of the cane required by the Estate Factory (which had been partially nationalized). There was an intense debate on this between the Estate managers and the Morogoro regional authorities between 1972 and 1974.

For reasons having to do with the synchronizing of processing, quality control and difficulties of price negotiation, the Estate would have preferred either to produce all the cane itself or else to incorporate the villages into its own capital-intensive farming system. This suggestion was rejected by the regional authorities as being against the norms of *ujamaa* which emphasized village self-management and self-reliance. Thus the Estate was directed to assist the villages in the manner mentioned above.[2]

Despite the fact that the Estate was now state property, the management's view of the peasantry and, in particular, of *ujamaa* villages, was not significantly different from that of the former capitalist owners. The Estate management tended to use purely economic criteria in dealing with the budding *ujamaa* villages, paying little attention to the other aspects of *ujamaa* community life. Three aspects of the resulting friction are particularly important.

First, the procedure is that the Estate enters into a contract with the villages. The contract stipulates that the Estate will provide all the necessary inputs, organize the cutting of the sugarcane and provide transport. But the charges, particularly for cutting, are high, and the balance paid and available as village reserve for expansion or reinvestment in other projects is usually very small.

Second, the Estate has been encroaching upon the cleared village land. For example, in the current expansion phase, the Estate has taken over substantial pieces of land from both Kidudwe and Lukenge. This limits the capacity of the villages to expand their own cane fields, particularly because the villages have little reserve that could be used in clearing new areas. The result may be further reliance on government assistance.

Third, the Estate has been attracting the village labour to work on its cane fields. Lukenge has been a victim of this; about 40 per cent of its labour force is hired by the Estate as casual labourers. Estate lorries go to the village regularly to carry the labourers to the Estate fields. This 'proletarianization' of the villagers seems deliberate. For example, in 1976/7 Lukenge had no sugarcane at all because the Estate broke the contract. The village had planned for 128 acres which the Estate ploughed in accordance with the contract. But the Estate did not send its experts to organize the planting; instead it attracted the village labour force away. Again, about 35 acres of cane which was ready for cutting was destroyed by fire set by Estate workers. The Estate promised to pay for this loss, but it is surprising that the village leadership has not shown much concern over it. The reason is clearly because some of the village leaders are hired by the Estate.

This has had several negative consequences for Lukenge's development. First, the *ujamaa* mode of production established in the earlier phase (1969-73) has virtually disappeared. Of course this disappearance is partly accounted for by the change in emphasis at the national level and the big influx of new entrants, most of whom were young men who were used to paid employment. Thus the dominant mode of production is now individual and block farming. Second, village production has fallen tremendously. Thus whereas the village produced goods worth about Shs 84,000 (gross) in 1973/4, it produced goods worth about Shs 45,000 (gross) in 1976/7 with a much larger labour force, and this despite ambitious production plans to cultivate over 400 acres of rice and cotton on a block farming basis, as well as 2 acres of food per household.[3]

Kidudwe, on the other hand, was able to resist the pressures from the Estate to hire its labour force; not a single man has been hired by the Estate, according to both the village leadership and the Estate management. Kidudwe was also able to resist the temptation to switch from *ujamaa* to development village status. Admission of new entrants to the village during the operation period was based on acceptance of the *ujamaa* mode of production in regard to the main crops and other development activities. It therefore became necessary to create Kidudwe II to take the non-*wajamaa*.

Village Organization and Leadership

The organizational structure of the two villages was outlined in the previous section. The Assembly meets once a year in October and the Council which meets monthly has 25 members. Both Kidudwe and Lukenge have shop sub-committees in addition to the legally required committees, and Kidudwe has a disciplinary and conciliation committee consisting of the village chairman and four elders who are also cell leaders. Elections for the main offices are supervised by the ward leaders who receive nominations and approve two names for each post (of chairman, secretary, cell leader, etc., offices which represent positions both in village government and in the party branch). The villagers then vote for them through secret ballot. Thus every village leader is expected to be an 'upright' party member.

The similarity of formal organizational structure at Kidudwe and Lukenge has not, however, been accompanied by similar leadership styles or effectiveness. Leadership at Lukenge has been unstable and ineffective whereas that of Kidudwe has been stable and effective, largely due to the dominance of one tribe (Pare). So far there have been only two village chairmen (1971-7) at Kidudwe, but rapid turnover at Lukenge, as shown in the following list:

Chairman	From	To	Length	1 Tribe	Comment
1. Daniel Lefani	1969	1974	(5 years)	Pangwa	(overthrown in a *coup*)
2. Juma Mambomambo	Jan. 74	Apr. 74	(4 months)	Zigua	(young men group)
3. Amos Luhenga	Apr. 74	Oct. 74	(6 months)	Bena	voted out
4. Antony Jacob	1974	1975	(4 months)	Pangwa	(resigned)
5. Abdallah Chinyonge	Feb. 75	Feb. 76	(1 year)	Zigua	voted out
6. Mrisho Jaribu	Feb. 76	77 (cont.)		Kwere	voted in by the new entrants

No chairman remained in office for more than a year after the *ujamaa* phase (i.e. from 1974 onwards). Apart from the rivalry between the Pangwa and the Zigua, the two major tribal groups of approximately equal numbers, there was also a generational rivalry. For example there was literally a *coup* in January 1974 launched by a 'young men' group. In one night a group of 40 young men gathered secretly to plan the *coup* and the following morning a new village government was announced. They accused the former leadership of inefficiency, old-fashioned methods of organizing work — sending only the younger people to the field, etc. — and inability to maintain proper records. However, the new leadership did not improve the situation, being popularly voted out within four months. Each new set of leaders has been accused of 'corruption', often because records are poor; village account books showing balances where there are deficits, and vice versa, because there are no trained book-keepers. There is also rivalry between the new and the old group. Thus those who entered after 1974 were able to put their candidate in power (a Kwere) to break the Pangwa-Zigua monopoly.

Moreover, the leadership at Kidudwe, by contrast, has been older, better educated and relatively wealthier than at Lukenge. The Secretary, who is also the village treasurer, has attended a book-keeping course at Moshi Co-operative College, and therefore financial control and internal auditing has been possible at Kidudwe.

There is also better work organization at Kidudwe than at Lukenge. At Kidudwe, Mondays are set aside for 'nation-building' activities — e.g. road works, maintenance of school buildings, dispensary building and similar social infrastructural activities. Tuesdays, Wednesdays and Thursdays are for communal work, mainly the sugarcane fields. Fridays, Saturdays and Sundays are for individual work. Sanctions have been effectively administered against failing to take part in village work. Enforcement is by a disciplinary and conciliation committee whose verdict is usually complied with. Lukenge used to have a similar work organization and enforcement machinery up to 1974, but with the erosion of the *ujamaa* mode of production, the organization has become so loose that it is even difficult to enforce the implementation of nation-building activities. As already pointed out, some of the leaders are themselves hired by the Estate. Further, the leaders command less authority, being younger, less educated and poorer than those of Kidudwe. For example, the current Secretary is a young bachelor, about 25 years old, with hardly any property in the village. Thus one finds that many simple cases — of theft, fighting, avoidance of nation-building work, etc. — which could have been settled at the village are handled by the ward officials or in courts.

What were the relative contributions of villagers and government agencies to the development programmes in these villages? The attempt to answer that question faces three major problems. First, there is the problem of quantifying the essential inputs since the key inputs are non-material. For example, getting people to agree to live together and work together for the benefit of all requires much more in the form of ideological mobilization than direct financial or material input. The cost of ideological persuasion is indeed difficult to assess. Second, even with physical or material inputs, analysis is hampered by the paucity of information due to poor records at both the village and district levels. Very often the figures given at the village are at variance with those found in district records. Very often, too, the figures do not include salaries of officials, travelling costs and many other expenses incurred by the officials responsible for particular projects. There are even fewer records for the output side. Third, the rapid changes in village labour force (especially at Lukenge), make it difficult to assess the inputs and outputs per capita over the period.

Even with these constraints, however, it is still possible to give an indication of the relative contributions of government and villagers to the various projects undertaken at the two villages. In Tables III.14a and III.14b, we give relative contributions by government and villagers (Kidudwe and Lukenge, respectively) to seven selected projects from 1969 to 1977. Although the level of self-help contributions by the two villages is virtually the same for the seven projects, 29 per cent and 27 per cent, Kidudwe has in fact done much better than Lukenge since roughly the same total labour contribution was made at Kidudwe by 100 workers (the average labour force from 1971 to 1977) compared with 160 at Lukenge. Furthermore, Kidudwe village was more success-ful in maintaining the projects than Lukenge. For example, there were more milk cows alive by 1977, giving sufficient milk to the village and a little surplus which was sold to the Estate workers. The care of the animals at Lukenge was sub-standard and the milk production was far below the cost of maintaining them. Similarly, whereas the carpentry shop at Kidudwe was able to meet the requirements of the village and provide a little surplus to sell outside the village, that of Lukenge was not able to meet the building needs of the village by 1977. Thus, overall, Kidudwe was able to get more out of government assistance than Lukenge.

Again, Kidudwe has been more successful in attracting further government assistance during the post-operation period than Lukenge. As mentioned earlier, the government has promised to provide it with a machine to make brown sugar to enable it to get more income from its

Table III.14a: Relative Contributions gy Government and Villagers to Selected Projects at Kidudwe Village, 1971-7

Project	Government assistance	Village self-help contributions
1. 5 classrooms, stores, etc.	Equipment and skills worth Shs 75,000	Labour worth Shs 25,000
2. Go-down/storage	Equipment etc., worth Shs 22,000	Labour worth Shs 8,000
3. Water supply (2 boreholes)	Equipment, etc., worth Shs 20,000	Labour worth Shs 2,000
4. 3-mile road	Allocated Shs 20,000	Labour worth Shs 9,000
5. Dairy	10 cows and a bull; plus building equipment all worth Shs 18,000	Labour contribution worth Shs 10,000
6. Carpentry	Equipment worth Shs 10,000	Labour in building worth Shs 2,000
7. Office and shop building	None	Labour and cash worth Shs 10,000
Total	Shs 165,000	Shs 65,000
Per cent of total cost	71 per cent	29 per cent

Source: Estimated from various sources, excluding salaries of officials, transport costs and other expenses.

Table III.14b: Relative Contributions by Government and Villagers to Seven Selected Projects at Lukenge Village, 1969-77

Project	Government assistance	Village self-help contributions
1. 6 classrooms and a teacher's house	Equipment, skills, etc., worth Shs 90,000	Labour worth Shs 30,000
2. Go-down/storage	Equipment, etc., worth Shs 30,000	Labour worth Shs 8,000
3. Water supply (1 borehole)	Equipment, etc., worth Shs 12,000	Labour worth Shs 1,500
4. 3-mile road	Allocated Shs 20,000	Labour worth Shs 10,000
5. Dairy	10 milk cows and a bull plus building equipment, all worth Shs 22,500	Labour in building worth Shs 8,500
6. Carpentry	Equipment worth Shs 10,500	Labour in building worth Shs 1,000
7. Office and shop building	None	Labour and cash worth Shs 8,000
Total	Shs 185,000	Shs 67,000
Per cent of total cost	73 per cent	27 per cent

Source: Estimated from various sources, excluding salaries of officials, transport costs and other expenses.

sugarcane. This contrasts with the charcoal project at Lukenge which has attracted little government support due to the lack of proper organization and sound plans at the village. All in all, however, both villages have, to date, received more material assistance from the government for their projects than from the contributions of their members. This is particularly true if account is taken of the fact that during the initial years the government supplied free services in clearing the bush, cultivation of the sugar plantations, etc. This initial massive support was undoubtedly necessary given the poverty of the villagers and the fact that most of the members had to establish themselves in new areas. The important question, however, still remains the extent to which this assistance has enhanced or stifled the spirit of self-reliance in the villages. We shall return to this question in Chapter 7 since village self-reliance is one of the main goals of Tanzania's village development programme.

Although in both villages officials were largely responsible for initially suggesting — and financing — the projects, it was at the second level of decision-making, concerning operation and maintenance, that problems developed and differences between Kidudwe and Lukenge are best seen. Since there was little supervision of the projects from outside, much depended on the internal cohesion and organizational strength of the villages themselves. As we have pointed out, Kidudwe had higher organizational capability than Lukenge and was therefore able to make binding decisions relating to government-assisted projects as well as to initiate plans for future village self-improvement. Thus, although it is correct to say that the bureaucratic element dominated the decision-making processes in initiating the projects, it can also be argued that the poor performance of these projects (especially at Lukenge) was partly due to lack of adequate government supervision on a regular basis. This raises the larger issue of the dilemma between grassroots democracy and productivity to which we shall return in Chapter 10 which sums up the lessons to be learnt from these case studies.

Notes

1. Interview with Ward Secretary, Diyongoya Ward, 12 May 1977.
2. For details, see S.S. Mushi 'Revolution by evolution', pp. 321-40.
3. Figures given by Ward Secretary.

7 EVALUATION OF PROGRAMME EFFECTS

These development efforts need to be evaluated in terms both of official goals — including the development of *ujamaa* relations of production and the fair distribution of wealth as well as raising production — and the villagers' own perceptions of goals and needs. This we shall try to do.

Production and Distribution of Proceeds

To begin with agricultural production, Table III.15 shows how much of the planned acreage was planted and finally harvested (the meaning of 'plan fulfilment') in two sample years. The table shows several interesting features and changes in the two villages between 1973 and 1976. First, the communal production which had existed in both villages in 1973 had disappeared at Lukenge by 1976, concentration being on individual farming (for food crops) and for cash crops on bloc farming in which the ploughing and spraying is done jointly by farmers working contiguous fields with the expenses shared. Second, whereas both villages had sugarcane as their main cash crop in 1973, this crop was marginal at Lukenge after 1973 and absent in 1976 due to factors we have already discussed. Third, Lukenge, which had plan fulfilment levels comparable to those of Kidudwe in 1973/4, had a very low plan fulfilment rate for its cash crop (cotton) in 1975/6 (25 per cent).

The main reasons for the low fulfilment at Lukenge are the instability of its labour force, poor village leadership and disruption of village plans by Mtibwa Estate. The Estate, far from achieving the target set by the Morogoro authorities in 1972 of getting, by 1977, 50 per cent of its sugar from surrounding *ujamaa* villages, was still, in 1976/7, taking only 12 per cent from any kind of outgrower, and less than 0.5 per cent from *ujamaa* villages — most of it from Kidudwe.

The post-operation period (1973-7) saw a marked improvement in labour productivity for Kidudwe but stagnation for Lukenge, at least if measured (Table III.15) in terms of acres cultivated per worker. (Kidudwe's 4.5 and Lukenge's 1.8 need to be set against the Morogoro Regional Agricultural Officer's estimate of an average 2 to 3 acres for the region.) This difference is also reflected in the figures for agri-

Table III.15: Plan Fulfilment at Kidudwe and Lukenge: Comparison of Individual and Communal Production, Food and Cash Crops, 1973/4 and 1975/6

Village	Communal				Individual				Total area cultivated per working person (acres)
	Cash crops		Food crops		Cash crops		Food crops		
	Planned (acres)	% Plan fulfilment	Planned (acres)	% Plan fulfilment	Planned (acres)	% Plan fulfilment	Planned (acres)	% Plan fulfilment	
1973/4									
Kidudwe	150	70	35	100	–	–	84	100	2.7
Lukenge	86	42	25	100	–	–	127	100	4.5
1975/6									
Kidudwe	152	59	–	–	–	–	977	86	1.0
Lukenge	–	–	–	–	412*	25%	300	100	1.8

*Cotton, not sugarcane.
Individual production plans are set in consultation with district officials.
Source: Kidudwe and Lukenge Village Offices.

cultural incomes set out in Table III.16 (for four other neighbouring villages, too, for purposes of comparison). The figures for total income, of course, would present a different picture, because of the wage income from the Estate in Lukenge, almost totally absent in Kidudwe.

Table III.16: Agricultural Earnings at Kidudwe and Lukenge, 1976/7: Comparison with Four Other Villages in Morogoro (Figures in Tanzanian Shillings)

Village	House-holds	Labour force	Value of produce sold	Av. income household	Av. income per worker
Kidudwe	90	156	72,240	800	463
Vigolegole	450	560	182,877	385	325
Bakira Chini	270	685	102,420	380	150
Kitungwa	506	1023	107,100	210	105
Matale	n.a.	600	54,452	n.a.	90
Lukenge*	142	272	20,337	145	75
Average				333	164

*The figures for Lukenge for 1973/4 were as follows: value of produce sold = Shs 83,939; average income per family = Shs 840; average income per worker = Shs 442.
Source: Morogoro District Office (derived from the buying agency, the National Milling Corporation) and village records.

Even in total income, however, Lukenge appears the poorer if household possessions be taken as a guide. There are 17 'modern' houses (with corrugated iron roofing) at Lukenge, as compared to Kidudwe's 26. Only about 22 per cent of the households possess radio sets, compared with about 45 per cent at Kidudwe. Less than 20 per cent of the villagers at Lukenge had a 'good' pair of leather shoes, compared to Kidudwe's 43 per cent, etc. Interviews also revealed that there was more 'longing' for these modern facilities at Kidudwe than at Lukenge except for bicycles and radios which every household wanted to have.

The better performance at Kidudwe has been accompanied by the emergence of elements of social differentiation. For example, the villager with the highest acreage in 1976/7 at Kidudwe had 15 acres of maize, 10 acres of rice and 5 acres of millet (totalling 30 acres); the lowest had a total of 3 acres, not too far from the village average of 4.5. At Lukenge, the highest had 5 acres and the lowest half an acre. There were also a few who cultivated no land at all, living at the village but earning their income from the Estate employment.[1]

Further, some Kidudwe villagers (five, including the chairman) have been able to take advantage of the tractor rental facilities available at

Mgongola rice rields, about five miles away. A number of important people from Morogoro and Dar es Salaam have established large rice farms in Mgongola area. The Kidudwe village chairman has about 60 acres in this area, but he was able to cultivate only ten acres in 1976/7 due to his leadership responsibilities which leave him little time.[2] There is little doubt that the trend towards 'kulakism' will continue at Kidudwe if the *ujamaa* mode of production slackens. In contrast, there is very little differentiation at Lukenge, and by 1977 there was only one 'progressive' farmer who had ventured to Mgongola, even though the *ujamaa* mode of production has virtually disappeared. The trend at Lukenge is towards 'proletarianization', and this is encouraged by Mtibwa Estate.

In sharing out communal proceeds, Kidudwe has continued to use the socialist principle of 'to each according to performance' based on the number of days one has worked on the communal farm or at other activities. Questioned as to why they did not use the complementary principle of 'to each according to needs', the village leaders argued that this would discourage the industrious members and lower the earning capacity of all.

The methods of calculating performance varied. The ten-household cell was for many purposes the unit to which tasks were allocated, and the cell leader provided an accounting to the village secretary. Performance might be measured in actual full days of attendance at work, or alternatively by a piece-work system — the system preferred at Kidudwe. A fixed task — to weed, say, so many acres of sugar — might be allocated to a cell (and thence to individuals) as so many days' work, but they could be left with a certain flexibility in deciding which particular days to work within the acceptable period. Pressure to take part in communal work was not insistent and individualists could spend more time on their private holdings than on the communal fields if they wished. Payment was by an immediate shareout when a crop was sold.

Records were similarly kept for nation-building activities, but in this case to secure compliance rather than to calculate remuneration. The system seems to have worked quite smoothly at Kidudwe with little dispute or pressure on record-keepers, whereas after 1976 at Lukenge it had broken down.

Villagers' Evaluation of the Programme

The effectiveness of a development programme cannot be evaluated

from the official goals alone; for ultimately it is the people who
'develop' and their understanding of the programme and satisfaction
with it are important for overall evaluation. We used a five-point
questionnaire to get some idea of the people's side of the equation. The
following questions were administered to a total of 100 villagers, 50
from each village.

1. What is the meaning of *ujamaa*?
2. In what ways have you benefited by living in this village?
3. What factors would you say have been responsible for the improvements in this village since you joined it?
4. What else do you think ought to be done to further improve the performance of this village?
5. What factors would you say have constrained the development of this village?

For each of these questions there was a 'probe' requiring the respondent to single out the major element or factor in his answer. These
major elements or factors were then recorded and analysed.

Villagers' Understanding of Ujamaa

The answers to the first question (Table III.17) reveal a clearer understanding at Kidudwe than at Lukenge of the official definition of
ujamaa in terms of the four elements: absence of exploitation, joint
ownership of the means of production, working together and sharing
joint production and a high level of self-reliance. The elements more
frequently chosen as the main characteristic by Lukenge villagers,
namely mutual help (28 per cent), living together and working together
(24 per cent) are close to the traditional, and in many areas still surviving, practice of *ujima* based on the principle of village co-operation,
reciprocity and mutual help.[3] The difference doubtless reflects the
fact that the norms of *ujamaa* are reinforced by praxis at Kidudwe
whereas they are not at Lukenge. This difference is also reflected in the
answers to the other questions.

Villagers' Perception of Programme Benefits

With samples of this size it is hard to draw conclusions concerning the
differences between the villages in the pattern of answers to the question asking in what way they had benefited from living in the village
(Table III.18). In both villages more were likely to single out material
benefits, security, etc., than 'becoming self-reliant', but in the context

Table III.17: Answers to the Question 'What is the Meaning of *Ujamaa?*' by Kidudwe and Lukenge Villagers

Answers/Villages	Kidudwe		Lukenge	
	No. of responses	%	No. of responses	%
1. Absence of exploitation	17	34	11	22
2. Mutual help	7	14	14	28
3. Joint ownership of the means of production	9	18	6	12
4. Living together and working together	4	8	12	24
5. Working together and sharing joint production	8	16	3	6
6. Self-reliance	4	8	2	4
7. Other	1	2	2	4
Total	50	100	50	100

Table III.18: Answers to the Question 'In What Ways have you Benefited by Living in this *Village?*'

Answers/Villages	Kidudwe		Lukenge	
	No. of responses	%	No. of responses	%
1. More income to family individual	10	20	7	14
2. More social services	11	22	12	24
3. More security	12	24	11	22
4. More government assistance	4	8	10	20
5. More self-reliant	4	8	4	8
6. A better life generally	8	16	3	6
7. Other	1	2	3	6
Total	50	100	50	100

of a question about 'benefits' that is perhaps not surprising.

Factors Associated With Village Improvement

From the long-term development perspective, the gains that the villagers get from government assistance are important only if the villagers are willing to use them as spring-boards or pillars for self-improvement. This intention is central to Tanzania's goal of self-reliance. Tables III.19 and III.20 tell us something about how well that intention has been realized.

There is a striking correspondence between the answers recorded in Table III.19 and the actual practice at the two villages. As expected, the efforts of the villagers themselves received more credit at Kidudwe (56 per cent) than at Lukenge (30 per cent). Similarly, the leadership at Kidudwe received more credit (20 per cent) than the permanently ailing one at Lukenge (8 per cent). On the other hand, Lukenge respondents gave more credit to government assistance (30 per cent) than those of Kidudwe (16 per cent), and more credit to the efforts of the local party organization (18 per cent) as against a mere 2 per cent of Kidudwe respondents. (Since the party and government leadership is almost completely fused at the sub-district level, 'government assistance' and 'party efforts' may have seemed synonymous to most villagers.)

On the other hand, this greater experience of successful self-reliance at Kidudwe is not (Table III.20) reflected in attitudes and intentions. If anything, more people at Kidudwe look to party and government help, and significantly more people at Lukenge speak of the need for the people's efforts (36 per cent and 10 per cent).

The equally low importance attached to '*ujamaa* life' in both villages in response to both questions (in spite of the fact that Kidudwe has retained important features of the *ujamaa* mode of production, especially in the production of cash crops, livestock and crafts) is probably due to the villagers conceiving of *ujamaa* not as a mode of production involving collective use of land, but more broadly for the whole complex of government assistance, party mobilizational effort, efforts of the villagers and their leadership, etc. — a common use of the term by many local leaders.

In view of the (understandable) reluctance of Lukenge respondents to give credit to their village leaders (Table III.19) it is perhaps surprising that when discussing the future they did not see leadership as an important factor that needed improvement. Only 10 per cent of the respondents stated the need to improve the quality of village leadership, as against Kidudwe's 20 per cent. This may well be because the village has never had good leadership since its inception. Election of leaders has been based on tribal rivalries rather than on development considerations. There has also been a tendency to choose leaders who will 'let the people alone', especially those who are not opposed to employment in the Sugar Estate. The election of the current chairman was partly based on this consideration. Lukenge's 'anti-strong-leadership' posture is also seen in the low emphasis placed on the need for improved party effort.

Table III.19: Answers to the Question 'What Factors Would You Say Have Been Responsible for the Improvements in This Village Since You Joined It?'

Answers/Villages	Kidudwe		Lukenge	
	No. of responses	%	No. of responses	%
1. Efforts of villagers	28	56	15	30
2. Good village leadership	10	20	4	8
3. Government assistance	8	16	15	30
4. Party effort	1	2	9	18
5. *Ujamaa* life	3	6	3	6
6. Other	–	–	4	8
Total	50	100	50	100

Table III.20: Answers to the Question 'What Else Do You Think Ought To Be Done to Further Improve the Performance of This Village?'

Answers/Villages	Kidudwe		Lukenge	
	No. of responses	%	No. of responses	%
1. More efforts of villagers	5	10	18	36
2. Improved village leadership	10	20	5	10
3. Further party efforts	9	18	4	8
4. Further govt. assistance	24	48	22	44
5. Strengthen *ujamaa*	1	2	1	2
6. Other	1	2	–	–
Total	50	100	50	100

With regard to the main factors constraining village development the two villages had similar views (Table III.21) though a dissatisfaction with the ward leaders seemed more strongly in evidence at Kidudwe, and complaints about internal co-operation at Lukenge.

Comments on Villagers' Evaluation

Generally speaking, the evaluation of the village development programme by the villagers was positive in both cases. The second question about the ways in which life had got better did offer the opportunity to complain, but nobody took it. Even the new entrants at Lukenge did

Table III.21: Answers to the Question 'What Factors Would You Say Have Constrained the Development of This Village?'

Answers/Villages	Kidudwe No. of responses	%	Lukenge No. of responses	%
1. Laziness of villagers	2	4	4	8
2. Lack of funds	15	30	16	32
3. Lack of co-operation at village	3	6	10	20
4. Bad village leadership	3	6	4	8
5. Lack of co-operation by ward/district leadership	12	24	5	10
6. Droughts and vermin	13	26	10	20
7. Too many projects	2	4	1	2
Total	50	100	50	100

not refer to the coercive style used in the operation period as opposed to the persuasive mobilizational style used during the *ujamaa* phase (1969-73), though how far this was because they identified the researchers with officialdom must remain problematic.

Another positive feature of the villagers' evaluation is that most of them, especially at Kidudwe, were able to diagnose their real problems and to suggest practical solutions. Lukenge was less successful in this, especially on the question of village leadership. The tendency at Lukenge was to 'externalize' the problems, attributing them either to natural catastrophes (e.g. droughts, vermin, etc.) or failure by the government or Mtibwa Estate to fulfil its promises or contractual obligations. Kidudwe has been more successful in examining its internal potential capabilities. We asked an additional question, 'What other development plans would you propose for this village?' About 75 per cent of Kidukwe's respondents had concrete suggestions, as against Lukenge's 18 per cent.

Most contrary to the declared intentions of government policy is the tendency towards greater reliance on government financial assistance. The need for government assistance (grants), subsidies or loans, to establish large village projects or to provide the basic social services is quite understandable. But in both villages there are many small and medium projects which could be established by villagers' own savings. It was striking that in talking about village plans and projects most respondents discussed government-sponsored projects with little reference to village-sponsored projects. The question of village savings was not tied to village plans. This orientation is partly a reflection of how development plans are conceived nationally. In the effort to make local plans part of a national 'comprehensive' plan, the tendency has been to emphasize sectoral projects financed and supervised by the government. This vertical orientation has overshadowed the horizontal possibilities available at the local level.

Another striking feature of the villagers' evaluation is that the local party organization was given less credit as an agent of change than is often expected. This is not entirely surprising considering the quality of the party leadership in Turiani Division. As we pointed out earlier (Chapter 6), the leaders are traditionally-minded, having been traditional leaders before independence; they are generally old, little educated and have not been exposed to intensive ideological training in the party ideological colleges.

Changes in the Marketing of Produce

In May 1976 the existing co-operative system was abolished and a new marketing system based on the villages was established. In the original conception of *ujamaa* villages it was expected that the co-operatives would eventually disappear after the villages had become viable collective economic units. However, given the slow rate of village development, it soon became clear to the national leaders that full village growth was a distant hope. Nevertheless there was 'impatience' within the leadership, resulting partly from the ineffectiveness and insolvency of most co-operative societies and unions and partly from the need to accelerate the approach of the village to maturity. There was also a need to improve the storage and transportation system which was intimated to be responsible for a sizeable part of the 30 to 35 per cent loss of potential grain production (along with plant disease and harvesting delays).

Organization of the New Marketing System

The new marketing system sought to give the villages more responsibilities and more benefits by removing the 'middle man' (co-operative societies and unions). The villages would act as marketing agents, selling the crop collected from farmers directly to the marketing authorities, the only legal buyers of agricultural produce in the commercial market. At the same time, the villages would benefit from levies paid to them, rather than to the former societies and unions. In Morogoro Region the National Milling Corporation (NMC) was the marketing authority for Morogoro and Kilombero Districts, and the Tanzania Cotton Authority (TCS) operated in Kilosa and Ulanga Districts as the marketing authority. As marketing agents, the villages would provide a link between the farmers and the marketing authorities.[4]

There were many problems in operating the new marketing system. Most villages were not ready to take over these activities, being at a formative stage, and few had trained manpower, safes, scales and go-downs. There was little time available to make arrangements for the 1976/7 harvest, and the marketing authorities could not provide all villages with finance for the crop purchases due to lack of transport facilities. A compromise solution had to be found through differential allocation of powers and functions to various villages (depending on their internal capabilities) and the crop authorities.

Power and responsibilities were allocated between different villages in the manner shown in Figure III.4. Villages which had both a go-down and a safe were made buying centre while villages with proper or provisional go-downs were made buying posts. Villages which could not provide storage facilities at all had either to deliver the crops to the nearest buying centre or post, or else the crop authority would make arrangements for immediate collection of the crop. Thus in Morogoro district 26 of the 168 registered villages were made buying centres, and another 89 buying posts or collection points.

We were unable to assess the actual size of the black-market channels shown on the left of Figure III.4 but there was evidence that some villagers managed to sell their crops outside the official market structure where they got better prices. This, therefore, calls for caution in interpreting the production figures given by the marketing authorities or Marketing Development Bureaus.

Prices to Farmers and Incentives

The new marketing system was expected to benefit the villagers in five ways. First, with the abolition of the middlemen, prices paid to the farmers would go up, serving as an incentive for expansion. Moreover, the government and the crop authorities would take other measures to stabilize the prices to avoid wide fluctuations from year to year which act as a disincentive for expansion. Second, the villages (as buying posts

Figure III.4: Marketing Functions Performed by Different Components in the New Marketing System in Morogoro Region, 1976/7

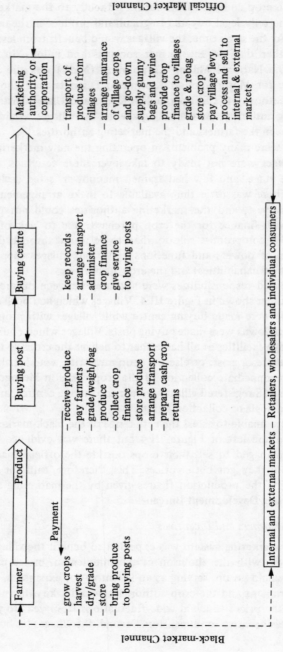

Source: Adopted with modifications from Mwihama *et al.*, 'A study in village marketing in Morogoro', p. 7.

and centres) would retain a crop levy for their own development. Third, credit and farm inputs would flow more smoothly to the villages, either directly from the government and banks or through the responsible crop authorities. Fourth, the villages would acquire greater internal capability by training the necessary accounting personnel and in improving storage facilities. Fifth, it was hoped that the villages would be in a better position to allocate resources more equitably among their members since they would have a growing fund from the crop levy. It should be borne in mind that these are long-term expectations; they have not yet been fully achieved.

Officially, the producing peasant has to sell his crops to the village organization which acts as a middleman for the designated crop authority. He is paid by the village according to fixed national prices which are announced well before the marketing season (often, before the cultivating season). It would seem that the extent of the black market has depended on the prices which have steadily risen, being on average 34 per cent higher than 1974/5 in 1976/7 and 84 per cent higher in 1977/8 (a crude average of the shillings per kilogram posted price for 13 major cash crops). Hence, price fluctuations in the world market are hardly felt by the farmers directly. Similarly, prices in the internal consumer market have also been stabilized to a large extent in the past decade.

The effects of price stabilization and subsidy policies on production are difficult to determine with any precision, because there are so many other factors affecting production such as the hazards of the weather, the villagization programme and the heavy 'life-or-death-farming' campaigns of the past three years (1975/6-1977/8) following the worldwide inflation and famine. But there is little doubt that price policies have had positive effects on peasant response to these campaigns.

Marketing Routines at Kidudwe and Lukenge

The new marketing system has produced different effects on our two case study villages, with Kidudwe benefiting more. Five villages in Turiani — Kidudwe Ujamaa, Kidudwe II, Lukenge, Kunke and Lusange — have been grouped in a marketing association or co-operative. In this network, Kidudwe *ujamaa* village became the sole buying centre since it had more facilities and better qualified manpower than any of the other villages. Lukenge and Lusanga villages, which had minimal facilities, became buying posts; and Kidudwe II and Kunke development villages, which had no storage facilities, became collection points or posts.

Farmers from the other villages brought their produce to Kidudwe *ujamaa* village which had to introduce a rotating system of buying days to avoid mixing of crops, and facilitate the purchasing routines. Separate records for the villages were kept, and the levy income was distributed according to the produce received from the villages.

Kidudwe finds the work of servicing the other villages enormous and challenging, but it has so far proved equal to the task, and the other villages in its marketing network said they were satisfied with the new marketing arrangement. Six advantages of the new marketing system were emphasized. First, the services rendered by the crop authority were considered superior to those rendered by the defunct societies and unions, and the levy of two cents per kilogram which it made for those services was less than the old co-operative societies took. Second, there was improvement in the distribution of crop finance, and gunny bags were supplied free of charge. Third, crop transport was considered smoother, more regular and reliable. Fourth, as the number of crop collection points had increased, there were shorter walking distances for the farmers to sell their crops. Fifth, with independent buying posts and centres, the villages considered themselves to be moving rapidly towards the goal of self-reliance, with their own storage facilities, secretaries, accounting personnel and related marketing capabilities. Finally, the villages thought they were now in a better position to provide their members with the necessary production and marketing services. In particular, they were more flexible with regard to opening hours of buying posts. Under the old system, in contrast, the societies were more strict in observing the official opening time. On some occasions they even refused to purchase crops from late farmers, resulting in long queues and congestion on marketing days.

The above advantages cannot, at present, be generalized for all the villages in rural Tanzania. The five villages in question are lucky in that they are not 'remote'; they are readily accessible and well served by Kidudwe buying centre. In many other areas the crop authority was faced with acute transport and storage problems. The inflation and famine of 1973/4 to 1975/6 had emphasized the need for better transport but also made it difficult to import a large number of vehicles since so much foreign exchange had to be spent on the importation of grains during that period. Furthermore, construction of storage facilities has lagged behind the demand despite the commendable effort that went into it in the past five years.

The new marketing system has other problems. First, there is the question of low marketing and accounting capabilities at the village level to which we have already referred. Second, as it has been operating during the past two years, the system has been heavily subsidized by the marketing authorities, especially in the remote areas where transportation costs are astronomically high. The levies charged to the farmer would have to be much higher to cover the economic costs of transportation, storage and distribution – higher even than the costs under the old system because of the additional conveniences such as the multiplication of buying centres. A way of minimizing these costs will have to be found. One possibility is to reorganize village marketing on a wider basis by linking villages within one ward in a marketing network with one fully equipped buying centre – the arrangement adopted in the five villages under discussion. This would reduce the replication of huge go-downs, safes, weighing scales, etc., at each village which, at any rate, most villages cannot afford at present.

However, such reorganization is likely to be resisted by the villagers. All the villages under Kidudwe buying centre (with the exception of Kidudwe itself) had interpreted self-reliance to mean self-sufficiency in production and marketing facilities for each village and complained about the 'satellite' relationship between them and Kidudwe. Indeed, the advantageous position of Kidudwe relative to the others in the network may lead to a rapid improvement in its marketing intelligence, storage facilities and even better farming methods, resulting in overall economic development. It will also stimulate manpower development to be able to meet the challenge of the marketing task for the network. Further, its more frequent direct contacts with the crop authority may also entail other benefits and 'favours'. However, it is possible to build into the network the norms of fair distribution of benefits to minimize the fears of 'satellization' of 'peripheralization' of the other partners. Moreover, rapid development in one of the partners may have a useful 'demonstration effect'.

Other Changes: Political and Sociocultural

Economic change outside the scope of the state-sponsored development programme has been very limited in scope: a charcoal project at Lukenge which involves a very few families and is not conspicuously successful; the growth of wage employment – which depends on the Estate – and the development by a few entrepreneurial individuals of rice farming – which also depended on a state initiative.

As for the other changes in the political and cultural sphere, it is hardly possible to ask whether they were part of the development programme or independent. As an attack on the 'three enemies' — poverty, hunger and ignorance — rural development is expected to be comprehensive. Political and cultural change is both an intended separate objective, and an implied concomitant, of economic change.

There is little doubt that the post-Arusha period has seen many changes in political attitudes amongst the workers and the peasantry. These changes have resulted from policy and demographic factors. At the policy level, the norms of 'popular participation' have been emphasized in various party documents and speeches of the central leadership. The 1971 party statement, known as *Mwongozo*, in particular sought to remove or reduce the 'fear' of authority that was instilled under the colonial administration. Thus clause 15 of the *Mwongozo* asserts boldly that any act which increases the power of the people to determine their own affairs is an act of development, even if the act does not provide more bread or better health. Clause 28 denounces the arrogance of the leadership in very strong terms and assures the people that they will not be penalized for 'bargaining' with their leaders or for demanding an account of their actions.

Although these norms may not greatly have altered official behaviour, there is some evidence of greater self-confidence in the villages and more courage to confront or bargain with the authorities than in the sixties. This courage has been reinforced by the radio — which has often reported cases of leaders who have been expelled for bad leadership or for mistreating the people. Indeed, the courage demonstrated by Kidudwe villagers in bargaining with the authorities (from the ward to the national level) over compensation for their property left at Kabuku shows a very high level of confidence. Examination of the correspondence over the issue shows that the villagers are not only 'aware' of their rights but also have the diplomacy necessary in playing a 'political game'. They have successfully struggled with the conservative ward leadership and in many occasions by-passed it with virtual impunity to seek audience with higher authorities.

There has also been a marked change in the overall 'political participation' of the rural population over the last decade. This change is particularly evident in the rising electoral participation. At the village level, Lukenge, among many other villages in Morogoro, has courageously used its democratic rights (which were reinforced by the *Mwongozo*) to throw out 'bad' leaders. At the national level, electoral registration and turn-out at the ballot has grown steadily from 1965. In the first elections under the one-party system in 1965, some three million people registered as voters and 45 per cent voted as compared with some six million of whom 80 per cent voted in the 1975 elections. The growth is large even after taking account of the population growth at the annual rate of 2.7 per cent and the lowering of the voting age from 21 to 18 years.

The changes in electoral participation are partly a result of the growing mobilizational capacity of the party machinery and partly a result of the concentration of people in village communities, which in turn has also made the task of political mobilization easier than when the villages were a mere conglomeration of isolated homesteads.

There is also some evidence that the *ujamaa* programme has led to significant changes in the sociocultural field. The radio has also played a revolutionizing role. There have been many programmes geared to dispelling the widespread belief in superstition in the villages, with some success. For example, the fear of witchcraft which constrained the rate of collectivization in the sixties and early seventies in Pangani, Handeni and Rufiji areas has been kept under control, although it has not been eradicated. When the massive collectivization drive started in 1974, the local leaders in Sumbawanga proposed to put all those who were named as suspected 'witches' in a separate village or a separate area within the village, but two years later those who had been called witches and isolated in 1974 were mixing freely with the rest of the community. Of course an intense educational campaign had been mounted by the local party organization.

The fear of witchcraft has also been a big problem at Lukenge. For example, until 1976, there was talk of a man-crocodile living in a nearby river. This monster, believed to be a creature of the village witches, had captured and killed several village children, according to village stories. The myth was similar to that of the 'man-lion' of Singida, Kendoa, Iramba and Shinyanga. The monster was believed to be under the full control of its master – the witch – who would instruct it to attack or cause damage to those who were in competition with him or whom he hated for some reason. It is not difficult to see how such a belief could lower village productivity; for the villagers fear to compete with the (unknown) master who controls the terrible monster. There have been some campaigns to dispel such beliefs and fears, but these have been half-hearted, and their results have not been significant. As we have pointed out, the ward and divisional leadership is a little too conservative. No such problems were reported at Kidudwe.

These changes are largely due to the heavy political and educational campaigns. As we have already pointed out (Chapter 6), the campaigns have led to (a) higher school attendance, (b) higher adult literacy, (c) compliance with health regulations (e.g. the latrine) and (d) higher self-confidence in the villages. We have further shown that Kidudwe is ahead of Lukenge on each of these scores. It is the task of Chapter 8 to explain this differential impact.

Notes

1. These were sent to court in mid-1977 for offending against the by-law that every household should cultivate two acres of food crops, but their cases had not been decided at the time we left the field.

2. He was even considering giving up leadership of the village so as to concentrate on his farm at the village and Mgongola.

3. For a distinction between *ujamaa* and *ujima*, see S.S. Mushi, 'Ujamaa: modernization by traditionalization', *TAAMULI* (1972).

4. Much of this and the following information on the new system in Morogoro as a whole has been covered in G.H.E.Mwihama, G.P. Shuma, M. Kuhu and K.M. Storm Roxman, 'A study of village marketing in Morogoro', copy of which is to be found in Kilosa District file no. UCK/69/II, folio 258. We have drawn liberally from this report although the specific features for Kidudwe and Lukenge are based on our own research.

8 EXPLANATION OF DIFFERENTIAL IMPACT

Why did the campaign have different outcomes at Kidudwe and Lukenge? The important explanatory variables have already been mentioned in passing in Chapters 5, 6 and 7. The task of this chapter, therefore, is to attempt a more systematic evaluation of these variables.

Such an attempt, it should be emphasized, faces serious methodological problems. 'Participant observation' in the villages enabled us to 'measure' (admittedly, rather crudely) the magnitude of the change over time and even to suggest the key variables involved, but it could not rank the variables themselves according to their varying impact. We can say that differences in educational attainment were important, for example, but we can not determine the relative importance of this variable *vis-à-vis* the others. Hence the order in which the variables are discussed below — characteristics of the village, of the campaign, and of policy — should be considered 'logical' (in a historical and implementational sense or sequence); and not an attempt to 'rank' the variables.

Background and Characteristics of the Villages

One way of distinguishing villages in Tanzania is by the manner of their creation, i.e. how they constituted themselves as 'village communities' in the context of the *Ujamaa Vijijini* policy. These distinctions yield three types of village. First, there are those which entailed no movement at all, '*ujamaa*' or 'development' villages being carved out of pre-existing populations in given geographical areas. These may be called traditional villages in that they do not have recent entrants. Second, there are those which include 'original' populations and new entrants in varying proportions. These may be called 'hybrid villages'. Third, there are those which have been established in entirely new or unsettled areas, with the entrants coming from all sorts of backgrounds. These may be called 'pioneer' villages.

In these terms, both Kidudwe and Lukenge are hybrid villages, so we must look for difference further down, and in, for example, the proportions of original members. In terms of proportions, both villages had a reasonable balance between 'native' and 'alien' populations. But whereas Kidudwe was able to control the rate of both emigration and

223

immigration, Lukenge was not. Apart from the original 17 families who have fully settled at Lukenge, the village has been losing and gaining members, particularly after 1974. This lesser stability has entailed a loose organizational structure; for it has not been possible to evolve and entrench widely shared norms of behaviour or community solidarity. We have already shown that the post-operation entrants at Lukenge have strong affinity for paid employment outside the village.

The backgrounds of later immigrants differed from the 'natives' in both places, but with more 'disintegrating' effect at Lukenge. At Kidudwe, both the guests and the hosts had farming experience and very few members had served in paid employment situations in urban or rural areas. There was, therefore, a commonality of occupational interest. There were three other integrating factors. First, just as the new entrants had two dominant tribes (the Pare and the Chagga), the traditional group consisted mainly of two native tribes, Zigua and Nguu. Second, the new entrants were further united by their joint struggle with the authorities over the issue of compensation for their Kabuku property. Third, the new entrants had a 'modernizing' influence on the traditional members since they were better educated and came from relatively more developed areas — Pare and Moshi. All these factors worked in favour of community solidarity and relatively rapid development.

At Lukenge, on the other hand, most of the new entrants were urban-oriented with little farming background. The original 17 families, who might have been expected to act as a stabilizing force, were preoccupied with tribal rivalries, and with mutual suspicion due to the widespread superstition to which we have already referred, and were also soon outnumbered by the new entrants. Moreover, the new entrants came from various backgrounds and joined the village as individuals rather than as a group, as was the case at Kidudwe. Again, neither group had well-educated members. Thus it is not entirely surprising that the community solidarity that emerged under the *ujamaa* phase (1969-73) was soon to disintegrate.

The geographical and land-ownership variables cannot explain the differences in performance in the two villages. As we have pointed out, each village had adequate land, and in both cases the Estate has claimed part of their cleared land. Moreover, the villages are sufficiently close together to make climatic and soil variations inconsequential. The background of the people and their organization, rather than land and climate, was the important influence on performance.

The Modalities of the Campaign

Our earlier discussion of the various agents involved in the campaign for *ujamaa* development left out an important element, namely the extent to which these efforts were co-ordinated. The decentralization reform of 1972 was supposed to promote 'integrated development' precisely by stimulating co-ordination at the local level. We will focus here on the functioning of three agents, namely the local party organization, Mtibwa Sugar Estate and the district administration.

The campaign for *ujamaa* development required proper co-ordination and utilization of three types of information, namely ideological information, technical information and operational information. Ideological information was primarily the task of the party which was supposed to raise the political consciousness of the villagers so as to make them accept the *ujamaa* mode of production and way of life. It would also strengthen the village leadership by closely supervising elections to ensure that those nominated had proper leadership qualities. The party would also mount a campaign to make the villages comply with the advice of the ward and district experts.

We have already pointed out that the local party organization was very inactive as far as campaign for 'local' development at the village level were concerned, though it was more active in 'national' campaigns and operations such as the health and agricultural improvement campaigns.

Technical information, and also essential supplies, were to be provided by the three field officers at the divisional level (agriculture, veterinary and *ujamaa*/co-operatives) and other experts (e.g. small industries and village crafts) at the district level. Their task was done admirably between 1970 and 1974, but thereafter there was little follow-up, especially at Lukenge. The technical personnel were more concerned with creation of new projects — what Professor Goran Hyden has termed *Hona ya Miradi Mipya* ('the fever of new projects'). Moreover, their co-ordination of the local party was poor. With regard to planning, for example, the 'rational' estimates of the experts were sometimes thrown overboard by the local leaders who instructed the villagers to expand their fields beyond the capacity of available village labour. This partly explains the great discrepancy between the planned acreage and the acreage actually harvested. As we have shown, the discrepency was particularly large at Lukenge. There is little doubt that such contradictory messages weakened the campaigns.

Operational information refers first to the proper co-ordination of local efforts and those of outside bodies — a feature notably lacking in the Mtibwa Estate's relations with Lukenge — and secondly, to proper sequential co-ordination of programmes. One major source of weakness was that the many 'national' campaigns and operations were not really incorporated into the village plans. For example, between 1973 and 1975, there were cases where the villagers faced a dilemma as to whether to attend literacy classes or to attend to their farms; for the central party leadership had arbitrarily ruled (1973) that full literacy must be achieved by 1975. The campaigns would have been more effective if they had been programmed sequentially, to a proper timetable, one after another. They were not weakened just by the weaknesses of the local leadership or so-called 'peasant conservatism'.

The Ambivalence of Government Policy

The above discussion suggests two things. First, there is a silent conflict between the goals of the villagers and the intentions of the leadership. This conflict is probably more at the operational level than at the ideological level. It is 'silent' because it is not expressed in loud protests but quiet non-compliance with arbitrary targets. For example, the villagers would not question the exaggerated acreage in so far as these were cultivated by government tractors; but they would then only plant, weed and harvest what they could. Further, during the *ujamaa* phase, the villagers complied with the directive to establish a large communal farm; but in practice paid more attention to their private *shambas*, as available statistics have already shown.

Second, the operational problems we have referred to were partly a result of the ambivalence and apparent contradiction in government policy over time. After the launching of the massive collectivization drive in 1974, the objectives of rural development appear to have changed in significant ways. At the level of ideology and political rhetoric, the various rural development programmes are still referred to as '*ujamaa*', but in practice communal farming which was central to the notion of *ujamaa* in the earlier phase has virtually been ignored. Thus there is a clear contradiction between theory (policy) and practice. The discrepancy could be removed by either revising the policy to fit the practice or revising the practice to fit the policy, as was attempted between 1969 and 1973. But the government and central leadership of the party have remained ambivalent on this.

The contradiction is particularly visible in three areas. First, there has been more emphasis on bloc farming than on communal farming, even though such *ujamaa* villages as Kidudwe have continued to receive praise and token rewards from the district leadership. Mtibwa Estate has thus managed to stop Lukenge's communal farming and draw labourers from it with virtual impunity. The Sungaji ward secretary showed his ambivalence when, on the one hand, he excused this prole-tarianization of the Lukenge villagers on the grounds that 'The Estate is in great need of labourers', and on the other went on to praise Kidudwe for continuing with *ujamaa* activities and for expanding its sugarcane fields. The local leadership, like the national, has been facing a dilemma between emphasis on *ujamaa* and emphasis on productivity. Unfortunately, they seem to see these two as necessarily conflicting or mutual exclusive. This assumption comes from the fact that during the *ujamaa* phase proper there was little effort to make the villages pro-ductive. There is little disposition to try to make the two objectives compatible if it takes time, little appreciation of the fact that no miracles could make the villages productive overnight.

Second, this impatience, resulting mainly from the bitter experiences of the inflationary period (1973-7), has opened the door for active participation by private individuals. In mid-1977, the new Prime Minister, Mr Edward Sokoine, declared openly that from then on pro-gressive farmers would be eligible for loans and government encourage-ment. The same theme was emphasized in various extemporaneous speeches by Mwalimu Nyerere, and the banks were instructed to process applications by private farmers as expeditiously as possible. This has of course had negative effects on the remaining *ujamaa* villages. They are likely to feel that they are being 'ignored' now that private individuals are being supported, and the net result may be further erosion of their *ujamaa* way of life and mode of production. Indeed, the responses of Kidudwe respondents discussed in the previous chapter indicate a trend in this direction. Lukenge, on the other hand, has taken advantage of this relaxation and ambivalence to revise its mode of pro-duction.

Third, a similar trend is also seen in the relative emphasis placed on technical assistance from the capitalist West as compared to the socialist East. Out of some 21 technical assistance teams which had assisted the regional authorities in the formulation of the Regional Integrated Development Programmes (RIDEP) by 1977, 18 were either from the West or Western-dominated multinational organizations such as the World Bank. There was participation by only one socialist country (Yugoslavia); by only one developing country (India) and by only one national institution (BRBLUB at the University of Dar es Salaam). There is also a certain irony in the fact that the post-Arusha *ujamaa* phase of Tanzania's community development was in fact a rejection of the 'transformation' model originally suggested by the World Bank; whereas by 1977 the Bank played a greater role in planning the villages and managing or consulting on various agricultural projects (such as the 13-region maize project) than any other single institution from outside. In Chapter 10 we shall comment further on this trend in the context of the three models of rural development we sketched briefly in Chapter 2.

9   COMMUNITY DEVELOPMENT AND THE NOTION OF COMMUNITY

There is little doubt that the presence of 'community solidarity' is an important factor in the success of any CD programme. But it is equally true to say that a successful CD programme promotes or reinforces community solidarity. For there is no solidarity *in vacuo*; solidarity always refers to mutual involvement in some joint activity. The activity may relate to the need for group security or survival, as would be the case in a harsh traditional environment; it may relate to production of material goods and services or even to the attainment of certain normative or social goals such as the need for affiliation, dignity, social recognition, etc.

Thus, in the context of Tanzania's rural development programme, we need to ask two questions. First, the extent to which community solidarity existed when the programme was introduced. Second, whether the level of success achieved during the period under review could sustain community solidarity in the villages. These will be discussed in the context of the normative and material goals of the *ujamaa* programme. For it is a combination of these that was expected to enhance community solidarity and the success of the programme as a whole.

The Normative Goals of Ujamaa

Tanzania's concept of *ujamaa* does not claim to be a rigorous sociological theory of socialist development in the sense that the Marxist 'scientific socialism' does. It is rather a statement of certain ideals which President Nyerere associates with a future Tanzanian society. The future society itself is supposed to be an outgrowth of the traditional communities. The new society would benefit from the communal solidarity and spirit of co-operation attributed to the traditional systems — from 'the social expectations of sharing what you have with your kinsfolk'[1] as President Nyerere called it, which derived from the traditional society where everyone was a worker, 'there was no living off the sweat of others', and little inequality of property. 'These things have nothing to do with Marx . . . Yet they provide a basis on which modern socialism can be built.' Africa's own contribution 'to the march of mankind', not just a borrowed ideology.

This conception raises a number of questions and poses problems at the level of programme execution. First, the conception overidealizes the traditional Tanzanian communities, for some of them — albeit a few — were quite differentiated. Second, the attributes themselves were a direct result of low production and insecurity. For example, lack of dependable storage facilities was the main reason for sharing perishable goods. The low technical level called for collective action in undertaking such activities as building houses, harvesting, hunting, etc. It was essentially 'co-operation for survival'. Third, it is questionable whether the norms of co-operation survived the colonial, capitalist interlude to the extent claimed, with the possible exception of the most remote villages. Yet *ujamaa* hangs on this assumption, as Mwalimu further elaborates:

> Certainly Tanzania was part of the Western capitalist world while it was under colonial domination, but it was very much on the fringe. Certainly our independent nation inherited a few capitalist institutions, and some of our people adopted capitalist and individualistic ideas as a result of their education or their envy of the colonial representatives whom they encountered. But the masses of the people did not become capitalist, and are not filled with capitalist ideas. By far the largest part of our economy is not organized on capitalist lines.[2]

Ujamaa, then, started with a belief that the characteristics attributed to the traditional communities still existed. These characteristics would be the pillars on which to build modern socialism. The assumed characteristics can be summarised as follows:

1. There was a 'spirit' (or instinct) of co-operation in undertaking community tasks and in activities which required mutual help;
2. In so far as everybody worked, there was no exploitation of man by man;
3. Lack of differentiation and absence of exploitation meant that there was mutual respect and mutual trust;
4. The community as a whole owned the means of production, chiefly land; and
5. There was equitable sharing of joint production.

Having assumed that these attributes still existed to a large degree and made for a high level of community solidarity, the implementers of the *ujamaa* programme went ahead to establish *ujamaa* villages. They did not take into account the fact that, apart from the traditional villages (to which we have referred), there were other hybrid or pioneer villages which brought in people from a variety of cultures and experiences, many of them from urban settings where the traditional norms of co-operation and sharing had been eroded by mercantile, capitalist and pecuniary aspirations. In such villages, therefore, the attributes of co-operation and sharing would need to be 'created' or 'recreated' through a carefully worked out programme of action rather than simply taken for granted.

Nor did the programme have any established methods of reactivating the supposed characteristics of traditional communities where they did exist. In many villages, one can indeed still observe the traditional norms of co-operation in the form of mutual assistance in building, cultivating and harvesting. As pointed out earlier, this phenomenon is called *ujima* (as distinct from *ujamaa*) in Swahili. This could form a good starting-point. 'Mutual assistance' groups provided the basis for socialist communes in some parts of rural China. But no advantage was taken of them in Tanzania even though they had been identified by the President.

In fact, throughout the *ujamaa* phase (1969-73), the local leadership campaigned against the use of existing 'solidarity' groups, particularly those with filial or clan ties. In 1972, for example, a village in Morogoro was denied financial and moral assistance because, in the words of the Regional Commissioner, it was 'a group of brothers who have pooled their farms and resources'. Yet this was then one of the promising villages. Assistance would only be given on condition that the village admitted people from other clans, or lineages. In reality, denial of 'solidarity' groups as a starting-point contradicted the President's own conception of *ujamaa*, for the word means 'family-hood', and he deliberately chose it for its African-ness and because 'it brings to the mind of our people the idea of mutual involvement in the family as we know it'.[3]

Furthermore, he wanted a 'step-by-step' approach, assisting existing groups and co-operatives to move to a higher level of co-operation and finally pooling their farms and other resources as they saw the advantages of co-operation. The speed and mode of this development should fit the ecology, local traditions and levels of development in different areas.[4] However, their frequent transfers (especially before the decentralization reform of 1972) meant that they did not have the opportunity to study the communities from within or see through the various projects they had initiated. Indeed, there was in most cases no sociological analysis of these communities, little of the 'scientific thinking' the President had advocated when he urged 'finding out all the facts in a particular situation, regardless of whether you like them or not, or whether they fit in with preconceived ideas . . . and then working out solutions to the problems you are concerned with in the light of these facts, and the objective you are trying to achieve.'[5]

The point we want to emphasize is that in practice, as opposed to political rhetoric, the *ujamaa* programme merely 'ritualized' what President Nyerere had stated so eloquently; the norms of co-operation still found in some communities became irrelevant (indeed, they were considered 'obstructionist' by some bureaucrats and local politicians) to the process of implementation. Just as *ujamaa* failed to utilize the social principles of the traditional communities, it also failed to use (having rejected) the principles of scientific socialism.[6] It is therefore not entirely surprising that the *ujamaa* programme seems to be reverting to the liberal-incremental model, as we shall further elaborate in Chapter 10.

The Material Goals of Ujamaa

The President has on several occasions emphasized that the best way to 'sell' *ujamaa* to the peasants is to demonstrate the advantages of the *ujamaa* mode of production by making *ujamaa* villages more productive — which they would become through the 'spirit of co-operation' which *ujamaa* would bring. However, the experiences of the period 1969 to 1973 (what we have called *ujamaa* phase proper) have shown that the 'spirit of co-operation' was not as automatic as had been assumed.

Frequently, in fact, the villagers have used the rhetoric of *ujamaa* to outsmart the bureaucrats in the process of bargaining with them for material goods and services. Thus, for example, during the planning season, the villagers would bury all their internal conflicts as they discussed their plans with the officials. They would unanimously accept a large communal farm which would be cultivated by government tractors from the Regional Development Fund (RDF). Since in many villages their private *shambas* were within the village (a few people had plots outside), they would also benefit from free cultivation of their private farms. They would also get free seeds, fertilizers and insecticides. That the villagers were using the *ujamaa* farm as a way of getting government assistance for their own individual purposes became clear at the planting, weeding and harvesting stages. In virtually all the cases we studied in Morogoro there was more emphasis on the private *shambas* than on the communal farm. In a few cases, the villagers even expected the government to mobilize 'harvesting hands' — National Service men, militia or school children — to assist in the communal farm.

Another example: the villagers would take advantage of a visit by a prominent government or party dignitary to read a long *risala* (message) outlining, often in very convincing terms, the progress of the village and wonderful future plans. They would then ask the dignitary for further assistance to ensure success of the village plans. Of course there were many cases where the *risala* was genuine, but we found cases where community effort was exaggerated in order to get further assistance. In most cases the *risala* bore fruits.

There is reason to believe that the local leadership was partly responsible for the exaggerations in the *risala*. The officials, quite understandably, associated village successes with their own 'promotion'. This was true of both the political and bureaucratic leadership. Thus one finds that between 1969 and 1973 the emphasis of the local leaders was on increasing the number of nucleated villages in their area; and the reports that were sent to the higher authorities referred to all such villages as *ujamaa* even where there was nothing like a socialist mode of production. In a few cases, the reports amounted to cheating the higher authorities, as when a visiting dignitary (in Tanga) was shown a 'village' which consisted of a few temporary houses which disappeared after the visit! This was, of course, an exception rather than the rule.

For both the villagers and the local leaders, therefore, *ujamaa* seems to have been interpreted simply as a means of allocating and reallocating government resources. Little attention was paid to the objectives for which these were supposed to be the means, namely the establishment of an effective communal mode of production and increasing productivity — objectives which, if achieved, could have led to a more lasting community solidarity in the villages.

This was partly the fault of the officials who, during the early phase, offered government assistance rather lavishly, often unconditionally. There was no serious attempt (with the exception of a few cases) to make government aid conditional upon having good leadership, clearly worked out plans and evidence of commitment by the members to the projects they were proposing. Such commitment could have been measured by the level of self-help contribution that had already been made by the villagers towards the project in question.

Such an approach would not only increase village self-confidence and self-reliance, but would also create a sense of community. For a sense of community grows out of joint activities which each member has 'sweated' for. Moreover, insistence that villages produce serious plans requires the villagers to think seriously about their future as a 'community'. The same conditions should be laid down for bank loans. During the *ujamaa* phase these were too 'soft' and repayment dates too generous for the villagers to take them seriously. Hence in a number of cases the loans were not repaid (especially those given to the former co-operative societies) and the government had to write them off.

The point we are making is that material incentives were used in a one-sided fashion. Emphasis was on the input side, that is, how much the government spent in establishing development projects and provision of the basic social services in the villages. The 'output', that is, production side of the projects, received very little attention. Thus both the villager and the official tended to measure village development in terms of the level of government funds flowing in, or number of government-sponsored projects established, each year. The productivity of these projects, out of the initiative and effort of the villages themselves, was a peripheral question. The same lopsided view was reflected in the local press and in the annual reports of the regions, which offer better statistics on government funds deployed than on actual production in the villages.

The Notion of Community at Kidudwe and Lukenge

What we have said generally about the weaknesses of the normative assumptions and administration of material incentives in the villages holds also for our two case studies, but more so for Lukenge than Kidudwe. Ideological persuasion seemed to have worked during the early phase; for both villages were organized along *ujamaa* lines till 1973, and there was then a relatively strong sense of community as evidenced by the many joint undertakings at the villages.

In the post-operational period, however, when there was a reduction in the use of material incentives by the government because so many more villages had to be attended to, the *ujamaa* mode disintegrated at Lukenge though it proved relatively more self-sustaining at Kidudwe where more projects continue to be initiated and maintained by the villagers themselves. The charcoal project at Lukenge, which could have been developed into an important village industry, has remained limited in size and very few members are participating in it. Again, with the exception of the original 17 families which have permanent, modern houses, the post-operation entrants have 'temporary' traditional huts which could be demolished any time the household head wanted to move. The former communal shop was also dismantled, and the new one has not taken off. This contrasts with Kidudwe which was able to reorganize a new communal shop following the dissolution of the pre-operation one. The funds were distributed to the members in accordance with their shares and immediately the members (new and old) contributed towards the fund to establish a new shop, revealing a higher community spirit than at Lukenge. One reaches the same conclusion if one looks at other indicators of community solidarity such as:

the number of communal activities undertaken in the context of *ujamaa*;
other joint activities undertaken in the context of traditional solidarity groups', such as those we have referred to as '*ujima*';
the presence of clearly formulated future plans initiated by the villages themselves;
level of compliance with set targets and the power of the leadership to enforce sanctions.

Kidudwe scored higher than Lukenge on each of these indicators. Besides having a large communal farm, Kidudwe villagers also organized mutual help groups along the traditional *ujima* lines to facilitate work on private *shambas*. Although this was still organized largely along tribal lines (especially amongst the Pare), there was some evidence that the practice could be extended to include members from different tribal origins. We observed nothing like this at Lukenge. Again, whereas Kidudwe had sound plans for future development, Lukenge had only vague ideas about the future, and whatever plans the respondents suggested related to what the government should do. Furthermore, as we have pointed out, whereas there was 'leadership legitimacy' at Kidudwe, there was a permanent 'leadership crisis' at Lukenge, making the enforcement of sanctions against non-compliance with set targets very difficult. Thus, whereas Kidudwe leadership was competent in settling most cases, Lukenge leadership referred most of its cases to the ward leadership or to the courts of law. There cannot be community solidarity where the leadership cannot make authoritative rules (or by-laws) and expect them to be followed.

To conclude then, it seems fair to attribute the low community solidarity found in the villages to both the official and the villagers' side of the equation. On the official side, administration of the normative and material incentives was weak. On the villages' side, solidarity varied with their internal organization and a host of sociocultural factors such as the origins of the villagers, their tribal composition, their educational attainments, and the cultural compatibility of old and new residents. It would be a one-sided view to attribute the weaknesses solely to so-called 'peasant conservatism' or 'possessive individualism', as some local leaders do.

Notes

1   1. J.K. Nyerere, *Freedom and Socialism* (Oxford University Press, Dar es Salaam, 1968), p. 16.
    2. Ibid., pp. 17-18.
    3. Ibid., p. 2.
    4. J.K. Nyerere, *Socialism and Rural Development* (Government Printer, Dar es Salaam, 1967).
    5. J.K, Nyerere, *Freedom and Socialism*, p. 16.
    6. The reasons for this rejection are outlined in Nyerere, ibid., pp. 14-26.

10 LESSONS TO BE LEARNED

A Summary

Analysis of Tanzania's community development started off with an outline of three models of community development, namely the liberal-incremental, the revolutionary-change and the guided-evolutionary models. We have shown that up until independence in 1961, CD was guided by the assumptions of the liberal-incremental model as it operated in the colonial context. From 1961 to 1967, the same assumptions prevailed in practice although CD programmes were undertaken with greater vigour and from a 'nationalist' standpoint. There were some organizational changes, emphasizing the role of co-operatives and self-help groups. At the ideological level, the central leadership sought to reactivate the traditional norms of behaviour which were expected to create a sense of community in the villages.

The resulting ideology was that of 'mixed economy', drawing eclectically from the traditional communalist organizational forms and the inherited Western values. However, this 'hybrid' ideology did not have a sound programme of action, and was unable to attract foreign resources as there was much uncertainty as to the ideological status of the independence government. Moreover, the mixed economy ideology left as much room for foreign exploitation as for a rapid growth of internal differentiation. These contradictions, among many others to which we have already referred, were the impetus for the Arusha Declaration of 1967.

At the level of 'pure' ideology, the Declaration made significant departures from both the liberal model of the West and the idealist-nationalistic model of the traditional African society. At the level of practical ideology, too, significant changes were introduced, the most important being state control of the major means of production and exchange, collectivization of the rural population into *ujamaa* village communities, decentralization of the administrative system and creation of participatory organizations for both the workers and peasants. These measures, coupled with the introduction of such 'revolutionary' programmes as the Workers' Self-Management programme (1970) and such policy documents as the *Mwongozo* (1972), showed clearly that Tanzania was moving away from the liberal-incremental model and closer to the revolutionary-change model.

Contradictions, particularly at the level of practical ideology, began to emerge after 1972. First, in that year, a decentralization package devised by a Western consultancy company was introduced. The package was clearly based on the assumptions of the liberal-incremental model. It emphasized the primacy of 'management procedures' entirely outside the ideological fabric advocated by the central leadership. For example, the mobilizational role of the party and the participatory functions of the people's organizations at the grass-roots level were given peripheral attention. Thus, in practice, the reform ended up consolidating the powers of the bureaucrats at the regional and district levels, contrary to the participatory norms of *ujamaa*.

Second, contrary to the well-articulated policy of self-reliance and selectivity in determining the source and nature of foreign aid, there has been more foreign aid pouring into the modern urban sector and the rural sector than during the pre-Arusha period. As we pointed out in Chapter 1, much of this aid came from the traditional Western sources. The aid included funds and personnel.

Third, the initial emphasis on socialist production in the villages gave way to bloc and individual farming after the launching of the massive collectivization in 1974. Thus, as we have pointed out, both the villagers and the local leadership seem to be rather confused as to the exact status of *ujamaa* as a mode of production.

From about 1972, therefore, there appear to be tendencies towards a reversion to the liberal-incremental model; emphasis having shifted from communal to individual or bloc farming; from aid from socialist countries (as observers had expected) to aid from the West; from equity to productivity.

These changes are due to several reasons. The first is the instability inherent in a guided evolutionary model, which seems to make claims to be 'revolutionary'. Second, the forces pulling the model towards the liberal direction were greater than those pulling it towards the revolutionary-change direction. These included the interests of Western financiers who apparently became more forthcoming and 'generous' after Arusha; the 'embourgeoisement' inclinations of the local elites, and the firm desire of the central leaders to maintain a sort of ideological non-alignment. In this 'non-alignment', the balance between Western and socialist aid depended on which bloc was more 'generous' in offering aid. In this, the capitalist world seems to have outbid the socialist world. Third, the famine and inflationary years (1973-6) also had a significant influence on the changes; especially the change from the initial emphasis on equity to emphasis on productivity.

The Lessons

Probably the most important lesson to be learnt from Tanzania's CD approach is the instability of the guided-evolutionary model itself. Apart from having many contradictions, it also hides opportunism within the ranks of the leadership, both local and central. Since the revolution is based on 'class collaboration' rather than 'class struggle', no systematic attempt has been made to identify the strata which are likely to support or obstruct revolutionary change either in Tanzania's relations with the world economy or in internal class relations. In this collaborative framework, it has been very easy for various groups within the leadership to attach the label *'ujamaa'* to a variety of actions, including those serving their own interests or those of the multi-nationals. This is possible largely because the political consciousness of the workers and peasants has not been systematically guided towards a struggle against such tendencies. Thus there has been very little challenge from below. In other words, 'political awareness' has come to be defined rather narrowly and conservatively to imply compliance with what the leaders say. This robs the workers and peasants of whatever revolutionary impulse they might have.   ⟵ P2 Coul

It should be noted, however, that at least President Nyerere is fully aware of the opportunistic and self-interested tendencies of some elements in the leadership. On countless occasions, he has appealed to the masses to expose reactionary leaders who hide selfish motives behind the label of *'ujamaa'* or *masilahi ya umma* (national, community or public interest), or even extension officials who were not doing their job. Some political leaders — both local and central — have been discredited or relieved of their duties for those reasons. All the same, however, these challenges from below have surfaced rather slowly and timidly except at election time. This is partly because political mobilization (in keeping with the notion of 'class collaboration') has been in the framework of a 'mass party' rather than a 'vanguard' party. Thus just as it is possible to have opportunism within the ranks of the leadership, it is also possible to have opportunism in the broad membership of the party from which a leadership cadre is selected. In other words, there seem to be few elements within the leadership and the broad party membership who can vigorously resist reversion to the liberal model.

The second lesson is that too much impatience by the leadership may lead to poor programme performance. Decision-making in Tanzania, particularly after Arusha, has been guided by the President's idea of 'running while others are walking'. This has meant introduction of too many projects, programmes, operations and campaigns at the same time, often without elaborate implementation guidelines or time-tables. Although this impatience is really a result of a genuine desire by the central leadership to improve the lot of the peasants, it has led to a number of problems. The main ones include: unfinished projects; little attention paid to the utility and maintenance of projects after completion; little time left to the peasants and local leaders to do feasibility studies or to evaluate their own successes or failures and draw appropriate lessons, and premature winding up of projects and programmes without examining the reasons for poor outcome.

Thus it is not entirely surprising that the implementers of CD programmes appear to have learned very little from the various approaches that have been attempted since independence. Mistakes made in one approach are repeated in others. For example, many of the mistakes observed in the transformation approach — such as oversubsidizing the settlers, bureaucratic decision-making and supervision, etc. — have been repeated in the *ujamaa* approach. Indeed, the bureaucrats have knowingly or unknowingly turned full circle by reinviting the World Bank (and other Western agents) to plan the villages, whereas the *ujamaa* approach was introduced as a rejection of the transformation approach recommended by the World Bank in 1961.

The tendency towards reversion to the liberal model is partly due to this impatience of the leadership — a genuine desire to see tangible results from CD programmes of which vested interests both within and without the country have been able to take advantage. This impatience has focused the dilemma of choice between productivity of projects and programmes in the short run, and the goal of grass-roots participation geared to the liberation of the productive forces as a long-term development strategy. Indeed, the management procedures devised by the McKinsey Consultancy Company (in connection with the decentralization reform) and those prescribed by the various Western technical assistance teams (in connection with the Regional Integrated Development Programmes) show clearly that current preoccupation is with productivity in the rather narrow economistic sense of 'optimizing' outputs from given inputs, irrespective of whether such optimization leads to the liberation of the (human) productive forces, utilizes local resources, increases local technological capacity or, more importantly, leads to a fundamental transformation of the economy and society.

The third lesson is that rural development is more than just providing funds for development projects or establishing the basic social services. It is, additionally, a mobilization process; for it is the people who must first be developed and in turn develop 'things'. This is the role of the party, but in practice it has not received due attention, particularly where the local party organization has been weak, as in the case of Turiani. Mobilization should not only entail communication of ideological messages but also communication of educational messages in the form of seminars, workshops, adult literacy classes, etc., at the village level to make peasants appreciate the need to change for a better life, to liberate them from superstitions and to give them a sense of self-confidence in tackling the development problems in their environment. The participatory approach was supposed to achieve this self-confidence but, as we have pointed out, its effectiveness has depended on several factors, including the level of political awareness in the villages, the dynamism of the local leadership and its willingness to decentralize some decision-making powers to the village level.

The final lesson is that village leadership is an important factor in rural development. Lukenge's poor performance, as compared with Kidudwe's satisfactory performance, was in large part due to its bad leadership. My studies of other villages in Morogoro have also shown a relationship between village performance and the stability and strength of its leadership over time.

A further problem is the frequent transfer and rapid turnover of officials which the government is trying to treble by posting or 'seconding' experts to the villages to act as village managers. Those appointed and posted between December 1977 and April 1978 were mostly graduates, showing the importance attached to the post. Since these graduates are as far as possible posted to their own areas, it is expected that they will be in a better position to understand the values and beliefs of the societies they are changing. Again, since they will normally not be transferred, except where a village demands it, they will provide continuity.

Along with this change, there are plans to give the villages a sounder financial base so that they are not completely dependent on the annual government budget. With the new marketing system, the villages will retain the crop levy and will probably be allowed to raise revenue from other sources as well (e.g. market fees, licence fees, etc.), as was the case with the pre-decentralization local government system.

The appointment of village managers may work well, but it may lead to conflict, with the appointed manager being accused of usurping the authority of the elected village chairman and secretary. This will of course depend on the personalities involved. The other possible source of tension may come from the fact that the official enjoys a relatively fat salary whereas the people he is leading are poor peasants who depend solely on their annual harvest. To reduce this envy, the government decided that both the village chairman and secretary should also be paid a monthly salary. This, it is hoped, will also encourage competent leaders to seek election and use much of their time in leadership activities rather than in attending to their own businesses.

But still a bureaucratically minded manager in a remote village where the people are not politically aware might further drain the villagers of their self-confidence, as in the settlement schemes of the sixties. However, the government seems to be aware of such possibilities, for it has issued guidelines discouraging such tendencies. It is to be hoped they will have some effect.

IV COMMUNITY DEVELOPMENT IN INDIA

V.R. Gaikwad

EDITOR'S FOREWORD

The project design for the whole four-country study, with its contrast between 'successful' and 'unsuccessful' cases of development, implied the existence of a development programme capable of making *some* positive impact on *some* villages. This study of community development in two Indian villages, and specifically of a farmers' credit institution, concludes that the initial presumption was, in the Indian case, unjustified.

In common with the other case studies, it started with the expectation that obvious differences in social structure between two villages — particularly in patterns of land ownership and wealth, and degrees of conflict and solidarity, or cohesion — would lead to a differential degree of success in implementing community development schemes. This is why the social and economic character of the two chosen villages is described and contrasted in some detail at the outset. It is clear that the one village (Seshagirihalli) was poorer, more internally unequal — both economically and ritually, more polarized in class and caste terms, and probably more prone to chronic factionalism, than was the other village (Ganakal).

However, the conclusion reached is that these structural differences explain very little in this case. While it is possible that this was because these two villages were not *sufficiently* different, or not different in other ways which might have proved more relevant (for example, their status in wider administrative, economic, commercial or political networks did not differ significantly, nor did their economic resources, physical environment or agricultural technology), this is not the explanation here advanced. Rather it is suggested that the community development programme was so constrained by its own limited resources, inflexible organization and underlying political motives, that it *could* not have achieved 'real' community development — here maximally defined as genuinely communal or co-operative productive activity. Even according to less exacting definitions of community development in terms of isolated initiatives to benefit individuals or small groups (with or without ramifying demonstration effects) and even considering initiatives in the (easier) welfare field rather than that of production, the sum total of successful actions by development agencies in these two villages was small.

The limitations of the community development programme itself, then, are put forward as the main explanation for its lack of impact. It might still be true that even a programme with more radical objectives and more resources would find some kinds of village much more open to change than others; it would be surprising if it were not so. But the study concludes this is a secondary matter. For the present, it is the aims, strategies and organization of community development programmes themselves which require most thought and probably a new beginning; the final part of the study suggests some of the directions this should take.

In the meantime, the section on the structure of the two sample villages, though somewhat redundant in terms of the original project design, does serve to indicate the kinds of problem that remain to be tackled, and the ways in which the various elements of the community development programme affected the two villages without having any real impact on the quality of life or the range and distribution of opportunities for their inhabitants.

1 THE NATIONAL BACKGROUND

For the last 25 years, India has struggled to achieve the social and economic transformation of its rural people. In this extremely heterogeneous society, fundamental change is only possible through persuasion; respect for democratic processes is deep rooted. The ideals of cultural coexistence and unity in diversity which have been responsible for the growth and continuity of Indian civilization over thousands of years continue to mould her society today.

Since independence, a two-fold objective has guided India's planned development: the building by democratic means of a rapidly expanding and technologically progressive economy, and a social order based on justice and equal opportunity for every citizen. The Five Year Plans have been the instrument designed to achieve these goals. The result is a strong industrial infrastructure. Today, India is the eleventh most industrialized country in the world. There is also a strong research and education base, especially in the technical and engineering fields, giving India, the third largest trained and qualified manpower reserve after the USA and the USSR.

Agriculture is very important; in 1974, agricultural and allied sectors accounted for 43 per cent of national income. Throughout the planning exercise, the complementarity of agriculture and industry has been stressed, and importance has been given to raising agricultural production and land productivity through irrigation, fertilizers, chemicals and improved and high-yielding varieties of seeds. Net production of foodgrains has gone up from 48.16 million tonnes in 1951 to 120 million tonnes in 1975-6. However, because India's population rose from 361 million in 1951 to 606 million in 1976, availability of foodgrains (cereals and pulses) has remained more or less constant.

Throughout this period, 125 million, or about 70 per cent of the workforce, depended on agriculture for its livelihood; employment opportunities generated in the industrial and other sectors were not sufficient to reduce the pressure on land. Of the total population of 606 million, about 485 million (80 per cent) live in 575,721 villages. Of the agricultural workers about 78 million are cultivators and 47.5 million landless and agricultural labourers.

The average size of an operational holding nationally is only 2:30 hectares, but that average conceals wide disparities. The 51 per cent of

247

holdings classed as marginal have about 9 per cent of the total land under agriculture; the 4 per cent with the largest farms, some 30 per cent.

Over the last 25 years, the absolute number as well as percentage of marginal and sub-marginal holdings has increased without any appreciable change in the average size. The number of landless has also increased — from 28 million to 48 million between 1951 and 1971. The average size of medium holdings has increased to some extent, while their number has declined. The share of large holdings has declined in both area and number.

The pattern of land distribution has been affected by agrarian reforms, population increase, continuous breaking up of joint families, inheritance laws, poor returns on agriculture, and inadequate employment opportunities outside agriculture. Today, there are no large farmers in India. The so-called large farms are managed by large, joint families composed of a number of nuclear families, with each constituent familiy owning a smaller medium-size holding from which it derives its livelihood.

Returns on agriculture have been very low and uncertain. There are many indicators of this. For example, the estimated income from agriculture in 1974 (at 1960-1 prices) was Rs 526.5 per hectare, or Rs 1210 per operational holding of average size of 2.3 hectares. Moreover, nearly 79 per cent of the total area under cultivation depends entirely on the monsoon. Abnormal monsoons, and occasional droughts, play havoc with the farmer's economy. The record production in 1975-6 came after 15 years of wide fluctuations. Between 1960-1 and 1974-5 there were six good years, three years of marginal improvement and six years of decline in agricultural production. Until 1971-2, every two-year period of progress was followed by setback in the third year. In 1965-6 and 1972-3, there was widespread drought.

The low income in agriculture is also reflected in per capita consumption expenditure. Dandekar and Rath[1] pointed out that in 1960-1 the figure for nearly 63 per cent of the rural population was below Rs 261.2 a year. In short, agrarian reforms leading to more equitable distribution of land, and agricultural development programmes for increasing productivity of land have not been sufficient to improve the economic conditions of the large mass of rural people. India has yet to evolve a planning model that will make a major dent in rural poverty, and improve the quality of life of rural people without reducing the pace of industrial development.

In the development strategy followed by India since independence the major priorities have been transport, communications and energy supplies, and industrialization as the chief means of achieving the long-term structural transformation necessary to raise per capita income. At the same time there has been little expectation that industrial growth could so outstrip population growth as to allow a transfer of working population out of agriculture and an improvement in the man/land ratio. Agriculture has received considerable investment of funds, especially for irrigation, but has not been envisaged as a major engine of growth in the economy, nor as the source of substantial investment funds for industry. The aims have been, first, to keep the growth in food production ahead of population growth, thus slowly improving consumption levels; and secondly to find employment for the growing numbers who cannot be absorbed in the other sectors of the economy.

The need to make sure that 'the benefits of economic development . . . accrue more and more to the relatively less privileged classes of society' (as the second plan document put it) has become stronger in the Fifth Plan which declares one of its basic objectives to be the raising of consumption levels for the poorest 30 per cent, to be accomplished by a variety of special schemes. The scheme described in this study belongs to that category.

Note

1. V.M. Dandekar and N. Rath, *Poverty in India* (Ford Foundation, New Delhi, 1970).

2 THE HISTORY OF COMMUNITY DEVELOPMENT IN INDIA

Community development had a long history in India even before the launching of the national programme in 1952. A number of isolated experiments in village reconstruction — usually under some religious auspice — were made during British rule. They all stressed self-help, but nearly all depended on the deep emotional involvement and enthusiasm of a leader and a small group of close associates.

Two projects in particular had an important influence on the subsequent programme. The first was an experimental pilot project at Etawah, initiated by an American engineer, which differed from earlier experiments in using a systematic organizational structure. So did the Nilokheri experiment directed by S.K. Dey, the Indian engineer who subsequently became Minister of Community Development, which sought to create a new township out of a camp for partition refugees — an attempt, through co-operative and public as well as private enterprise, to create an agro-industrial centre that might provide India with a model unit for a future pattern of decentralized industrialization.

Further impetus was given by an extensive 15-village pilot project very largely modelled on the Etawah experiment, begun with a Ford Foundation grant in 1951, and to be followed next year by the launching of the community development programme proper. In this model, which was to set the pattern for subsequent developments, the term 'community development' (CD) implied two rather weak assumptions: (i) that the economic interests of *all* the people in a village were common and for the purposes of economic development they would operate as a community; and (ii) that the programme itself would develop community feeling in a village settlement, if it did not already exist. The repeated use of the term 'community' in speeches and documents strengthened the first assumption to such an extent that for a long time development programmes were introduced in rural India without challenging its validity. But in fact the operational agreement that defined the programme was couched chiefly in terms of individual improvement, induced by project workers able 'to mobilize the enthusiasm and co-operation of the people'. There was no built-in collective element.

For example, there *had* been much discussion in India, particularly in the Gandhian tradition, of the desirability of co-operative farming both as the means of *creating* community spirit and as an essential precondition for efficient modern agriculture. The first five-year plan had declared it to be an objective, and set aside Rs 4 million for it, but there was no reflection of such thinking in the initial CD programme (CDP). Declarations in favour of co-operative farming have continued to appear in the plans but have had little effect in practice, beyond the fact that a few thousand joint farming and collective farming societies do exist, at least on paper.

Many considerations entered into the adoption of this particular CD model: the shortage of investment funds and the priority given to heavy industry in the early plans which ruled out the more expensive alternative of developing agro-industrial townships on the Nilokheri model, the emphasis on the urgency of increasing agricultural production and, not least, the persuasive offer of American assistance for precisely that sort of programme from Chester Bowles who was convinced that it was the sort of programme which would have saved China from communism if Chiang Kai-shek had only had the wit to adopt it. It was, in short, a convenient low-cost strategy for social welfare and agriculture-based economic development which, planners hoped, would keep the hopes and aspirations of the rural people, as well as their faith in government, alive till the fruits of rapid industrialization reached them.

From the beginning, the basic administrative unit for the CDP has been the 'block' — a unit comprising some 100-odd natural villages. Each block is headed by a block development officer with a staff of eight specialist extension officers. Then there are a dozen village-level workers (VLWs) with responsibility for about ten villages each. A medical team, storemen, messengers, clerks, drivers, etc., could bring the total establishment at the peak phase up to 45.

The assumption was that a programme in any particular block would go through a sequence of stages with varying intensity of operation, different levels of expenditure and staffing. Thereby, as resources were shifted, the whole country would be covered — and, indeed, by the late sixties, the whole country had been reached.

By the mid-1950s it became obvious that the results of the CDP were not impressive. The chief measure adopted to give an additional fillip was democratic control over the block officers by an elected assembly. At about the same time the Central Directing Agency was elevated to the status of a Ministry of Community Development and Administration. It was a period of great optimism which, however, gradually faded. Ten years later the Ministry was downgraded to the status of a department within the Ministry of Agriculture, and, although most of its staff remained in post, its reduced funds (4.8 per cent of the Second Plan expenditure, 0.7 per cent for the fourth) have covered little more than salaries and contingencies, plus, in the 1970s, some additional earmarked expenditure for the new programmes intended to concentrate attention on the 'weaker sections of the rural population'[2] — programmes such as the Small and Marginal Farmers and Agricultural Labourers Development Programmes, Drought Prone Areas Programme, Tribal and Hill Areas Development Programmes, Pilot Intensive Rural Employment Projects, etc.

Throughout the active life of the CDP there had been debate over priorities — how far it should concentrate on productive activities, how far on social services, amenities and social welfare. It was with the Third Plan and the scheme for Intensive Agricultural District Programmes that the main thrust of agricultural improvement work moved outside the CDP proper, leaving it with the special programmes which were seen by the more hard-headed planners as being justified not by potential contributions to GNP but either by (a) their experimentation with new social forms (as in the Whole Village scheme) or (b) their distributive effect in 'doing something for the poor'.

By the end of the 1960s the pretence of a vigorous CDP had in effect been abandoned; whatever else brought the Green Revolution to parts of India, community development rarely receives credit. Acknowledging its failure, a former minister ascribes it to a variety of reasons. Rapid expansion meant that resources were spread too thinly on the ground; one young village-level worker with a bicycle could have little impact on 10-15 villages. The responsible staff at the block level were recruited largely from the existing administrative staff with their predominantly revenue-collecting, law-and-order-preserving orientation; the staff newly recruited as village-level workers, even if they generated some initial enthusiasm, were reduced to bureaucratic conformity, especially after the 1961 'blue book of instructions' reduced opportunities for individual initiatives. The technical staff was often inadequate and in conflict with the administrators; factional conflict within the ruling party was reflected in the block assembly and served to deflect the development objectives of the CDP, while the sheer shortage of resources exacerbated the intensity of every conflict.[3]

Notes

1. Chester Bowles, *Ambassador's Report* (Collins, London, 1954), pp. 132-5.

2. Government of India, Ministry of Agriculture and Irrigation (Department of Rural Development) Report: 1974-5, p. 5.

3. S.K. Dey, *Power to the People? A Chronicle of India 1947-67* (Orient Longman, Bombay, 1969), pp. 94-110.

3 THE VILLAGE SETTING

Location

Seshagirihalli and Ganakal are two small villages with 87 and 94 households respectively, located in Ramanagaram block of Bangalore district in Karnataka State (Figure IV.1). It is a dry, chronically drought-

Figure IV.1: Location of Sample Villages in Bangalore District

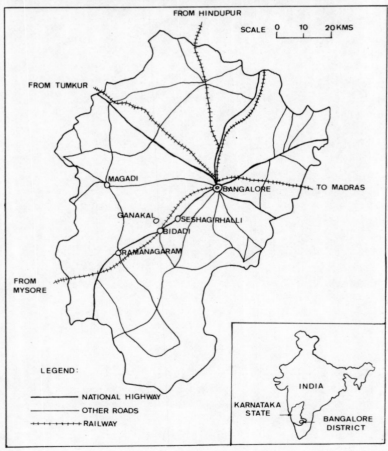

affected region with average annual rainfall of about 100 cm. The terrain is undulating, with sandy red soil and hard granite rocks. There are no rivers near the villages.

Seshagirihalli is well connected with the outside world. Situated on the Bangalore-Mysore state highway, it is about 29 km from Bangalore (the state capital and district headquarters), 19 km from Ramanagaram (block headquarters), 5 km from Bidadi (FSS headquarters), and 1.5 km from Hejjala (railway station) (Figure IV.2). Ganakal was more remote, being 8 km from Bidadi along a *kuchha* road with very steep gradients, and passable only by motor cycle or jeep. A heavily loaded cart would need a very sturdy pair of oxen to pull it through, and cyclists had to walk half the distance. To take a bus, the villagers had to go to Bidadi. The trains could be boarded at Bidadi or Hejjala which was also about 8 km from the village. Since Bidadi and Hejjala were common points for both Ganakal and Seshagirihalli, bus and train servces were the same. Seshagirihalli was one of the four villages forming a panchayat with its headquarters at Bannikuppe, about 4 km away. Ganakal was the headquarters of a panchayat which also had three other villages under it. A VLW who lived in Magadi, about 48 km away from Bannikuppe, served both panchayats, having Bannikuppe as his headquarters. The Bannikuppe panchayat secretary's headquarters was at Bannikuppe itself, while that of Ganakal was in Borehalli, about 1 km from Ganakal.

Even though Ganakal was situated in the interior, it was not isolated. Since it was the panchayat headquarters, government functionaries from revenue, block and public works departments paid frequent visits to the village. There were also some educated families in the village, whose members, while working in nearby towns and cities, continued to keep close ties with their families, and the village community.

Seshagirihalli covered an area of 749 acres, about 40 per cent cultivable land, the rest being waste, grazing and reported fallow. Ganakal covered 502 acres of which roughly half was cultivable, with 8 acres under settlement.

Population

According to the 1971 census, Seshagirihalli had 80 households with 402 members. By 1976, the number of households had increased to 87 and the population to 445, with average size of household 5.1. There were 240 adults and 205 children.

Figure IV.2: Bidadi Hobli

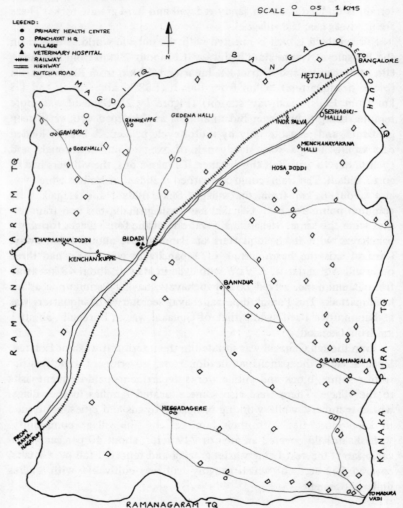

In 1971, Ganakal had 80 households with 455 members. By 1976 the number of households had increased to 94 and the population to 507. The average household size was 5.4, with 297 adults and 210 children.

Caste Composition

Both Seshagirihalli and Ganakal were multi-caste villages. Seshagirihalli had four castes; Lingayat (18 households), Vokkaliga (29 households), Adi Karnataka (38 households), and Bovi (one household). There were also a Muslim household and two scheduled tribe households. Lingayats and Vokkaligas rank high in the caste hierarchy. The Adi Karnatakas are former untouchables, known as Harijans or 'scheduled castes' (SC) because, with the scheduled tribes (ST) they have certain compensatory privileges such as reserved places in college and government services. The average size of higher caste households in this village was larger than that of the scheduled castes (Lingayats 6.4; Vokkaligas 6; and Adi Karnatakas 3.7).

Of the eleven castes in Ganakal, Vokkaliga (with 71 households) was the dominant caste numerically, socially and politically. Most of the other castes in the village — the Achari (goldsmith), Kammara (blacksmith), Kumbhar (potter), Barber and Dhobi (washerman) — seem to exist to service the Vokkaligas. The Ediga (backward class), Naik and Adi Karnataka came to the village as agricultural labourers. A few of them now own some land.

In Ganakal, the average size of most of the SC households was higher (7) than that of the cultivator castes (5.5), but again SCs had smaller households (4.5), partly because few owned the land necessary to support larger families, but also because of a tradition of splitting into nuclear units.

Settlement Pattern

In Seshagirihalli, there were three separated or segregated clusters of dwellings (Figure IV.3), each being inhabited by only one caste group: 18 Lingayat households in Inorpalya, 29 Vokkaliga households in the main hamlet, and 35 Adi Kanataka, one Bovi and two tribals in the Harijan colony. The Lingayats of Inorpalya had their own temple, and the Vokkaligas a prayer hall, whilst the Harijans had no religious building. Each caste settlement had its own well, though the Harijans' often dried up. The physical segregation was not a new phenomenon; it was as old as the village itself.

All three hamlets were one-street settlements. The streets were unpaved and there was no drainage system. Out of a total of 87 dwellings, 36 were merely huts belonging to Adi Kanatakas and tribals,

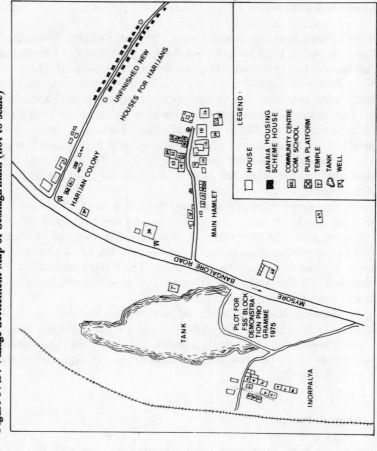

Figure IV.3: Village Settlement Map of Seshagirihalli (not to scale)

LEGEND:

☐ HOUSE
▨ JANAIA HOUSING SCHEME HOUSE
▣ COMMUNITY CENTRE COM. SCHOOL
⊞ PUJA PLATFORM
⊡ TEMPLE
〰 TANK
⋉ WELL

HARIJAN COLONY

UNFINISHED NEW HOUSES FOR HARIJANS

MAIN HAMLET

BANGALORE ROAD

MYSORE

PLOT FOR FSS BLOCK DEMONSTRATION PROGRAMME 1975

TANK

INORPALYA

nine were *pucca* (four of these were Vokkaliga, two Lingayat and only one Harijan) and the rest *kuchha* houses mostly with thatched roofs.

The settlement pattern of Ganakal, with its one dominant caste, was very different from that of Seshagirihalli. It could be described as a nucleated village (Figure IV.4). Within the cluster of dwellings there

Figure IV.4: Village Settlement Map of Ganakal (not to scale)

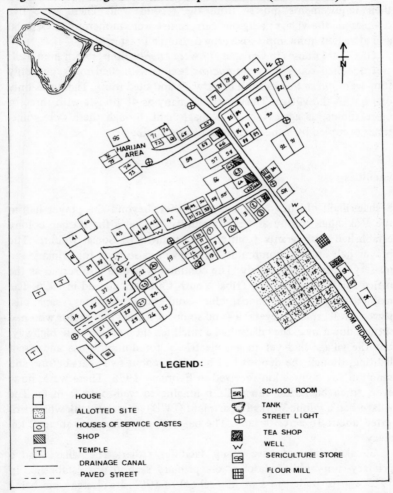

LEGEND:

HOUSE	SCHOOL ROOM
ALLOTTED SITE	TANK
HOUSES OF SERVICE CASTES	STREET LIGHT
SHOP	TEA SHOP
TEMPLE	WELL
DRAINAGE CANAL	SERICULTURE STORE
PAVED STREET	FLOUR MILL

were, however, sub-clusters, each separated from the adjoining one by lanes and open spaces. About 200 metres of one of the village streets passing through the closely clustered dwellings were stone-paved and along the entire length of this street there was a drain.

Also in 1972 the village acquired electricity. So far, only six households have domestic connections, but there were eight street lights provided by the electricity department.

Ganakal had three drinking wells, roughly located in three corners of the village and used by all the castes, though the SC households drew their requirements mostly from the second well. There were five temples in the village; religious ceremonies were numerous in Ganakal and attracted quite impressive crowds from all castes.

Of the 94 houses in Ganakal, 77 were *kuchha* houses with mud walls and thatched roofs, 12 were *kuchha* houses with tiled roofs, and only four were *pucca* houses with brick walls and tiled roofs. There was only one hut in the village. There were as many as 48 houses with three or more rooms, as against 25 in Seshagirihalli, though these were sometimes occupied by as many as four or five families.

Facilities

Seshagirihalli did not have many facilities, beyond the prayer hall in the Vokkaliga colony and a community centre in the Harijan colony established with grants from the Department of Social Welfare. The prayer hall and the community centre were also used for primary and nursery schools respectively. The community centre also served as the office for the Harijan and Tribal Youth Club, established in 1976. The main hamlet had two shops, which sold grains, cigarettes, soaps, oils, jaggery, salt, spices, vegetables and so on. A former contractor who had settled down near the village had a small tea shop on the state highway, but the village had yet to get electricity for domestic use and street lighting, though the deposit had been paid about two years before, and sanction for connection received in February 1976. There were, however, three energized tubewells belonging to well-to-do farmers. The village had a Public Works Department (PWD) irrigation tank which irrigated about 16 acres of land. The nearest post office was about 2 km away.

Ganakal did not have many facilities either. The village had a primacy-cum-middle school whose primary section was established in 1925 and upgraded to a middle school in 1951. Its classes were being organized in three different places. Ganakal was the headquarters of the *gram panchayat* but there was no panchayat building. There were four shops, a small tea shop, and a flour mill. The village had received electricity in 1976, but so far, only six households had taken connections. Out of four tubewells in the village, two were energized. There was a sub-post office in the village.

Bannikuppe, which was within four km of these villages, had a veterinary sub-centre. There was also an auxiliary nurse (midwife) posted at Bannikuppe. Bidadi was the nearest point with facilities such as a primary health centre (PHC), dispensary, and family planning clinic. For serious cases, people had to go to Bangalore. Education to primary level was available in the villages themselves, but for high school education, Bidadi was the nearest place. It also served as the main centre for purchases of most household and other requirements, and had a veterinary hospital, post and telegraph, and bank facilities.

Schooling

In both villages only a minority of adults had been to school, and only in the last few years has primary school attendance become the norm, at least for boys. The higher castes tended to have more education, but not entirely so: three of Seshagirihalli's four graduates were Harijans.

Sanitation and Health

In both villages disposal of cattle dung and garbage very near the dwellings was quite common. Even though the digging of compost pits was one of the programmes of the CD scheme, none were dug in all these years. There were no latrines, and, in Seshagirihalli, soakage pits had been constructed to prevent used domestic water from forming puddles in the roads. The cleaning of streets and lanes was not a community responsibility.

The PHD at Bidadi provided medical facilities to people of both the villages. There was also an Auxiliary Nurse and Midwife Centre (ANM) at Bannikuppe. During 1975-6, there were fifteen births in Seshagirihalli and seven in Ganakal. All deliveries took place at residences without any assistance from the PHC or ANM. For some years there were no smallpox cases in these villages. Even then, in 1975-6, as a precautionary measure about 35-40 per cent of the village population was given smallpox vaccination.

During 1975-6 there were eleven deaths in Seshagirihalli, out of which five were adults and six infants. The adults died from old age and illness. Four out of six infants died at birth, and two of illness later. Out of fifteen births in the year there were six infant deaths. In Ganakal, there were five deaths in the year, including two infants out of the seven births.

The family planning (FP) programme was not popular in Seshagiri-halli; in fact, people belonging to all castes had developed a strong hostility towards it. There was not a single case of sterilization and none of the 65 couples in the reproductive age group was using any method of family planning. At one time, the fear of being forcibly steril-ized was so overpowering among the Harijans that many among them were not prepared to go to Bidadi to file membership forms for the Farmers' Service Co-operative Society (FSS). The reasons for the strong opposition to family planning were two-fold: (a) spread of news from neighbouring villages about the inept handling of sterilization cases by the family planning personnel resulting in deaths in previous years; and (b) reports about harsh methods, such as threats of withholding grants, licences, facilities and inputs needed by farmers, followed by the revenue and development officials responsible for achieving FP targets.

However, in Ganakal, despite the fact that the community was deeply religious and orthodox, FP had had some impact. A total of sixteen sterilizations had been recorded. The number of couples in the reproductive category at the time of the survey was 70. During the two years 1974/5-1975/6 five female sterilizations had been completed and two women had opted for IUCDs.

4 VILLAGE ECONOMIC STRUCTURE

Land Distribution

Of the two villages, Seshagirihalli had the more skewed distribution of landholdings. About 44 per cent of its households were landless as against about 20 per cent in Ganakal (Table IV.1). One of the reasons could be that about 45 acres of cultivable land in Seshagirihalli was owned by wealthy people living in Bidadi and Bangalore, and used for vegetable cultivation, grape orchards and coconut plantations. Tube-wells were installed on these lands and provided employment for about 25 Adi Karnataks from the village. Given the land shortage, some of the local people were illegally cultivating part of the land recorded as waste and grazing lands.

Largely because Ganakal was in the interior, only 19 acres of its land was owned by outsiders, and they were from nearby villages. Here also, an unspecified but quite large area was illegally cultivated. In Table IV.1, cultivators of such land are not included.

In both the villages, most holdings were under 2.5 acres. (Seshagirihalli 63 per cent, and Ganakal about 55 per cent; for India as a whole it is 51 per cent.) In neither village were there farmers with very large holdings. The largest in Seshagirihalli was 15.78 acres, and in Ganakal 19.70 acres. In general, hldings over 10 acres were owned by joint families.

In both the villages landownership was concentrated in the upper caste households (Tables IV.2 and IV.3). This was much more so in Seshagirihalli where the Vokkaligas and Lingayats with 53 per cent of households owned 90 per cent of the land, whilst the Adi Karnatakas who were 43 per cent of households, owned only 10 per cent of the land. And of the 38 landless households, 36 were Adi Karnatakas. (It is interesting to note, however, that one of the four large landholders in Seshagirihalli was an Adi Karnataka.) In Ganakal, the Vokkaligas were 76 per cent of households and owned 83 per cent of land, but there were also 10 Vokkaliga households which were landless.

Within the upper caste in each village, however, the size of land-holdings varied considerably. In Seshagirihalli, the 22 Vokkaliga households which had less than five acres owned about 42 per cent of land held by the caste, and the six households with more than five acres controlled the remaining 58 per cent. In Ganakal, the 56 Vokkaliga

Table IV.1: Distribution of Households According to the Size of Landholdings in Seshagirihalli and Ganakal

Size of landholding	No. of households		Percentage of landholders under each category		Cumulative percentage		Percentage of the total land owned by each category	
	Seshagirihalli	Ganakal	Seshagirihalli	Ganakal	Seshagirihalli	Ganakal	Seshagirihalli	Ganakal
Up to 1 acre	3	11	6.1	14.6	6.1	24.0	1.4	2.6
1.1-2.5 acres	29	30	59.2	40.0	65.3	54.7	32.2	25.1
2.6-5.0 acres	8	28	16.3	37.3	81.6	91.9	15.6	44.4
5.1-10. acres	5	3	10.2	3.4	91.8	95.9	20.0	9.5
10 acres +	4	3	8.1	4.0	100.00	100.00	30.8	18.4
Total landholders	49	75	100.0	100.0	–	–	100.0	100.0
Landless	38	19	–	–	–	–	0.0	0.0
Grand Total	87	94	–	–	–	–	100.0	100.0

Table IV.2: Castewise Distribution of Landholdings in Seshagirihalli

Caste	Size of landholdings (acres)				Total	Percentage of total land owned
	Landless	Up to 2.5	2.6-10.0	10.1 +		
Lingayats	1	10	7		18	28.8
Vokkaligas	1	19	5	4	29	61.1
Adi Karnatakas and others	36	3	–	1	40	10.1
Total	38	32	12	5	87	100

Table IV.3: Castewise Distribution of Landholdings in Ganakal

Caste	Size of landholdings (Acres)				Total	Percentage of total land owned
	Landless	Up to 1.0	to 1.1	to 2.6	to 5.1 +		
Vaishnava and Lingayat				2		2	4.2
Vokkaliga	10	8	25	23	5	71	83.4
Service castes	4		2	2	1	9	8.4
Naik and AK (SC)	5	3	3	1		12	4.0
Total	19	11	30	28	6	94	100

households with less than five acres owned 71 per cent, and the five households with more than five acres controlled 29 per cent of the total land owned by Vokkaligas. Thus within the dominant caste in both villages there was concentration of land in a few families, most markedly in Seshagirihalli.

Occupation

Agriculture was the main occupation in both villages, either through cultivation or hired labour. Of the 38 landless households in Seshagirihalli, 42 persons reported their main ocupation as agricultural labour, one as mill labour and one as school teaching. Most of these were Adi Karnatakas or from the backward classes. The only reported subsidiary occupations were: priest (1); wayside shop (2); agricultural labour (1); and tea shop (1).

Since there was not enough work in Seshagirihalli all the year round for the daily wage workers, about 15 of them went to nearby villages in the sowing and harvesting seasons. Nine people had more or less permanently migrated to a village about 10 km away, to work in a small textile mill, but still kept up social relations with their kin in Seshagirihalli.[1] There was also some inflow. Recently 15 Adi Karnatakas had moved into the Harijan colony from nearby villages, having been given house-sites under the Ganata (People's) Housing Scheme sanctioned by a former Minister of Social Welfare who was also an Adi Karnataka.

In Ganakal, the pattern of main occupation was similar, and it is clear that in neither village have any new sources of income appeared. Of the 137 workers in Ganakal 102 were primarily cultivators and 23 were agricultural labourers. Only 12 had other main occupations, which were: goldsmith (2); potter (1); barber (3); washerman (1); tea shop (2); provision store (1); and government service (2).

There were 49 who reported subsidiary occupations, 37 being Vokkaligas engaged in: sheep-raising (11); agricultural labour (11); shop-keeping (5); sericulture (6); carpentry (2); service (1); and tailoring (1). Of the lower castes, 12 combined service work with agricultural labour or sheep-raising. As in Seshagirihalli, shortage of work produced seasonal migrations; as many as 25 from the lower castes go to neighbouring villages for the sugarcane harvesting and crushing every year. About 25 others had permanently migrated from the village to various towns in the area. But at harvest-time there is in-migration to meet the peak in labour demands.

The traditional *jajmani* system was still in evidence in both villages, though for the farmers of Seshagirihalli the relevant castes who were paid in kind for the services they provided were outside the village. There were some instances where payment in cash was sometimes more common, and in Ganakal the service castes had acquired some independence through subsidiary occupations such as wage-labouring, but in general the traditional economic relationships seemed strong.

Agriculture

About 10 per cent of land in Seshagirihalli, and 15 per cent in Ganakal, was irrigated — by public tank and private tubewells. So as much as 85-90 per cent of the land depended entirely on rainfall which was scanty and uncertain. For almost all the farmers, therefore, there was only one crop season, namely *kharif*, when 90-95 per cent of cultivable land would be sown, as against only 5-13 per cent in the other seasons. So the farmers' economy depended effectively on one crop and on rainfall.

Ragi (a coarse cereal) was the major crop accounting in *kharif* for nearly 42 per cent of net sown area in Seshagirihalli and 50 per cent in Ganakal. Pulses and vegetables (which could be conveniently transported to Bangalore city) were the secondary crops in Seshagirihalli, and groundnut in Ganakal. Small amounts of high-yielding varieties (HYV) of wheat, maize and paddy were grown in the other seasons. Ganakal generally had more land under HYV (23 per cent of gross cropped area) than Seshagirihalli (13 per cent), mainly because irrigation was more available.

Animal Husbandry

Sheep, goat and poultry were reared in both villages primarily for home consumption, though the skins and wool could be sold to provide a little additional income. But in neither village did animal husbandry develop as a major occupation. No efforts were made to improve the production of grass for fodder, nor to introduce improved breeds of animal.

Cottage Industry

In Ganakal, some of the big farmers had sericulture as a subsidiary occupation, but this did not go beyond the cocoon production stage. The cocoons were sold off at the government-controlled cocoon centre at Bidadi. The total area under sericulture in Ganakal was about 10 acres, and, on average, the net return per acre was about Rs 1200. There was no sericulture in Seshagirihalli.

Fifteen Adi Karnataka and tribal households in Seshagirihalli and seven Adi Karnataka and Naik caste households in Ganakal were engaged in weaving from coconut and palm leaves, but there was no regular production for sale. Production beyond a family's own requirements was sold in the village itself, and generally paid for in kind.

Net Village Income

There were many channels for the inflow and outflow of money which are shown in Figure IV.5. Most were common to both villages.

The main source of institutional finance was the Farmers' Service Co-operative Society (FSS) which gave credit for agricultural inputs, tractor hire, and purchase of sheep and goats. There was more institutional finance in Seshagirihalli than in Ganakal because of the special FSS 'block demonstration programme' there. In a sense institutional finance took away more (in repayments and interest) than it injected into the village, unless it increased productivity significantly. Since it was borrowed primarily for purchase of industrial products such as fertilizers and chemicals, and equipment (oil engine, pump-sets, etc.), most of it went out of the village economic system. All such transactions took place outside the village, so no profit from trade accrued to the local people. Agriculture was a means for supporting and benefiting the industrial urban sector.

Private investment in agriculture by urban-based landowners was most evident in Seshagirihalli, where about 45 acres of land was owned by outsiders. Only a part of the earnings by these outsiders was reinvested in Seshagirihalli. The sale of agricultural products was the main source of income, while expenditure on agricultural inputs such as fertilizers, high-yielding varieties of seeds, pesticides, etc., water and electricity charges, and investment in equipment and implements such as pump-sets were major items for the outflow of money. Often even sheep, goats and cattle had to be purchased from outside.

Figure IV.5: Major Channels of Inflow, Outflow of Money and Exchange Within the System

In-flow	Village Economic System	Out-flow
1. Institutional finance (FSS)		1. Loan and interest
2. Private investments by urban-based landowners	**Exchange Within System**	2. Money taken away by urban-based landowners
3. Government grants and salaries: a) School building, prayer hall, community centre, Harijan housing colony, village tank, etc. b) Salaries – school teacher	— Wages in cash and kind to agricultural labourers of the village	3. a) Payment by government to contractors for public building construction — building material — outside labour b) Government revenue duties
4. Sale of agricultural and allied products: a) Food grains b) Vegetables c) Sericulture d) Sheep, goat & cattle e) Animal by-products; hide, skin and wool	— Payment in cash and kind for services and goods (earthen pots, mats, agricultural implements and repairs thereof, house construction, washing of clothes, tailoring, grinding of grains, money spent in tea shops, purchase of goods from the local grocery shops, temple priest, expenses at the time of birth, death and marriage, etc.)	4. Agricultural inputs a) Fertilizers b) Seeds c) Pesticides d) Water charges e) Electricity charges f) Sheep, goat and cattle g) Implements and machines h) Packaging
5. Wages earned by agricultural labourers from other villages		5. Wages paid to agricultural labourers from other villages
6. Earnings of family members living in other places		6. Wages for services and certain goods in cash and kind
7. Pension		7. Household consumption: a) Food articles b) Fuel and light c) Medicine d) Household goods e) Education f) Construction g) Transport h) Others

Since, in the two villages, there was both in- and out-migration of agricultural labour, the net effect on money flow is hard to assess.

Government grants through the village panchayat and other agencies also added to the income of the villages, and allowed them to construct schools in both villages, and the prayer hall, community centre and Harijan housing colony in Seshagirihalli also brought an inflow of government grants. Again, a major part was spent as payment to contractors, for building materials and outside labour. Thus, only a small portion of these grants, in terms of wages paid to local labour, contributed to the village economy.

The most important outflow was expenditure on items for household consumption bought from outside, such as foodgrains (especially in years of scarcity), and many other basic and luxury goods.

Within the village economic system there was exchange of goods and services, payment for which was in cash, kind or both, depending upon the nature of goods and services. Wages to agricultural labour were paid in both cash and kind. The kind component generally covered grains at the end of the week or agricultural season, food for breakfast and lunch and some *bidi* (country cigarettes) or tobacco for smoking or chewing. In Ganakal the service castes were paid in cash and kind for their services. A part of the money spent by the people in the local tea shops and on purchase of goods from the local grocery shops remained within the village.

The net annual income of the village (NVI) as a whole had two main components: (a) net income of farming households; and (b) income earned by those agricultural labourers who seasonally migrated to other places for employment. Exact income figures were difficult to obtain for the wage-earners, marginal and small farmers, and those in traditional occupations, as they found it difficult to recall the income earned during a year by them and the members of their families. This was also the case with most of the medium and big farmers since few kept any records. They mostly provide only rough estimates of their previous year's income. To get a higher degree of reliability, the following checks were used: (a) comparison of estimates of income of households having same occupation, size of holding and number of earning members; and (b) cross-checks with village-level officials such as the village accountant, VLWs and police patel (headman), and other knowledgeable persons. Table IV.4 is based on the income estimates arrived at in this way.

Table IV.4 indicates that NVI in these villages (col. 8) was very low. It was from this low income that the households had to take care

Table IV.4: Estimates of Total Net Annual Income of Households and Net Village Income (NVI)

Village	Farming households	Landless households Agrl. Labour		Others	Total landless	All households	Total net annual income (7)+(9)	Average household income		Per capita per month income	
		Earned within village	Earned from outside*								
(1)	(2)	(3)	(4)	(5)	(6)	(7)	(8)	(9)	(10)	(11)	(12)
Seshagirihalli 87	164,560	17,760	4,050	10,000	31,810	196,370	168,610	2,257	1,938	37	32
Ganakal 94	260,780	9,790	6,750	6,950	23,490	284,270	267,530	3,024	2,846	47	44

*From Seshagirihalli and Ganakal about 15 and 25 landless labourers respectively migrated seasonally to other places for about two months in the year for employment. Average daily wage is Rs 4.5. It was assumed that all their earnings had come to their respective villages.

of household consumption needs, investments in agriculture and allied activities, emergencies like drought and sickness, social and cultural activities at the times of birth, death, marriages, festivals, and so on. The level of living and quality of life of the people of these two villages was found to be very low. Capital formation, if any, in these villages would be very slow and would threaten an already very low standard of living.

The population of Ganakal seems to be better off than that of Seshagirihalli. The average annual income of farm households in Seshagirihalli and Ganakal was Rs 3,358 and Rs 3,477 respectively. The average annual income of landless households in these villages was Rs 606 and Rs 1,378 respectively. It seems that the better position of Ganakal was primarily due to its landless households earning more than their Seshagirihalli counterparts.

Income Distribution

The distribution of land and occupations, and the standard of housing discussed earlier gives a fairly good picture of economic conditions and stratification in the two villages. The distribution of estimated annual household income provides additional evidence.

In Seshagirihalli, 20 out of 87 households (23 per cent) were extremely poor, with estimated income of less than Rs 500 per annum, i.e. about Rs 40 per month. All were landless Adi Karnatakas with no occupation other than agricultural labour. In Ganakal, only five families suffered extreme poverty. Two of these were landless, depending entirely on daily wages, while the remaining three were marginal farmers with no other source of income. In the second and third categories (Rs 502-2,000 and Rs 1,001-1,500) also there were higher percentages (24 and 15) in Seshagirihalli than in Ganakal (18 and 8.5). In Seshagirihalli, 15 out of 21 falling in the second category, and 1 out of 13 falling in the third category were from landless households depending entirely on daily wages. Thus in Seshagirihalli, 36 out of 38 landless households depended entirely on daily wages. Of the remaining two, one was an Adi Karnataka school teacher and the other was a mill worker. In Ganakal, 12 out of 19 depended entirely on daily wages. The remaining seven were either in such traditional occupations as barber, washerman, blacksmith, or were owners of wayside shops. Thus, in both the villages almost all the landless households fell in the two bottom income categories, namely, less than Rs 500 and Rs 501-1,000.

For all but one of the income categories over Rs 1,500, the percentage of households was higher in Ganakal than in Seshagirihalli. In most cases it was nearly double or more than double that in Seshagirihalli. There was a corresponding difference in the position of the landless. In Seshagirihalli, the average annual earnings of the 36 landless households was Rs 606 per annum compared with Rs 1,378 for the 12 landless households in Ganakal.

The presence of a large landless population in Seshagirihalli also had a marked effect on the income of marginal and small landowners who fell in the income categories between Rs 1,501-2,000 and Rs 4,001-5,000. It seems that landless households were competing with the marginal and small households (most of whom were underemployed due to their very small land base and single crop cultivation) for the limited employment opportunities in the village, and were getting a major share of these opportunities, probably because, since they had no other income source, the big farms found them more dependable or easily controlled. So, even if employment opportunities increase, the outlook for marginal farmers is bleak.

As mentioned earlier, there were a few big land-holders in the village and some outsiders owned substantial acreages. These farmers had tubewells. In addition to normal crops they also had vegetable cultivation and grape and coconut plantations. These farmers fell in the income category of Rs 8,000 and above. They employed a large number of the landless, a few on an annual basis but most as and when required. In fact, one of the two important reasons for the presence of a large number of landless labourers in Seshagirihalli was the employment opportunity on the land offered by the big farmers. The second was the distribution of houses under the Janata Housing Scheme. These landless people, almost all Adi Karnatakas, were in a way an appendage to the basic social and economic structure of the village.

So far we have analysed income distribution among households, but obviously per capita income within households is a better guide to the quality of life for many purposes. A detailed analysis shows that the distribution is less skewed for per capita than for household income, as one might expect. (Those with bigger incomes can afford larger families.) The evening-out effect of taking per capita income is, however, more marked in Ganakal than in Sheshagirihalli as Table IV.5 shows. The bottom left and the top right cells for each village (households high on one of the two criteria but not both) contain jointly 23 per cent of households in Ganakal, and 6 per cent in Seshagirihalli: Seshagirihalli clearly has a more skewed distribution of income whatever criterion is used.

Table IV.5: Distribution of Households According to Total Annual and Per Capita Income (Grouped Data)

Per capita	Seshagirihalli annual income			Ganakal annual income		
	Up to Rs 2,500	Above Rs 2,501	Total Rs	Up to Rs 2,500	Above Rs 2,501	Total Rs
Up to Rs 500	67 (77)	5 (5.8)	72 (82.8)	42 (44.7)	9 (9.6)	51 (54.3)
Above Rs 501	—	15 (17.2)	15 (17.2)	13 (13.8)	30 (31.9)	43 (45.7)
	67 (77)	20 (23)	87 (100)	55 (58.5)	39 (41.5)	94 (100)

Note: Figures in parentheses are percentages.

Note

1. These persons, however, are not included in the household census.

5　SOCIAL STRUCTURE AND ORGANIZATION

Family

Both Seshagirihalli and Ganakal had joint families and nuclear families, as well as families with adult unmarried sons. Ganakal had more joint families (66 per cent joint, 34 per cent nuclear) than Seshagirihalli (48 per cent and 52 per cent). In general, the joint family pattern did not seem more common at any particular caste level, though there *were* more nuclear families among the Adi Karnatakas of Seshagirihalli, mainly because of their landlessness and the migration of their children.

Inter-caste Relationship

It was difficult to state the exact rank of each caste in the caste hierarchy. For an outsider it is only possible to say categorically that the Vaishnavas (Brahmin), Lingayats and Vokkaligas ranked high on the social ladder. The Lingayats had higher ritual position than the Vokkaligas. The Ediga, Naik and Adi Karnatakas came last in the rank. Achari, Kammara, Kumbhar, Barber and Dhobi were service castes. For them also, the rank order was quite ambiguous. These could, however, be ranked as middle castes. The maintenance of social distance between the high, middle and low groups of castes was apparent, but the social distance between the castes constituting each group was less clear.

The physical separation of dwellings in Seshagirihalli reflected an acute form of segregation based on caste. Ganakal, with its one numerically dominant caste, was different; the service castes were not segregated, though the Adi Karnatakas were, their houses being concentrated in the north-west part of the village.

The maintenance of social distance was reflected in the spontaneous behaviour of members of different castes towards each other. For example, in Seshagirihalli, untouchability was not practised in the presence of senior government functionaries. Water, tea and sometimes even snacks like biscuits were accepted by the members and leaders of the upper castes such as the Vokkaligas from the Adi Karnatakas. An influential leader of the Adi Karnatakas had taken the lead in organizing communal feasts in the village to which important officials from the Bidadi *hobli* and Ramanagaram taluka were invited. But generally, only leaders from the Lingayat and Vokkaliga castes attended the feasts; others from these castes generally reported 'sick', or 'urgent work' at some other place.

Behaviour in institutions such as the village school, nursery school and *bhajan mandali* (prayer group) perhaps reflected the maintenance of social distance most clearly. Except for two, the Lingayats of Inorpalya did not send their children to the village primary school in the main hamlet. There were fifteen students (twelve boys and three girls) from Inorpalya who went to the primary school located at Menchanayakahalli. Parents explained that the village school was only up to primary standard, and eventually their children would have to go to other schools, and as the village school was far away, children would have to walk over the tank bund and cross the highway. (The other school was even farther away and also on the other side of the highway.)

The village primary school was conducted in the prayer hall located in the Vokkaliga locality by a lone teacher. It was observed that generally the Adi Karnataka children occupied the back seats in the class even though there was no deliberate attempt by the teacher at segregation. Cooking and distribution of midday meals in the school (provided with CARE funds under the Applied Nutrition Programme) created problems because they were supposed to be prepared by housewives in rotation, but in fact only the Vokkaliga housewives were involved in the end.

The maintenance of social distance in these villages was measured on the following dimensions: marriage relations, eating together, acceptance of food, water and *bidi*, attending social and religious functions, and use of the common well for drinking water. Table IV.6 indicates the traditional and present position of each caste on each of the above items. From the table it emerges that in both villages, the rigidity of constraints once exercised by various castes in social interaction had been modified, but in varying degrees for the leaders, elders and young people in each caste group.

In general, caste practice in Ganakal was noticeably less extreme than in Seshagirihalli. Untouchability, for example, was no longer practised in Ganakal, and this was not because of any government measures. It was a change caused by social pressure generated within the system. The subtle versions of untouchability practised in schools, temples and other similar public places, and not so subtle version reflected in the settlement pattern in Seshagirihalli, were absent in Ganakal. The distribution of midday meals in the Ganakal village school was without prej-

Table IV.6: Caste and Commensality in Seshagirihalli and Ganakal

Caste	Item		Traditional stand in the past	Seshagirihalli	Ganakal
VAISHNAVA* and LINGAYAT	(a)	Marriage relations	Not outside the sub-caste	Can marry with other sub-castes, but not outside the caste	Would not marry their own daughter outside the sub-caste, but would accept the daughters from other sub-castes
	(b)	Eating together	With the same caste group	Most of them eat with the Vokkaligas but only on special occasions. Leaders however eat even in normal course. No eating together with other caste groups	With Lingayats/Vaishnavas only. On special occasions with others
	(c)	Accepting food	Not from any other caste	Do not accept food from others, however, do eat in restaurants outside their village. In Bidadi and Ramanagaram quite a few of the restaurants are owned by the Lingayats, where they prefer to eat.	Do not accept unless it is cooked by themselves or another Brahmin – eating in restaurants allowed
	(d)	Accepting water	Not from scheduled caste/tribes and Muslims	Same as in the past	Same as in the past
	(e)	Accepting *bidis*, cigarettes	Smoking not allowed *Did not accept from any one	Accept from Vokkaligas	From all castes
	(f)	Attending social & religious functions	*Those of Vokkaligas generally; special invitees in case of other castes	Participation intimate in case of Vokkaligas; notional in case of other castes; none in case of Muslims	Those of all castes

Caste	Item	Traditional stand in the past	Seshagirihalli	Ganakal
	(g) Physical contacts	Avoided scheduled caste/tribes	Not avoid any	Not avoid any
	(h) Using common drinking water well	Not allowed	It is not resented now although it is not required in their case since Inorpalya is an exclusively Lingayat locality	Use of common well
VOKKALIGAS	(a) Marriage relations	Not outside the sub-caste	Can marry among any sub-caste of Vokkaligas, even other farming caste such as Reddy, Patel and Patil; not with other castes	Can marry any farming caste, such as Reddy, Patel, Patil
	(b) Eating together	With Lingayats, Vaishnavas, Acharis, Bovi and other castes, except scheduled caste/tribes. *Avoided SCs/STs	The majority with Lingayats, Vaishnavas, Acharis, Bovi and other non-scheduled castes/tribes; the younger and educated among them with all castes (without telling their parents/elders)	With all
	(c) Accepting food	From none	From none	From none
	(d) Accepting water	Only from Lingayats, Vaishnavas, Acharis, Bovi and non-scheduled caste/tribes	Younger elements from all castes, elders from Lingayats, Vaishnavas, Acharis, Bovi nd and non-SCs/STs only	From all
	(e) Accepting bidis, cigarettes	– do –	From all	From all
	(f) Attending social and religious functions	In case of all castes, but did not share drinks, and food; just watched and sat through ceremonies *All cases except SCs	In case of castes; also eating and full intermingling in case of non-SCs/STs; only notional participation in case of SCs/STs	All castes

	Column 1	Column 2	Column 3
(g) Physical contacts *Avoided SCs/STs	Did not mind Avoided SCs/STs	Not avoided	Not avoided
(h) Use of common well for drinking water	Avoided drawing water from well used by SCs/STs *Resented use by SCs/STs	Do not mind now (one Vokkaliga lives in Harijan colony and draws water from the common well there)	Not avoided
ACHARIS*, KUMBHAR, KAMMARA, BARBER and DHOBI			
(a) Marriage relations	Not outside their own caste	—	Not outside their caste
(b) Eating together	With Lingayats, Vaishnavas, Vokkaligas, and Backward Castes (BCs)	—	With all except scheduled castes
(c) Accepting food	From all except SCs	—	From all except SCs
(d) Accepting bidis, cigarettes	From all	—	From all
(e) Accepting water	From all except SCs	—	From all except SCs
(f) Attending social and religious functions	Of all castes	—	Of all castes
(g) Physical contacts	Of all castes	—	Of all castes
(h) Use of common drinking water well	Shared with all	—	Shared with all
SCHEDULED TRIBES			
(a) Marriage relations	With own caste	With own caste	—
(b) Eating together	With all, except SCs and Muslims	Eat with all others excepting Muslims	—
(c) Accepting food	From all, except from Muslims	From all except Muslims	—
(d) Accepting water	From all except Muslims	From all except Muslims	—

Caste	Item	Traditional stand in the past	Seshagirihalli	Ganakal
	(e) Accepting *bidis*, cigarettes	From all	From all	—
	(f) Attending social and religious functions	Of all except Muslims	Of all except Muslims	—
	(g) Physical contacts	Most castes avoided them; they avoided Lingayats	Do not avoid any	—
	(h) Use of common drinking water well	Resented by other castes	No restriction now	—
SCHEDULED CASTES†	(a) to (h)	Same as in case of STs	Same as in case of STs	—
NAIK and BOVI (A.Ks.)*	(a) Marriage relations	Within own caste	—	Within own caste
	(b) Eating together	With only own caste groups, all others avoided	—	With all
	(c) Accepting food	From all	—	From all
	(d) Accepting water	From all	—	From all
	(e) Accepting *bidis*, cigarettes	From all	—	From all
	(f) Attending social and religious functions	Of all castes	—	Of all castes
	(g) Physical contacts	Most castes avoided them	—	Do not avoid any
	(h) Use of common drinking water well	Resented by higher castes	—	No restriction now

*Only in Ganakal.
† Only in Seshagirihalli.

udice and quite often the scheduled caste boys were associated with the distribution of food.

These differences between Ganakal and Seshagirihalli can be attributed to three factors: (a) enlightened leadership; (b) the presence of a number of middle, service castes; and (c) the fact that there were several landless households among the dominant caste, namely, Vokkaligas. Interdependence and interaction between the upper caste and service castes could have led to greater commensality and more humane treatment of the lower castes. Also the poor economic condition and number of landless among the Vokkaligas could have been a contributing factor in reducing the social distance between the castes. In contrast to Ganakal, in Seshagirihalli the two caste groups of Lingayat and Vokkaligas on the one hand, and Adi Karnatakas on the other hand, were at the extremes of the ritual status hierarchy. Moreover, almost all the Adi Karnatakas were landless; class division reinforced caste division.

Interaction in Formal Institutions

Bannikuppe village panchayat covered Seshagirihalli and three other revenue villages. It has 14 committee members. The socioeconomic background of the members of the present and previous committees is given in Table IV.7.

The Bannikuppe village panachayat's headquarters was at Bannikuppe. The past and present chairmen and vice-chairmen of the panchayat came from Bannikuppe. Vokkaliga was numerically the dominant caste of the region, and as such had the largest representation in the panchayat. Well-to-do Vokkaligas had dominated this body since its inception.

For some years, indeed, the 14-member committee had been dominated by its former chairman who had strong support in the other three villages, where he had managed to get his supporters elected as panchayat members unopposed in the three elections held so far. Only in Seshagirihalli was voting necessary. His opponents, DN (a Vokkaliga) and N (an Adi Karnataka) had held their seats, but the contests had left a trail of bitterness. It was alleged that this division in Seshagirihalli had provided an excuse for the other members of the panchayat to neglect the development of Seshagirihalli. Many persons in Seshagirihalli resented the attitude of the chairman and his supporters toward their village. In 1975, when enmity between the chairman and an Iyengar (a Vaishnava Brahmin — Iyengar is the surname for the Vaishnava

Table IV.7: Profile of the Leaders of Present Bannikuppe Panchayat

	Name	Village	Caste	Age	Education	Landholdings (in acres)
1.	D (Vice-chairman)	Bannikuppe	Vokkaliga	47	1st std.	7.00
2.	BNN	– do –	– do –	58	4th std.	15.50
3.	(Mrs) N	– do –	– do –	36	–	5.00
4.	B*	– do –	– do –	55	3rd std.	20.00
5.	R	Hejjala	Adi Karnataka (S.C.)	48	–	2.00
6.	DN	Seshagirihalli	Vokkaliga	60	4th std.	15.78
7.	N	– do –	Adi Karnataka (S.C.)	45	4th std.	2.00
8.	H (Chairman)	Kurubakaranahally	Vokkaliga	52	4th std.	10.00
9.	R	– do –	– do –	55	3rd std.	75.00
10.	HT	– do –	Adi Karnataka (S.C.)	48	–	4.50
11.	(Mrs) R	– do –	Vaishnava	46	–	2.50
12.	G	Jadenhallipalya	Vokkaliga	55	–	10.60
13.	CR	– do –	– do –	52	2nd std.	5.00
14.	(Mrs) B	– do –	– do –	46	–	3.40

*Since died.

community in some states) from Seshagirihalli, came to a head, the latter gave evidence to the District Collector that the chairman had misappropriated funds. The chairman was removed from office by the Collector, but he saw to it that the Iyengar was completely excluded from Seshagirihalli village through a complete socioeconomic boycott. The electoral battles and personal animosities of leaders had embittered the relationships between the members of different castes as well as within each caste.

Apart from the Farmers' Service Co-operative Society (FSS), which will be discussed in detail later, the other formal organization was the School Betterment Committee, established in 1975. It was expected to perform two functions — to persuade reluctant parents to send their children regularly to school, and, since the school had no building of its own, to try to get grants for the building and for equipping the school. The committee consisted of the village panchayat chairman as president, three Vokkaligas from the main hamlet and one Adi Karnataka from the Harijan colony as its members, and the teacher of the village primary school as member-secretary. The committee was expected to meet every month but did not do so. The lone Harijan member felt that the committee was a farce. According to him, the only thing the committee discussed was how the CARE food was to be cooked and distributed, and it did succeed in persuading Vokkaliga housewives to cook the food by rotation.

Like Seshagirihalli, the population of Ganakal also had links with two formal institutions, namely, Ganakal village panchayat and the FSS. Both these institutions had jurisdiction over a wider area. The panchayat covered three other villages, and the FSS covered eight other village panchayats.

The panchayat had thirteen members and was dominated by big farmers, who constituted ten of its members, eight of whom were Vokkaligas. They were elderly and not highly educated (Table IV.8). After 1968, PG was replaced by GB, another Vokkaliga from Ganakal, who remained as panchayat chairman thereafter. After 1968, the socio-economic character of the panchayat members had also changed. In the present panchayat, the landless and small farmers are better represented, their number having gone up from three to seven. Also there is better representation of the backward class, and the scheduled caste and service caste, whose number went up from three to six.

Table IV.8: Profile of Members of Present Ganakal Panchayat

Sl. No.	Name	Village	Caste	Age	Education	Landholdings (in acres)
1.	GB (Chairman)	Ganakal	Vokkaliga	48	8th std.	10.00
2.	S (Vice-chairman)	– do –	– do –	48	4th std.	8.00
3.	(Mrs) H	– do –	– do –	50	–	5.00
4.	M	– do –	– do –	48	4th std.	4.00
5.	PM	Kempadapana-hally	Kumbhar	45	4th std.	12.00
6.	SR	– do –	Reddy	38	4th std.	20.00
7.	(Mrs) LD	– do –	Banajiga (BC)	38	–	–
8.	V	Betengere	Tigadara (BC)	52	3rd std.	15.00
9.	MB	– do –	Bovi (SC)	48	–	–
10.	MVB	– do –	– do –	68	–	2.00
11.	V	Kakaramana-hally	– do –	60	4th std.	4.00
12.	M	– do –	Vokkaliga	50	4th std.	20. 00
13.	KSB	– do –	– do –	45	4th std.	3.00

There had been a long battle for the leadership of the panchayat between PG, the previous chairman, and GB, the present chairman. PG was an elderly man who had excellent contacts outside the village. His eventual electoral defeat was ascribed to his indifference towards the well-being of the general public, and concern to profit himself and his supporters. In particular, he alienated himself from the Harijans who were a significant group in Ganakal and Betangere (another village in the panchayat). GB, on the other hand, helped some Harijans in getting land from the surplus land available after the operation of the land ceiling Act, and thus won their support. GB was popular because he was ready to listen to others and willing to help them. This helped him a great deal in his first term as panchayat chairman since at that time his supporters were in a minority. Afterwards he gained complete control of the panchayat.

Factional politics persisted even after GB took over. However, it never reached explosive proportions, due mainly to the efforts of GN who was a retired school teacher and was related to GB. He played a moderating role between the parties and kept the conflict within reasonable limits. The panchayat, therefore, functioned as an institution for the village as a whole rather than for a particular group.

The Role of Informal Leaders

The five influential persons of Seshagirihalli were: P, a Lingayat from Inorpalya; DN and VN, two Vokkaligas from the main hamlet; and N and R, two Adi Karnatakas from the Harijan colony. DN and N were also members of the village panchayat. Each of these five was leader of a faction. The disposition of these leaders towards each other decided the functioning of various activities undertaken in the village, P, DB and VN could generally work together since their interests normally did not clash. They did not, however, see eye to eye with R and N, who represented Harijan interests. R was a newcomer in the village. He was formerly a social welfare minister in Karnataka State. In 1975 he decided to settle down in this village and purchased a six-acre piece of land. R did not establish any rapport with P, DN and VN, thinking that, being a politician of some standing, he would be able to exercise influence over the local people. This, however, did not happen. He also antagonized the panchayat chairman, a Vokkaliga, by more or less demanding permission to build an outhouse on his own land. The chairman resented ths approach and saw to it that permission was refused. R, however, went ahead with the construction of the outhouse, which was still going on at the time of the study. The outcome was awaited with interest.

There were other reasons why R was not popular with the other local leaders. When he was a minister he sanctioned the Janata Housing Scheme for the scheduled castes of Seshagirihalli. He also brought another 15 Harijan families from outside to settle in their colony. It was a device to strengthen his local power base. He organized the local and new Harijans in the Harijan and Tribal Youth Association. His expectation was that since both Lingayats and Vokkaligas depended on the Harijan labour for their farming operations, placing the Harijan labour under this control would establish his power position in the village completely. There was a general feeling among the local Lingayats and Vokkaligas that R had a vested interested in the continued poverty and destitution of the SCs and STs. According to them, once their lot improved, they would disown R's leadership. Even VN, the Vokkaliga leader of the Harijans, was at odds with R. As a government functionary (the school teacher), he was to promote the family planning programme. But R's supporters took advantage of the programme's having acquired a bad name and tried to discredit VN. Since then VN and R have fallen out.

It was alleged that R had forbidden the SC and ST people under his influence even to talk to government officials and outside visitors without consulting him. Due to this they were not getting the benefits of many government programmes. He himself employed about 15 local Harijans as daily workers on his farm and the general belief was that he did not pay them adequately.

The formation of the Youth Association provoked some reaction from the Vokkaligas and Lingayats. In the last two cropping seasons, the number of Harijans employed by the farmers of the main hamlet and Inorpalya had declined considerably. Secondly, through their contacts with the revenue officials, the Vokkaligas saw to it that the members of SCs and STs were ordered to stop cultivating government waste-land which they had been doing illegally for quite some time. Thus, the formation of the Harijan and Tribal Youth Association led to further polarization of caste groups and increased tensions.

The *bhajan mendali* (prayer groups) had once been a meeting point for members of all castes. In the last three or four years, however, it had become the preserve of the Vokkaligas alone. Though there was no prohibition for Adi Karnatakas or Lingayats, they did not attend the meetings any more.

In Ganakal, there were three influential persons, namely PG, the ousted village panchayat chairman; GB, the present chairman; and VH, the sub-postmaster, who was a rallying point for the Harijans and SCs.

PG and GB were Vokkaligas while VH himself belonged to a scheduled caste. GB held a formal position in the panchayat, and VH in the FSS, and each was influential in village life. These three leaders each had a well-knit support group.

PG drew his support from among the Vokkaligas, particularly the well-to-do. He was quite old and PS, the police patel, who had been acting as his right-hand man, was in the process of assuming the mantle of leadership of the group.

GB, on the other hand, not only had as his supporters the Vokkaligas, but also members of other castes, notably the service castes. He was also on good terms with VH, the scheduled caste leader, through whom he was assured of the vote and support of SC members. GB was tutored as a leader by GN, a retired school teacher and close relative. It was GN who operated behind the scene and charted out the strategies for the group. He also exercised a moderating influence on the factional politics in the village.

Three factors contributed to making VH a leader: (a) he was educated and had a job as sub-postmaster; (b) the Vokkaliga group was evenly divided, and members of SCs constituted an important segment that could tilt the scales in favour of either of the two groups; and (c) he had the support of some non-SC leaders at the district level who made him a director of the FSS. VH was not very assertive, but by deft handling of his SC group, he succeeded in getting land for quite a few SC members in Ganakal.

Cohesion and Solidarity

Seshagirihalli, with its three distinct caste-based localities, did not operate as a single social unit. For the solution of most of the issues facing them, such as drinking water, irrigation, electricity, housing, land distribution, and other social facilities, people in the three localities did not come together, mainly because their interests did not coincide. Housing and land distribution were of concern mainly to the landless Adi Karnataka households, irrigation and power were problems mainly for the Lingayat and Vokkaliga farming households. Since the localities were widely spaced, each group wanted its own drinking well within its locality, not so much for caste reasons as for convenience.

There was only one occasion in the whole calendar year when the entire village participated in a single activity. This was the *Puja* of the Gramdouta Mutreya (worship of village deity), organized some time in the month of April. Every household participated in the *Puja*. However, the participation itself was both collective and individual. The ceremony did have some elements of community solidarity inasmuch as all the households offered ownership to the same village deity, on the same day and time, at the same place, and took part in the procession. But the offerings and the eating parts of the ceremony were individual/ kin-group activities. While there was 'eating together' there was no sharing of food.

There was no other instance where the village demonstrated its cohesiveness. On the contrary, it seemed divisions in the village had enabled successive panchayat chairmen to ignore problems of village economic development.

Compared to Seshagirihalli, Ganakal showed a higher degree of cohesiveness and solidarity. People were used to coming together for social, religious and economic activities. Over a period of time, the community had constructed five temples – two within the settlement, and three just outside the village, towards which the people contributed about Rs 20,000. Labour was offered free by people belonging to different castes. The response for the construction of these temples was spontaneous, since it was believed that different deities would bestow their favours on the entire village. These temples were constructed through collective efforts, and as such were collectively owned by the entire village community.

Religious ceremonies involving the whole village were common. Arrangements for these were quite elaborate. The five temples had five separate priests. Three among them were from the priest castes, namely, Vaishnava and Lingayat. The remaining two were Vokkaligas. This itself indicated the broader outlook of the Ganakal population. There were particular days for the worship of each deity. People of all castes participated with equal enthusiasm in all the activities associated with it.

The village celebrated Independence Day (15 August), Republic Day (26 January), and Children's Day (14 November), which was Nehru's birthday. All these were celebrated at the village school and consequently the participation was limited to the school children, the teachers and the panchayat office-bearers and a few other educated villagers. The panchayat spent Rs 25 on Independence Day and Republic Day distributing sweets to the children. On children's day it distributed slates, books and school dress to SC and ST children.

On many social occasions such as birth, *Mumdan*: ceremonial first shaving of head; *Upanayam*: ceremony for wearing the sacred thread by

Brahmins and some other higher castes; marriage or death, people helped each other. Participation on some of these occasions (e.g. death) was restricted to the affinal and consanguineous relatives. On other occasions, the villagers participated in different capacities. In a marriage of a daughter of one Vokkaliga, for example, the non-Vokkaligas helped the family in various ways such as lending utensils and cots, helping in the cooking; and at the time of the feasts, attending to the bride's relatives and so on. Close relatives and friends also provided help in the form of material and monetary contributions.

In addition to co-operation among people on religious, secular and social occasions, there were instances of co-operation and mutual assistance during farming operations. This type of co-operation, however, was apparent at the individual level. At the times of sowing and harvesting, help was sought and given, generally on a reciprocal basis. There were also instances when help was given, especially to medium and large farmers, in return for the use of their implements and bullocks.

6 DEVELOPMENT EFFORTS

The Community Development Programme and its Impact

This section will describe the CDP as it operated in the two sample villages, indicating in the process the inadequacies of its approach; it is these which prompt a detailed examination of a more specific programme — the Farmers' Service Co-operative Society.

The CDP was introduced in Mysore State (now Karnataka) in 1952 on the pattern followed all over India. By 1963-4 the entire state was covered by 268 CD blocks. On the all-India pattern, a block covered a population of 66,000-100,000. The Ramanagaram taluka (or lower level revenue district) in which Seshagirihalli and Ganakal were situated, was comparatively small (population about 140,000 in 1971), and so was covered by one block, Bidadi Hobli — see Figure IV.2 — being situated within it. (Some of the bigger talukas were subdivided into as many as three blocks.) Initially, it had a Block Development Officer, (BDO), eight Extension Officers (for agriculture, animal husbandry, rural engineering, co-operation, social education — male and female, panchayat and rural industries), twelve village-level workers (VLWs), of whom two were women, and a supporting office staff. Again in accord with the all-India pattern, it was given Rs 12 lakhs for a Phase 1 of five years and Rs 5 lakhs for a Phase 2 of another five years.

In the programme's early stages, the BDO acted mainly as a co-ordinator for the activities of the various extension officers of the government technical departments, and the extension staff were also under the control of their respective state departments for technical advice and guidance. An attempt to co-ordinate these technical efforts and put them under popular control came, in Mysore State, with the Panchayat and Local Board Act of 1959, which introduced a three-tier system of (1) village panchayats, (2) a taluka development board (TDB) or panchayat samithi at the taluka/block level, and (3) a district development council at the district level.

The village panchayat was elected by secret ballot. For the TDB each taluka was divided into constituencies, each electing two or three members. Finally, the district development council consisted of the presidents of the TDBs within each district. The MLAs, MLCs and MPs within the district were its *ex officio* members. There was also provision for co-option of SC/ST members onto the district council and the TDB. There was no direct link between the village panchayat and the TDB or the district council, since elections to the two latter bodies were direct. Neither had powers to sanction or modify the budget of the village panchayat. However, the TDB exercised general control over the activities of the village panchayat, while the district council sanctioned the TDB's budget and advised government on the distribution of grants to TDBs in the district.

The main sources of village panchayat income were property tax, cess on land revenue or rent, and vehicle and professional tax. Of the total land revenue, 35 per cent was given to the village panchayat as grant. The main sources of income for the TDB were funds from the CDP, funds from other plan and non-plan schemes, and taxes and cess. Initially, 30 per cent of land revenue was received by the TDB in addition to a local cess on land revenue and water rate. In recent years, the distribution of land revenue between village panchayats and the TDB has been in the ratio of 40:60. The district council, being a supervisory and co-ordinating body, received no share of land revenue or taxes.

Each village panchayat had a secretary who worked under the administrative control of the *sarpanch* (chairman) of the village panchayat. At the TDB level, the original block staff were transferred to the Board. The BDO served as the chief executive officer of the TDB, and was under the President of the TDB. The Collector (the senior civil servant of the whole district) was the *ex officio* chairman of the district council.

There were several administrative repercussions of the new arrangement. Kulkani[1] reported three direct results of decentralization. The technical departments, such as agriculture, animal husbandry, minor irrigation, etc., transferred to the TDBs a number of schemes for implementation on terms and conditions prescribed by the government, but the field officials of the technical departments then often did not assume as much responsibility as previously, and many development schemes suffered. Secondly, the technical departments at the state level often tried to shift responsibility for their own shortcomings onto the development department which was handling the CD institutions. Thirdly, the state development and technical departments both issued directions on day-to-day functions, and asked for reports in such numbers from the field officials that in practice very little time was left for extension officers to attend to field programmes.

In 1969, the government directed all departments to operate their programmes through the TDBs in so far as they could be split up on a taluka basis. The extension staff from the respective departments were to work increasingly through the TDBs to implement their programmes. 'But a trend set in during the Fourth Plan for different departments to create their parallel independent staff at block (taluka) level on one ground or the other. The horizontal administration gave place to the vertical hierarchy.'

Some idea of the activities of the programme can be gained from the breakdown of its expenditure in the years when it was at its peak between 1960-1 and 1965-6. For the whole state it was as follows: expenses of block headquarters took 33 per cent: agriculture and animal husbandry 9.5 per cent; irrigation and land reclamation 22 per cent; education 5 per cent; social education 5 per cent; health and sanitation 10 per cent; communications 4 per cent; village industry 5 per cent; housing of project staff 5 per cent; and rural housing 2 per cent.[2] Thus during this period, nearly 37 per cent of the amount was spent on block staff and their housing, and about 31 per cent on agriculture, animal husbandry and irrigation. While 5 per cent of expenditure went on housing block staff, only 2 per cent went to the housing of the rural poor.

Supplementary contributions by the people had been substantial in the early period — equivalent to about 25 per cent of total government expenditure in the 1950s. This contribution, however, rapidly declined therefore, from 13 per cent in 1961 to 5 per cent in 1966.[3]

The Ramanagaram TDB: 1971/2 to 1976/7

The total impact of the TDB can perhaps be gauged from the fact that its annual expenditure in this period averaged some Rs 1.8 per inhabitant, with revenue and expenditure showing a declining trend, due to loss of grants and contributions which made up about 20 per cent of income. As for expenditure, about 61 per cent went on public development works — construction and repair of buildings (mainly schools), new welfare buildings — e.g. the community and prayer halls, roads and bridges, drainage works, hotels, houses for teachers at special Harijan schools and a further 3 per cent on small irrigation works.

The second highest expenditure (17 per cent) was on 'General Administration' which covered the expenses of the TDB (monthly honorarium for president and vice-president, travel allowance to members, meeting and election expenses, receptions for VIPs, salary of

officers and staff (including office expenditure), and 'public' welfare
expenditure, employees' pensions, purchase and repair of jeep, petrol
expenses, audit fees, rent and tax on building, legal expenses, etc.).

Education received a little over 3 per cent of total expenditure,
which was divided between adult education, books and maps, assistance to kindergarten schools, women's and youth clubs, community
training, and taluka sports. The salaries of the school teachers were paid
by the state government and so were not part of the TDB budget.

Direct expenditure for health was again relatively small (about 2
per cent plus another 1.5 per cent from the construction budget)
because salary costs were borne by the state. The TDB established a
Public Health Centre (PHC) at Bidadi in 1965. It has also posted trained
auxiliary nurses and midwives (ANM) to various places in the taluka.
Between 1970 and 1975, 15 to 20 per cent of the population used the
services of the PHC at Bidadi every year, the annual average number of
patients per day varying from 60 to 80. In spite of maternal and child
welfare services provided by the doctors, trained midwives, auxiliary
nurses and *dais*, the rates of infant and maternal mortality and of still
births remained very high.

The health services also looked after preventive programmes such as
vaccination for typhoid and smallpox, the collection of blood smears
under the National Malaria Eradication Programme, and the distribution of medicines under such programmes. They also handled the
family planning programme. Between 1970-1 and 1975-6 the numbers
of vasectomies, tubectomies and IUCD insertions were 103, 1,928 and
691 respectively. The number of persons using conventional contra-
ceptives was 2,156.

It is worth noting that in its expenditure statement the TDB does
not treat irrigation, agriculture, animal husbandry, forestry, industry,
mining, etc., as major heads of expenditure. These occur incidentally
under other heads. The TDB's central concern is not economic and production-oriented activities which would lead to economic development.
The total expenditure on irrigation, agriculture and animal husbandry
(scattered through the expenditure statement in various places) was only
7.5 per cent of total expenditure, which included small irrigation
works, exhibitions, conferences on agriculture, the construction and
running of veterinary hospitals, dispensaries, an artificial insemination
centre, extension efforts to popularize high-yielding varieties and plant
protection measures, and the development of fish-farming. Activities
such as dairy and various agro-industries, small-scale and household
industries, forestry, mining, etc., which could generate employment in

the region, and consequently increase income, were not within the juris-diction of the TDB.

It is necessary to emphasize here that the TDB was not the only agency undertaking development work in the region. Various technical departments continued to implement directly a number of plan and non-plan schemes. For example, the Public Works Department (PWD) through its district-level agency was responsible for the construction and maintenance of district roads. The TDBs were made responsible only for village roads. Similarly, major and medium irrigation projects were handled directly by the irrigation branch of the PWD. Major area development projects and programmes financed by the World Bank such as the Drought Prone Area Programme, and Command Area Pro-gramme, were handled by separate project authorities. A number of agri-cultural development and animal husbandry programmes, as well as health and family planning programmes, were handled directly by the respective technical departments of the state government.

Development Work by the TDB and other Departments in the Sample Villages

The development work undertaken by TDB Ramanagaram in Seshagiri-halli and Ganakal over the last ten years (either with its own funds or those of other agencies) is listed in Tables IV.9 and IV.10. In Sesha-girihalli almost the whole amount was spent on the construction and maintenance of buildings and roads. Very recently, an amount was directly spent on the construction of houses for the SCs and STs. Only in Ganakal did funds directly reach the small marginal farmers in the form of a subsidy for implements, a wheat demonstration, and sheep loans.

To these lists should be added the initiatives taken by other govern-ment departments and directly implemented by them rather than through the TDB. In Seshagirihalli, several years ago the PWD con-structed the tank bund which contributed to proper water storage in the village tank. In all, 37 farmers were able to irrigate about 16 acres of land using the tank water. They paid a water cess of Rs 544 per year. The Bannikuppe panchayat also earned a revenue of Rs 100 per year by sales of humus gathered in the tank. The Education Department gave an annual grant for running the primary school in Seshagirihalli, though there was no separate school building in the village. The Land Development Bank (LDB) gave a loan of Rs 11,500 to a big farmer

Table IV.9: Development Work Undertaken in Seshagirihalli Village by TDB Ramanagaram

Programme	Year	Units	Amount spent (Rs)	Funds provided by
Kitchen room for ANP	1965-6	1	255.00	SWD
Bhajan Mandir building	1967-8	1	2500.00	SWD
L-shaped drain	1971-2	1	364.08	CD
Repairs to temples	1971-2	1	55.95	SWD
Drinking water well	1971-2	1	6,062.00	CD
Community centre building	1975-6	1	13,900.00	Rs 10,000 by state government and Rs 3,900 by TDB
Construction of a culvert	1975-6	1	2,500.00	CD
Approach road	1975-6	1	1,744.00	CD
House sites	1975-6	30	(land-free)	SWD
Janata housing	1975-6	20	30,000.00	SWD
Total			57,381.03	

SWD: Social Welfare Department
CD: Community Development

Table IV.10: Development Work Undertaken in Ganakal Village by TDB Ramanagaram

Programme	Year	Units	Amount spent (Rs)	Fund provided by
School buildings	1969-70	2	4,000.00	
Drinking water well	1970-1	1	343.00	
House sites	1975-6	26	741.00 (land free)	SWD
Implement subsidy	— do —	1	17.00	
Wheat demonstration subsidy	— do —	1	200.00	
Sheep loan subsidy to marginal farmers	— do —	4	1,980.00	SFDA
Sheep loan subsidy to small farmers	— do —	4	1,500.00	SFDA
Total			8,781.00	

SFDA: Small Farmers' Development Agency

(living in Bangalore) for developing a coconut garden, and installing a pump-set. No other person received any loan from the LDB.

In Ganakal, between 1965 and 1971, four farmers received loans totalling Rs 16,200 from the LDB for digging wells and installing pump-sets. The PWD repaired the Ganakal tank several years ago. The Education Department gave a grant for running the primary-cum-middle school at Ganakal. One of the five buildings in which the school was being run was in a very dilapidated condition. The Forestry Department has so far not taken any interest in Seshagirihalli or Ganakal. In a nearby cluster of villages it had, however, developed a large tract of eucalyptus forest which proved very useful to the local population. The Department of Sericulture had introduced a sericulture scheme in recent years.

It is clear from the above that there were no planned, systematic efforts by the state departments for the development of Seshagirihalli and Ganakal, and for that matter of any village. Their efforts were isolated and sporadic.

Development Work by Village Panchayats

The onus did not only rest on the TDB and the various departments of the state government; the village panchayats were also expected to contribute to general development work as well as undertaking projects with their own funds. The functions given to the village panchayats were:

to maintain health and sanitation in the village
to provide drinking water
to maintain approach roads and streets
to provide facilities for education (including contributions towards the building of schools, and free clothing and textbooks to SC and ST students)
to provide house-sites to the landless
to maintain government land
to celebrate national festivals.

The village panchayats were involved to some degree in executing the projects listed in Tables IV.9 and IV.10, but took very little initiative of their own. In Seshagirihalli, the only major effort of the Bannikuppe panchayat was a contribution to the construction of two drinking wells. Even though permission for electrifying the street lights had been received five years earlier, the panchayat had not shown any interest in following this up. Two individual farmers, however, got electricity connections for their tubewells through their personal influence at higher levels.

In Ganakal, the village panchayat had contributed about Rs 5,000 to the cost of school buildings over the years. It also contributed Rs 450 for the construction of two drinking wells. The other development works undertaken by the panchayat in the village were: construction of part of an approach road from Ganakal to Bidadi (3 km), repairs to the village tank, drainage for part of one street, the electrification of the village and provision of nine street lights, an approach road from Ganakal to Betengere (2 km) and distribution of clothing to SC/ST students. As mentioned earlier, the entire cost of construction of five temples was borne by the villagers themselves. These temples were constructed between 1936 and 1976.

Neither Bannikuppe nor Ganakal panchayat had an income large enough for it to undertake any major development programme. In 1975-6, their budgeted income was Rs 6,660 and Rs 2,967 respectively — mostly raised internally by rents and taxes. Consequently, the panchayats were hardly involved in development work. The Bannikuppe panchayat, for example, budgeted to spend its Rs 6,310 in 1975-6 on the following items: general administration, Rs 925; public protection, Rs 925 (street lights, insurance and malaria preventive measures); panchayat public works, Rs 2,500 (on drainage); public health, Rs 60 (on transportation of garbage, vaccination and control of rabies); public facilities, Rs 500 (for radio, library, Independence Day arrangements); grants and contributions, Rs 200 (to Red Cross, free-aid medicine, etc.); and miscellaneous expenses, Rs 1,200.

It is not surprising, in consequence, that where there has been innovation and increased productivity in agricultural extension work, only 23 and 13 per cent of gross cropped area was under high-yielding varieties in Ganakal and Seshagirihalli respectively, primarily due to lack of irrigation. Only a few farmers could afford to invest on their own in items such as wells and pump-sets. After acquiring the means to irrigate his land, one farmer in Seshagirihalli (who lived in Bangalore) had switched over to a coconut plantation from food grain crops. A second opted for sugarcane and vegetables. A third had switched over to growing tuber-roses which he supplied to Bangalore. In Ganakal, too, ten farmers had dug wells. Six of them had pump-sets (three energized and three diesel operated). All of them were economically better off. After developing irrigation facilities they went in for commercial crops such as sugarcane, groundnuts and vegetables. Conditions for the rest of the farmers and the landless remained comparatively unchanged. The official development programme, it seems may have added a few welfare trimmings to village life, but had very little impact on its economic structure or the distribution of wealth and opportunity. We turn therefore to a particular programme whose aims were more explicitly geared to promoting the economic development of one disadvantaged group, the small and marginal farmers.

Notes

1. H.L. Kulkarni, 'Panchayati Raj in Mysore', in R.N. Haldipur and V.R.K. Paramahamsa (eds.), *Local Government Institutions in India: Some Aspects* (National Institute of Community Development, Hyderabad, 1970), pp. 172-3.

2. Paul Karipurath, 'Community Development and Extension Programme in Mysore State' in T.K. Medi (ed.), *Economic Development and Social Change in Mysore State* (Kamataka University, Dharwar, 1971), pp. 272-3.

3. Ibid., pp. 274-5.

7 THE FARMERS' SERVICE CO-OPERATIVE SOCIETY

Background

The Farmers' Service Co-operative Society (FSS) is the latest in a line of institutional innovations to promote the productivity and welfare of small and marginal farmers. The concern with such farmers has a long history. Between 1965 and 1970, the Planning Commission sponsored a few studies on the problems of small farmers. The findings of these and many other studies[1] clearly indicated that the administrative machinery and credit institutions had, by and large, ignored this group. The outcome, after a committee had considered the matter,[2] was a provision in the Fourth Five Year Plan to set up 46 Small Farmers' Development Agencies (SFDAs) in various parts of India, and an additional number of Marginal Farmers and Agricultural Labourers Development Schemes (MFALS).

In the Fourth Plan period, four SFDAs and three MFALs were sanctioned for the government of Karnataka, and one of the first SFDAs was in Bangalore. Its task was to use subsidies, interest support grants and technical advice to improve the flow of credit, supplies and know-how to small farmers, defined as those with five acres or less, or half that area of Class 1 irrigated land. (Marginal farmers were defined as those with less than half these amounts.) Up to the end of March 1975 it had identified 45,114 small farmers distributed in 705 villages in Bangalore district. Out of this, 29,269 (about 65 per cent) were reported to be enrolled and 27,742 (about 61 per cent) were reported to have benefited,[3] the loans they received — through the SFDA's interest support — amounting to about Rs 750 per capita during the four-year period or an average of Rs 188 per annum.[4] In physical terms these 27,742 small farmers received: dug-wells, 1469; pump-sets, 840; milch-cattle, 1475; poultry units, 43; sheep units, 830; piggery units, 73; and the number of rural artisans helped was 320.[5] Even if it is assumed that different small farmers received these benefits, the total number of beneficiaries would be 5,050, the rest presumably received working capital — or consumption support.

Farmers' Service Co-operative Society

The farmers assisted by the SFDA still had to compete with large farmers for loans from regular credit institutions. The need for a new institution to provide credit specifically for the small and marginal farmers had already been indicated by the National Commission on Agriculture in 1971. It urged that small and marginal farmers needed, not funds alone, but the timely availability of a package of inputs and services, along with technical advice and supporting services for storage, transport, processing and marketing, preferably through a single contact point.[6] It recommended that

a Farmers' Service Society should be formed as registered cooperative body, with bye-laws to ensure autonomy, efficient management and freedom from official intervention to provide the integrated agricultural credit service to the small and marginal farmers and agricultural labourers . . .

the Farmers' Service Society will be the sole agency taking care of all the developmental needs of the small and marginal farmers and agricultural labourers, either directly or by special arrangements with other agencies.[7]

To exclude large farmers, the Commission recommended that '*only* those farmers, agricultural labourers, and village artisans who qualify for receiving assistance under the SDFA and MFAL projects should be eligible for membership of the Farmers' Service Societies. Other sections of the farming community might be made eligible for associate membership for services without enjoying the rights of voting. As agriculture includes animal husbandry, fisheries, and farm forestry, involvement of the bigger farmers in the service societies might be beneficial in some cases — for example in milk-processing and marketing, if a Rural Milk Service Organization were to be set up in a particular area.[8]

The Bidadi FSS

The Farmers' Service Co-operative Society Ltd, Bidadi, was the first FSS to be registered in the country. It was sponsored by Canara Bank and was registered in June 1973. The listed objectives of the society were:

1. To grant short, medium and long-term loans to members, with special preference to small and marginal farmers and agricultural labourers.
2. To procure, purchase and supply agricultural inputs such as fertilizers, seeds, manures, implements, cattle-feed, pesticides and raw materials, machines, appliances, etc., for cottage and small-scale industries undertaken by members, and domestic requirements and other necessary supplies.
3. To procure, purchase and sell agricultural produce, products of dairies, poultries, etc., and cottage/small-scale industrial products of its members to their best advantage, directly or through co-operative marketing societies or other agencies.
4. To promote or own or hire agricultural-processing units such as handpounding, rice and flour mills, oil crushers, etc.
5. To organize agricultural service activities by owning or hiring agricultural machinery such as tractors, power tillers, bulldozers, sprayers and pumpsets, etc., for the benefit of the members.
6. To improve the breed of the members' live stock by owning or arranging for the provision of stud bulls, breeding rams, pedigree stock, etc., and also to run or support a model dairy farm, etc.
7. To own or hire go-downs to provide facilities to store the products of agriculture and agro-based industries for sale, or to store the agricultural inputs meant for sale, or for such activities as are in the general interest of the community.
8. To purchase, own, or obtain on lease, land for running a model farm for carrying on agricultural operations and for the dissemination of modern agricultural techniques.
9. To undertake the construction of roads, sinking of wells, construction and repair of buildings, tanks, canals, irrigation works and other job works, etc., by entering into contract with the government, local bodies or individuals and carrying out the contract through, or with the help of, members, with a view to providing seasonal employment.
10. To organize, execute, own and maintain lift irrigation schemes.
11. To encourage generally thrift, self-help and co-operation among the members.
12. To open branches, depots, shops, showrooms and workshops in furtherance of the objectives under the by-laws.
13. To provide an agricultural extension service for the benefit of members by employing the necessary technical personnel.
14. To raise funds by way of deposits and borrowings from members

and non-members, including co-operative and commercial banks, financial institutions and the government.

15. To act as an agent of the LDB or the marketing or processing society which has jurisdiction over the area of operation of the society, for the disbursement and recovery of long-term loans or the supply of agricultural inputs or consumer goods or the sale of agricultural and dairy produce.

16. Generally to undertake such other activities as may be conducive to the promotion of the economic interest of members, the overall development of the area and the objects specified above, as may be approved by the financing bank.

It is worth noting that the by-laws specifically mentioned that, while granting short, medium and long-term loans to its members, the society was to show special preference to the small and marginal farmers and agricultural labourers. In case of all other 'objectives' (2 to 16), there was no compulsion on the society to show such preference to this class.

The authorized share capital of the society was Rs 205,000, made up of 10,000 A class shares of Rs 10 each, 100 B class shares of Rs 1,000 each, and 5,000 C class shares of Rs 1 each. A-class share were allotted to individual members above the age of 18. B-class shares were allotted only to the state government, and C-class shares to nominal members. A-class shares were divided into two parts: part I included those who were identified as small farmers, marginal farmers, and agricultural labourers; part II included all other individual members. No fixed number or proportion was reserved for part I or part II. Thus, the original recommendation of the National Commission on Agriculture that *only* small and marginal farmers, agricultural labourers, and village artisans should be members of the FSS was not taken seriously.

There was, by contrast, an attempt to bias *control* of the society towards the small farmers. Five of the seven elected members of the Board of Directors were to be part I A-class members and only two from the part II group. They were balanced, however, by five nominated members — four by the Registrar of Co-operative Societies, and one by the financing bank — in this case the Canara Bank. The Managing Director, appointed by the Board with the bank's approval, also sat on the Board.

In fact, no elections have yet taken place. The by-laws provided for nomination of the first Board and elections thereafter. However, at the end of the first term (plus a six-month extension) the State Registrar of Co-operatives used his legal powers to reduce the area of jurisdiction of the society from 50 to 36 villages (15 to 9 panchayat areas), an area thought to be more manageable, given the society's resources. This 'fresh start' in September 1976 was deemed to justify another three years under a nominated Board.

Of the five 'elected, part I' members, two belonged to a scheduled caste, and were marginal farmers. The other three were small farmers only in the technical sense of the term, since the landholdings in their individual names were small. However, all three were reported to be very well off, and politically influential at the taluka level. The two members in the 'elected, part II' category were also well-off persons. The six nominated members of the Board were: (1) Assistant Registrar of Co-operative Societies; (2) Assistant Director of Agriculture; (3) Assistant Director of Animal Husbandry; (4) Block Development Officer; and (5) Manager, Canara Bank, Bidadi branch. Apart from one of the SC members who was replaced by a caste fellow, all the Board members were retained for the second term.

The by-laws and rules of the FSS did not provide a geographical jurisdiction for each elected member of the Board. However, an informal 'sharing out' of panchayats did take place, and each member scrutinized and processed the loan applications of the FSS members belonging to the villages under his jurisdiction. Each thus acquired an 'influence zone'.

The society had 11 persons on its roll; a managing director, a manager, two clerks, two attendants, one driver and one cleaner. There was also a technical cell which consisted of one agricultural extension officer and two VLWS. The managing director was an employee of the Canara Bank on loan to the FSS. His salary was paid by the bank. The three employees of the technical cell belonged to the Agriculture Department of the state government, and were also on loan. Their salaries were paid by the government. The main functions of the technical cell were to assess the credit requirements of the members, help them to get credit and also take an active role in the recovery of loans. The society paid the salary of the remaining staff. Other assistance to the society came from the SFDA in the form of a risk fund, subsidies for medium-term loans, and payments of share capital for a number of small and marginal farmers.

Performance of FSS Bidadi

The performance of the society can be measured by (a) the percentage of small and marginal farmers, and agricultural labourers who received benefit from it, (b) the magnitude of benefit received by them, and by other classes of farmers and household, (c) the nature of activities undertaken, and (d) profit made. These areas are considered below.

Membership

Tables IV.11 and IV.12 provide basic information about the society and its activities. There were certain deficiencies in the basic information provided in the FSS documents, as indicated by the footnotes to Table IV.11. Apart from the uncertainties there noted, it is not clear whether the number 41 reported against agricultural labourers (Table IV.11) was of individuals or families. Agricultural labourers (as individuals) and small or marginal farmer families are clearly not exclusive categories.

Table IV.11: Basic Information on FSS Bidadi (as at 31 Aug. 1976)

1.	Date of registration	6 Jun. 1973
2.	Date of commencement of business	28 Jun. 1973
3.	Area of operation	Bidadi Hobli
4.	No. of panchayats	15
5.	No. of villages	50
6.	Total area (acres)	49,517
7.	Total cultivable land	28,502
	(a) Total wet land 2,725	
	(b) Total dry land 25,767	
	(c) Total garden land 1,136	
8.	Total population	34,909
9.	Total number of families	6,982 (7,500)*
10.	Total population of SCs & STs	6,400
11.	Estimated number of SC/ST families	1,200-1,300†
12.	Total number of small farmers	1,909 (2,194)*
13.	No. of marginal farmers	1,098
14.	No.of agricultural labourers	953
15.	Total number of farmers enrolled as members of FSS as of 31.8. 1976	2,277
	(a) Small farmers 912	
	(b) Marginal farmers 241	
	(c) Agricultural labourers 41	
	(d) Others 1,083	
16.	Share capital:	
	(a) Authorized share capital	Rs 205,000
	(b) Share capital from members	Rs 241,501
	(c) Share capital from government	Rs 30,000
	(d) Share capital from SFDA	Rs 6,160

*There were some discrepancies in the figures given in different documents.
†No. of SC/ST families not available in official reports. Only the SC/ST population figure was available from which this estimate is made.

Table IV.12: Credit and Other Activities of FSS Bidadi (up to 31 Aug. 1976)

A. Short-term Loan (crop)

Year	Small farmers No.	Amount	Average	Others No.	Amount	Average	Total No.	Amount	Average	% Amount	Recovery %
1973 Kharif	161	80,000	497	260	99,650	383	421	179,650	427	6.6	98
1974 "	356	215,450	605	226	257,777	1,141	582	473,227	813	17.2	90
1975 "	263	368,000	1,399	370	485,690	1,313	633	853,690	1,349	31.1	60
1976 (from Jan.'76)	392	536,750	1,369	340	700,400	2,060	732	1,237,150	1,690	45.1	62
Total	1,172	1,200,200 (43.7)	1,024	1,196	1,543,517 (56.3)	1,290	2,368	2,743,717 (100)	1,159		

B. Medium-term Loan

Purpose	Small farmers No.	Amount	Average	%	Marginal farmers No.	Amount	Average	%	Others No.	Amount	Average	%	Total No.	Amount	Average	%
1. Sheep loan	159	204,500	1,286	63.4	106	159,000	1,500	93.5	53	79,500	1,500	29.8	318	443,000	1,393	58
2. Sericulture	24	24,000	1,000	7.4	11	11,000	1,000	6.5	11	11,000	1,000	4.1	46	46,000	1,000	6
3. Farm finance	5	41,550	8,310	12.9	–	–	–	–	7	53,500	7,643	20.1	12	95,050	7,921	13
4. Pump-sets	8	52,350	6,544	16.2	–	–	–	–	17	122,650	7,215	46.0	25	175,000	7,000	23
Total	196 (48.2)	322,400 (42.5)	1,645	99.9	117 (29.2)	170,000 (22.4)	1,453	100	88 (21.9)	266,650 (35.1)	3,030	100	401 (100)	759,050 (100)	1,893	100

C. Loan Advanced to SC/STs

Members – 342: Amount Rs 268,750; Average Rs 785.8.

There was also some confusion in categorizing the members of FSS as small, marginal or agricultural labourers. Not all the 1,083 included under the category of 'others' were necessarily large farmers. As a matter of fact, the number of large landholders itself was very small in the entire Bidadi *hobli*. The category 'others' was inflated because so far many small farmers had not been 'officially' identified as such, and certified by the SDFA and block agency. In the absence of an official certificate, they were included under the category 'others', and were not entitled to subsidy and other benefits from SFDA. The bulk of the SC and ST members had been identified, however. They were 36 of the 1,083 'others' but 329 (more than a quarter) of the 1,194 small and marginal farmers and agricultural labourers.

Thus, the official figures indicated that about 70 per cent of the farm families of the region were so far not even registered as members of FSS (assuming that each of the 2,277 registered members represented a family). Similarly, of the estimated 1,200-1,300 SC and ST families, about 70 per cent were not enrolled. The percentage enrolment of small and marginal farmers and agricultural labourers (who were entitled to SDFA subsidy and other special benefits) was 42, 22 and 4 respectively.

The percentage of families who were members varied from panchayat to panchayat — from 3 per cent in one to 85 per cent in another. There was a similar variation in the proportion of members who received services from the society — all except two of the 224 members in one village panchayat area, only a third of the 176 members in another. Overall the proportion was about 63 per cent; 80 per cent of the small farmers, 64 per cent of the marginal farmers, 27 per cent of the agricultural labourers and 60 per cent of the others. In total they made up about 20 per cent of all the farming families in the region.

Among its long list of objectives, in its first four years' of existence the society concentrated on the following activities:

providing short-term crop loans;
providing medium-term loans for sheep-rearing, sericulture, irrigation wells and pump-sets;
trading in essential consumer items, namely kerosene, sugar, foodgrains and cloth (non-controlled and controlled);
input distribution (sale) of fertilizers, seeds, implements, pesticides and insecticides, and other agricultural chemicals; and
hiring out the tractor.

Loans

A summary of the society's loan activities will be found in Table IV.12. As far as single-season crop loans are concerned it will be seen that less than half of total loans went to small farmers, and that the share of 'others' is increasing. In terms of coverage, the 392 small farmers who received loans in 1976 amount to a mere 12 per cent of the small and marginal farmers in the region.

As for the medium-term loans, small and marginal farmers did get the bulk of the loans for sheep, but for the larger items, again the 'others' take a predominant share. Once more, it is a tiny proportion of farmers who benefit from this facility.

The exiguous nature of the resources available is clear. If one assumes that all the loans (totalling Rs 3.7m), irrespective of their length, yielded a 15 per cent income to their borrowers, the total increase in income averaged over the whole area for the five years would be Rs 75 per household and Rs 16 per acre. This would amount to 25 paise per capita per month — if the average size of family was assumed to be five. It hardly needs pointing out that this maximum increase in income of 30 paise per capita per month would neither improve the household's quality of life nor increase its rate of capital formation. In short, the impact of the lending operations of the FSS (there were, of course, some other lending institutions in the area, both commercial and co-operative, but no others concentrating on small farmers) would be negligible on these two counts. Some impact would be visible only when (a) limited credit facilities were concentrated on a few households out of many who need it and/or (b) farmers defaulted on their repayments.

Trading Activities

The society had two shops, one at Bidadi and the other at Kenchana-kuppe, for the sale of consumer items and agricultural inputs, the latter generally being linked with crop loans. Details are given in Table IV.13. From these total sales of some Rs 4m, the gross profit had amounted to Rs. 0.1m or about 2 per cent.

Tractor Hire

The society owned a 35 hp tractor with two trailers, and ploughing accessories, costing approximately Rs 74,000. For the purchase of these, it received an outright subsidy of Rs 23,000 from SFDA Banga-lore. The society employed a driver at a salary of Rs 200 per month and a cleaner at Rs 105. The tractor was mainly used for hauling and

Table IV.13: Trading Activities of FSS Bidadi (to 31 Aug. 1976)

Item	1973-4	1974-5	1975-6	Total
A. Input distribution (sales)				
1. Fertilizers	0.62	6.65	10.32	17.59
2. Seeds	0.03	0.09	0.17	0.29
3. Implements	0.08	0.06	0.01	0.15
4. Pesticides and insecticides	0.005	0.17	0.21	0.385
5. Agricultural chemicals	0.20	0.18	0.21	0.59
Total A	0.935	7.15	10.92	19.005
B. Consumer goods				
1. Cloth (non-controlled and controlled)	–	1.48	1.98	3.46
2. Foodgrains, etc.	–	–	0.85	0.85
Total B	–	1.48	2.83	4.31
Grand Total (A + B)	0.935	8.63	13.75	23.315

ploughing. For cultivating, the tractor hire charges with cultivator were Rs 20 per hour for small farmers and Rs 30 per hour for others. The hauling charges per day of 7-8 hours were Rs 150 with one trailer and Rs 225 with two trailers. No concession was given to small farmers if they hired the tractor for hauling purposes. The tractor was given to all farmers, members as well as non-members on a first-come-first-served basis.

During 1974-5 and 1975-6 the income from the tractor unit was around Rs 37,000 and Rs 28,000 respectively. However, in the same period expenditure (including depreciation) on the unit was Rs 53,000 and Rs 56,000 respectively. So the society has so far suffered a net loss of about Rs 43,500 on account of the tractor unit.

Attempted Innovations

Since July 1975, the society had undertaken three special agricultural development programmes: two attempts at collaborative farming (the one in Seshagirihalli village will be described in the next chapter) and one hybrid maize programme in conjunction with a new irrigation scheme executed by the PWD.

Profit and Loss Account

Table IV:14 gives the profit and loss account for 1975-6, and Table IV.15 a summary account for the three years as a whole. Over the period, losses amounted to a little over 10 per cent of expenditure, and this in spite of subsidies amounting to 13 per cent of expenditure.

The tractor loss accounted for a good deal of the total loss, but even without the tractor (to which nearly a half of the total subsidy was tied) the loss would still be around 5 per cent. What these tables do not show, of course, is the additional subsidy in the shape of the salaries of the Managing Director and the three members of the technical staff — probably in the region of Rs 1.4m. If that sum is added, the subsidy element rises to 35 per cent of expenditure. The loss that would have been incurred if those subsidies had not been received and the tractor operation still carried out (Rs 2.3m) would more or less equal the society's Rs 2.4 capital.

None of this takes account of the quite large, and growing (Table IV.12), proportion of unrecovered loans.

Self-appraisal

The society, and especially its Managing Director, was quite eloquent on the topic of its own achievements and limitations, as may be seen from the following abstracts taken from various documents and reports (mostly mimeo) prepared by the Managing Director. Of course most of these are concerned to defend the role of the society, sometimes with a particular audience in mind:

> If the performance of the society is measured in relation to the area of jurisdiction, it is not satisfactory; if measured in relation to the other financing institutions in the area of jurisdiction of the society, it is satisfactory; and if measured in relation to the help it has given to the small farmers it is very satisfactory.

> The society has been functioning for the past three years and has discharged its responsibilities to the community in satisfactory manner in terms of its objectives and goals . . . in comparison to what has been done for the community for the past decade, and to astronomical heights in relation to the cooperation and guidance received from the different government agencies, officers who are on the Board of Directors of the Society, and the attitude of the financing Bank towards the society.

> What cooperative movement and the government extension agencies

Table IV.14: Bidadi FSS Profit and Loss Account for the Year 1975-6 (Tentative)

Expenditure		Amount (Rs)	Income		Amount (Rs)
To salary (office staff)		17,495	By gross profit from trading account		36,008
To salary (technical staff)		24,893	By miscellaneous income		993
To rent		5,310	By interest on loan from members		99,933
To TA and DA (office staff)		548	By sprayer hire		248
To TA and DA (technical staff)		2,807	By levy commission		130
To DD Commission		194	By discount:		
To GB meeting expenses		458	(a) To Rudraradhya & Co.	8,971	
To repairs of weighing machine and sprayer		585	(b) PACT	332	
To wages		4,425	(c) EID Parry & Co.	100	9,403
To printing and stationery		9,932	By subsidy from government	14,961	
To post and telegraphs		1,336	Add: Sanctioned amount	6,300	21,261
To electric charges		315	By interest on deposits		5,962
To miscellaneous expenses		4,449	By books and forms		3,163
To audit fee (1972 to 1975)		1,359	By tractor subsidy as per B/S		23,160
To interest to Canara Bank:			By net loss		49,020
Farm finance	4,648.00				
Pump-set	5,137.00				
Sheep loan	10,196.25				
Sericulture	1,840.00				
Crop loan	1,10,011.90				
OCC A/c	12,566.50	1,44,399			
To audit fee (approximately) 1975-6		2,000			
To depreciation of furniture @ 10%		812			
To tractor loss		27,969			
Total		2,49,277	Total		2,49,281

Table IV.15: Bidadi FSS Summary Table for Profit and Loss Account for the Period 1973/4 to 1975/6*

Expenditure	Year	Amount	%
A. Salary, etc.	1973-4	10,082	
	1974-5	20,652	
	1975-6	76,916	
	Total	107,650	29
B. Interest paid to Canara Bank	1973-4	13,419	
	1974-5	62,009	
	1975-6	144,399	
	Total	219,827	59
C. Tractor loss†	1973-4	–	
	1974-5	16,014	
	1975-6	27,969	
	Total	43,983	12
Total expenditure	1973-4	23,502	
	1974-5	98,675	
	1975-6	249,285	
	Total	371,462	100
Profit & Loss			
Loss	1973-4	8,213	
Profit	1974-5	18,069	
Loss	1975-6	49,020	
Net loss		39,164	

Income	Year	Amount	%
A. Gross profit from trading	1973-4	3,982	
	1974-5	63,081	
	1975-6	36,008	
	Total	103,071	31
B. Interest on loan from members	1973-4	9,894	
	1974-5	42,341	
	1975-6	99,933	
	Total	152,168	45
C. Discount commission from input supply companies	1973-4	–	
	1974-5	4,000	
	1975-6	9,403	
	Total	13,403	4
D. Tractor and other subsidy	1973-4	–	
	1974-5	4,450	
	1975-6	44,421	
	Total	48,871	14
E. Others (interest on deposits, books, forms, etc.)	1973-4	941	
	1974-5	2,873	
	1975-6	10,497	
	Total	14,311	4
F. Profit on tractor	1973-4	470	
	Total	470	
Total income	1973-4	15,288	
	1974-5	116,745	
	1975-6	200,264	
	Grand Total	332,297	

*Figures for 1975-6 are tentative.
†Including Rs 4,309 interest paid to bank.

have not achieved in a decade, the society has been able to establish and achieve with a certain degree of success. This can be judged from the increase in transactions and turnover from Rs 9 lakhs to Rs 34 lakhs to Rs 55 lakhs in three years' time.

The society has not received any guidance from the government officials who are on the Board in co-ordinating programmes, etc. They have always shown a tendency to be indifferent to promotion or execution of any programmes. They try to find faults, but claim credit for the success of programmes. The programmes of the society are formulated and worked out by the team of extension staff in consultation with the local village leaders and Directors.

In complaint against the Canara Bank, it was observed that:

The Bank which sponsored and financed the society expected other financing institutions to cease lending for agricultural operations in the area of jurisdiction of the society. However, its own branch was extending credit to farmers who fell within the society's juris-diction. It was pointed out that the manager of this Bank had the power to sanction loans and disburse the same immediately but the Bank did not feel that the same powers should be enjoyed by the Managing Director of FSS who was either an assistant registrar of cooperative societies, an officer of gazetted rank, or an officer of the financing bank.

The financing bank has to guide us, keeping in view its policies, in framing subsidiary rules for lending, viz., types of loans, repayment schedules, security, and method of disbursement, etc. The Bank has not given any powers to the Managing Director to execute its policies. The Bank has followed the same procedures it adopts in financing primary cooperative societies. The Managing Director in the society is just a figurehead, attending to the routine work and just that. The Bank had advised us to have sub-rules for loan dis-bursements, etc. But power has not been given to the Managing Director to sanction and distribute loans, when he can be sued or held liable for his actions as far as cash baaalance and stocks are concerned.

The concept of the society was to find a solution to the ills of coop-erative institutional finance but the direction in which we are proceeding will not make things better for the rural community.

These then were the subjective judgements of those involved in running the society and they draw attention to some of the problems experienced by those on the inside, particularly in relation to the parent bank. The language of administrative self-defence and complaint contrasts rather with the more objective assessments presented previously. On those terms, it is clear, first, that the FSS could not be rated commercially successful, but that, as a primarily subsidizing agency, it was not serving only, or even a majority, of its intended clientele. However, it *was* serving a reasonably substantial group of small farmers who had previously found it very hard to get credit.

Notes

1. For a review of this literature, see V.R. Gaikwad, *Small Farmers: State Policy and Programme Implementation* (National Institute of Community Development, Hyderabad, 1971), pp. 1-13.
2. *Report of the All-India Rural Credit Review Committee.* Ch. 18, 'Small Farmers Development Agency' (December 1969), pp. 537-89.
3. Government of Karnataka, *Rural Development with Social Justice in Karnataka* (Rural Development and Co-operative Department, Bangalore, May 1975), p. 77.
4. Ibid., p. 79.
5. Ibid., p. 80.
6. Government of India, *Interim Report of the National Commission on Agriculture on Credit Services for Small and Marginal Farmers and Agricultural Labourers* (New Delhi, December 1971), p. 22.
7. Ibid.,p. 27.
8. Ibid., pp. 28-9.

8 FSS'S OPERATION IN THE SAMPLE VILLAGES

Enrolment of Members

The Managing Director of the society had been an extension officer (EO) with the sponsoring bank for over seven years and so had experience of this approach to agricultural development. He decided to visit a few villages to familiarize himself with the farmers and their problems, and encourage them to enrol as members of the society.

Efforts to enrol the farmers of Seshagirihalli as members of the society started sometime in July 1973. In a small impromptu meeting he talked about the FSS and what it was expected to do for the farmers. No government or FSS official accompanied him on that day. The immediate response of the audience was not very encouraging. They listened silently and, after the talk, there was no show of enthusiasm. The MD recalled that when he left, he had a feeling that he had not made any impact and that his efforts were wasted.

On his return from the village he shared his assessment with the President and some of the directors of the society. One of the latter was a Vokkaliga who owned land in a village near Seshagirihalli. He was fairly well known throughout Bidadi Hobli. He suggested that the MD pay another visit to the village after a few days. In the meanwhile he sent messages to two Vokkaliga leaders of main hamlet and a Lingayat leader of Inorpalya about enrolling members for the society.

The MD visited Seshagirihalli again in August 1973 and found that a number of farmers were willing to become members. This time he had with him a couple of assistants who helped the farmers fill in the application forms. During 1973, seven farmers from the village became members of the society, and in 1974 another 17 did so. By November 1976, there were 39 members, but 38 of them were from the 10 landowning households, and only one from the landless.

While, according to the official land records, there were only 13 small farmers in the village, according to the society's records 21 persons were registered as members in the category of small farmers. There were three reasons for discrepancy: more than one member from the same household joined the society; some who had been illegally cultivating government land while not covered by the official land records also did so; and so did some who did not own any land but had rights of cultivation.

313

Till recently, there was a general feeling among the landless that the society was not meant for them. There was also a fear among them that if they approached any official agency for a loan or a grant they would be forced to undergo sterilization. The society officials had made no effort to remove this fear and persuade the landless to become members. But in October-November 1976, the EO and VLWs of the society met these landless people and clarified the position of the society *vis-à-vis* the family planning programme. As a result, immediately afterwards a batch of 19 landless agricultural labourers, all from the Harijan colony, became members. (Since most of the fieldwork for this study was already over before this date, these members are not included in the analysis presented in this chapter.)

Unlike Seshagirihalli, in Ganakal the MD and the society's staff did not bother to take any initiative in enrolling members since one of the directors himself belonged to the village. He took responsibility for persuading people to join, and also helped them fill in the forms which were later collected by the society's VLWs. In 1973, 4 farmers became members of the society; 9 in 1974, 12 in 1975, and 21 thereafter. Thus, with 94 households in the village, 46 persons became FSS members, including the three big farmers.

Main Programme and Beneficiaries

In the sample villages, the society extended only two types of loan, namely, short-term crop loan and medium-term loan for sheep-rearing. In Seshagirihalli, during the three-year period (1973-4 to 1975-6) the society distributed Rs 33,000 as loan, about 80 per cent in the first category and 20 per cent in the second. Almost all of this went to small farmers (56 per cent) and marginal farmers (44 per cent). Of the 39 members (as at November 1976) 35 received a loan from the society at some time. There was only one landless agricultural labourer who was a member, and he did not receive any loan. More than half of the crop loans were given in the second year and in the context of the block demonstration experiment to be described below. The only obvious trend in the loan figures is for the average size of loan to increase — from Rs 307 in the first year to Rs 807 in the third — chiefly because, in the third year, five of the eleven beneficiaries took more than a thousand rupees each.

In Ganakal, during the first four years, the society extended a total loan of Rs 44,850, half as crop loan over the period, and the remainder as sheep loan in 1975-6. About 44 per cent of the crop loan was given to big farmers, 25 per cent to small farmers and 31 per cent to marginal farmers, whilst sheep loan was given to only small and marginal farmers. Out of 46 members, 28 received loans at some time (never more than 13 in any one year), whilst 18 received none. There were only four landless persons who were members. The trend towards giving larger loans to fewer farmers is again apparent. In the year 1976-7, only two farmers received loans – one of more than Rs 2,500 and one of half that amount – compared with an average loan of Rs 450 in the first year when ten people took loans.

The Block Demonstration Experiment (BDE)

In July-December 1975, the society conducted a BDE in Seshagirihalli. The idea was that, since not all the villages covered by the society could be worked on simultaneously, some villages should be selected for concentrated efforts to produce the maximum demonstration effect.

The experiment was also referred to as 'Joint Collaboration in Farming'. The collaboration was between the society on the one hand and 35 individual farmers on the other hand.

The broad objectives of this experiment were to provide know-how and on-the-job training for farmers. The specific objective was

to bring about increased productivity and income for small and marginal farmers – but not excluding medium type farmers – by making available, especially to the former, loans in kind for inputs (improved seeds, fertilizers, pesticides, etc.) at the right time, and technical guidance and on-the-job training to the farmers from soil testing and the beginning of the sowing season until harvest when the loans were recovered and the remaining produce was handed over to the respective farmers or marketed on their behalf.[1]

The experimental area was 15.2 acres of wet land under the *ayacut* of the Seshagirihalli PWD tank. The area was cultivated by 35 farmers who owned plots of varying sizes. The experiment was to introduce improved varieties of paddy. It began in July 1975 with a meeting at Seshagirihalli between local farmers and the society functionaries, namely, the MD, the EO and the VLWs. The objectives of the experiment were explained and the farmers' agreement obtained. According to the report, the following methods and procedures were agreed upon:

soils would be analysed and tested; loans would be given to individual farmers according to the respective size of their holdings; the
improved paddy seeds that would be used would be mainly MR 272;
the loan would be in kind, i.e., the seeds, fertilizers, etc., would be
brought in bulk, and its use pro-rated on the basis of the size of the
holdings; vouchers and other records would be maintained for each
'collaborator' and copies of receipts would be given to each of them;
labour would be provided by each 'collaborator'; technical assistance
at all stages would be given by the technical cell of the co-operative
society free of cost; all work which was of common benefit would
be undertaken by the technical cell; the harvesting and other operations would be undertaken under the supervision of the co-operative
society; the loans would be recovered after the harvest; the remaining produce would be given to the respective farmers in proportion
to the size of their holdings or any part of it would be marketed on
behalf of the owners by the co-operative society.[2]

The society came to an agreement with all the 35 farmers to farm their
lands as a single unit on a collaborative basis.

Under this agreement, the co-operative society was vested with the
over-all responsibility for cultivation; to provide all the inputs on
loan; and to give technical guidance from the initial soil testing till
completion of harvest. The farmers provided their labour and
received on-the-job training in science-based agriculture. The understanding was that the farmers *would not lose anything* under this
agreement and that there was a good possibility that their net income would be appreciably greater than the average during previous
years.[3]

The next day (7 July) a benchmark survey was conducted by the EO
and VLWs to record the agricultural practices generally followed by the
farmers. The chronology of events thereafter is given in Table IV.16.
Throughout the period of about five months, the EO and VLWs of the
society were involved in the experiment and the MD visited the village
frequently. The results of soil testing were available within ten days.
In the meantime the input requirements were worked out and the
implications of soil testing were explained to the farmers. Various agricultural operations, such as seed treatment, were explained in the
meetings with farmers before they were actually carried out. And then
the guidance and supervision of the EO and VLWs were available to all
the participant farmers.

Table IV.16: Chronology of Block Demonstration Experiment in Seshagirihalli

	Item of work	Date
1.	Meeting at night in Seshagirihalli at the school building to convince the farmers about the BDP and to take their consent	6. 7.75
2.	Benchmark survey to record the existing agricultural practices and production	7. 7.75
3.	Collection of soil samples from individual plots and its despatch to the laboratory	10. 7.75
4.	Meeting at night for method demonstration at the school building (detailed analysis of agricultural operations for the benefit of 35 participants)	12. 7.75
5.	Working out the requirements of inputs and submission to the MD	14. 7.75
6.	Stock of inputs	16. 7.75
7.	Getting analysed results of soil samples from the laboratory	20. 7.75
8.	Night meeting to repeat the content of method demonstration and explain the implications of soil sample	21. 7.75
9.	Seed treatment (actual operation of treating the seed with Agrason and Serosan-Wet) and sowing of seed in nursery beds	22. 7.75 to 25. 7.75
10.	Application of farmyard manure to the fields	26. 7.75 to 30. 7.75
11.	First spraying of plant protection (PP) chemicals in the nurseries	4. 8.75 to 5. 8.75
12.	Second spraying of PP chemicals in the nurseries	12. 8.75 to 13. 8.75
13.	Application of basal dose of fertilizers	14. 8.75 to 20. 8.75
14.	Application of zinc sulphate solution	15. 8.75 to 21. 8.75
15.	Paddy transplantation	15. 8.75 to 21. 8.75
16.	Application of Solverix to the fields	– do –
17.	Application of Weedicide	20. 8.75 to 25. 8.75
18.	First top dressing	5. 9.75 to 10. 9.75
19.	First PP spraying	11. 9.75 to 13. 9.75
20.	Second top dressing	28. 9.75 to 2.10.75

21.	Second PP spraying	2.10.75
		to
		4.10.75
22.	Harvesting and yield data collection	25.11.75
23.	Harvesting	5.12.75

Source: *Joint Collaboration in Farming* (cyclostyled).

The responsibility for all the decisions about farming operations rested with the society. The farmers only helped the society functionaries in the implementation of these decisions. The society saw that all the necessary inputs were available in time and were actually used on the experimental plots, and ensured uniformity in the application of the recommended package of practices.

According to the society, the results of the experiment were quite encouraging. The data provided by it is given in Table IV.17 and Table IV.18. It can be seen from Table IV.17 that under BDE all the 35 farmers used the treated seed at the recommended rate (as against only four farmers previously), all used farmyard manure (as against 22 farmers earlier) and all used the recommended doses of fertilizers. All of them followed the recommended practices, namely, timely sowing, planting, spraying of nursery, application of basal dose of fertilizers and plant protection measures.

According to the society's report, the average yield in pre-experimental years was about 1,100 kg of paddy per acre; the maximum was 1,240 kg per acre and the minimum was as low as 600 kg per acre. As a result of the experiment, the average yield was about 2,000 kg per acre. The maximum yield was 2,300 kg and the minimum was 1,700 kg per acre. Thus, in the case of a minimum yield the increase was about two-fold. The loan requirement averaged Rs 964 per acre.

According to its financial analysis (Table IV.18), the society claimed:

At the open market price, the gross income from paddy and by-products was Rs 2318 per acre, and the net income after recovery of loan and 13 per cent interest was Rs 1354 per acre. This excludes the cost of labour furnished by the respective farmers, and the SFDA subsidy of Rs 200 to which 23 of the small and marginal farmers were entitled.

It observed:

Table IV.17: Analysis of High-yielding Variety of Paddy Block Demonstration for Kharif 1975-6, Seshagirihalli, Bidadi Hobli, Ramanagaram Taluka, Bangalore District

	Particulars	Benchmark year	Block demonstration year
1.	Type of soil	Clayeen loam	–
2.	Source of irrigation	Seshagirihalli tank	
3.	Area involved (in acres)	15.20	15.20
4.	No. of cultivators involved	35	35
5.	No. of small farmers	12	12
6.	No. of marginal farmers	11	11
7.	No. of medium and big farmers	12	12
8.	Recommended seed rate per acre	15 kg	25 kg
9.	Average seed rate used	18 kg	25 kg
10.	No. of farmers using lesser seed rate	Nil	Nil
11.	No. of farmers using recommended seed rate	4	35
12.	No. of farmers using: (a) Madhu	4	20
	(b) MR 272	–	14
	(c) S 701	29	1
	(d) IR 20	2	Nil
13.	No. of farmers using treated seeds	4	35
14.	No. of farmers using FYM to the main field	22	35
15.	No. of farmers using fertilizers	35	35
16.	No. of farmers using recommended dose of fertilizers	Nil	35
17.	No. of farmers using below the recommended dose	18	Nil
18.	No. of farmers using above the recommended dose	3	Nil
19.	No. of farmers using only N & P fertilizers	9	Nil
20.	No. of farmers using only nitrogenous fertilizers	5	Nil
21.	Recommended dosage of fertilizers as per package	25:15:15	40:20:20
22.	No. of farmers who tested their soils	13	28
23.	Soil test recommendation	–	40:20.3:20.
24.	No. farmers taking up timely sowings	16	35
25.	No. of farmers taking up timely planting	18	35
26.	No. of farmers spraying the nursery	8	35
27.	No. of farmers applying basal dose of fertilizers	21	35
28.	No. of farmers taking up spraying to main fields	12	35
29.	No. of farmers taking up cured urea	Nil	4
30.	No. of farmers taking up urea spraying	Nil	5
31.	Maximum fertilizers used per acre	40:13:13	40:25:20
32.	Minimum fertilizers used per acre	23:0:0	40:20:20
33.	Maximum yield per acre (in kg)	1,240	2,300
34.	Minimum yield per acre (in kg)	600	1,700
35.	Average yield obtained per acre (in kg)	1,110	2,000

Source: *Joint Collaboration in Farming* (cyclostyled).

Table IV.18: Financial Analysis of BDE

1. Total loan: Rs 14,146. + Interest Rs 510.00		Rs 14,656
2. Total yield: 310 qtls. or 31,000 kg		
3. Total gross income (at free market prices of Rs 1.14 per kg of paddy)		
	(a) For paddy Rs 34,300	
	(b) For by-products Rs 940	
	Total Rs 35,240	Rs 35,240
4. Total net income (excluding cost of labour provided by individual farmers and SFDA subsidy to 23 eligible small and marginal farmers)		Rs 20,583
5. Total area of land cultivated		15.2 acres
6. Average loan per acre cultivated		Rs 964
7. Average yield per acre cultivated		2,000 kg
8. Average gross and net income per acre cultivated (excluding labour provided by the farmers and SFDA subsidy to 28 eligible small and marginal farmers)		
	(a) Gross	Rs 2,318
	(b) Net	Rs 1,354
9. SFDA subsidy @ Rs 200 for each of 23 marginal farmers		Rs 4,600
10. Average size of a holding (35 farmers cultivated 15.2 acres)		0.43 acre
11. Average net income of a marginal farmer, assuming that his land was of the average size (0.43 acre and adding Rs 200 as SFDA subsidy for each of 23 such farmers)		Rs 782
12. Same as Item 11, but excluding SFDA subsidy		Rs 582
13. Since 4½ months elapsed from 'seed treatment to 'date of harvest', the average income *per month* during these 4½ months of a marginal or small farmer with an average landholding of 0.43 acre, even though the yield was double that of previous year	(a) *With subsidy:* Rs 175 p.m. (b) *Without subsidy:* Rs 129 p.m.	
14. Assuming that a similar 'collaboration' is extended for the summer season also, and the above figures are approximately the same for the summer season harvest, the figures in items 11 and 12 would presumably apply also for the summer season. Therefore, the income *per month* of a small or marginal farmer averaged over a twelve-month period will be twice the amounts in items 11 and 12 divided by 12.	(a) *With subsidy* Rs 130 p.m. (b) *Without subsidy* Rs 97 p.m.	
15. Without loans made available in the 'collaboration' experiment, the farmers might have had to borrow from the usual sources, viz., money-lenders who lend at exorbitant rates of interest. The average yield from their land during previous years was only about one half (in the case of some farmers in fact it was about one-third). Assuming that their net income was only one half of what was achieved in the 'collaboration' experiment, the maximum average income during the year would have been only one half of item 14 (without subsidy)		Rs 48.5 p.m.
16. 'Indirect costs', viz., estimated cost of staff services rendered by the co-operative society		Rs 2,000

Source: *Joint Collaboration in Farming* (cyclostyled).

This analysis indicates that by granting a loan of Rs 964 per acre to a small farmer of irrigated land and if he utilizes this loan in approximately the same effective manner as in the above experiment, his net income can be expected to be about Rs 1354 per acre.

The society was aware that there was a substantial element of indirect cost, in terms of the time and labour of its staff who provided the managerial and technical assistance, which was not passed on to the farmers. According to its calculation this administrative cost was about Rs 2,000 for the entire project.

Immediately after the harvesting, the financing bank recovered all its loan of Rs 14,164 with interest of Rs 510. Encouraged by the results, the society decided to take up a much larger area of about 250 acres at Kenchanakuppe village during the ensuing summer season (1976).

According to the society the success of the experiment was due to:

(a) the availability of efficient management and technical skill in the FSS;
(b) the inputs being available when needed; and
(c) the economy of farming 15.20 acres as a single unit instead of 36 separate units.

It was observed that 'one of the by-products of such a venture would be *de facto* consolidation of land'.

Analysis of BDE

As mentioned above, the BDE was also referred to as an experiment in 'collaboration in farming', but it was, of course, collaboration only between the society and individual cultivators, and not *among* the cultivators. It was, moreover, only for one cropping season. Apart from a certain amount of mutual aid of a traditional kind, the actual performance of agricultural operations by the 35 participants was confined to individual plots. The only common agricultural operation performed by the society's functionaries during the entire experiment was spraying of the plant protection chemicals. Apart from sprays, the inputs used and outputs obtained were the sole concern of the individual participants. Yet the BDE did have an element of co-operation in the sense that the 35 participants agreed to grow the same varieties of paddy and to synchronize their individual actions. To make 35 farmers think and operate on more or less the same wave-length was no mean achievement for the FSS. The achievement looks much more impressive when one realizes that in the past the people of this village have come together only on religious and ceremonial occasions and have never engaged collectively in economic, production-oriented tasks.

Not all the 35 participants were actually from Seshagirihalli; as many as nine were from adjoining villages and hamlets. And it was a mixed group in terms of landholding and and caste. Ten were marginal farmers, 13 small farmers and 12 medium to large farmers. Castewise the distribution was as follows: Vokkaliga, 16; Lingayat, 13; SC/BC 4; Muslim, 1; and Iyengar, 1, though he sold the land and left the village during the year of the experiment.

The plots covered under the experiment varied from one tenth of an acre to two acres, with an average of 0.43 acres. Equally varied was the size of the loan taken, though not necessarily in proportion to acreage. The per acre loan varied from Rs 305 (Rs 251.60 for a plot of 0.825 acres) to Rs 6,667 per acre (Rs 1,000 for a plot of 0.15 acre), with the average just below a thousand rupees. The five farmers who received very high per acre loans were three marginal farmers and two small farmers.

Among the participants, there was sharing of nursery work and some sharing in the preparation of main plots, compost application, transportation, watering, etc. Such sharing, however, was not uncommon in the village generally. The co-operation extended to the society and the ressponse to its recommendations were not uniform. P (Lingayat) from Inorpalya, VN, DN and G (all Vokkaligas) from the main hamlet, and R (Vokkaliga) from the nearby village extended their full co-operation to the experiment. They were progressive farmers, belonging in the medium-large landholding size, educated and receptive to new ideas. P, for example, raised a larger nursery on his plot which he allowed the society to distribute among those participants who could not raise the required quantity of seedlings. On the other hand, N (Lingayat) from Inorpalya disposed of part of his nursery, miscalculating his requirements, and at the time of transplantation fell short. S, another Lingayat, sowed a local variety instead of the recommended MR136/MR272. R (Vokkaliga) and B (Muslim) were lukewarm in their response to the society's recommendations. Generally, those farmers who did not own bullocks and implements, and were dependent upon others, were not very enthusiastic about the experiment. They were suspicious and not sure whether they would get good returns. Their number, however, was small.

The net income of Rs 1,354 per acre looks quite attractive. One would expect that the actual experience of getting such a net income would motivate all the participant farmers to take loans in the subsequent year from the society to buy inputs and to follow the already tried practices. In fact, however, if credit facilities are any guide, there was little or no carry-over.[4] Only 10 of the 35 farmers who took part in the experiment took loans the following year — compared with six in the year before the experiment. The main reason for the reluctance to continue the recommended practices would seem to be the increased initial costs and consequent risks. Unfortunately the society did not collect cost data — either for the pre-experimental year or for the experimental year; the calculations in Table IV.18 are based on the assumption that costs equalled amount borrowed, perhaps because the loans were all in kind. But this is patently false, if for no other reason than that the borrowers were also farming other land during the period in question.

Leaving labour aside, costs were increased in several ways. The recommended doses of fertilizers were bigger than the farmers had been using. The plant protection measures were an additional charge. So was seed; the HYV had to be purchased, whereas the traditional varieties were saved from their own previous year's crop. All the farmers used farmyard manure in the experimental year where only 22 claimed to have done so before, so that the other 13 probably had to purchase theirs.

One can make certain rough calculations, accepting the cost figures of Table IV.18 (Rs 960 per acre) plus an estimate of costs of Rs 500, for the previous year, an additional income of Rs 1,030 gross or Rs 570 net. For the smallest farmer in the scheme with only a tenth of an acre, this means a net increase of Rs 57 for an extra Rs 46 risked — the equivalent of about 12 days' wages for a labourer. But these calculations assume the *average* yield of 2,000 kg. If he were one of the unlucky ones with the minimum 1,700 kg yield, that Rs 46 would be reduced to Rs 22.

And if one assumes that the Rs 2,000 estimated administrative costs to the society in the experimental year would have to be borne by the farmers thereafter, and subtracts the Rs 4,600 subsidy from the SFDA which the experiment attracted, that Rs 22 gain to the low yield farmer with a tenth of an acre turns into a loss of Rs 21 — i.e. an extra Rs 90 outlay for a gross Rs 69 additional return.

The experiment was able to get the farmers' co-operation because in the experimental year the society accepted entire responsibility for the risks involved. The farmers were guaranteed to get no less than the previous year. The society was lucky that year: the rains were normal and it got its money back. But in the absence of such guarantees, past experience of rains and pest attacks (and, perhaps, price fluctuations) makes farmers reluctant to accept — for relatively small prospective returns — a large increase in the investment they have at risk.

One may summarize the conclusions to be drawn from this demonstration experiment as follows:

1. Even under this intensive and scientific agriculture, because of the very small size of plots, the absolute increase in consumption income was really very insignificant. In most cases, given the choice, the farmer would prefer working for wages for a few days, to having to (a) wait for 5½ months to get the small amount of extra income, (b) take additional risk on the increased outlay, (c) put additional labour into this intensive agriculture, and (d) change his methods of working.

2. Farmers were not averse to the idea of transferring their right to take decisions on agricultural operations for food crops to an external agency if (a) that agency also took the entire responsibility for the investment, (b) accepted all the risks involved, (c) the individual farmer's right on land was preserved, and (d) there was an increase in the net income of the farmers. This was true for all categories of farmers, marginal, small and medium-large, with either dry or irrigated area.

3. To be effective, the transfer of risk to an external agency should not be a one-off short-duration affair, but should be continuous for many years so as to give a strong foundation to the farmers' economy and develop a sense of security and confidence.

Notes

1. These objectives and other details about the experiment were taken from the brief report, *Joint Collaboration in Farming* (cyclostyled) provided by Small Farmers' Development Agency, Bangalore, as well as by the FSCS, Bidadi, p. 1.
2. Ibid., p. 2.
3. Ibid. (Summary), p. 1.
4. This is not a unique phenomenon. Even under the Intensive Agriculture District Programme (IADP) the farmers responded in similar fashion. *See* V.R. Gaikwad, Gunvant M. Desai, Paul Mapilly, and V.S. Vyas, *Development of Intensive Agriculture: Lessons from IADP* (Indian Institute of Management, Ahmedabad, 1977), pp. 333-43.

9 OVERALL ASSESSMENT OF CDP AND FSS

It will be recalled that the four basic elements of the CDP design were:

1. a focus on individual cultivators;
2. a restructuring and reorganization of district administration, especially by the establishment of new administrative units, on an area (block) basis;
3. the provision of necessary facilities (including knowledge) for agricultural production to the individual cultivator through co-operatives and the block agency; and
4. the provision of welfare facilities by the block agency at the block level and the rural settlement level.

The micro-level realities at Seshagirihalli and Ganakal villages have shown how these four basic elements of the DC design worked out in practice.

Focus on the Individual

In neither village did the CDP and other programmes following the CD design try to develop a sense of community feeling among the people, or succeed in improving the economic condition of all segments of the community. In all economic activities, the focus was on the individual. There is the example of the PWD and the TDB constructing a tank bund in Seshagirihalli which helped 37 farmers to irrigate about 16 acres of land. Neither the community (nor even the immediate beneficiaries) were involved in the construction, and the benefit was not shared by the entire community either. The SFDA and the FSS followed the same principle. Their approach was also individual-oriented and they had nothing to offer to the village community as a whole. The FSS's block demonstration experiment, however, was a slight departure from the normal individual-oriented approach. But there was still little the community or the small group of 37 farmers could do. The society had an agreement with each farmer; the farmers had no agreement among themselves for sharing either inputs or outputs.

In neither village were economic assets developed and owned by the

325

entire community. The only community assets were the school building, community centre (both built and owned by the government and managed by its grants) and temples.

Under the CDP design there was no encouragement and organizational support for collective or co-operative economic efforts. In the absence of any task-oriented organization, the village people could not organize either to assert their rights in other respects, nor to demand due returns on their investment on labour and capital. To keep the rural population atomized and away from the fold of any organized effort was the latent philosophy of CDP. Therefore between the villages there was no basic difference in terms of community life, community initiative of community action in relation to economic activities. It seems that our expectation of finding differences between the two villages due to community action or the efforts of one or more individuals for the economic development of the total community was itself based on a mistaken premiss. Superficial differences lasting for a short time always exist between villages. But these do not provide a base from which to work in planning rural development in India's half million villages.

Focus on the Cultivator

The CDP's focus was not merely on the individual, but on the individual *cultivator*. It ignored those who had no land. In both villages (as well as in nearby areas) there were no activities under CDP which could provide permanent, gainful employment to people outside farming and thereby reduce the pressure on land. There were no efforts to develop village or cottage industries, or agro-industries. Apart from the recent granting of loans to a few farmers and landless households for sheep-rearing, no efforts have been made even to develop the existing subsidiary occupations. In short, the emphasis on crop husbandry was more or less absolute, despite the fact that the agricultural resources of the area — the shortage, chiefly, of irrigated land — were such that agriculture could not possibly utilize all the available manpower.

The CDP could not even offer prosperity to those who had a larger than average share of land. The so-called 'better off' farm families were better off only in comparison with other farm families in the village. The proportion of net annual income from land available for consumption purposes for the 'better off' family was generally less than that earned by a member of the urban lower middle class, such as a clerk or semi-skilled worker — and lacked the protection from monsoon vagaries and price fluctuations, and the annual increments, bonus, pensions, provident fund and various fringe benefits enjoyed by the urban worker.

So it is only when the responsibility for investment and risks is transferred to an external agency, and when the rewards — monetary and otherwise — are sufficiently attractive, that farmers will work as a group or community. The 'Collaboration in Farming' experiment of the FSS only worked because the society took over the risk — but it did so for only one crop season. If the return on agriculture under this kind of intensive, scientific cultivation were really financially attractive, then commercial, profit-oriented organizations would not hesitate to come forward to take care of the 'risk' element on a long-term basis. That none has so far done so indicates that these institutions realize no commercial institution would survive if it took the type and magnitude of risk the Indian farmer takes year after year. The only way it could survive would be with the aid of regular subsidies and grants from the government, i.e. through a transfer of resources from other sectors. But the transfer of resources from other sectors, especially the industrial sector would have far-reaching consequences, since it would affect industrial development, the growth of employment opportunities outside agriculture, socioeconomic mobility, etc. Under the circumstances of constrained resources in the developing countries, it would appear that a generous transfer of resources from the developed countries to the developing countries will be the only solution.

Restructuring and Reorganization of Administration

Broadly speaking, the three sub-systems operating within the boundaries of a district were: (1) producer farmer sub-systems; (2) a credit and input supply sub-system composed of co-operative institutions; and (c) the district administrative sub-system which performed service, regulatory and co-ordinating functions. In 1951, this third sub-system was reorganized to establish the administrative unit on an area (block) basis. There were no major changes in the structure and management of the second sub-system. As mentioned earlier, the CDP design did not encourage any reorganization among farmers.

The reorganized block level administrative machinery of the Ramanagaram block has been in operation for the last 25 years or so. However, during this period it has not contributed much to the socioeconomic development of the region, and especially of the people of Seshagirihalli and Ganakal. Its income has been meagre and confined to traditional revenue sources and its pattern of expenditure equally traditional — chiefly on construction and repairs of building and roads. It has not been involved in economic and production-oriented activities of its own which would encourage economic development.

Nor did the introduction of elected bodies change matters much. They were designed to dovetail with the organization and structure of district administration. There were village panchayats at the bottom with very little power of authority, and two more tiers of panchayats (at block and district level) above them, corresponding to the existing levels in the district administrative machinery. Although a segment of the district administrative machinery, along with the CD block machinery, was transferred to these bodies, they did not have any power to change or redesign the administrative set-up given to them. There were no changes in control procedures, information systems, or reward and appraisal systems. There was no change in the traditional colonial style of administrative behaviour, nor any recognition of the need for creative thinking. Throughout the succession of 'programmes' — SFDA, MFAL, DPAP, CADA, FSS, etc. — titles have changed, but the style, activities and organizational design have remained basically the same. Even the FSS, which was for all practical purposes controlled by the district bureaucracy, could not generate any new ideas, except perhaps the block demonstration experiment.

The system of local bodies with traditional functions and rules, was found very convenient by the bureaucracy for two reasons. First, it was not required to make any major change in its overall structure and recruitment policies. Secondly, its power was unaffected. Its culture and its expertise could continue to be mostly regulatory with a secondary welfare element. The CDP design did not encourage either the people or the state bureaucracy and local bodies to take up responsibilities for economic and production-oriented activities.

Facilities for Supplying Inputs

Under the CDP design, although extension was the function of the block agency, co-operative institutions were expected to provide credit and inputs to the rural population. They could only do so, however, under the indirect control of the administrators. The latter provided the estimates of demand to the government, sanctioned licences to suppliers, and regulated and controlled the quantity and quality of inputs. No loan could be sanctioned without a certificate of landowner-ship from the revenue officials, even under schemes such as the SFDA. Nor was that the full extent of administrative control. As mentioned earlier, the first board of directors of the FSS was nominated by the Registrar of Co-operative Societies. Even subsequently, four out of the thirteen directors were to be district/block level government func-tionaries nominated by the Registrar. The general impact of institu-tions, even after 25 years of operation, on the economic development of the farming and non-farm population of Seshagirihalli and Ganakal was negligible. It is not surprising, therefore, that even SFDA was unable to make much of a dent on the economic condition of small and marginal farmers.

This system of providing credit and necessary inputs to farmers, especially to small and marginal farmers, was costly and uneconomical. For example, under SFDA, to distribute a subsidy of Rs 100 to small and marginal farmers, the government had to spend Rs 43 in the form of risk fund, managerial cost, establishment and administrative cost, etc. The FSS was supposed to work on sound, commercial lines. In addition to income from lending, it earned a sizeable income from trading; however, even then its operation was uneconomical. If the total administrative cost (including the salary of functionaries at present paid partly by the bank, and the subsidy paid by the SFDA) was taken into account, then the loss incurred by the FSS over the first three years of its operation was nearly equal to the share capital of its members.

Provision for Welfare Facilities

The welfare facilities provided under the CDP were limited to certain aspects of health and education. Under the health programme, a public health centre was established in each CD block. A number of auxiliary nurses and midwives were also posted in the block. Health services at district level and below also had responsibility for the preventive pro-grammes such as vaccination for typhoid and smallpox. The health ser-vices also handled the family planning programme.

Given the size of the population and the threats to health, the health programme was inadequate. The elementary needs of human beings — clean drinking water, sanitation and nutritious food — remained unsatis-fied for the vast majority of the people who, as a result, remained vulnerable to microbial attack. As in the case of agricultural production, here also the approach was individual-oriented. There was little attempt to stimulate community efforts to keep the surroundings clean. That malnutrition led to various diseases and infections was apparent. In spite of there being maternal and child welfare services, the rates for infant mortality, maternal deaths due to childbirth, and stillbirths all continued to be very high.

The education programme was equally ineffective. The most it was able to do was to provide primary education of extremely poor quality to village children. Enrolments increased, but the schooling received was of little practical value in the context of village life, nor could any but a microscopically small number of village children continue their education even up to the level of high school and thereby compete with urbanites for the blue-collar and white-collar jobs in urban areas.

All welfare facilities were entirely designed, managed and controlled by the block and district administrative machinery. The village community had absolutely no say whatsoever in either deciding on social welfare priorities or in managing programmes. With its meagre income, the village panchayat itself could not provide welfare services to the community. The community's dependence on block and district bureaucracy for welfare measures was absolute. It could only wait and hope to get the facilities that the bureaucracy thought fit and could provide for the community.

10 LESSONS FOR THE FUTURE

India has invested many a precious year in experimenting with the four-element CD approach. This and the subsequent 'area approach' have had a very limited impact on the poverty and the quality of life of the rural masses. The persistence of poverty in rural areas throws doubt upon the very relevance of the CD model to the present-day environment.

An important lesson from the CD experiment is that a mere restructuring of the district administrative machinery and building of various agencies and institutions managed and controlled by government functionaries cannot improve the conditions of the rural people. The prolific growth of agencies, institutions and programmes for the development of the rural population over the last 25 years has not and could not overcome the basic need to build people's organizations in the countryside. An enlargement of the bureaucracy and a continuation of its power over the rural citizens have been the two major achievements of the institutional and programme approach to rural development. Such efforts have for some time merely diverted attention from the basic needs of the society.

Indian rural society today is an atomized mass, composed of individuals who are not in any organized fold except the family and the extended kin-groups which form the sub-caste. They are primarily exposed to influences exercised by the family and the caste, which keep them tradition-bound. They have no collective voice to exert pressure on the rest of society to give them their due opportunities for growth. The CD design encouraged the process of atomization and discouraged the formation of people's organizations. The desired social transformation could not take place in the absence of new forms of people's organization.

The very process of industrialization and urbanization is also contributing to a weakening of the existing structure of political and economic power in the rural areas. The just demands of the urban blue-collar and white-collar workers for a reasonable income and quality of life have resulted in larger monetary incomes which allow them to purchase basic goods. However, it has also resulted in the creation of a system which tries to satisfy their demands without necessarily giving them a greater share of industrial production. Thus, food prices are kept low, through subsidies or through procurement of foodgrains at low prices, or through some combination of these. The minimal amenities of life are provided at subsidized prices. The increased cost of production, due to higher wages and better amenities for workers, is transferred to the farming population through higher prices for agricultural inputs. High input prices and low procurement prices directly reduce farmers' incomes. Thus, an improvement in the economic condition and quality of life of urban blue- and white-collar workers is inevitably gained at the expense of the rural people. It is to be emphasized that the urban lower classes and the slum-dwellers are at best only marginally better off than the rural poor. Most of them are in fact migrants from rural areas.

The breakdown of the old centres of rural power, with the disappearance of large landowners and the breaking up of joint families, and the absence of any new people's organizations, explains in part why food is kept cheap and agricultural inputs dear — even though, as a result, it is only the more articulate and better-off sections of the urban population who genuinely benefit. Flows of welfare funds back to the rural areas are likewise limited. It is the rural community which has to bear the cost of schemes to guarantee minimum wages or to provide house plots for the growing number of landless.

A new direction is needed. Both in order to increase the political organizational power of rural people, and for economic reasons, there is a need for the reorganization of production in more viable, bigger units (a feature of all developed countries, whether capitalist, socialist or communist). Only in this way can the contacts of the extension agencies be sufficiently concentrated to be effective, and the costs of covering the risk through an external financing agency minimized.

Such a reorganization is needed not only because it would enhance agricultural production; as we have seen, even considerable increases in productivity have a limited impact on consumption levels. The point is that the new units will really prove their value only if they provide a framework for organizing permanent, non-agricultural, and possibly non-land-based, production-oriented activities which can provide a higher net income.

The crucial role of the management of such organizations will therefore be that of searching for new ways of utilizing natural and human resources, improving the existing products and skills, undertaking new production, and consequently increasing the level of investment in rural areas.

It is likely that in the initial period of operation of these organizations, the increase in net income of the members, due either to higher agricultural productivity or new economic activities, may not be attractive enough for them to continue their membership. In such a situation in particular, and even in general, the provision of welfare services such as health and medical facilities, schooling, distribution of essential commodities such as foodgrains and clothing at subsidized rates, and housing, through these organizations, is likely to motivate people to continue their membership. Common social welfare services and facilities will reduce the social gap and provide equal opportunities for all to develop and will operate as a binding force at the same time — and such a binding force is necessary, given the existing social organization and structure of India villages. Compassion, patience and careful planning will be necessary. Perhaps, for example, the attempt to create new interest-oriented, politico-economic organizations could best begin among castes which maintain a low degree of social distance among themselves.

In this context, it maybe worthwhile to recall two indigenous models ignored during the CD experiment era, the Nilokheri township and co-operative farming, both of which existed before the official CDP began. The Nilokheri model was designed to build new settlements (townships) in rural areas, in which new ways of organizing people were to be developed for industrial production-oriented activities, possibly on a co-operative basis. Its primary focus was vocational training and small industry. The primary and crucial element of the co-operative farming model was a reorganization of the unit of management of agricultural production. Its approach was to increase the size of this unit and to develop new co-operative organizations to manage the pooled land. Left to itself, India could perhaps revive these two models. Possibly a combination of the two models could provide a more effective method of socioeconomic transformation and of improving the quality of life of rural people, than could CD.

What role can agencies external to India play in such efforts? We have earlier observed that, given the technology, the low risk-bearing ability of the farmers is possibly the most critical constraint on agricultural productivity. It is evident that similar, if not greater, constraints would be faced in connection with other development activities. While new organizations, as suggested above, and a redistribution of internal resources could provide better risk cover than at present, it is likely that even these efforts will have only limited potential because of the limited resources available internally. Indeed, it may well be that this situation is characteristic of most developing coun-

tries. This is an area where external agents — namely, the developed
countries and international agencies such as the World Bank and the
United Nations Development Programme — could play a meaningful
role. Through an international development risk fund, they can help
cover the risk to a much greater extent than can be managed by the
developing countries on their own.

Note

1. I am grateful to my colleague, Professor Shreekant Sambrani, for a discussion of this chapter.

V COMMUNITY DEVELOPMENT IN MEXICO

Ignacio Algara Cosío

COMMUNITY DEVELOPMENT IN MEXICO

1 THE COUNTRY AND THE SOCIETY

Mexico is sometimes considered a part of Central America; sometimes, a part of North America. That question of nomenclature apart, the relevant matter is that Mexico is the dividing point between two worlds: the highly developed industrialized state of the United States of America on one side, and on the other Guatemala and Belize, countries which are even poorer and more underdeveloped than itself.

Although Mexico is thought to be a middle-sized country in terms of the American continent, it is actually the fifth largest in area (1,972,000 square km). Mexico has two long coastlines (9,903 km in total), one along the Pacific Ocean and the other along the Gulf of Mexico and the Antilles — but it lacks a tradition of seamanship.

Claude Bataillon's description of the different environments in Mexico shows that distribution of major regional areas is a of the country's geological structure.[1] The mountains of the country form two ranges that descend from the north along the coasts and meet at the middle of the country, forming a large plateau at the centre and lowlands near the shores. Other mountain ranges continue down to the south. The mountainous configuration of the land makes both communication and irrigation more difficult since the coastal plains are limited and the rivers coming down from the mountains flow rapidly into the sea. The major part of the valleys of the central plateau (1,700 to 2,200 m) have little terrain under irrigation.

The Tropic of Cancer crosses the country in its central part, but because of great differences in altitude there is a wide variety of climates ranging from the very hot at the lowland shores to the cold or perpetually icy in the mountains with a height of over 5,000 m. There are also deserts and arid zones in the north and north-west, and very humid areas in the south-east. A great variety of vegetations corresponds to these climates: desert, prairies, forests and tropical jungles.

Since the arrival of the Spanish, the mineral resources of Mexico have been well known and these resources have had great economic importance. At present, gold and silver are still mined, but other industrial minerals such as iron, lead, zinc, copper, etc., are also important. Mexico also owns vast oil fields and recent discoveries promise rapid increases in oil exports in the next few years.

Figure V.1: Mexico, Geographic Situation

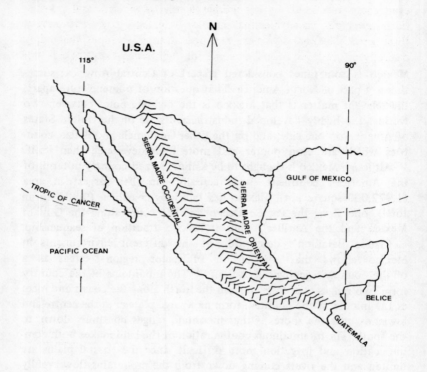

Political Structure

Since 1824, Mexico has been a Federal Republic. The Republic now consists of 23 states and a federal district, where the federal government offices are located.

Both the federal and state governments are formally organized on the principle of the separation of the legislative, executive and judicial powers, though the dominance of the executive headed by elected officials — the President and state governors — is marked. Both the latter are elected for six-year terms, though the elections are not normally held simultaneously.

The state's autonomy, both executive and legislative, is limited, and the federal government reserves to itself most forms of taxation. The *municipios* (municipalities) into which the states are divided are divided even more restricted, having neither legislative nor judicial powers. Each *municipio* has a municipal president, elected by direct vote every three years. The *municipios* are very poor in their resources, depending basically on state and federal agencies for their public works or services.

Population

Table V.1 shows both the very high growth rate of the total population (3.4 per cent per annum in the recent years) and the strong urbanizing trend. In spite of the percentage decline of the rural population, however, absolute numbers in rural areas (villages with less than 2,500 inhabitants) rose from nearly 13 million to nearly 20 million.[2] Of these, some 3 million were indigenous peoples, speaking languages other than Spanish.

Table V.1: Population of Mexico, 1940-70

Year	Total population	Rural	Urban
1940	19,653,552	64.9	35.1
1950	25,791,000	57.4	42.6
1960	34,923,129	49.3	50.7
1970	48,225,238	41.3	58.7

Source: Dirección general de Estadística – SIC.

Many rural settlements were tiny – 55,650 villages had fewer than 100 inhabitants in 1976, and at the other extreme, the urban concentration of Mexico City contained 12 million people. There was consequently wide variation around the average population density (1970) of 25 inhabitants per square kilometre. In the Federal District (Mexico City), for example, it was 4,674; in the state of Guanajuato, 74 and in the extreme northern and southern states only 2 inhabitants per square kilometre.

Productive Infrastructure

Until 1860 Mexico was a country with poor communications, largely because of its vast area and its mountainous terrain. Railroads were steadily developed thereafter and they became the basic communication system by the time of the Revolution. They were marked by two characteristics typical of the country: centralism — all roads converged on Mexico City — and dependence — they led also to the northern frontier.

In this century and principally after the Revolution (1910-20), roads and highways received great support from the government, and so also did irrigation and electricity (Table V.2).

Table V.2: Roads and Irrigated Land, Mexico 1940-70

Year	Kilometres of roads	Hectares of irrigated land	Millions of KWH by of electricity consumption
1940	9,929	1,125,000	2,528
1950	21,422	2,158,000	5,336 (1952)
1960	40,770	3,343,000	15,748 (1964)
1970	67,995	4,000,000	22,731 (1968)

Source: Data from 'Bienestar campesino y desarrollo socioeconómico' — FCE.

The building of great water dams, irrigation systems and hydraulic power plants has been a characteristic of the last 30 years. But still, in spite of these efforts, a good many villages lack roads; 47 per cent of homes had no electricity in 1975 and only 16.5 per cent of the cultivated acreage was under irrigation, a critical situation for a country where rain-fed agriculture is very uncertain.

Social Infrastructure

Education has been another field in which governments have made considerable efforts. But still, in 1970, two-thirds of the approximately 32 million people over 15 years of age had not finished primary school. The census breakdown of figures according to educational levels is as follows:[3]

22.6%	without any instruction
31.4%	only up to three years of primary school
12.6%	only up to five years of primary school
19.0%	with complete primary school
7.3%	some grades of secondary school
2.2%	preparatory school
2.3%	technical schools

2.5%   professional school
0.01%   postgraduate school

It is calculated that universal basic education (nine years) could be achieved by 1980 if the public expenditure on education was increased from 3.1 per cent to 4 per cent of GNP but such an increase does not seem probable.[4]

Compared with other Latin American countries, Mexico has made larger investments in economic infrastructure than in social welfare. Nutritional intake for the average Mexican is below the recommendations of the National Institute of Nutrition, mainly with respect to animal protein consumption, but, in spite of a basic diet of corn pancakes and beans, mortality has rapidly decreased in the last 30 years from 33 per 1,000 inhabitants in 1940 to 9.9 in 1970.[5] Social welfare is provided by an Institute of Social Security which was created in 1945. It began to function in urban and industrial areas, but has since expended to some rural areas. This institute and a similar one for public office employees are calculated to benefit a population of 16,000,000.

Economic Growth

Since 1940 the Mexican economy has grown at an annual rate of over 6 per cent, over 3 per cent per capita, an achievement often called the 'Mexican miracle'. As Roger Hansen says, 'maintaining this rhythm for over thirty-five years may not be miraculous but it is impressive'.[6]

The transformation of the economy is clear from Table V.3 which shows the changing importance of the main economic sectors over the last 30 years, and their share in employment and contribution to GNP.

Table V.3: Share of Sectors in Mexican Economy 1940-70

Sector	1940		1970	
	% employment	% output	% employment	% output
Agriculture	65.4	24.3	39.5	11.6
Mining	1.8	8.5	1.4	5.2
Industry	10.9	22.6	21.5	29.2
Services	21.9	44.6	37.6	54.0
Total	100.0	100.0	100.0	100.0

Source: Clark W. Reynolds, *La Economía Mexicana; su Estructura y Crecimiento en el Siglo XX* (Fondo de Cultura Economica, Mexico, DF, 1973).

Agriculture has not been stagnant, with growth rates well above rates of population increase, but has declined relatively in its share of employment and output, because of the much faster growth of manufacturing. From 1910 to 1964, according to studies made by Nacional Financiera, the GNP corresponding to primary activities increased three and a half times, and that of the industrial sector increased eleven times in the same period.[7]

By 1970, Mexico was mostly self-sufficient in food production, basic oil products, steel and the greater part of consumer goods, and, as Hensen points out,

> an indicator of the vastness of Mexican industrialization is the fact that the fastest growth has been experienced in production goods. Between 1950 and 1960 steel production and other metallic articles grew at an annual rate of 11.5 per cent production of machinery at 10 per cent, vehicles and transportation equipment at 10.7 per cent and chemical products at 12.5 per cent.

> The manufacturing sector presently produces, among other articles, automobile motors, hydraulic brakes, tractors, industrial motors, bulldozers, colour televisions, electric transformers, air conditioning units and electric equipment for offices and business.[8]

Figure V.2: Growth of GNP 1934-72

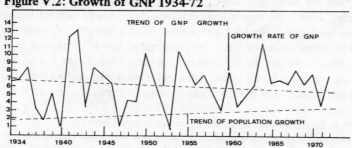

Source: Padilla Aragón, *México: Desarrollo con Pobreza.*

A less optimistic view of the Mexican economy is given by Padilla Aragón who sees an underlying tendency for the growth rate to decline — which he attributes to the slow growth of internal demand, thanks to the backwardness of agriculture, and to the failure to expand foreign trade — and a converging trend for the population growth rate to increase.[9]

The other source of pessimism and concern revolves around

increasing dependence. In 1970 foreign enterprises controlled 13 per cent of total industrial production, and 45 per cent of the modern manufacturing sector.[10] The external debt by the mid-seventies was of formidable importance, and technological dependence on the US — and the volume of payments for foreign technology — was growing every year.

Agricultural Development

According to Reyes Osorio: 'The agricultural sector must perform three main functions: a) provide agricultural and animal products for national and foreign markets, b) provide a sufficient income to agricultural producers and c) provide an adequate basis for the development of the other economic sectors.'[11]

Some data may help us understand if these functions have been carried out. First, agricultural production increased satisfactorily from 1935 to 1967 at an annual rate of 4.4 per cent. Importation of food products almost ended (only 1 per cent of the entire value of agricultural production in 1960) though it has recently started to increase again. The nutrition provided by agricultural products has also improved, going from 1,800 to 2,654 calories per day between 1938 and 1960, even though that is still an unsatisfactory level. The three most important commercial crops which are exported and contribute earnings of foreign exchange are cotton, sugar and coffee. Agricultural exports constituted 24 per cent of total exports in 1974, though the trend is for the trade balance in agriculture to deteriorate. Corn and wheat imports have become necessary since 1970, and the amount of sugar available for export is steadily declining.[12]

Agriculture has shown positive achievements, but, on the other hand, peasant incomes remain well below those of the rest of the country. In 1960, the ratio between agricultural and non-agricultural average incomes was 1:5.9 and within the same agricultural sector there were also profound differences. For example, in the same study Reyes Osorio shows that 50.3 per cent of the land units produced only 4.2 per cent of the entire value of the national agricultural product, and these producers earned an average income of $60 a year.[13] At the other extreme, 0.5 per cent of the land units generated 32 per cent of the product, with an average income of $30,800 a year. The polarity of the income distribution is evident.

The majority of the poor producers apart, the situation of the landless labourers in agriculture (*jornaleros*) is even bleaker. They number some three million. In 1950 they could work an average of 190 days a year, but in 1960 they could only work around 100 days. Even when they do get work the wages paid are normally below the legal minimum, which is in itself very low.

With respect to the last function of agriculture, that of providing a basis for other sectors, an attempt has been made to measure the extent of the intersectoral transfer of capital in the period 1942 to 1962.[14]

The following are the estimated total flows into and out of agriculture:

from the tax mechanisms	+	$340 million
from the bank mechanisms	−	$200 million
from the price mechanisms	−	$280 million
Total capital transfer		$240 million
(agriculture to other sectors)		

In brief, agriculture has bolstered the economic development of the country, providing food and raw materials for national and foreign markets. It has also supported Mexican foreign trade, provided labour to the other sectors and contributed capital in considerable amounts.

The Beneficiaries of Growth

The inequalities described above within the agricultural sector are characteristic of the whole society. According to an ECLA study, 'the average income of the richer 5 per cent of population is 32 times that of the 20 per cent of population constituting the poorer classes. 50 per cent of the population receives only 15 per cent of the total income.'

In comparatively few nations in the world are the rich so rich, and the poor so poor. Alongside a small group of privileged Mexicans and foreigners, who are owners of a considerable part of the national wealth, in 1960 Mexico had, according to the census:

more than a million people who spoke only Indian languages
about 2 million peasants without land
more than 3 million children between 6 and 14 years who had no access
   to schools
4.6 million workers who tried to cross the American border illegally
   and seek jobs in the United States (between 1948 and 1957)

almost 5 million Mexicans who walked barefoot and nearly 2.7 million
who did not usually wear shoes
more than 5 million families with an annual income of less than $960
about 4.3 million homes without running water
more than 8 million people who never ate meat, fish, milk or eggs and
more than 10 million who never ate bread
almost 10 million non-unionized
almost 11 million illiterates.[15]

And as for the number of unemployed, Fidel Velázquez, a national
worker's union leader, recently estimated their number at around four
million,[16] and the director of the National Institute on Work Studies
said that from a labour force of 16 million, the underemployed represented six million and the unemployed were around 1,200,000.[17]

A Global Picture

The problems of agriculture and rural development are closely related
to the general structure of inequality and dependence. The problem is
not solely one of land tenure, technical assistance, credit, productive
infrastructure, commercialization, or administration and organization.
The problem is not the sum of all these needs either. They are all
crucial, but it is much more important to remember that Mexico has a
capitalistic economy which is in addition dependent, and that it chose
an industrialization model of development.

All this has meant, first, that the major part of the resources available has gone into industrialization, credits, infrastructure, price
policies, import substitution protection; everything has been pointing
to the miraculous hope of development through industry. Agriculture
received 20 per cent of total public investment in 1947-52, but never
more than 15 per cent since.

It has also meant a process of capital accumulation at the expense
of the peasants and workers. A long chain of exploitation integrates the
labour force from top to bottom. Peasants without land work for very
low salaries in agricultural and non-agricultural work. Farming enterprises profit by giving low salaries, but in turn they transfer their
surplus to industrial or commercial enterprises, and, through various
mechanisms, some of that surplus flows abroad.

The question is whether the system can sustain itself. According to
Reyes Osorio:

346 *Community Development in Mexico*

The agricultural sector has serious maladjustments, that may turn into a 'bottleneck'. This strangling point will not be a function of the misunderstood productive incapacity of the rural sector, but, on the contrary it will be a function of the limited demand the rural population has for agricultural and non-agricultural products. The very deficient income distribution in Mexico, [which] is even more acute in rural areas, prevents the country from establishing a wide and firm basis on which to expand its industrial production and even its agricultural production.[18]

Notes

1. Claude Bataillon, *Las Regiones Geográficas en México* (Institut des Hautes Etudes de l'Amerique Latin, Université de Paris, 1967).
2. Benitez Zenteno, Raúl Gustavo Cabrera, *Proyecciones de la Población de México, 1960-1980* (Banco de México, S.A., 1966).
3. Dirección General de Estadística. SIC, *Censo General de Población de 1970* (Mexico, 1972).
4. Carlos Muñoz Izquierdo, 'Evaluación del dessarrollo Educativo en México (1958-1970)', *Revista del Centro de Estudios Educativos*, vol. III, no. 3 (Mexico 1973), pp. 22-24.
5. Enrique Padilla Aragón, *México; Desarrollo con Pobreza*, Ed. Siglo XXI (Mexico, 1975), p. 55.
6. Roger Hansen, *La Política del Desarrollo Mexicano*, Ed. Siglo XXI (Mexico, 1975), p. 7.
7. Nacional Financiera, SA, *La economía mexicana en cifras* (Mexico, 1966).
8. Roger Hansen, *La Política del Desarrollo Mexicano*, Ed. Siglo XXI (Mexico, 1975), p. 55.
9. Padilla Aragón, *México: Desarrollo con Pobreza*, p. 23.
10. Bernardo Sepúlveda *et al.*, *Las Empresas Transacionales en México* (El Colegio de México, 1974).
11. Sergio Reyes Osorio, *El marco económico del prolema agrario Mexicano'*, *Lecturas Sobre Desarrollo Agrícola* (Fondo de cultura económica, Mexico, 1974), p. 387.
12. Jesús Puente Leyva, *Distribución del Ingreso en un Area Urbana: el Caso de Monterrey*, el mundo del Hombre: Economía y Demografía (Siglio Vientiuno, Mexico, 1969).
13. US dollars throughout.
14. Reyes Osorio *et al.*, *Estructura Agraria y Desarrollo Agrícola en México* (Fondo de Cultural Económica, Mexico, 1974).
15. Quoted by Padilla, *México: Desarrollo con Pobreza*, p. 101.
16. *Excelsior*, 13 September 1975.
17. *El Sol de México*, 20 December 1975.
18. Reyes Osorio, *Estructura Agraria*, p. 386.

2 ORIGINS AND PURPOSES OF COMMUNITY DEVELOPMENT IN MEXICO

Unlike other countries, Mexico has never had a single nationwide community development programme, though many of the projects sponsored by federal and state governments have been referred to as community development projects, or at least could have reasonably claimed to conform to an early UN definition of community development as:

> the set of procedures by which the inhabitants of a country join their efforts to those of the public powers to improve the economic, social, and cultural situation of the communities, to involve these communities in the life of the nation and so to contribute fully to the progress of the country.[1]

In Mexico, as in other countries, one can discern, in the past history of movements that conform to the broad definition just quoted, a variety of approaches which may be usefully categorized using Dr Mushi's tripartite distinction between a liberal-incrementalist model that appeals primarily to individualistic motives for improvement in a stable capitalist framework, a guided evolutionary model that is more collectivist, more concerned with distributional equity, more willing to use state direction, and a revolutionary-change model that relies on mass mobilization under strong party leadership, and seeks a fundamental change in the distribution of wealth and power between the classes.[2]

Perhaps, 'guided evolutionary' is the best category in which to put the first actions that resemble community development. They date back to the time of the colony (1535) and the work of Vasco de Quiroga who developed, with the Tarascan Indians, a master plan based on the Utopia of Thomas More. Within the context of the terrible exploitation of indigenous populations, Vasco do Quiroga created regional islands of integral development and understanding. After 400 years the social and economic organization of this region still preserves some of its vestiges.

Thereafter during the colony, and the first years of the Republic, such interest as was shown in rural areas and the poor of the urban centres led to individual philanthropic and charitable endeavours with no systematic aims or organization. The first modern form of community development was the 'Cultural Missions' formed by the Ministry of Education in 1923 when the armed period of the Revolution was coming to an end.

These missions consisted of an itinerant group of teachers who visited remote villages and organized courses for rural teachers which lasted three weeks and had the following objectives:

1. Cultural and professional improvement of the rural teachers.
2. Improvement of family domestic practices.
3. Economic improvement of the community, through the development of agriculture and small industries.
4. Community sanitation.[3]

In 1936, a 'social service' of medical students was started. As a prerequiste for obtaining the professional certificate, they were required to do one year of work in a rural community. In 1944 a new law made such social service obligatory for almost all students, but nevertheless only in a very few universities and institutions has the social service scheme really worked.

From 1934 to 1940 the pace of land redistribution under the agrarian reform increased enormously, and the greatest emphasis was placed on turning the *ejido* lands into collective farms. An *ejido* bank provided credit for this purpose and also to individual peasants – and some other supports were also provided. These supports, however, started to be withdrawn from 1940, after the change of president.

Up to this moment most of the schemes described could be classed as guided evolutionary, still influenced by the expectations of the recent revolution. But from 1940 onwards something closer to the liberal-incremental model was the dominant one. The policy of industrialization was demanding a net flow of resources in a different direction.

Regional development plans started in 1947, with the Papaloapan River Basin project, which was intended to offer a solution to agricultural, demographic and political problems. It was also considered to be the answer to the general development needs of the country, and to show the possiblities for developing backward and poor regions. Large expenditures were made on public works: dams, electricity generation, roads, highways and buildings. Similar projects were launched in the basins of the rivers: Lerma, Balsas, Fuerte, Grijalva and other important ones.

At first these project plans had little place for community development and local participation was not promoted to any great extent. In the 1950s, however, the situation changed and they began to incorporate specialized departments for rural community development. Although not well defined, or understood, 'community development' was a term that raised many hopes. The support it received from international organizations and the interest of the various public agencies in expanding their political sphere of influence and their budgets, resulted in the fact that all ministries implemented some national, regional or local pilot plans; some referred to as community development, and some by other names. Technical assistance was expanded, school buildings, electricity, drinking water, health centres and roads for rural areas have received greater attention and budgets from 1956 to the present day, and so also have housing, nutrition and sanitation.

In 1954 agricultural extension services were reorganized and expanded. Young peasant clubs have been promoted by the extensionists since then and in 1956 a 'rural home improvement plan' was launched by the Ministry of Agriculture. The National Institute of Mexican Youth (government sponsored) organized its first rural development brigades in 1958. In 1962, the Lerma River Commission, dependent on the Hydraulic Resources Ministry, started a Community Development Plan, and the other commissions, such as that for the Papaloapan Basin, did the same in 1967.

In 1963 the Ministry of Public Health established the 'Co-operative Programme for Rural Community Development' to build public works in rural villages. It was given food by American organizations to use as incentive payments and also, since 1967, by the United Nations World Food Programme. Besides the existing Cultural Missions, the Ministry of Public Education created, in 1969, the 'Brigades for Rural Community development'.

These are only a sample of the programmes described in a survey undertaken in 1970,[4] and since then new institutions have been created, some of them concerned with organizing production and collectivizing the *ejidos*.

The competition between ministries which results from this proliferation of programmes has been seen as a major problem, and there have been several attempts at co-ordination. In 1958 three ministries established a common programme of 'Rural Improvement Missions' with personnel from those three institutions. This programme did not last very long. Another effort, commenced in 1963, was the creation of a Community Development Office depending directly on the Ministry of the Presidency which survived only two and a half years, and only worked in two pilot project zones. Then, in 1970, the National Institute for Rural Community Development and Popular Housing (INDECO) was created, but this Institute had almost no possibility of acting as either co-ordinator or promoter, since it also received a very reduced budget.

In 1973 the Ministry of the Presidency organized the PIDER programme (Public Investments Programme for Rural Development) which concentrated investments from different ministries in poor regions. It also organized a 'Committee for Socioeconomic Development' in each state with the participation of federal and state agencies, the private sector and university representatives. These committees attempt to control investments and works and decide on priorities in terms of the provision of services to communities. Complaints are still made concerning the lack of co-ordination.

As regards the private sector, during the sixties there were also many associations and groups that launched community development programmes; most of them were pilot projects for particular geographical zones, adult education, protection of indigenous ethnic groups and students' social service were some of the types of these programmes.

Since the end of the sixties, the concept and experience of community development has entered into a crisis of a different order from the problems of administrative co-ordination. In the universities the term is greeted with mistrust. Many social work schools have been in internal turmoil and a complex reconceptualization of the task of the social worker is being undertaken.

Put briefly, the liberal-incremental model is being challenged in terms of the revolutionary change model. Community development projects are seen as a means of imposing the values and way of life of the promoters on others, as programmes which treat marginalized populations as mere 'obstacles' to development, and above all as manifestations of mere philanthropic 'assistentialism' designed to 'buy off' discontent with concessions which do not tackle the underlying cases of backwardness and poverty, but merely obscure the need for fundamental structural change.

What has to be changed, it is argued, is the structure of (dependent) capitalism itself. Even though peasants produce a part of their harvests for their own consumption, a considerable part enters the market. Many peasants can only survive by additionally selling their labour in the market for cash. Through these mechanisms, surplus is transferred from the rural to the industrial sector. The so-called conservatism of the 'obstructive' Mexican peasant is a natural consequence of centuries of exploitation: peasants are unwilling to risk innovations, for fear of losing the little they already have.

Some who hold this view work through local popular movements to seek to change the structure by mobilizing people against established powers, taking as their point of departure the expressed needs and problems of the community — for example, the lack of cultivable land, public services, or housing, the level of wages or transport fares. Others, taking what might be called the 'opportunity' approach, join in official community development schemes, and seek not only to improve the material conditions of life in accordance with the project's aims, but also to raise the consciousness and the level of organization and information of the people within the limits of political tolerance accorded them by the project's sponsors. Thereby they seek to create the conditions for the subsequent acquisition of power by the majority.

Public Agencies in Rural Areas

Perhaps the most important ministry working in rural areas is the Ministry of Agrarian Reform (SRA). This ministry receives demands for land, establishes the procedures for land allocation, legalizes all expropriations, defines measures and limits, issues and registers titles to land, and controls the elections and operations of the *ejido*. These were lands attributed by the agrarian reform collectively to village units. They remain collectively owned, although parts of the *ejido* can be worked individually. They coexist along with small-scale individually-owned land units in Mexico. The ministry also gives courses to peasants on legal rights, organization, administration and productivity.

Recently the SRA has made a great effort to collectivize ejidal production. In addition, it controls the FONAFE (National Fund for the Improvement of *Ejidos*) which finances small-scale industry and infrastructural works.

SRH (Ministry of Hydraulic Resources) constructs irrigation works and maintains and controls all water resources for irrigation. In a country such as Mexico which has a high percentage of poor rain-fed lands, irrigation water becomes a key to improving productivity. Many problems arise from the way water is managed by different proprietors. The SRH also trains peasants in water handling, fertilizing, cultivation and soil protection techniques. For the very large river basins of the country the SRH has formed Commissions for Regional Development.

CONASUPO (National Company for Popular Subsistence) purchases basic crops (corn,beans, wheat, etc.) at guaranteed prices. It also deals in other crops and other consumer products all over the country. It also runs training programmes for the peasants with whom it deals.

The SAG (Ministry of Agriculture and Livestock) is obliged to offer free technical assistance for production, to build small irrigation water deposits, to control the movement of cattle, agricultural and wood products and also to control plagues and diseases. The SAG maintains other kinds of small project in rural areas, such as those associated with home improvement. Most agricultural research is undertaken by SAG specialized centres.

The SEP (Ministry of Public Education) controls the official system of education. Almost all villages of over 500 inhabitants have a primary school. Besides formal education, the SEP controls over 200 Community Development Brigades and a similar number of Cultural Missions.

The SSA (Ministry of Health) controls the Rural Health Centres (small hospitals), conducts vaccination campaigns, constructs drinking water systems, improves communal and home sanitation, nutrition and housing. For a considerable period of time it sponsored a community development programme, which has now been diversified in several ways.

The INPI (National Institute for the Protection of Infants, and the Family) has established many lines of action in the cities. In rural areas it distributes *Nurtinpis* — nutritional breakfast package — among school children. It also controls a community development programme operated through 'community development centres' (a building, some sewing and typing machines, a nurse and some social workers). A local branch of INPI sponsored the programme to be evaluated in this study.

SOP (Ministry of Public Works) builds and maintains roads, highways, railroads and large public buildings. For small villages the SOP sponsors the construction of access roads by a labour-intensive method. It also has a programme for the provision of sportsfields (mainly basketball) and a productive activities programme to establish small industries and workshops.

The CFE (Federal Commission of Electricity), as well as installing and operating electricity networks and rural electrification schemes, also sells a basic home appliances package and a communal package. Huge dams for hydro-electric generation are also built by the CFE.

A final but perhaps decisive institution working in rural areas is the Rural Credit Bank. This was formed last year by the amalgamation of three different official banks that previously operated separately. The bank not only provides the money but also promotes the organization of *ejidatarios* and small proprietors in co-operatives and solidarity groups and gives technical assistance. Sometimes the bank buys and provides fertilizers, machinery and pesticides, hires personnel for the harvest and sells the products. This happens mostly for commercial crops.

Many other smaller institutions also work in rural areas: state and municipal governments, religious, independent and philanthropic institutions all have small programmes which are limited geographically as well as in terms of objectives.

It is within the context of this complex network of institutions and interests that the programme to be described took place. A detailed exposition of the origins, objectives and organization of the programme is presented in the following chapters.

Notes

1. Social Progress through Community Development, UN Bureau of Social Affairs; quoted by Marco Marchionia in *Comunidad y Desarrollo* (Editorial Terra-Nova, Barcelona, 1969).
2. See the Tanzanian case study in this volume.
3. Santiago Sierra Augusto, *Las Misiones Culturales* (Sepsetentas, Mexico, 1973), p. 23.
4. Witold Langrod, *En el Campo de México* (Universidad Iberoamericana, Mexico, 1970).

3 THE PROGRAMME AND ITS SETTING

Origins and Chronology

The particular programme we chose to evaluate was first promoted at the beginning of 1973. At that time, elections for governor were to be held in the state of Guanajuato. The only candidate running for election invited a specialist in community development to participate in his campaign as an observer and also as an adviser.

Political campaigns for governor are extensive and intensive. Even though there was no other candidate, the candidate and his entourage travelled throughout the state, holding meetings in large cities, in municipal towns and in many smaller villages over a period of three months. At that time, José Trueba — the specialist — was in charge of the Social Development Department of INDECO (National Institute for Rural Community Development). When the campaign ended, Trueba presented to the elected governor plans for a project to be started in the poorest region of the state, which included eight *municipios*. The governor was also interested in this zone because he was born in one of these *municipios*.

After a series of analyses the project was finally approved by the governor and a contract was signed in January 1974 between the state government, represented by the INPI (Institute for the Protection of Infancy), and Trueba as head of the team of 'promoters' or 'animators'. The contract was for one year and aimed to evaluate the possibilities of expanding the project to other zones of the state. The project was named PRODECOR.

A basic document exists in which objective, criteria, organization and budget were established. However, the objectives sought by the state government and the promoting team were slightly different. The governor was concerned with the poor conditions in the zone, and with enhancing his prestige as a rising politician by finding solutions for a difficult problem. The promoting team saw the programme as an opportunity to improve the standard of living of the zone but principally as a means to facilitate the education, organization and participation of peasants.

The programme began in the field in March 1974 and the first year produced politically acceapable results. A new contract was signed in 1975, and promotion activities were extended to other *municipios*. All seemed to be going well. However, several difficulties arose, at the end of 1975, between the promoting team and the Director of the INPI (representing the state government). Salaries, current expenses and other administrative aids began to be reduced and the team considered the possibility of resigning.

Finally in March 1976 some of the promoters were dismissed or resigned and the same happened to the rest during the following months. The INPI kept only two promoters and a veterinary surgeon after the team left; the programme was practically ended after a little more than two years of operation. Not all the projected stages of the programme were completed, therefore, a fact which slightly impairs its value for case study purposes, but not to a fatal degree.

The chronology is outlined below:

	1973	1974	1975	1976
Campaign and election	xxx			
Preparation of the project	xx			
Approval of the project		x		
Formation of the team		x		
Initiation of activities		x		
Development of programme		xxxxxxxxxxxxxxxxxxxxx		
Expansion to a second area			xxxxxxxxxxx	
Withdrawal of promoters				xxxx

Contents of the Programme

Let us begin by summarizing the basic document of January 1974[1] which set out the objectives of the programme.

After specifying that the programme was in the nature of a pilot project which could later be expanded and which should serve as a training ground for promoters, the document lists the four main objectives in each village as:

1. To reinforce the peasant's existing institutions and organizations and to promote the creation of new ones legally compatible with those already in existence.
2. To carry out an education programme for adults within the rural villages already included in the programme.
3. To promote and establish a programme of economic improvement for peasants.

4. To promote and establish a programme of social welfare — improvement of public services, nutrition, housing, health, etc.

The following section on the basic criteria for the operation of the programme reflects the compromises which had to be achieved. On the one hand, material improvement is not enough. 'The personal development of peasants . . . will not be encouraged if thinking, organizing and critical capacity are not increased.' Likewise, the programme will concentrate on the poor — the landless, the *ejidatarios* and the small proprietors, and atomization of individual efforts has to be countered by integrating them in a 'collective force'. But, on the other hand, there should be no adventurism; 'we accept the institutional and legal framework created by the government for the execution, development and consolidation of the agrarian reform as well as compatibility of such objectives and criteria with those guiding this programme', and 'this programme will work in co-ordination with those official ministries that operate in our zone . . . supporting the actions and programmes these ministries are developing'. Then came a list of the detailed activities to be carried out:

Education:
  better use of the school's demonstration plot[2]
  primary education up to fourth grade in those places where it does not exist
  a radio programme with orientation towards change and development
  literacy campaigns through the University Social Service Programme
  programmes for the support and encouragement of rural teachers in the area

Health
  distribution of *Nurtinpis* (nutritional packages with breakfast for those children attending school) in villages where it is not yet distributed
  distribution of medicines in collaboration with the Public Health Ministry. We shall ask this agency to send a Doctor to instruct and advise local caseworkers and to provide them with a basic set of medicines and first-aid kit.
  construction of facilities for running water in schools located in villages that are without drinking water.

Economic improvement

> developing co-operatives for savings and general marketing of agricultural products, also special co-operatives for fruit producers, cattle-raisers, handicraft producers, and supporting the activities of CONASUPO (arranging communal buying of fertilizers, etc.)
>
> promoting livestock production — poultry, sheep, goats, rabbits, pigs and bees
>
> experimenting with improvement of pasture grasses and maguey and nopal cactus
>
> promoting fish culture by dams
>
> constructing forage deposits

Sectoral promotion

> youth clubs
>
> women's and children's clubs

Cultural and recreational

> several events

Housing and public services

> according to the needs and characteristics of the villages, an effort will be made to satisfy these.

The Objectives in Practice

This list of objectives needs elaborating, partly to 'situate' the programme in the general spectrum of community development programmes, partly to take account of modifications in practice by the promoters.

First, on the external links of the communities to the nation, the programme was clearly designed more to transfer resources into the villages from the towns than vice versa. Food rations, technical assistance, building materials, equipment, tools and government credit were all to be provided, though internal improvements in production were hoped for as the main means of enrichment.

Economic improvement projects were directed, in a first phase, toward self-consumption, in a second phase toward local markets and in a third phase toward regional or national markets. When this last phase was reached it might well be that some transfer, from agriculture to industry, would take place via an unfair price system, but the intention was always that the wealth created in the zone would go to the population of that zone and that only a minimal part would diffuse to other regions.

As for the political effects of the programme, rather than trying expressly to develop a national consciousness, the programme sought to create and develop an authentic class consciousness in the peasants, as a basis for the autonomous development of the communities.

There were no intentions to give support to the ruling regime. Neither were there attempts to defuse the peasant's demands by articulating and placating them, thereby reducing social tensions. Rather, these were channelled to other official agencies directly in charge of those problems. Peasants were told of their rights and the ways in which to proceed.

As for the means of inducing economic change in the villages, given the restricted ecological possibilities, the choice was made to diversify production towards cattle raising. Nevertheless, fertilizers and improved trees for fruit cultivation were also promoted. Economic projects were always directed towards an equitable distribution of benefits. In this sense, participation of the largest number of peasants was sought, and the intention was, at least, to encourage the participation of the poorest. Since the zone has traditionally had one of the highest migration rates in the country, the creation of new employment was also stressed.

Internal political change was sought by attempting to discover, support and develop natural leaders, in order to present a new alternative to *cacicazgo* the traditional authoritarian leadership. At no moment was there any intention to assure political stability for the central government. Great importance was placed on the active participation of peasants at all levels of community activity. Furthermore, there were attempts to promote the participation of peasants in the policies of the programme itself, mainly in the last months of work. In order to avoid technocratism and manipulation, it was intended to have a 'peasants' programme in which the promoters and technical staff carried out plans of action which had been decided on by the peasants. Whenever possible the programme attempted to increase the opportunities for political expression, thus promoting participation in the decision-making process of the village with respect to day-to-day matters, in the hope that organizations with political as well as economic objectives might eventually result. In the cultural and educational field, the programme did attempt to introduce new behaviour patterns and values. Solidarity was fostered, as against individualism; creativity as opposed to existing passivity; participation and self-reliance instead of dependence. The participation of women, as well as a more democratic decision-making process at the family and communal level, were promoted.

At the same time there was no wholesale sweeping away of local values and technology which were valued whenever they were useful within the economic and cultural context of the region. It was also a matter of concern that the technology introduced should be appropriate — should exploit local agricultural and animal resources more rationally, should not exceed the learning and organizational capacity of the peasants and should have low capital-labour ratios.

In the same way, rational exploitation demanded the creation of technical and managerial capacity in order to develop the work organization. Training in those aspects was always sought to be framed in co-operative organization forms. All economic groups were designed to work on a co-operative basis.

The programme also sought to modify women's role in family and community life by urging their participation as members of the co-operatives, or as children's instructors or health promoters giving services to the community. It was assumed that such participation could lead to a breakdown of the father's traditional and despotic authority.

In the consumption field, the emphasis was on nutrition and health. Nutritional improvement included increased protein consumption through rabbit-breeding at household level, and also greater caloric and vitamin consumption through keeping bees and vegetable plots. Preventative health measures concentrated on improving home hygiene. In addition, peasant girls were trained as health promoters, trained in pregnant mother and infant care, the recognition and treatment of common diseases, and first aid in the villages.

No specific family planning activity was attempted. Interested persons were advised to consult family planning advisers at health centres belonging to the Ministry of Public Health, and might be helped with transport.

The consumption, savings and credit co-operatives were expected to help transform the consumption habits of the population. The goals were to look for cheaper prices, and to acquire and practice the habit of saving, to be free from local money-lenders and rationalize house expenses.

Not all these objectives received equal attention. The promoters' views of priorities are best given in their own words.

Political and educational objectives were doubtless the most important ones, and those that received our greatest efforts. Organization and education of the peasants were the true aims of the programme. The other objectives would be considered as the means to reach such goals.

The economic objective became important as a means of attaining educational-organizational objectives. The very poor material conditions of the people in the geographic area showed that no educational activity can be undertaken if, at the same time, the economic situation of poor peasants is not changed. Organization also demands a common interest, over a specified time period, such as the interest produced in a communal or co-operative economic project.

The Setting

The State of Guanajuato

The state of Guanajuato in which the programme took place, is located in the Mexican Central Plateau (Figure V.3). Compared to other states,

Figure V.3: Location in Guanajuato State

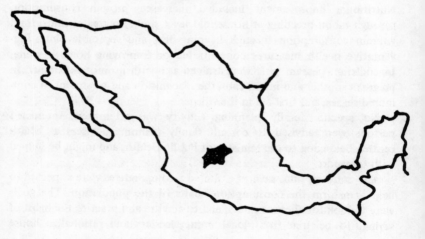

Guanajuato is not very large; it has a surface area of 30,589 square km, i.e. 1.5 per cent of the country's total area. Nevertheless, it is one of the most densely populated states, with 74 inhabitants per square kilometre, three times the average for the country as a whole.

Its population is *mestizo* and the greater part of its large communities were founded in the early phases of the colonial period. Forty-eight per cent of the population lived in rural areas in 1970 and the rate of out-migration was among the highest in the country — largely out-migration in search of casual work in Mexico City, in other states, and in the United States. A smaller proportion of the economically active population is employed in the secondary sector, working in a roup of fairly well-industrialized cities.

As well as its own executive, the state has its own judiciary and its own legislature. The *diputados* of the latter, in addition to their legislative task, also play an intermediary role in channelling the concrete demand of different population groups or villages to the state of federal agencies. The branch offices of these agencies are all located in the capital city (which in this case is also named Guanajuato.) Almost all demands, applications or procedures for obtaining public services or solving the needs or problems of the communities need to be presented in the city of Guanajuato.

The state of Guanajuato is made up of 46 *municipios*, each of which is run by a committee (a 'delegation') whose size depends on its population. The rural *municipios* have few resources and little opportunity to build and operate public services. Running water, schoolrooms, electricity and roads depend basically on the investment programmes of the federal agencies, in co-operation with the state government and the villages.

Physically, the state is divided into two regions (Figure V.4). The poorer upland zone to the north is higher, more rugged and has less rainfall as well as less flat land. To compound its ill-fortune it has received less government investment.

By contrast, the other zone, El Bajio (the lowlands), has a higher rainfall and more flat land. It contains the majority of the roads, 74 per cent of the irrigated land and the state's major industrial activities. It also has a higher population density, and is the centre of commercial agriculture characterized by the intensive use of fertilizers, improved seeds and machinery. High yields from export products allow the irrigated lands to be profitably and intensively used. The number of these farmers is relatively small, and they have no difficulty in getting bank credits to sustain a high level of modern agricultural technology.

Figure V.4: The State of Guanajuato

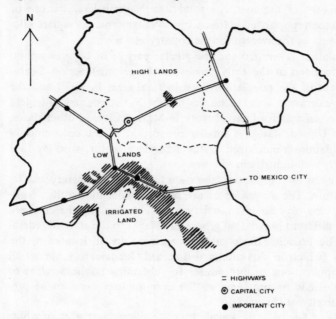

The Project Area

The northern zone, by contrast, in which the project was located, is populated by peasants controlling limited resources and operating under conditions of low productivity because of the lack of water. Insufficient production obliges them to go for seasonal work in the irrigated lands of El Bajio, or of other states and to search for work in other activities such as building labour.

The eight *municipios* in which the programme was carried out are in the poorest north-east corner of the state. As can be seen from the map (Figure V.5), paved roads running from the main national highway hardly penetrate beyond the two small towns of San José Iturbide and San Luis de Paz. Beyond that there are dirt roads, vast areas of flat lands owned by private farmers, and two canyon river basins, offering small areas for cultivation along which settlement takes place. The total population of these eight *municipios* was approximately 100,000 inhabitants in 1970, but the programme concentrated in fact on 40 villages, mainly located in the poor areas of the mountainous region.

After much reconnoitring we selected two of those villages for our

Figure V.5: The Project Area

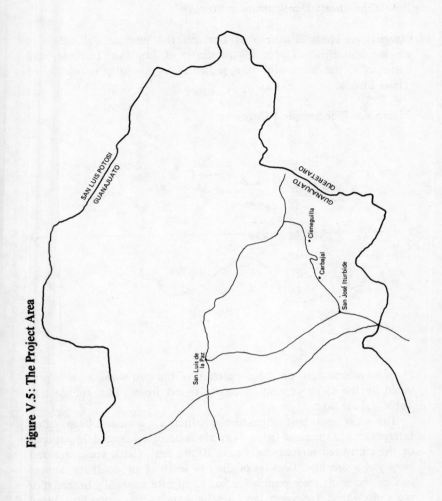

SAN LUIS POTOSI
GUANAJUATO

GUANAJUATO
QUERETARO

San Luis de la Paz

• Cieneguilla

• Carbajal

San José Iturbide

comparative study (Figure V.6). *Carbajal*, the 'unsuccessful' village, is on the hinterland edge of the *municipio* of San José Iturbide, and *Cieneguilla*, the 'successful' one, is in the neighbouring *municipio* of Tierra Blanca.

Figure V.6: The Sample Villages

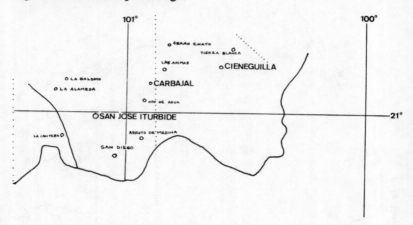

Basic information on the population of the two *municipios* is provided by the 1970 population census report from which the data in Table V.4 are taken.

The most important agricultural products are corn and beans often interplanted in the same fields. Corn alone occupied around 75 per cent of the cultivated surface, and beans 20 per cent. Cattle are scarce and crop yields are low. Because of the low levels of productivity, almost half of the adult male population has to migrate seasonally in search of work elsewhere. Ten years ago a new economic activity was introduced into the area, namely home knitting machines which are operated mainly by women. In an interview held with the municipal president of San José Iturbide we were told that approximately 10,000 machines were to be found in the north-eastern zone, i.e. approximately one machine for every two families.

Social Organization

The following description of 'social classes' in the zone was given in a draft 'The Story of San José Iturbide' found in its municipal files. It is significant not only for what it says, but for the fact that it can be said

Table V.4: Population and Housing Data for Sample Area

Municipio	Total population	Economically active	Primary activities	Industry	Commerce and services	Literacy	Attend primary school	With primary instruction or more
					Population data in %			
Tierra Blanca	8,428	24.4	72.6	10.5	8.4	39.1	39.5	4.1
San Jose Iturbide	23,490	23.0	62.3	17.4	11.9	54.0	38.9	7.4

Municipio	Total population	Total number of houses		With running water		With sewage	With electricity	With radio	With TV
			Own	Inside	Outside	Housing data in %			
Tierra Blanca	8,428	1,595	91.4	2.6	3.6	3.0	6.2	42.4	2.9
San Jose Iturbide	23,490	3,867	77.7	18.1	9.6	20.1	29.1	66.8	10.2

Source: *Census Report* (1970).

so matter-of-factly as if describing part of the order of nature.[3]

The difference between these two classes is evident with respect to their economic position, level of nutrition, degree of education and kind of clothing. The attitude of those of the humble class towards the middle class is to a certain point indifferent, since there are only a few persons who have an interest in overcoming their situation. The middle class eats three meals a day, and the humble class only two.

With reference to the economic organization of the zone, this same document mentions that 'there existed a commercial organization named the *Union of acrylic knitting workers of San José*, but this organization does not function at all, even though the advantages of such an organization have continuously been insisted upon'. It goes on: 'for these three types of employees [domestic, agricultural and knitters] social benefits do not exist, wages are below the legal minimum and their rights are limited'.

The characteristics of the area in summary are:

mountainous and rocky land
little cultivable land
lack of water for drinking and irrigation purposes
low agricultural productivity
predominant production of crops for self-consumption (corn, beans)
lack of wage work
high rate of seasonal migration
low incomes
scarce and difficult means of transportation
lack of public services such as electricity, drinking water, health centres
high rate of illiteracy
a new occupation, mainly for women — knitting acrylic fibres with
   home-based machines.

After years of neglect, several government programmes were initiated in the area within four years. PRODECOR was one of them.

Notes

1. Programa del Gobierno del Estado de Guanajuato y del Instituto de Protección a la Infancia de Guanajuato, para promover el dessarrollo de las com-

unidades rurales en el noreste del Estado, 1974-5.

    2. Each rural school usually has a plot of land used for agricultural experiments.

    3. 'Notas de la historia de San José', typed document, municipal files of San José Iturbide, 1975.

4 ADMINISTRATION AND ORGANIZATION

The most important elements in the administrative structure of the programme were; the formal organization, the territorial and operational organization, and the resources which were invested. These elements are explained in detail in this chapter.

Formal Organization

The structure of the work team wwas as shown in Figure V.7. From Figure V.7 we can see that there were, in fact, four types of work. All the positions involved were held by official personnel who were paid by the programme. The main functions and training levels of the people holding these jobs are as follows.

The coordinator was responsible to the state government and the INPI, for carrying out the programme. He was in charge of relations between the programme and the existing authorities in the region as well as the planning and co-ordination of activities. He had a postgraduate degree, with long-term experience in research and social promotion. His assistant, the sub-co-ordinator, was a college graduate.

The technical staff advised the social promoters about the diverse technical aspects of their work. This group planned the actions to be taken, maintained the technical training of the promoters and peasants, supervised the work undertaken and produced the necessary educational materials. The administrator, who was nominated directly by the state governor, had graduated from secondary school (*preparatoria*) and had experience in business and farm administration.

The promoters worked in pairs (one man and one woman), one for each micro-region consisting of four to seven villages. These teams were responsible for the programme's basic fieldwork. While living in these villages in constant contact with the peasants, they carried out the promotional tasks as well as giving general advice and encouragement. The promoters' origins were varied, ranging from peasants with very little education to peasant girls who had graduated from a social work school (secondary level), to university students and young professionals.

The actual functioning of the programme was in fact organized on the lines shown in Figure V.8.

Figure V.7

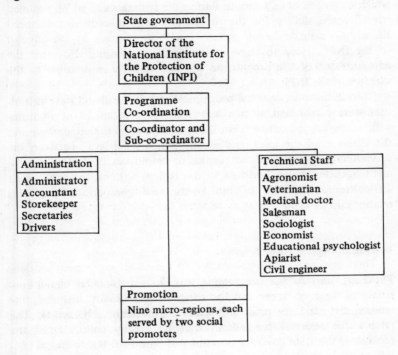

Figure V.8

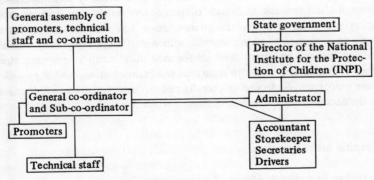

The changes brought about in the formal organization diagram were due, on the one hand, to the introduction of democratic mechanisms enabling the promoters, technical staff and co-ordination to participate in the decision-making. Decisions were made in a general assembly which convened once a month during the seminars and which assumed overall responsibility for the programme. The co-ordinator balanced the decisions made by the assembly with those made by the director of the INPI, trying to arrive at intermediate measures. However, the administrator of the programme was also directly responsible to the director of the INPI.

The relations between the programme and the local and state authorities were established at two levels: first, by means of negotiations which were carried out between the co-ordinator of the programme and the director of the INPI, and secondly at a local level, between the promoters and the local authorities or employees of diverse government agencies which operated in the region, with all the consequent difficulties arising out of the institutional competition that this relationship entailed.

Territorial Organization

The basic unit of the programme was the micro-region which consisted of four to seven neighbouring villages usually including the municipality and its most important surrounding settlements. The criteria for selecting the villages were principally political, i.e., the request of the state governor or municipal president. But technical considerations were also taken into account: that is, the villages chosen should not be too isolated or be marred by too many local conflicts between the peasants. One pair of promoters worked in each micro-region and lived in one of its communities. The fact that there was a man and a woman working together allowed of more integrated action, since in this area it is very difficult for men to relate to women and vice versa. It is also important to note that the promoters worked in groups. Team effort helped to prevent the loss of enthusiasm often experienced by the social promoter working alone.

Recruitment of Personnel

Given the fact that in Mexico there are very few promoters with solid experience, the participants in the programme were selected on the basis of their interest in working with the peasants and of their willingness to accept the difficult conditions and low salaries which were offered. Training was provided essentially inside the programme by means of seminars and technical advice given by the staff and co-ordinators.

Transport

The programme owned two lorries, three cars and one VW minibus which are reported to have been insufficient. For this reason the programme resorted to paying for the petrol used by the private cars of some of the participants. The promoters who did not own cars used bicycles and were given allowances for bus trips. Theoretically, they were supposed to take turns in using one of the programme's vehicles once a week, but this system frequently did not work. The staff and co-ordinators, on the other hand, made their visits to the villages in the cars belonging to the programme.

Work Routine

The work cycle applied in the programme was as follows: five weeks of fieldwork followed by one week of seminars. During the period of fieldwork, each pair of promoters planned their activities, usually visiting one village every day of the week. Generally, the mornings were dedicated to house visits and the afternoons to meetings with the organized groups.

Reports

Every one and and a half months the promoters handed in a report of their activities. The co-ordinator himself turned in three monthly reports to the governor.

Team Meetings

Informal weekly meetings were held between the promoters who operated in neighbouring micro-regions. However, because of the difficulties in getting together, most of the decisions were made in the seminars. These lasted for five days and were dedicated to training the promoters, evaluating the work which had been done and planning future actions. The evaluation and planning activities were carried out on a democratic basis with everyone participating.

Meetings with Peasants

Since the promoters lived in one of the villages of their micro-region and visited the others frequently, they were in direct contact with the peasants. At a more formal level however, there were meetings and assemblies. The meetings were held with small groups of villagers, or with the whole community, to discuss some particular problem which affected the village and also to request their participation in some new activity or to explain a new programme. Sometimes, one of the co-ordinators or technical staff attended the meetings and assemblies.

Supervision and Evaluation

Supervision was mostly indirect, being exercised during the seminars when all the team members could participate. Evaluation was the assessment of the whole team, though an external evaluation by specialists from the Mexican Institute of Social Studies was planned. However, for lack of funds, this only worked during the first six months of the programme. Whenever a serious problem cropped up, or when a new promoter joined the team, the co-ordinators directly supervised the promoter by accompanying him in his fieldwork.

Training of the Promoters

This was effected during the week of seminars by the workers in the programme themselves. However, outsiders were also invited from time to time to discuss some topic related to the work of the programme.

Training of the Peasants

This was accomplished in three ways. The first was technical instruction in the development of the projects. For example, the veterinarian gave instructions during his consulting visits to a pig-raising co-operative.

The second method took the form of short courses (two to three days) or seminars in the subject, for example bee-keeping, fruit-growing etc., but other aspects related to the general situation of the peasants in Mexico were also discussed, with special attention to the area in which the programme operated.

The third method consisted of visits to other communities or groups within the same area which were more advanced in some aspect of their projects, and external visits when it was necessary to get acquainted with social or technical experience outside the region.

Technical Assistance

The technical team visited the communities at the request of the promoters or the peasants themselves, to provide the technical assistance that the organized group might need and at the same time to give the peasants advice on how to run their businesses.

Promotional Strategy

Originally, the promoting team had only an approximate idea of the sequence of activities to be undertaken. Retrospectively, however, the co-ordinator saw their work as going through the following stages.[1]

Contact with the Community

This stage of initial contact is also a stage of study and socioeconomic research to discover the needs of the village. The first simple and feasible projects can also be initiated. The promoter is supposed to gain the people's confidence and to be serious, punctual and not to promise things that the programme is unable to fulfil.

Formation of Groups

Once the promoters have interested people in participating in simple improvement activities, the work is focused on the formation of economic production or consumption units. Specific training then becomes of importance and courses are begun at the headquarters. Legal registration of groups and applications for credit are commenced. Depending on the cost of the projects, sums of money are advanced by the programme in order to begin the building of the required facilities, and to maintain the level of interest of the population.

In order to facilitate promotion, the programme considered a series of 'economic modules', consisting of a basic unit of operation that could easily be understood and explained by the promoter. The programme prepared and edited instructions for modules related to the following areas of production:

beehives
goats
lambs
pigs (suckling and fat pigs)
poultry (chicken fattening)
rabbits (home-consumption and commercial)
fruit trees
market gardening.

The instructions for each module contained: a general idea of the project; the requirements for a solidarity group; its practical functioning; investment and credit requirements; expected benefits and repayment of credit; perspectives for expansion; and the regional dimensions of the project. Technical staff supported the interested groups.

Technical Training

The programme anticipates the creation at this moment of a 'Peasant Training Centre'. Technically, the centre should provide adequate training for the activities promoted. It should also set the problems related to the role of agriculture in their national economic and ideological context, pointing out, for example, the need to replace individualistic by collectivist attitudes in order to transform society. Educational activities take place through the use of courses, assemblies, written and illustrated materials and information, small meetings, visits, etc.

Economic Consolidation

Economic groups are already working at this stage and are supported by the credits they applied for. Installations should be completed, or at least have started production. Some will face marketing and other external problems, also internal problems of organization and human relations. Some associates leave the groups and new members can then be admitted.

Administrative

The attention of the programme is now focused on the consolidation of economic groups. As peasants do not usually have an entrepreneurial mentality, training concentrates on administration and accounting. During this stage economic groups at the community level come together to form producers and consumers societies at the regional level. Moreover, the economic groups form 'Local Peasants Councils' in each village. The technical services of the programme should be transformed into a self-financing Service Centre and the promotional activities of the programme should greatly decrease.

Peasant Responsibility

By this stage the groups should be economically independent and the producers and consumers societies should also be working normally. A 'Regional Peasants Council' must be formed with representatives from the local councils to take responsibility for the Training Centre, the Service Centre, and a fund established with contributions from the profits the groups make. The programme would then have succeeded and should be ceased.

The whole process, in the estimation of the project workers, should have taken three years with each stage lasting about six months, though with flexible target times as all groups or communities do not develop at the same rate. In fact, as we noted in dealing with the limitations of the programme, the total duration was only two years. Administrative consolidation was beginning to take place only in the most advanced groups, as will be seen in future chapters.

Resources

Budgets for 1974 and 1975[2]

$192,000 was allocated for 1974 but only $152,000 was spent. In 1975, the programme was expanded to cover three more *municipios* and ten new promoters had to be hired, as well as some complementary personnel. This represented a 50 per cent enlargement of the programme. Thus, $248,000 was budgeted but again, though for different reasons, only $200,000 in effect was spent.

The categories of expenditure were approximately as follows:

	1974	1975	Total
Salaries	$80,000	$120,000	$200,000
Operational costs (petrol, offices papers, etc.)	19,200	25,600	44,800
Promotional support (short-term loans, grants for materials, tools, rabbits, seeds, etc.)	24,800	18,400	43,200
Equipment (vehicles, office furniture, audiovisual, etc.)	28,000	36,000	64,000
	$152,000	$200,000	$352,000

At the end of the programme, the equipment was valued at over $40,000. All the above funds were provided by the state government through the INPI.

Other Financial Aid

Approximate sums of other allocations were:

Food rations given during the building of public services or works, provided by the Health Ministry	$83,200
Truck lent for 9 months by the Ford Programme	2,160
Building tools lent by the Public Works Ministry	3,200
Grants from individuals and groups	8,000
	$96,560

Credits approved by the Rural Credit Bank for the following activities:

two pig-breeding groups	$104,000
three goat-breeding groups	24,000
four bee-keeping groups	25,600
one fruit-growing group	6,400
one poultry group	2,400
	$162,400

Notes

1. José Trueba *et al.*, *Modelo de Organización para el Desarrollo Campesino y Fomento de la Productividad: el Sexenio 1976-1982* (mimeo, 1976), p. 226.

2. In order to provide an easier base of comparison, we shall express all monetary sums in US dollars at the rate then prevailing, namely, 12.5 Mexican pesos to the dollar.

5   THE 'UNSUCCESSFUL' VILLAGE: CARBAJAL

Description of the Village

Carbajal is a small community of about 560 inhabitants in about 100 households. It is located on the south-east border of the municipality of San José Iturbide, about 14 km along a good dirt road from the main highway.

It has a mild climate, not very extreme, since it is situated on a plateau about 2,150 m above sea level. Some of its houses and land nevertheless are in the foot-hills of a mountain range. Vegetation is of the arid type: cactus and small bushes. Rainfall is sparse, about 400 mm annually, and lack of water is therefore the most important problem the people have to face. There is a small river flowing through the village, though it brings water only during the rainy season from August to November. The soil in Carbajal is thin and the lack of water causes production to be low. The nearby hills have pine trees, but these are not exploited.

We could not find reliable data on the origins of Carbajal, since the municipal files were destroyed by fire in 1929. It has certainly been settled for over 120 years however; older people recalled that their grandparents had lived there.

Land is privately owned. Sixty per cent of households have from two to four hectares, and only two have no land, but eight own over 15 hectares and about twenty own less than one.

The settlement pattern is scattered (Figure V.9). At the centre of the village there is a small dam, and a chapel. All roads — little more than paths — are unpaved. The population is completely 'mestiza' and only Spanish is spoken.

The nuclear family is the common household form, but families are closely interrelated in three or four kin networks of which the larger are the Zarazua and Gutierrez families.

According to the census of 1970, 24 per cent of the population is economically active, and agriculture is the main activity of 90 per cent of them, with commerce and industry claiming 5 per cent each. Of the 10 respondents to our questionnaire four worked only on their own land, four had to work as *jornaleros* (day labourers) to supplement the income from their own smaller holdings of land, one was a merchant owner of two stores, and another was a mason.

377

Figure V.9: Plan of Carbajal

Cultivation Land

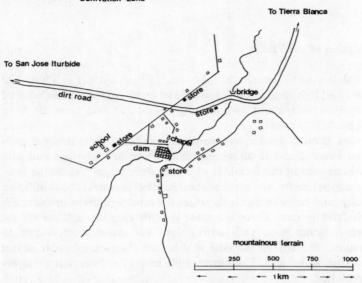

Most of the households have at least a piece of land, which they work for home consumption and cultivate corn and beans, usually interplanted. Productivity is very low. Dom Camilo, the Municipal Delegate, who seemed to be a good cultivator, said that in average years one hectare produced 500 kg of corn and 300 kg of beans. His family of five members consumed 1,650 kg of corn and 270 kg of beans per year. Three to four hectares, therefore, provided the necessary corn and a small surplus of beans. Houses with less land and more dependants need other sources of income.

Nor is productivity obviously improving. Fertilizers are not applied, because of the lack of of irrigation water. People say 'the fertilizer wants water', plants grow high at first but decline later and produce little corn. Pesticides for beans have been applied for four years by two of our ten respondents. Some people in the village own a spraying pump. Improved seeds were also not used, because of bad results when two of them were tried. Traditional corn seeds reach full growth in three months, and hybrid improved seeds take about six months. As the rains start late in July, they have only a little over three months before the arrival of frosts in November.

Of the ten families interviewed, all kept some kind of domestic animals.

	Number of households	Average number of animals
hens	4	4
pigs	3	1
cows	3	2
sheep	2	15
mules	1	1
beehives	1	4

Eggs, poultry and honey are used for domestic consumption. Pigs are a means of saving, because they feed only on offal, and sheep are commercial stock. Some milk is sold within the village, and the wool and animals are sold to outsiders.

As agriculture is not very productive, the temporary migration of men is very common. In some seasons, over 60 per cent of the adult male population leaves the community, some to places such as Nayarit (600 km away) to harvest beans, or to Torreón and Apatzingán to harvest cotton, and to the cities for building activities. Much of this work, especially harvesting work, is piecework, with earnings varying from $4 to $8 a day. After paying lodging, meals and transportation not much is left to bring back to the family, after a two- or three-month absence.

It is not surprising that a new source of income — knitting of acrylic yarn garments — should have been quickly accepted in recent years. The 1970 census did not record women as economically active, but we found at least one knitting machine in every house, and a large proportion of the girls and women work steadily at them. On average they produce five garments a day at 32 cents each. This makes a monthly income of about $40. To pay for a machine bought on credit takes $16 a month over two years. Middlemen provide the credit, and the yarn, and market the finished products in the cities — at a very considerable profit.

Knitting is hard work. Many girls end up with muscular and lung problems after some years, and they do consider themselves exploited, but they are glad to have the money, since the environment offers few alternatives. In these circumstances savings are almost impossible, and when people have an unforeseen need or problem, they sell an animal, or borrow from a money-lender at an interest rate of 20 per cent a month, or from a friend. Only one of the people interviewed had obtained credit from a bank — he was the owner of the two stores. Cash incomes of the population were very difficult to calculate, so we preferred to look for some other indicators of living levels.

The normal meal of the families interviewed, consists of tortillas (corn pancakes) and beans. Soups and *nopalitos* (a kind of cactus) are often included. As many as 40 per cent of the sample never ate meat, milk consumption is also very low: 60 per cent never drink it and 30 per cent only once a month. Fruit and vegetables are very rare, so besides the lack of animal protein, intake of minerals and vitamins is also low.

Housing is poor by Mexican standards. Most houses are of *adobe* (mud brick) with tiles for roofing, and consisting of two rooms plus kitchen. Six out of ten houses visited had dirt floors; windows were small, and ventilation and illumination poor. There are no bathrooms or latrines, and physical needs are satisfied in the extensive backyard common to all homes. A few homes have additional facilities such as a place to keep grain, cultivating tools, etc.

Clothing seems to be adequate for the climate. Except for two very poor families visited, young girls and boys wore clothing that was clean, in good condition and even fashionable. It would be difficult to distinguish between a girl from Carbajal and one from San José Iturbide by their appearance.

There is a shortage of public services. Drinking water, electricity, health centres, telegraph and sportsfields are lacking. A primary school has been functioning for 15 years, but when the programme started in Carbajal it was incomplete, having only the first four grades. During the time that programme was being conducted the fifth and sixth grades were added.

To solve the need for drinking water, they have had a dam built on the small river (Figure V.10). It was built over 80 years ago and holds water from November to March. Cattle consume water directly from the dam, and water for home use comes from three small wells sunk on the upstream edge of the dammed water. In this way water filters through to the well and comes out cleaner. Transportation to the home is by buckets, and water is kept in clay jars.

The water in the dam dries up about March, and the wells one month later. Thus they are without water for three months until the rains start again, and in some years they have to travel for several km to get water.The programme helped the community to enlarge the dam, but the problem remains, and in our interviews water dominated all other matters in answers to questions about the most important problems facing villagers, clearly outranking mentions of electricity or jobs, with entertainment and sports facilities not mentioned at all, and

Figure V.10: Water Sources in Carbajal

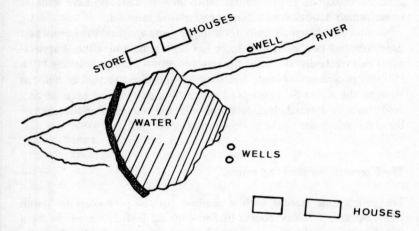

health facilities rarely, though people have to travel to San José or Tierra Blanca (14 or 20 km) to see a doctor in the Health Centre when they are sick. The most important diseases are gastrointestinal and respiratory.

Clearly, although not perhaps perceived as such, another important problem is the lack of organization and the high level of factional conflict. There are practically no organizations. The school has a parent's association, but at present it does not function. There is also a committee to build a bell tower for a small chapel, but this is basically the initiative of one person. Occasionally, action committees are formed to make demands for public services, such as electricity, school and water, but these are usually only activated by the visit of a candidate for the post of governor or deputy, which end in the presentation of verbal petitions with no effective pressure on governmental authorities.

Several informants from San José Iturbide and El Capulín insisted that the people of Carbajal were suspicious and inhospitable and jealous of their women. For many years no Carbajal girl has married out of the village. A nurse from El Capulín remembers that some years ago girls from Carbajal could have no friends outside the village. There is also a certain amount of internal mistrust and there have been thefts and fights between villagers. The reputation of the people of Carbajal is now at its lowest point; three years ago a young man from one of the important families was responsible for three murders, one in and two outside the village. He is still at large and protected by his family in spite of occasionl police hunts. Most men in Carbajal have guns at home, which doubtless adds to its aggressive reputation.

Besides the dirt road built about eight years ago, and the school and dam enlarged two years ago, there has been almost no other improvement or investment made by the government — excepting in the PRODECOR programme. People feel they have received very little help, in view of the 40 or 50 pesos per hectare they pay in land taxes to San José Iturbide. Nevertheless, relations with the municipal authorities or the state government have not been ones of conflict.

The Execution of the Programme

The programme started with a seminar for the promoters in March 1974. After a five-day course in San Luis de la Paz, the whole team travelled around the zone to get a first overview, and finally chose the micro-region and the village in which each one would live. Carbajal was included as one of the villages in the Capulín micro-region. The pair of promoters would be in charge of a total of four villages. Amparo — the girl promoter — was appointed first. Gonzalo arrived one month later, when the second seminar for promoters was held at San Luis de la Paz. Amparo is a young girl who had studied rural social work for three years beyond primary school at 'La Labor' — a school specializing in rural promotion — near the zone in the same state of Guanjuato. Gonzalo had studied chemistry for a year but then left university. He had had experience in poultry and pig farms, but not of promotion work. Both lived at Capulín, a village of 2,000 inhabitants, which served as the headquarters for the micro-region.

Their first task was to do research on the village, to identify the problems, needs and resources, and to make contacts, with the aid of the school teacher and the municipal delegate (elected as the contact man between Carbajal and the municipal administration). They fixed one day a week to visit Carbajal, and usually called a meeting which they got the delegate to organize. Gonzalo said of these meetings:

Carbajal is a backward village. They had many problems like the lack of water, but they didn't seem positively interested in anything. At the first meeting forty turned up, but by the fourth meeting only seven. The meetings were held at the school. In the beginning people were curious to hear about the programme, and that is why they went. They started to show interest in electricity and also in a water tank for the school, but it was a very slow village. At the meetings almost nobody spoke except for the municipal delegate. People were apathetic. Maybe they were used to drinking muddy water.

The programme had a number of projects in mind, such as introducing rabbits, beehives and kitchen gardens to improve nutrition, or chicken, pigs and goats, to improve cash income and to provide more local employment. A water tank in the school for children's consumption was another one of these projects. Ganzalo and Amparo, usually accompanied by the agricultural technician, proposed these ideas at the meetings, and tried to explain the advantages of each idea. The full list of projects which they finally decided, after the first month, to try to promote was:

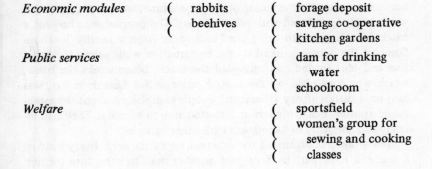

Economic modules	{	rabbits beehives	{	forage deposit savings co-operative kitchen gardens
Public services			{	dam for drinking water schoolroom

Welfare			{	sportsfield
				women's group for
				   sewing and cooking
				   classes

On these proposed projects, only the dam and a girls' group with fifteen members had begun six months later, when the evaluation by IMES (Mexican Institute of Social Studies) was done. The girls' group was started partly as a response to declining attendance at the meetings, in the fifth week. Amparo offered sewing and cooking classes and hoped to gain the confidence of the girls and young wives so that they would start kitchen gardens and begin keeping rabbits. Meanwhile, Gonzalo used to talk to a few individuals who were interested in kitchen gardens, and he also sought out the *Delegado*, the school teacher, to discuss possible projects. At one of these meetings they decided to build a water tank for the school, so that children could drink safe water. It was to be fed by rainwater collected from the roof in the rainy season.

A committee was formed and they asked the programme to provide free industrial materials (iron rods and cement) and food rations. Food rations are a standard device used by the Mexican government during the past ten years to encourage local labour in public works. The committee went to San Luis de la Paz to pick up the rations and the materials but the water tank was never built. They had started to dig the hole but then stopped the work. It seems, having discovered they could get material help from the government, they decided to aim at a larger objective, to keep the small amount of material they had got and ask for a larger quantity to build a small dam for general village use. Gonzalo, however, persuaded them not to build a new dam, but to raise the level of the one they already had. By raising the dam wall by about a metre — to make a total depth of about 4 metres in the middle — and lengthening it somewhat beyond its original 60 metres, it could be made to hold a good deal more water.

The programme gave them about 14 tons of cement in August 1974, six months after the beginning of the programme, and people started to work very rapidly and with great interest. The programme also sent a truck once a week to bring sand and rocks from a nearby location. Some of the people worked on the construction while others (between five and ten) loaded and unloaded the truck. Some weeks the truck, which was controlled by the central office in San Luis de la Paz, was sent on a different day from usual. People complained about the established routine being broken and started not to turn up. They had already had this kind of experience with other agencies.

The work was organized by a committee of six men. Every head of household took part in it or paid another man to substitute for him when he could not work himself. The committee registered the total number of work days (*faenas*) everyone had done and also distributed the food rations. By January 1975 the dam was almost finished. In the sixth month evaluation Gonzalo reported that only the water project was being supported. Some of the other promotions had been positively rejected — migration of the men made the economic modules very difficult to establish. There was no organization of a knitting co-operative as happened in other villages. All Amparo did was visit homes and collect information about this activity.

In January 1975 Gonzalo resigned and left the programme, as did Amparo a few weeks later. In April a new girl promoter — Susana — was sent to the micro-region and a fortnight later Aurelio joined her. Aurelio says he then tried to overcome the programme's reputation for delay and inactivity, and gain peoples' confidence by being punctual. But he did not start any new promotions; by then what people were thinking about was enlarging the total distance of the dam wall so that it could hold more water (Figure V.11).

Figure V.11: Planned Extension of Dam

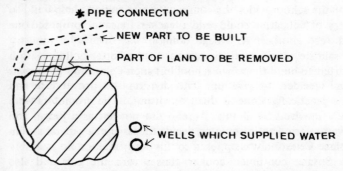

In April they started on this new work, but a problem arose over a villager named Celestino, the owner of the two small stores, who lived next to the dam. For many years he had had an underground pipe connection to the reservoir, and a water tank inside his home. He had also built a larger tank of about 300 cubic metres to irrigate is corn and vegetable garden. Because he had a pump which could be used at any time, people mistrusted his promise only to use the dam's overflow in the rainy season, and many were in favour of his privileges being removed. Because of these disputes and even litigations, the *Delegado* resigned — he was the son-in-law of the affected merchant and preferred not to be mixed up in the conflict. A new committee was formed, led by the strongest opponent, José, a man with some land, cattle and a pick-up truck in which he transports acrylic yarn and knitted products, acting as a middle-man.

At the end of August 1975, the majority of the people decided Celestino's pipe connection should be closed off. Then they started to work on the enlargement of the wall. In the end, they decided to contract a mason and some workers to finish the job. It was all accomplished in three weeks with co-operation all round. The dispute of the pipe connection is still continuing. On one of the visits we made in September 1976, the affected man invited us to his home for a drink. He showed us 'official papers' from the Ministry of Hydraulic Resources which he claimed supported the case for an individual using the water, since it had not ben designated national or communal property. He complained about the municipal president — a woman — of San José Iturbide, because she had not supported him. He had also brought legal action against José for obstruction of the pipe, without success. By then he had spent $240 in lawyer's fees (about three or four months' salary for a common *jornalero* of the region).

Fifteen years ago these two men had had a similar dispute about the location of the school which the community was going to help build so the Ministry of Education could send a teacher. Celestino proposed one place and José another. As village opinion was divided, a ministry inspector said he would send the teacher to the better building. Both groups started to build their own school but soon Celestino's group was behind and decided to give up. The division did not endure and Celestino is practically alone in this later dispute. The promoters were not actively involved in all this. Aurelio did not act as a judge, and would have preferred to let opinion decide the issue in a general assembly. But since Celestino was opposed to this confrontation no assembly was held. Susana continued cooker classes with the girls and also started a guitar group, and a savings group for them. Otherwise the two promoters did not want to start any new promotions. Aurelio commented that the people themselves said they would not participate in any other project until they finished the dam. Nevertheless in the same period a new schoolroom was built, which meant that education could continue up to the sixth grade, and the village also made a formal request for electricity, even though many people did not consider it to be as necessary as water for irrigation. A bell tower for a small chapel is also being built.

People talked to Aurelio about building a big irrigation dam up in the hills, but no formal steps were taken. The idea of digging a deep well was also discarded. An engineer who visited them during a political campaign told them that the water was deeper than 300 m; Aurelio also thought that it was not the time to insist on new projects. In March 1976 the whole programme had problems with the state authorities and the promoters resigned. A 'Cultural Mission' of the Ministry of Education continued going to Carbajal and kept in contact with the girls' group, changing the classes slightly — now they also teach nursing. The dam was finished in 1975 but only held a small amount of water partly because, due to the disputes, the rainy season was over by the time it was completed, and partly because the failure of efforts to scour out sand inside the dam had led to its clogging up. In 1976 a visit made in November showed the dam to be almost filled but because of leakages, people thought the water would only last for more or less the same time as the previous year. When the dam runs dry, they are planning to make the necessary repairs.

The Results

The two results of the programme were the enlarging of the dam and the functioning of a women's group. But during the two years, a schoolroom was also built, and requests were made by the village for a huge irrigation dam and electricity.

The costs of enlarging the dam were considerable. The estimated value of materials provided by the government (cement, food rations, truck) was $2,000. The villagers provided the labour; about 900 *faenas* which at a rate of $2 per day gives a total cost of $1,800. Administration overheads (operation costs and salaries) are difficult to calculate accurately, but the approximate cost per village served would be $4,800. The larger dam has proved useful to the village, and the assumption is that its benefits will be equally distributed. Celestino antagonized the majority because he was taking larger amounts of water for irrigation purposes. In the case of water for domestic use, people from other villages are even allowed to take a share in dry years.

The women's group was intended to help promote other activities such as a savings co-operative and a health and children's instructor. But nothing developed beyond the girls' attendance at courses in cooking, nursing, sewing and music. There is no way to measure benefits precisely, since the outputs are not quantifiable. Most of the girls in the groups are economically active in the knitting industry, but no action was taken to improve their situation.

The other relevant activity was the building of a schoolroom. A specialized committee from the Ministry of Education took charge of the work. School attendance increased from 120 to 160 and fifth and sixth grades were added There are other changes, particularly in family income as a result of the knitting activity. About seven years ago, people started buying machines at San José or working with borrowed ones. By now almost all families have one, and many have two or three, depending on the number of girls able to operate them. The work is hard, and very badly paid (about $1.60 per day), but now women and children's labour has an economic value, sometimes higher than men's. The interviews showed only one man working in the village itself and he had an income of $2 per day, either from collecting and selling wood, or from general labouring.

Labourers who went to other states could earn $3 to $6 a day but had to pay travelling expenses, as well as lodging and meals, reducing their net income by half. As agriculture is mostly for consumption, knitting is the most important cash activity in Carbajal. Income has actually increased, as is apparent from the clothing of the people. Agriculture has not changed significantly. Fertilizers are hardly used because of the lack of water. Fumigation of beans started to be practised about four or five years ago. A few people — like the *Delegado* and Don José — have a spray-pump. Improved corn seeds have been tried but produced bad results because they take six months to grow, so running into the time when the rains start and frosts come. Local seeds develop in only three months. Changes in attitude were not directly observed, and changes in solidarity will be specifically detailed in Chapter 7.

6 THE 'SUCCESSFUL' VILLAGE: CIENEGUILLA

Description of the Village

Cieneguilla is a village of about 400 inhabitants. It belongs to the *municipio* of Tierra Blanca, and with 15 small villages around it forms what is called a 'Congregation'. It dates from 1593 and is one of the oldest villages in the state of Guanajuato. Its name means a small marsh. Perhaps the first settlers chose the place because it had water, a scarce resource in the zone.

The climate is mild and the vegetation typical of arid zones: cactus and small bushes. Although the stream which runs through the village dries up sometimes it provides enough humidity in the sandy soils alongside for water to be obtainable all year round from small wells. There are trees such as avocado and walnut at the bottom of the river basin, while the higher elevation yields only cactus and bushes. In the mountains there are pine trees. Cieneguilla also has a thermal water-spring, with a small but permanent flow, that is used as a public bath, and visited by people from other communities.

The village is situated in a valley at about 1,750 m above sea level. This valley is long and narrow and follows the course of the river. There are only a few flat areas used for agriculture; most plots slope steeply because they are located at the foot of the mountains.

The settlement is dispersed. There is a church and small square at the centre, but no streets as such; just houses widely spaced along old tracks (Figure V.12).

Figure V.12: Plan of Cieneguilla

The indigenous Otomí constitute the ethnic base of the population. The entire valley is populated by Otomíes, which differentiates it from other valleys and plateaux which are *mestizo*. Older people still speak the Otomí dialect, and some wear traditional costume, unlike members of the younger generation. Many traditions, such as religious festivals, continue to be observed. There are six festivals during the year. The most important takes place in January on the feast days of San Ildefonso who is the patron saint of the village. During the festivities pilgrims take an image of the saint around the village. They are accompanied by music and firecrackers and food is given to everyone. The Congregation is so organized that each feast is sponsored by a group of four *mayordomos*. Consequently there are 24 *mayordomos*, who keep their position for two years. The job entails an outlay of about $320, but also carries a certain prestige, and the right to find a successor.

Until 1851 Cieneguilla belonged to a great *hacienda* which included the present land of the Congregation. The proprietors sold the land — about 1,200 hectares —to the *peones* (wage workers), who thus became small proprietors. Subsequent division of land among the descendants of the *peones* greatly reduced the size of plots, and even though at present about 80 per cent of household heads own a piece of land, the area of such plots varies from 0.25 to 3 hectares.

Almost all the land is rain-fed, but the average annual rainfall is only 400 mm. Only a few plots alongside the stream and thermal waterspring benefit from moisture or irrigation. Productivity is very low. The two major crops — almost the only ones — are corn and beans, with annual yields per hectare of around 750 kg and 300 kg respectively. Fertilizers and insecticides were used by all the peasants interviewed, and have been for eight years. Production is basically for subsistence.

Before the programme started, the following animals were owned by households in the sample of 13 interviewed: chickens (6), pigs (3), cattle (2), sheep (2), and goats (3). Husbandry was traditional; animals fed on garbage of natural pasture, with no special measures taken. Chickens were for home consumption. pigs provided a means of saving for immediate needs, while cattle, sheep and goats were for commercial purposes.

As in Carbajal, low production obliges many peasants to seek other forms of income. Almost 85 per cent of the interviewed adult male population worked as *jornaleros* on farms in El Bajio, and during the harvest in other states, or worked in Mexico City as masons. A few even went to the United States. They accept having to leave their families for several months a year, because there is no other way to supplement their basic income.

Wages for agricultural *jornaleros* range from $3 to $5 per day in the nearby Bajio, and masons in Mexico City may earn $8 a day. These earnings may be decreased by expenses if the peasant cannot use contacts or special facilities to help cover cost. One mason commented that he had a 'relative' in Mexico City, and he slept at his home, and paid him only a small amount. Masons are sometimes allowed to sleep in the building they are working on.

Years before, about half the households produced bamboo baskets. The whole family helped in this craft and the village was noted for it. Current sales have decreased because of the appearance of plastic substitutes, but 10 per cent of the population is still engaged in this activity. Daily earnings range from $1.60 to $3. The peasants buy the bamboo at Santa Catarina (about 20 km away) and sell the baskets in Queretaro (about 80 km away) or to a middleman.

Weaving palm leaves is another activity, and about 10 per cent of the population works at this activity. Middlemen from the neighbouring state of San Luis Potosí provide the peasants with the leaves and buy the woven product at a very low price. The finished product is used to make hats, but outside Cieneguilla.

A last but very important economic activity is home knitting of acrylic yarn for baby sweaters and dresses. More than 70 per cent of the households own a domestic knitting machine, operated by young daughters or even by boys. As in Carbajal, piece work is the norm, with a middleman providing the yarn and buying the finished goods. Average earnings are around $40 US a month per working machine. Some families have two or three machines. People complain about exploitation but realize that knitting is a way of adding to the very limited income of each household.

Bamboo baskets, palm-tree hats and acrylic garments are made for popular consumption, and have low prices on the national market. Even so, middlemen make a high profit, almost 100 per cent for knitted products.

Total family income was not calculated, but some indicators of the standard of living may be presented here.

Daily meals consist of beans and *tortillas* (corn); 50 per cent of those interviewed also ate noodles and vegetables once a week, 20 per cent ate fruit, 38 per cent ate meat, but 80 per cent drank milk only once a year. Nutrition seems to be better than in Carbajal, but it is still very low in animal protein.

Most houses are built with *adobe* (mud bricks), though we also found some (15 per cent) with walls built with a kind of cactus plant. Roofs are tile and asbestos; 30 per cent of the houses had three rooms, 40 per cent had two and 30 per cent had only one room. All have a separate room for the kitchen, and most had a room for washing in; 90 per cent have dirt floors.

Cieneguilla now has running water and public faucets, and 25 per cent of the homes have a domestic connection. Electricity has also been installed and 85 per cent of the homes now have this service. At the beginning of the programme these services did not exist.

There is no entertainment other than watching TV. There are only a few sets and one has to pay to see programmes. Playing volley ball in the school field is the only sport.

Cieneguilla is joined to the main all-weather road from San José to Tierra Blanca by a short dirt road which is frequently flooded and impassable. There are frequent buses from the junction to San José (29 km distance) and Tierra Blanca.

Twenty-five years ago a small two-classroom school was founded and run by a group of nuns. In 1969 a new school was built with the co-operation of the federal and state governments, which has eight school-rooms and facilities for complete primary education (six grades). There are eight teachers and over 300 pupils. Education is one of the major concerns of the people in Cieneguilla. Of the sample interviewed, 54 per cent of the adult men (heads of household) had finished primary school — a very high percentage compared with the national average — and all had attended school for several years even if they had not completed it. As many as 78 per cent of the sons and daughters over 15 years of age have finished primary school and 16 per cent are already in secondary, technical or normal schools, much higher ratios than those normally encountered in rural areas.

There is no health centre or attending physician at Cieneguilla. Two untrained village women help at births. People have to travel to Tierra Blanca to go to the Health Centre. Only a few — 15 — go to San José to see a private doctor. The major diseases are intestinal and respiratory. Health is another main concern of the people from Cieneguilla.

It cannot be said that there is a clear-cut division of classes within Cieneguilla, on economic grounds. Landownership is not a determining factor, since total land area and plot size are both so small. Families cannot subsist without wages from elsewhere. There are no large proprietors who contract labour in Cieneguilla, and work relations are symmetric — reciprocal lending of labour between peasants. There are no 'rich people' who have emerged in the village, nor are there local middlemen in the knitting business or basket production. The existing main organizations are religious: the *mayordomos* and the Catholic action groups, which exist but are not active. At present there is only a women's Catholic action group.

However, there are also some specialized committees in the village, the most relevant and permanent being the parents' school committee, which deals with the continuing problems of operating the school. At the time the programme was instituted in Cieneguilla there were also committees for constructing the drinking-water system, installing electricity, building the square, and arranging the church garden. Some of them disappeared when the work was completed, and by the time the research was undertaken, several other committees or groups were active: a technical secondary school, a group interested in drilling a well for irrigation, a group interested in building a modest spa near the thermal water springs, and a committee for a health centre.

Most of these committees, once they have defined the interest and the demands to be made, send representatives to the state capital of Guanajuato to start the procedures and meet all the requirements. Occasionally, demands would be made on home ground when candidates for election posts passed through on their campaign trails. This petitioning process illustrates how much it is assumed that change can only be supplied by the government, a kind of dependency which must have affected reaction to the promoters. Several more organizations are functioning as a result of the programme, but they will be described later.

Cieneguilla also acts as an administrative 'centre' for the Congregation in its relationship with the *municipio*, and the municipal delegate usually lives there. Each of the other villages has a sub-delegate. A definite competitition between Cieneguilla and Tierra Blanca (the municipal head) has developed, with conflicts of authority and tense relations from time to time.

For years the accepted way to build public works locally has been to work in common, with each head of household donating one or several days of work. They call this custom *faenas*, and public works such as the school, some dirt roads, water pipes, had been accomplished in this manner. At the time we were interviewing, the most important needs expressed by the people were for more jobs, and for a health centre.

Previous experience with government officials from other agencies and programmes had been mixed. The construction of the dirt road in 1967, and of the school, was a positive experience even though the townspeople had to insist on obtaining the latter, against obstruction from the municipal president of Tierra Blanca. In many other cases the image of the government which people form has been negative because of the many promises made and not satisfied, such as the building of a basketball field. For this purpose a piece of land was donated, worked over and sand and stones brought to it. But the officials of the agency never came back. There have been many other similar cases, and such experiences meant the programme started in an atmosphere of mistrust.

The Execution of the Programme

Cieneguilla was one of the 40 villages chosen for the programme. Ricardo and Virginia were nominated as the promoters for the micro-region which included Cieneguilla and Tierra Blanca, the municipal capital, where the promoters decided to live.

Ricardo first contacted the municipal president of Tierra Blanca who advised him not to work in Cieneguilla because the people were difficult and lazy and no results could be expected. As the village had already been chosen, Ricardo said his job was to visit it anyway. His first task in Cieneguilla was to talk with the delegate, who also invited six other important people of the village. The promoters explained the objectives of the programme, but in retrospect they believed their listeners were not convinced.

According to the steps to be followed in the programme, the promoters started going to Cieneguilla twice a week, and visiting their families to collect information. Sometimes they were invited by the schoolteachers to meetings of the parents' committee, but they had no general meetings with the townspeople. They tried to get the people's confidence by being punctual and courteous, two of the qualities which previous government officials had not possessed and they seem to have succeeded. A letter written in November 1975 to the wife of President Echeverría by a member of one of the groups set up by the programme said:

> we have been working with enthusiasm, taking advantage of the material elements, but mainly of the human elements . . . which at the beginning inspired no confidence in us, but when we saw the work they did, they convinced us, not only in their technical capacity but in their ability to deal with human beings.[1]

In the first month of the work the promoters finished the research and various problems became evident. For the second month of work they proposed the following projects to be carried out:

drilling of a well to benefit approximately 80 hectares. A group of 78 interested people already existed, and Don Pancho was its president;
establishing a fruit growers' group, with 10 associates, to improve their present fruit cultivation;
forming groups of livestock owners to improve handling techniques for peasants who had goats and lambs;
forming a women's group to learn first aid, and sewing and cutting techniques.

These projects were discussed in assemblies, with huge attendances initially, but declining attendance thereafter as interest waned.

In an evaluation carried out by the Mexican Institute of Social Research projects actually undertaken were listed as:

rebuilding of the square (all the Congregation)
formal demands by the irrigation well group (78 persons)
establishment of the savings and credit co-operative (41 associates)
formation of a beehive group (9 associates)
formation of a sewing group (15 girls)
improvement of fruit trees (10 persons)
planting and sowing of kitchen gardens.

The rebuilding of the square was especially significant for the promoters because of the diplomacy involved. The programme had provided five tons of cement and the municipal administration, one ton. As Ricardo had begun to gain people's confidence he felt able to get an engineer to draw up plans, but the municipal president intervened and insisted on a different design. Ricardo discussed this with him and since there were other factors the situation became very tense. People from Cieneguilla gave support to Ricardo and this confirmed their confidence in the programme.

Because the programme needed a promoter in another micro-region and because of the situation, Ricardo left Cieneguilla. A new promoter — Jorge — took his place in October 1974 and was introduced to all the village groups by Ricardo. He had studied industrial relations for two years, and had then changed to law school. Later, in France, he took a special course in public administration. Virginia stayed in the micro-region. She had been born in Tierra Blanca, and had attended only primary school, but she was a natural leader who had headed a group of knitters to demand that the governor intervene to establish better prices, though this initiative was unfortunately never linked with any organization amongst the knitters themselves.

The first actions Jorge undertook were to invite groups or interested people to the first technical courses for peasants held at San Luis de la Paz. Two people from Cieneguilla attended the first three-day course. Don Pancho, who was one of them, became very interested in a pig farm. When he came back, he convinced several other people to form a co-operative. As this co-operative was one of the most important economic activities, it is relevant to describe its development in detail. Around 25 persons were interested at first but only 15 finally signed the bank credit application in December 1974. Don Pancho was elected president. Invitations were issued through open meetings and personal contacts, but the original group was not enlarged. Its members were not all from the 'centre' of the Congregation, since Don Pancho had sent invitations to people from other nearby villages. When we asked why ony 15 had entered the group they said that many people considered them fools for taking on a large debt, which they would never be able to pay off.

The group bought a piece of land and worked sporadically to arrange and clear it. The programme gave them a small loan for cement and iron rods to start building, pending credit from the bank. Most of the members normally had to leave Cieneguilla for paid work so in March 1975 when the building demanded full-time work, they had to ask for food rations from the programme. A daily ration consists of 1 kg of corn flour, 150 gr of rice and 0.5 kg of beans, which is insufficient for a family of more than four members.

They then started to work six days a week and this provoked an internal crisis since some of them began to send a *peón* (day labourer) in their place. The promoter insisted that the co-operative character of the group should exclude paid labour. The group then decided to set a maximum of two *peón* days a week per member. One of the associates resigned and they accepted a new member who paid for his membership with the equivalent of the days the group had already worked. Two of the members went to León to take a one-month practical course in farm handling, while the construction continued. For the size of the village, the farm is large, close to 1,000 square meters of covered surface, enough to house 30 female breeding pigs and two male breeding pigs, and with a monthly production of 40 fat pigs.

The group provided most of the construction materials themselves.

They made their own adobe and transported sand and stones using a truck sent by the programme. The credit from the bank did not come until August 1975. They received an amount of $50,000 to cover the cost of the building, the breeding animals, and a mill and mixer for feed. An application for a second loan for rotating capital was never approved, so the group had to finance the feeding of the first animals from the considerable savings they had accumulated by building with their own cheap labour and materials. Even though construction was not completed by August 1975, they started to bring in the first breeding animals.

Building continued for six days per week until June 1976 – a little more than a year in total. The food rations were then finished, and they decided to work only enough days to maintain the operation of the farm and finish the building. Now, three of the fifteen members work each day by shifts, so every one has to spend a complete day every five days, and during the rest of the time can work his own land, or go away, or weave baskets. In this way they can assure the cultivation of their own lands and also have some ready cash to meet their family's needs. Also in June 1976 they sold the first fat pigs produced on the farm, and from then on the production rate has varied, despite satisfactory performance in management and growth.

With the same loan, the group also bought a truck, to transport grain, concentrated feed, animals and building materials. Occasionally they transport merchandise and people, but not as a business. The group also sold some female pigs for breeding to a similar co-operative promoted by the programme in another village. As the other group had not obtained its loan, they provided the pigs at a value of $1,200 to be paid around ten months later or whenever the new group obtained its loan.

Two other ideas were accepted, though not carried out: first, the lending of the male breeding pigs, so that people outside the co-operative who had pigs could improve their breed. The second idea was to improve the housing of the members of the co-operative, because they all gained experience as masons.

This co-operative was important because it served to catalyse other activities developed at Cieneguilla, which are now described.

Since the beginning of the programme, eight bee-keepers, each with one hive, have formed a group and kept the beehives together. In May 1975 this initial group was increased to 18, 15 of whom were also members of the pig co-operative. The rest of the members had been invited by Don Pancho. A total of 30 hives were set up on a collective basis. They were received on credit from the programme, payment pledged in money, honey and beeswax, or swarms of bees. This credit amounted to approximately $1,000. The normal yearly production of a single beehive is about 50 kg of honey, and assuming a selling price of $1 per kg, the co-operative had a potential annual income of $1,500. In less than a year, they could pay off the credit and make a profit. However, in the first year of the programme, there was a condition that the honey should be consumed by the co-operative and that an application should be made for a bank loan to increase the number of hives to 100. (This was in fact rejected.)

The 30 beehives were erected in August of the same year, but, due to lack of time, there was no crop in November. The April harvest was lost because a late frost killed the flora. The group admitted having neglected the bees during this period and later because they were very occupied with the construction and operation of the pig farm. This resulted in a November harvest of only 160 kg of honey or about 9 kg per family. During the last period — April to November 1976 — other groups in nearby areas had harvests that were five times greater.

When the group was constituted, six members took courses on management technique. They held meetings every two weeks, worked out their own rules, and took turns caring for the beehives. The zone where the programme was established budgeted for an apiarist to lend technical assistance. However, he had very little time to give to the programme since he had to divide his attention among 30 groups that had been formed. The bee-keepers with other neighbours, also cleared underbrush shrubs and trees, and levelled off about 1.5 km, to open up a road between the site of the apiary and the village.

Another of the potentially important groups in the area is the Savings and Loan Co-operative. Although founded since the programme started, it had remained almost inactive. Up to August of 1975, 40 members had promised to save a specific amount of money weekly, but actually half of them did not. At that time, the co-operative had only $240 in hand, and had not granted any credit. Two months later, under the insistence of the organizer, the group revived its interest, savings increased to $480, and loans were issued. In January of 1976, the Board of Directors was changed and several new committees formed — for vigilance, credit and education. Aristeo, Don Pancho's brother, a self-educated teacher from the village, became president.

Thus motivated, the membership increased to 49 and savings were made and credit extended. Each member was entitled to a loan equivalent to twice the amount of money saved, to be repaid in three months at a 2 per cent monthly interest rate. The credit committee screens the applications. Each applicant must have a backer who will guarantee the full payment of the loan if the borrower defaults. No losses have been suffered, and there has only been a need to extend the term of payment when delays have occurred. Most of the people have found the savings bank to be of great help from the time that it started to issue loans. This way they can readily solve their expenditure problems in case of sickness, for small purchases or trips. Previously such credit was only available from money-lenders at a monthly rate of 20 per cent.

This same group has also thought of becoming a consumer co-operative and of establishing a *nixtamal* (prepared corn used to make *tortillas*) mill. Interests elsewhere in the community would be affected by the competitition from both these projects. The owner of the existing mill went to Leon (an industrial city in the state) to prevent officials at the Department of Industry and Commerce from giving permission for the mill. Neither project has got beyond the planning stage.

Another activity of the Savings Co-operative was the buying of fert-ilizer worth $1,280 at the beginning of the year, and its resale at cost price to the community, including non-members of the co-operative.

There were other activities of less importance which were proposed and taken up. For example, Virginia organized a group of women of varying ages. They held weekly meetings where she taught them how to sew, cut patterns, use a knitting machine, crochet, cook and make stuffed and paper toys. They continued to meet periodically since they strongly depended on the organizer's presence. The sewing machines that they used had been distributed in rural villages on instructions from President Echeverría's wife so that the housewives could make and mend clothes for their families. The organizer, Virginia, had formed this group by visiting the homes and personally inviting the women to attend.

Other activities stemmed from this women's club. In March of 1975, two programmes were organized — health and nursery school. Three members of the club (one from Cieneguilla and two from other com-munities) registered for the health programme. They attended a one-week course each month in San Luis de la Paz. They were taught first aid and how to apply injections, dress wounds, grow garden produce, plan proper diets for children, and build cooking stoves and latrines. On their return they would teach the housewives of their community what they had learned about proper diets, pre- and post-natal care, and promote vegetable gardening as well as the construction of cooking stoves and latrines. A group of 24 women was formed in Cieneguilla but only 8 had vegetable gardens. Not one cooking stove or latrine was built. The vegetable seeds were sold in small packages containing several varieties.

They organized several *kermesses* (a fair with food, games and rides) in order to raise money. With the proceeds, they equipped a medical dispensary with penicillin injections, antibiotics, common cures for gastrointestinal and respiratory disorders, and bandages. This way the villagers no longer had to go to Tierra Blanca or San José to be treated for minor illness by a doctor.

This clinic was in operation for only two months because the woman in charge (a nurse from the programme at the Public Health Ministry) left. Now the organizers — the three girls who originally registered for the course — give injections to those who ask for them and give advice or prescriptions, but the people have to go outside the village for medicine or have it sent in. The women continued to attend the monthly courses from March until December 1975. At the same time, a nurse came once a month on a cultural mission to talk to the men, women and children about personal hygiene.

The women involved in the nursery school programme followed a similar plan of action. They took a one-week course in San Luis de la Paz and afterwards worked for three or four weeks in their community. They established a kind of nursery school or kindergarten with a group of children. They sang and played with the children and taught them manual arts with paper, cardboard, colours, etc. Four girls registered as leaders. Two of them worked with a group of 40 children in Cieneguilla and the other two with a group of 70 in a neighbouring community. During the afternoons they used the school and a site prepared by the parents. This continued only until December when the funds ran out. The cost in food and expenses for the courses per leader was $24 per month or $400 in total to cover expenses for the leaders of the health programme and $480 for the nursery school leaders of Cieneguilla.

A knitters' group which grew out of the original women's group might have developed into a much larger co-operative to encompass the whole zone. The registration reached 90, but the co-operative had to be legally constituted first (a long and complicated process) and, in the end, the bank did not grant the loan to purchase the machines and yarn, mainly because they had stipulated that the co-operative be formally registered but this was very difficult to clear with the Ministry of Commerce. The co-operative never reached its full potential.

Another project was the rearing of rabbits, to supplement the diet with animal proteins. Fifteen families, the majority of whom were also members of the pig farm, formed this group. Each family received a female rabbit on credit. They had to build a cage and promise to repay the programme with two baby rabbits (a doe and buck) one month after the first litter was born. The 15 female rabbits were serviced by one male that each household received by turn. The original idea was that each family would have four does and so could eat meat once a week. In practice they have one or two and the rabbits from the litters *are* consumed although once in a while they are sold.

The rabbits are fed with the leftovers of the meals, some with alfalfa — although it is difficult to obtain for lack of water — and others with concentrated feed, but not on a regular basis. Since they do not keep adequate records on operating costs, the profitability of this activity cannot be ascertained.

Another activity that is underway is the construction of a town square in the middle of the village where a space had been reserved for it. It was one of the first things that the people wanted to do with the programme. Work was assigned on mutual agreement. The IPI programme donated part of the cement: a total of nine tons was used, of which the programme gave five, a Congressman three and a mayor of Tierra Blanca one. The programme lent them a truck to bring in sand and stones. Each head of a household, not only from Cieneguilla but also from the rest of the farms in the area, contributed by completing five or six work assignments. Food rations were an additional aid. Not everyone participated in this voluntary work, which was organized by a municipal *Delegado*. They trucked in the material and prepared the stone pavement during the month of July. In March 1975, they resumed work and laid the cement floor. A pavilion that was included in the plans has not been built and therefore the town square is still unfinished.

The aid extended by the programme can be estimated at a total worth of $880 in the form of five tons of cement, about 600 food rations, and a loaned truck. The community's contribution was work and local materials.

Fruit-growing was also given support, but on a more individual basis. An initial group of ten were interested in grafting avocado trees which are cultivated in the area. Through the programme they bought small, fine-quality avocado trees that could be sold at a very low price, but the results are not know, since this was a one-day activity with no follow-up. In a similar way 1,000 vine shoots were distributed but with minimum instructions for planting and care. Jorge, the organizer of all this activity, feels that it was not successful because it was not well located and neither he nor those interviewed had satisfactory results. Many trees or shoots were killed by frost. The opinion of one of the persons interviewed is that 20 or 30 people still have small vineyards.

Besides these activities, there were others which either pre-dated the programme or started during it, but were not a direct part of it. One of these was the installation of a drinking water system. The village applied for it in April of 1974 through a committee, and, with the support of the governor of the state, it was quickly approved. The Construction Committee of the Department of Health carried it out and it was financed by PIDER, a programme that was operating in the area.

The system included a well, located near a river, a reservoir to store water, 1000 m of tubing and three public hydrants in different parts of the village. The community's contribution was $12 per household, the sites for the well and reservoir, and the labour involved in digging ditches, laying the pipes, and covering them up. Each household head contributed nine work assignments and in the end, the cost was waived. During the work assignments, the men received food rations. If the people living near the pipelines wished to install running water in their homes, they could do so by purchasing, for $16, a kit containing a faucet, 10 m of hose and 1 m of tubing. PIDER and its crew drilled the well and constructed the reservoir.

The installation of electricity was another important achievement. A committee had been applying for it since 1969. In 1974, the Federal Electric Commission approved it and asked the community to contribute $2,800, but no labour or materials. This cost was to have been shared by 60 households, which meant $47 per family. Electricity was brought to the centre of the village and to the pump of the well, and by February 1976 the rest of the village had electrical power. However, by November of the same year, ten or twelve homes were still not connected because they either did not pay, or were absent when the contracts were drawn up or the connection installed. Only half the money has been paid and the committee is still collecting the deficit.

Finally, there are four additional activities people have been promoting, although with small result as yet. Before the arrival of the programme, a group of 78, led again by Don Pancho, had requested the Department of Water Resources to drill a well. The department replied that there was not sufficient water to make it profitable. But Ricardo succeeded in getting a geologist, on behalf of the programme, to make studies, which showed the venture to be worthwhile. A diviner was then asked to indicate places where there would be sufficient water for drilling. Otherwise, no further progress has been made. Now they are considering a bank loan.

Another idea is to use the hot springs in the village, at present just a local open-air bathing place, to build a spa. A group of 100 started a fund, each contributing $80, but to date only $720 has been collected. Since very little can be accomplished with this amount, they want to ask for a bank loan for the building but any plans are very hazy.

The levelling and preparing of a site for animal husbandry and vocational agricultural high school was another enterprise worked on during November. At present, high school students must go to Tierra Blanca. A similar request for an agricultural school at Cieneguilla had been made before, but since Tierra Blanca has more political influence the school had been constructed there. On this occasion the people of Cieneguilla offered the large site required and quickly began work. So far they have also cleared about five hectares through work assignments by the heads of households.

The last endeavour that deserves mention is the creation of a small hat factory. Previously, middlemen from San Luis Potosi supplied the palm leaves which were woven by hand in Cieneguilla and then bought back at very low prices for hats to be made elsewhere. But in response to a petition from Don Pancho, the government offered a loan to start the factory, and twelve young people, selected from many by Don Pancho, were to be given a month's training at a factory in the city. However, the factory never materialized.

These last four activities were not instigated by the promoter, but arose from initiative and interest in the community.

The Results

The most impressive result is the building of the pig farm. The major part of the resources came from outside the village, with credit of $50,000 and $2,800 estimated cost of food rations giving a total of $52,800, whilst the cost of labour proviced locally could be calculated at $10,000. The ratio of total project outlay ($62,800) to estimated programme overhead costs per village ($4,800) seems quite healthy in this case.

The building of the farm provided work for 15 men over 13 months, and almost four full-time operators are needed. But the capital/employment ratio is very high — near to $16,000 per job. In future, the mill, warehouse and transport will demand more labour, and the promoters

Community Development in Mexico

believe new related activities will emerge such as packing. A lowering of the ratio would make this model more acceptable for promotion elsewhere. So far it has been very difficult to gauge the economic performance of the farm. There have been sales since June 1976 but costs (not including capital replacements) have exceeded income ($24,000 in expenses and $16,960 in sales). Up to April 1977 it seems the size of farm population and level of production will be as expected.

Actual estimates of returns per animal are $24, or a total of $1,440 a month, a very reasonable amount for a rural area. Nevertheless pork prices fluctuate rapidly and may threaten the farm's viability. Time will tell.

The use of the co-operative's truck has not been very well planned. Generally they use it only once a week to bring the prepared food for the pigs, thus saving $160 a month. The rest of the week they do occasional trips — sometimes taking sick people to a doctor — but otherwise the truck is unused. The mill is still not connected and is inactive. Milling their own grain would save them about $800 a month, but still they have no idea how much their costs in electricity and maintenance would be.

All income is shared equally among the members. Up to November they had paid themselves three shares, with a total of $280 for each associate. Don Pancho normally dedicates more time than the others to the co-operative, but preferred not to take any more than the others.

The arranging of the village garden or square also meant an inflow of resources. Materials and food rations given by the government were around $960. There were no financial returns from this activity.

The apiculture group received credit of about $960 and generated no significant work for the installation of operation of the beehives. Prices after the recent harvest were bad, and the group decided not to sell the honey but to distribute it equally among themselves.

The health and infant welfare promoters received very limited financial support and their results were very difficult to assess. During the two months the medicine box operated, cheap medicine was provided and savings made on travelling expenses to Tierra Blanca. Afterwards, the trainees' only function was to give injections, and some advice. Regarding the promoters who worked with the young children, the only opinion we had came from one of the school teachers who said that the children who had gone to rural kindergarten were more eager to learn and better adapted socially than their peers.

An important group, with good results at the moment, is the Savings Co-operative. Operating with no direct cost to the programme it has the largest coverage of all the groups. It is estimated that $250 per month is now being saved by the villagers over what they would have been paying in interest on private loans.

The installation of electricity in the village has also been a clear benefit. The state and federal governments have each matched the villagers' supposed input of $2,800. So the total contribution from outside has been $5,600.

The water system accounted for about $6,400 of direct government investment and $300 in food rations. The gain has been reliable drinking water, all year round.

Note

1. Letter from the Saving and Loan Co-operative of Cieneguilla to the wife of President Echeverría, 25 Nov. 1975.

7 EXPLANATIONS

Differences Between the Villages

The fate of the community development programme in the two villages
studied seems to provide a startling contrast. In part this is to be
explained by the different impact of the programme on the two
villages, in part by differences in the situation and structure of the two
villages themselves.

Let us begin with the latter. The first question to ask is whether
there are important differences in the way the two villages relate to the
wider socioeconomic structure of the country as a whole. The picture
is paradoxical: in many ways Carbajal seemed the more likely to
develop wider links — its population was Hispanic and *mestizo* rather
than Otomí, and it was physically closer to the main road, to a large
town and the railway. And yet it was Cieneguilla which was the more
open and receptive village. It seems, then, that such general links were
not important. What probably mattered far more in Cieneguilla were
the links and rivalries between the local administrative units, as will be
described later.

So it is within the local situation that the most important differences lie. The following descriptions are based on information from
open-ended interviews, and a standard questionnaire in both communities.

Ecological Conditions

Cieneguilla has the advantage of water availability. Although its stream
does not carry water all year round, sub-soils maintain adequate
humidity. In Carbajal — on the contrary — even water for domestic
consumption disappears completely for a period of weeks. The economic activities promoted, such as rabbit and pig-breeding, and cultivating of kitchen gardens were not feasible in Carbajal.

Existing Organizations

Cieneguilla is a Congregation that unites 15 villages for religious festivals.
Since the colonial period there has existed a tradition of working communally for public works or feast-days. The fact that the people have
an *Otomí* origin also gives them greater internal cohesion.

Carbajal does not seem to have a tradition of organization. All

406

public works in the community had been built through *faenas*, but there are no permanent organizations. Kinship is one source of internal cohesion, but only in the face of outsiders — over questions of immigration or marriage.

Certainly kinship provided no basis for internal *unity*. Apathy in the beehive groups (feasible because not dependent on water) was attributed by many to the difficulties of integrating a group of ten associates as the programme required.

3) Previous Experiences with Other Programmes

It is common to find mistrust towards government plans based on previous negative experience with public agencies. Since this was true of both villages, it cannot explain differences. The relevant point is the kind of relationship the communities maintained with their municipal head, and thus with government in general. Cieneguilla has an advantage in its competitive position with Tierra Blanca. Since Tierra Blanca had previously obstructed several demands for public services the Congregation had made, people were eager to support any agencies which now seemed willing to extend services to them.

The relationship between Carbajal and San José Iturbide, the municipal head, seems non-existent by comparison. The committees formed by the villagers have presented their demands only when a candidate visits the village. They have not attempted to go and exert pressure where decisions are actually taken.

4) Previous Promotion in the Village

About six years ago a French priest lived in Cieneguilla and promoted several activities such as saving and consumer groups, beehives and knitting machines. He offered the means to buy beehives and knitting machines at low prices, and some people took up these activities.

We found no evidence of previous promotion in Carbajal. Before the present dirt road was made in 1967, there was a priest who got people to co-operate in improving the old road, but this was a one-off event.

Don Pancho told us in Cieneguilla that one of the best results of the programme there was the boosting of expectations and confidence for future projects, so it seems reasonable to assume that the promotion carried out by the French priest provided a more receptive environment for the programme in Cieneguilla.

5) Local Leadership

This is one of the clearest differences between the two villages. In

Cieneguilla, Don Pancho is a leader, and once he decided to take on the pig farm almost all the other activities gained impetus.

Don Pancho has been involved in politics and pressure groups for the past 15 years. In 1961 he was the president of the school's parents' association, and also secretary and treasurer until 1963. He was born in a nearby village — but moved to Cieneguilla in pursuance of his activities. The parents' association enabled him to 'get to know many things, many ways of working, and many people in the government'. From 1963 to 1967 he was municipal delegate (a locally-elected agent of the municipal authorities) and from 1967 to 1969 he became municipal president of Tierra Blanca. He then gained the support of the Ministry of Education for the building of the school, after obstruction by previous administrations. So, apart from the direct effects of his participation in village activities, Don Pancho's political links have also helped Cieneguilla. He has known personally several governors of the state and many other authorities.

In Carbajal there is no equivalent single leader and recurrent but unstable factionalism. In the case of the enlarging of the dam, one of the protagonists was supported by the majority in closing the pipe connection, but at the same time this man seems to be opposed to the building of a large dam upstream, because this would affect his own lands, and this will no doubt provoke new groupings. In addition to the limited leadership, the most prominent people have basically commercial rather than political or social interests. One of them owns two of the local stores and the other is an intermediary in the acrylic knitting business and so a competitor of the municipal president of San José who is also in the business.

Characteristics of the Population

From the questionnaire we found that all the heads of household in Carbajal had always lived there, while in Cieneguilla 30 per cent came from other nearby places. Also the average age of the people interviewed in Carbajal was higher. These factors suggest that it might well be less open to outside promotion, and that the younger generation emigrates more than in Cieneguilla.

The level of schooling of the heads of household of Cieneguilla was also higher. Fifty per cent of the people interviewed had finished primary school, and in Carbajal none had, and 80 per cent had never gone to school at all. In Carbajal none of the sons over 15 years of age had passed the fourth grade of primary school, whilst in Cieneguilla 75 per cent had completed primary school, 40 per cent had reached secondary school and 25 pr cent were in technical school or teacher training college. All this may be a factor in the relatively easier promotion in Cieneguilla.

Land Tenure and Agricultural Techniques

The kind of tenure in both Cieneguilla and Carbajal is small private holdings. There are three kinds of land. The first is the plot or backyard that almost all households have, of 0.25 to 0.5 of a hectare. Another kind is the labour land, more extensive, from 2 to 15 or 20 hectares, and these are usually on the outskirts of the village. About 10 per cent of the population did not have this kind of land. The majority had between 0.5 and 3 hectares, and in Carbajal the average plots were slightly larger than in Cieneguilla. A third kind of land is the hilly mountainous land, normally used as pasture. Only a few people, mainly in Carbajal, owned this kind of land, in 60 or 70 hectare plots. Detailed observation of holding size was impossible because of technical difficulties in the municipal files to which we had access, and also because people were suspicious of our insistence as there had been demands for land distribution made to the Agrarian Reform Ministry.

It seems that landownership is not an important factor in explaining differences between the two villages. In Cieneguilla, for example, the people who joined organized groups did not seem to differ from the majority in the amount of land they owned.

The people of Cieneguilla did enjoy superiority of agricultural techniques; 85 per cent of them use fertilizers and 54 per cent use insecticides while in Carbajal only 20 per cent use either, though it must be remembered that Cieneguilla has more wet land.

Attitudes to Collective Work

We asked in the questionnaire whether working land collectively or individually was thought better; 25 per cent in Cieneguilla (all from either the pig farm or the savings collective) said collectively, but added that they saw difficulties in this kind of work. Though this group was not a majority, at least it was clear that the idea of working collectively was known and favoured by some. After all, before the programme started, Don Pancho had collected a group of 78 who wanted to co-operate in drilling a well. But in Carbajal no one answered the questionnaire by choosing collective work, giving such reasons as: 'in a society it is difficult for everyone to agree; we do not all have the same enthusiasm', and 'we are already used to working on our own'.

This all seems to indicate that there were better conditions in Cieneguilla for the kind of co-operative or solidarity groups proposed by the programme.

A Comparison of Present Situations

In Cieneguilla more than 80 per cent answered that their present situation was better or equal to previous years whereas in Carbajal only 50 per cent felt things were better now, and 40 per cent answered that conditions had worsened, mainly because of the cost of living. Of course in Cieneguilla running water and electricity had recently been installed.

In both villages it was considered that young people and children now live in better conditions than when the respondents were young.

The opinions of Cieneguilla seem more positive, but it may be that this is the effect of the programme because they may now be influenced by the installation of public services unconnected with the programme, and, as yet, not enjoyed by Carbajal.

Expressed Needs of the Village

We asked which were the three most important needs of the community. Answers in Cieneguilla were: jobs, a health centre, and the completion of the public square. In Carbajal they were: water, electricity and jobs. The lack of water is a key to understanding the position of the people in Carbajal. On several occasions they commented to the promoters that first they should solve that problem and then other projects could be thought about. In Cieneguilla the lack of jobs is now seen as the most important problem, though Don Pancho thinks there is a positive need for organization.

Confidence in the Actions of the Government

Attitudes toward government are different in the two villages. More than half of those questioned in Carbajal stated that the government never fulfilled its promises, a view no doubt reinforced by the fact that many of their requests have been made to visiting political candidates. The people of Cieneguilla seem less pessimistic about government. The demand for a school building was their first experience of local politics, and this had a successful outcome. Also they are currently receiving services from various government agencies.

Don Pancho says that in the first meetings they mistrusted the promoters, but that after some weeks they accepted their sincerity. Aurelio — the promoter of Carbajal — describes the population as exacting and easily offended. If the promoters failed to turn up on the appointed date, or arrived late, people were dissatisfied and withdrew from meetings.

Conflicts within the Community and with Other Communities

The questionnaire seems to reveal more internal and external conflict in Cieneguilla than in Carbajal. This may, however, be misleading.

In Cieneguilla the internal tensions arose from the building of the school. Some members of the PAN (National Action Party, a conservative group) tried to insist that the cost of the building should be entirely borne by the government without local co-operation. There were some who never did join the scheme, and this destroyed the unity of the village. Lesser conflicts over land boundaries have also occurred but mainly within families.

Cieneguilla has had conflicts with Tierra Blanca, due to their competitive positions. As described earlier, at one point this situation helped the original promoter — Ricardo — to gain people's support, because he also had certain conflicts with the municipal president of Tierra Blanca.

People at Carbajal initially said there were no internal or external conflicts, but further conversation changed this first impression. The fact is that they have a violent reputation in the area. As mentioned above, in the past three years a young man from Carbajal has shot several people and is still free, but in hiding. The police do not try to arrest him because he can count on the armed support of his closest relatives.

During several of the interviews outside homes, people gathered to listen, which made people cautious about what they said. Twice people came to look for us afterwards to make comments or to add information they could not give with others present. In this way we learnt there had recently been robberies and conflicts over and above the tensions produced during the building of the school and the dam.

For years Carbajal has had the reputation of being a closed place. Kin-groups are important for everything, and people from outside are not accepted. Unlike other villages in which young girls were allowed to take part in courses at San Luis de la Paz during the week, the girls from Carbajal were never given permission to leave. Although it took the promotion team a few months to detect these problems, it may well have deterred them later from being too persistent in their promotion.

Elements of the Programme

We shall start by analysing the work of the promoters, and the differences in their performance and professional training.

Promoters' Activities

Everything seems to indicate that the promoting team in Cieneguilla performed better. They visited the village twice a week and were relatively punctual, whilst the Carbajal team went only once a week, and sometimes missed going either because of transport problems or promoters' meetings at San Luis de la Paz.

When there was a change of promoters, Carbajal experienced a disruptive gap, whilst in Cieneguilla there was a month's overlap, with the two promoters working together, and the new man being introduced to key people and groups.

Another aspect worth pointing out in Carbajal is that, once the people showed no interest in activities other than enlarging the dam, the two promoters spent most of their time merely talking to people. The only established activities were the classes for the girls. The promoters seemed to have no other plan or activity to suggest in Carbajal.

The Choice of Objectives

In Cieneguilla, unlike Carbajal, a good deal of emphasis was placed on economic activity, with some notion of self-help. In Carbajal the work with the girls was the main project and this was very much a matter of supplying services rather than stimulating independent activity.

A Clear Conception of Needs

It is clear the Carbajal promoters did not even grasp the limitations and needs of the village. In the second month of work, they drew up a list of projects to be done, which included 'the adaptation of the existing dam, in order to irrigate lower cultivable lands' and 'the building of a water deposit in the school'.[1] Neither of these projects corresponded to reality. The capacity of the dam is not sufficient even to provide domestic water, so irrigation was out of the question, and a water deposit in the school could not solve the need for drinking water for the whole community.

Promoters' Preparation

The educational background of the promoters is known to be varied. The first one in Carbajal had completed preparatory school (three years more than secondary) and the second only primary school. Cieneguilla had the advantage since one promoter had preparatory school and the second postgraduate studies. It is true that the girls who worked in Carbajal had more education then their counterparts in Cieneguilla, but this did not mean very much since the girl promoters mostly came from a social work school for rural promoters. This sounds impressive and generated expectations, but was in fact disappointing because it was essentially an assistance approach.

Adaptation of Projects to Needs

The Cieneguilla promoters managed to use the set of possible actions the programme offered to address the specific conditions of Cieneguilla, foremost among which was the need for extra water for several uses. And even though the limited economic resources of the programme put the irrigation dam the people saw as the first priority outside the scope of the programme (it required very specialized and detailed studies from the Ministry of Hydraulic Resources), nevertheless the promoters got involved in helping the demand to be expressed, and were instrumental in having some action taken.

Of course, the promoters also found more receptive conditions in Cieneguilla, with its particular attitudes and organizational forms. It is necessary therefore to look at solidarity as a special factor in explaining programme success.

Assumptions on Existing Solidarity

How far did the programme assume the existence of community solidarity, and that it, rather than self-interest, could be relied on to further community development objectives?

The basic programme document said:

the atomization of individual effort is considered a basic problem to be solved. Thus it is necessary to integrate and unify these individual efforts in a collective force in order to attain common objectives.[2]

So the programme sought from the start deliberately to promote solidarity and assumed Mexican peasants to be individualistic. And solidarity in the rhetoric of the programme did refer to the community — the solidarity of a whole territorial unit.

At the outset, the promoters certainly had little knowledge of the level of existing solidarity in the two villages. They knew that Cieneguilla formed part of a Congregation, and had indigenous origins, which might have suggested a degree of internal cohesion. But Carbajal was unknown when the programme started; the problems of aggression and violence became apparent only with time.

The general degree of community solidarity might be relevant to some aspects of the promoter's job (for example, public works were to be undertaken by the whole community) and certainly could affect the atmosphere in which he worked, as the description of the two villages bears out. But, as pointed out above, when it came to the substance of his job, it was less relevant since most of the projects were designed to work through small groups or co-operatives which might well either cause division in the community at large or flourish where division already existed. So the relevance of solidarity, and of solidarity at various levels, is a matter for investigation. We must also ask whether it is solidarity itself which is the explanatory variable, or whether we should seek further for the conditions which promote solidarity.

Incidence of Solidarity and Collective Action in the Programme

The question is how far did the degree and type of solidarity affect the success of the programme? There is certainly more evidence for solidarity at the level of the community in Cieneguilla than in Carbajal. In Cieneguilla it was not only public works which called forth widely based combinations of efforts, but various kinds of productive activity.

It may be useful here to list the needs expressed and actions undertaken in each community so as to highlight the different cases of combined activity. The data on needs derive from the questionnaire and appear in the order of priority people gave them.

Cieneguilla

Expressed need	Actions
1. Employment	15 associates started a pig farm co-operative
	a committee made a formal request to set up a palm hat factory, and so to provide work for 12 young men
	100 associates are initiating a fund to improve the facilities of the thermal water springs, (including some from neighbouring communities)

2. Health centre	a committee was formed and made a formal request for the centre
	they collected a communal fee, and bought a plot where the centre could be built
3. Laying out of the public square	the village built all the cement paths and arranged the green spaces
	all the villages belonging to the Congregation contributed
4. Technical secondary school	a committee was set up and formally requested the school
	some individuals donated the land for the installation of the school
	a group of all the interested parents of students are preparing the land by means of *faenas*
5. Water for irrigation	78 interested people formed a group and formally requested the drilling of a well
	they made explorations by themselves, with a geologist, and also with a local water diviner
6. A bridge	we had no information about any action
7. Work on the church	three years ago the whole Congregation co-operated to build the floor of the exterior esplanade
	they are about to initiate the decoration of the roof and ceiling of the church
8. Instruction in using communal sewing machines	we had no information about any action
9. Housing improvement	the associates of the pig farm co-operative decided to undertake this after the farm building was completed but they have not started

In addition to meeting most of these expressed needs, the community undertook several other activities:

1. Running water	they formed a committee and formally requested the service
	they co-operated through *faenas* to dig the trenches for the pipe installations
2. Electricity	a committee formally requested the service
	all heads of household are now paying their co-operation fee
3. Raising agricultural productivity	the Savings Co-operative bought 1,280 dollars' worth of fertilizer, and sold it at cost price to everybody interested, even if not members of the co-operative
	the pig farm has lent their fine breed male pigs to anyone in the village interested in improving the breed of the ordinary pigs, even to non-members of the co-operative
4. Nutrition	18 people formed a group for communal bee-keeping
	15 families formed a group for rabbit-keeping, with individually owned female rabbits and a male
5. Cash income	50 families are in the Saving and Loans Co-operative

Some of the above activities refer to combined action at the level of the Congregation, others to the village of Cieneguilla and others to the level of organized groups within the village. The activities also vary, from those where co-operation could be just one way of serving individual interest — as with the pig farm or the bee-keeping — to those where there seemed to be a genuine expression of community solidarity, as with the work on the church and square.

It was difficult to know whether all the activities really were voluntary. For example, in communal tasks, the tradition of giving a day's work (*faena*) is of feudal origin, and it is not easy to be sure they are not now coercive. However, today's authorities do not have the strong powers they used to have. For example, it is agreed that if somebody is unwilling or unable to give his *faena*, he has to pay its equivalent. But even this is not very strictly observed; working outside the village exonerates one. Such instances suggest that co-operative action in Cieneguilla is comparatively freely engaged in.

Let us now consider *Carbajal*.

Expressed need	Actions
1. Water for irrigation	the village has a committee which has informally requested the building of a large dam
2. Drinking water	it is the same committee that is in charge of the water for irrigation
	the community enlarged the existing dam, through co-operative work and also by means of donations
	the majority of the people rejected the continuation of the privilege of individual use of water, and they have even discussed this point with federal agencies
3. Electricity	there is a committee, which formally requested the service
4. Employment	it is expected that the irrigation dam will provide more work on the cultivable land
5. Schools	there is a permanent school parents' association
	we had no information about any other action
6. Raising of (low) incomes	we had no information about any action in this area
7. Improved nutrition	we had no information about any action in this area

8. Increased unity

if this opinion relates to the problem of the dam, it could best be considered an act of solidarity of the majority against the privilege of an individual

if it is considered as referring to the general situation of the village, we saw no attempts at a solution

There were other activities undertaken by people of the village, which were not listed by them as expressed needs:

1. School classroom

there is a permanent committee, and a formal request to enlarge the school

the village enlarged the school with two more classrooms, through cash co-operation

2. Girls' group

around 25 girls formed a group

they had weekly meetings to take courses on cooking, sewing and nursing

3. Chapel bell tower

a small committee is collecting donations and distributing work

they have brought in stone and sand to start the building of the small bell tower.

We found sometimes that the same committees were carrying out more than one of the activities listed above. During the fieldwork we found that many people did not know who were on such committees, and they were also not informed about the progress of their petitions to the official agencies.

We can also observe that some of the villagers' expressed needs could have been met by projects offered in the programme; it seems it was the necessity of operating in groups or co-operatives which made them unacceptable. On the other hand, they mentioned that in drought years they allowed other villages to take from their dam, and this seems to be an example of solidarity with neighbouring communities faced with a need they feel strongly.

So it is the clear reluctance of people in Carbajal to forge links outside the individual or family economic unit which is its distinctive characteristic and the most important for explaining the programme's comparative lack of success. This is also distinct from the issue of community solidarity. Indeed atomization may sometimes be compatible with expressions of community solidarity; for example, the voicing of antagonism towards other communities, or willingness to further the prestige of the community (as with Carbajal's bell tower). There are then two dimensions; Carbajal was certainly low on community solidarity, but, more than this, it was so atomized that there was little potential for association between families into the kind of small groups the programme demanded.

Solidarity as an Objective and a Result of the Programme

How far was it an objective of the programme to strengthen the sense of community solidarity? The basic programme document gives as one of its objectives:

> to reinforce the peasant's existing organizations and institutions, and to promote the creation of new ones in legal accordance with those already in existence.[3]

Of course, 'peasant solidarity' could be interpreted to mean class or sectional solidarity, but in context, it is clearly the community which is referred to.

And why was it an objective? As a means to more effective change in other spheres? Or because fraternity and solidarity are seen as desirable ends in themselves? There seemed to be confusion about this, both in the programme and the promoting teams.

If solidarity is taken to be a feeling or an atitude, it is difficult to determine whether there was significant change, since the data on the two villages before the programme started is impressionistic only. But if we read solidarity from observable action, then we can say that in Cieneguilla there was a strengthening of group solidarity in particular. The number of organizations trying to meet the village's needs is greater than before the programme. We cannot say the same about Carbajal.

The conditions for, or even symptoms of, group solidarity were certainly evident in Cieneguilla, with its high degree of organization, participation of the people in decision-making processes (such as the election of the municipal delegate in Cieneguilla and the sub-delegates in the other villages), and the tradition of co-operation in communal works. But perhaps the root explanation is the higher degree of social and economic equality in Cieneguilla. Its more organized, participative and egalitarian structure could accept more easily the organizational models proposed by the programme, such as the co-operative or solidarity groups. And the fact that Cieneguilla was a 'one leader village' was certainly an important factor. Don Pancho has the personal contacts and political skill which could secure concrete results.

Carbajal, by contrast had a higher degree of social and economic differentiation — land distribution was more unequal than in Cieneguilla, and there were more marked occupational and income distinctions, especially as some of the villagers were middlemen in the knitting industry. But there was no tradition of combination outside the family unit, which made co-operation unacceptable even in the pursuit of individual economic interest, while the lack of general organization or of a dominating leader meant that expressions of community solidarity were limited and sporadic. Even the factionalism which appeared from time to time was not sufficiently solid to provide a base for group organization. So the village had neither the participatory organization of economic equals, nor the solid divisions which may arise from inequality.

The Programme as a Whole

We have dealt in the two previous sections with explanation at the village level and we would like at this point to consider the programme as a whole.

On the economic front the programme produced these results:

a net transfer of resources to the villages through credit and public services, although with great variation between villages;

diversification of livestock production, again affecting some communities more than others;

increases in local production, through diversification. In Cieneguilla, for instance, the value of the pig farm's annual production is three times that of agriculture's;

whether *income* has been increased is not yet clear. The pig farm, for example, is not yet breaking even, even disregarding capital repayments;

equal distribution of project benefits is assumed to be achieved through
the cooperatives;

creation of new jobs, but this has been very limited in proportion to the
number of groups and participants;

on the other hand, the programme has done almost nothing to modify
mechanisms of exploitation in two of the main activities of the
zone: the knitting industry and migrant wage labour;

neither did the programme affect exploitation or productivity in agriculture, which is also an important source of livelihood in the area;

the livestock projects were in general capital intensive, so their capacity
to spread or grow would be limited.

In the political field, the results could be summarized as:

creation of economic groups which will have political significance;

limited participation of peasants in the administration of the programme, brought to an end when the promoters tried to establish
the 'Regional Peasants Council';

the provoking of some discussion among peasants about national and
peasant politics;

a reinforcing of local modes of decision-making through the building of
public services.

In the area of education:

solidarity was promoted, but only within the groups that were set up;

female participation was increased through the work of health and rural
kindergarten promoters;

school attendance was sometimes increased because of the programme,
but often the communities had already demanded that the Ministry
of Education provide school rooms and teachers.

Regarding changes in consumption:

in those villages where there were active health promoters, nutrition
and health were improved;

savings groups, where they operated, served to reduce the cost of
money loans:

several public services were installed, either through the programme
directly or by other agencies with support and help from the programme.

The programme also had its effects on the promoting teams, leading to:

the writing of two documents, one on the role of peasants in the
Mexican economy, and the second a proposal for a vast plan of
action. Both were reproduced in mimeographed form;[4]
follow-up meetings with other promotion teams so that experience
could be discussed and exchanged.

Finally, is there some overall measure of efficiency which can be set
against the total cost of the programme — $240,000 including salaries
and operational costs? One possibility is to take the ratio of total cost
to total credit obtained for the programme's clients, which in this case
was $160,000, or two thirds of total cost. The index of 1.5 compares
unfavourably with other Mexican development programmes, such as
some of the service centres of the Foundation for Rural Development
(FMD) which have indices from 0.05 to 0.10. On this criterion, their
efficiency is 15 to 30 times greater.

However, there are other points to be made in defence of this programme in comparison with FMD. The promotion team insisted that
their approach was different; unlike FMD they did not try to establish
capitalist enterprises, which would favour those already in control of
resources. Of course the 'progressive farmers' promoted by FMD were
eager to accept innovations. They also said FMD could rely on contacts
with easy credit, while they had to fight even for approval of their
projects. They also said the credit comparison was not valid because at
the time they left the programme, there were too many credit applications pending to the total was underrepresented. Nevertheless, perhaps
the two programmes do have something to learn from one another.

In summary we may say that:

there was no attack on entrenched patterns or institutions such as
existing agricultural technique, or the structure of local industry;
the number of new jobs created, and productive activities introduced,
was small, and limited to a group of people who chose to be
interested;
ideological and organizational change was also limited;
it is hard to see whether these limited changes will have any future
effects.

We shall now suggest some possible reasons for these limitations.

Political Limitations

The programme lacked both time and support. In its own terms, it did not allow sufficient time for any real organizational groundwork with the groups. And then by 1975 the programme's support from above — it was vertically dependent on the government — had almost completely disappeared. Differences of opinion with the INPI (Institute for Protection of Infancy, which sponsored the programme) were also a sign of the growing gap between it and the state authorities. In its last three months it could hardly function.

It would have been possible to devise tactics which served the political and ideological interests of both government and promoters, but it seems that neither was clear about their aims. When in the course of the programme, the promoting team reached a clearer position and started to set up the Regional Peasants Council, the government reacted adversely and for this and other reasons decided to withdraw the promoting team.

The new organizational structure proposed by the team — of Local and Regional Peasants Councils — was regarded with suspicion in political circles. In any case the programme attempted to be relatively autonomous in carrying out activities such as public works which were also undertaken by other agencies, and so it encountered opposition from its competitors and rivals.

Planning Process

Despite minor modifications over time, the programme's objectives were never either radical or comprehensive. The three most important economic activities of the zone were not substantially affected and regional strategy seems to be missing from the beginning, with villages being treated in isolation. Later there was an attempt to tackle the knitting situation, but with little result.

Further the most important economic modules promoted — pigs and poultry (which absorbed 60 per cent of the credit) — did not correspond to the criteria of low capital intensity and high labour requirements, so they were costly and did not provide many jobs. They were also risky from the market point of view. The livestock diversification projects, such as rabbits and beehives, assumed a marketable surplus would be produced in the second stage, but even so there would not be much job creation. However, perhaps for peasants with subsistence plots it is more appropriate to think in terms of work that can be shared, rather than of discrete jobs.

The pig farm in Cieneguilla illustrates this point. Considered as full-time employment, there would be jobs for only 4 of the 15 associates; but at present, if each works one or two days a week in the farm, it is sufficient for none to have to leave the village. Given this approach, the farm provides a job for the 15 associates.

It was decided at the beginning that evaluation would be a part of the programme. Though the promoting team made critical revisions of their work during their monthly meetings, this was overtaken by the problems with the state authorities, and internal rifts between promoters. There was one formal evaluation, undertaken by an external research institute; IMES (Mexican Institute of Social Studies) but no resources for any others.

Promotional Strategy

The programme's main instrument was the promoting team which was assigned in pairs (one woman and one man); it was expected that the girl promoters's activities would serve as the key to gaining the confidence of the village. However, although confidence had been developed in most villages after the first weeks, girl promoters continued the same kind of activities thereafter. They did not get beyond an 'improving' approach and lacked the perspective or vision to understand that economic activities and organization of such groups were basic. The men were not exempt from this limitation either.

A considerable amount of the budget was invested in these promoters, as well as the time and energy of the rest of the team.

According to the opinion of three of its more important members, the limited results of the programme could be explained principally by the lack of a good promotional team. The 'improvement' approach was common, but, on the other hand, there were radical promoters who were most interested in theoretical criticism and spent less time on field action of any kind. Of course, fieldwork may well attract woolly idealists or those with psychological problems, and the programme had to cope with such cases too. The principal officials of the programme themselves thought that the team as a whole could not be considered to be good promoters, despite spending one week a month on training.

In terms of substance, the programme offered a list of possible actions to be carried out, but in fact only a few could depend on reliable material support. For many others, the projects depended on the budgets and programmes of other agencies or on credit to be obtained from the Rural Credit Bank. The obvious problems of co-ordination meant that many such projects could not be carried out.

Under these circumstances, the global nature of the programme (attacking the whole variety of projects the people were interested in) seemed overambitious. The important projects are those related to economic production, which have the potential of increasing income and redistributing wealth, which in turn may have political and organizational effects. Public works could well be done by other agencies.

Notes

1. INPI – PRODECOR, 'Segundo Reporte Mensual de Activades' (Mayo, 1974).
2. 'Programa del Gobierno del Estado de Guanajuato' (1974).
3. 'Programa del Gobierno del Estado de Guanajuato' (1974).
4. Trueba Jose, and others, *op. cit.*

8 LESSONS TO BE LEARNED

We must relate the lessons to be learned to two levels. We deal first with the national level — the national development plan, in which community development programmes have a specific role to play.

The second level refers to community development programmes themselves. The subsequent three sections will present recommendations on the basic conditions for their operation, the planning process and promotional strategy.

National Structure

There are Mexican and Latin-American scholars who feel that our countries cannot develop satisfactorily within the capitalist system. This of course implies structural change. We cannot think of profound improvements for the peasants and urban marginalized classes without eliminating capitalism, or at least, reducing its effects.

So the first lesson is: community development programmes must recognize the limitations of the national socioeconomic system, and not treat communities as isolated entities. There are no longer any pure subsistence villages. And if the links with the national economy are exploitative, they must be recognized as such, and taken into account.

The Location of Community Development Programmes

However, our economic and political structure is not completely inflexible. Some improvement in productivity and income distribution can be achieved within the limits of the whole system by rationalizing resource use and cutting down corruption. In the political field, there is also a margin for independent action. Information can be channelled and organization increased. It is possible to press demands for social services, and to increase the negotiating power of the peasants for a better distribution of the benefits of growth. Community development programmes would then have a double purpose:

to procure resources to improve the living conditions of the peasants and poor; and

to recognize the need for structural transformation and to further this by organizing and mobilizing the peasants to defend their interests.

A programme with these aims would require strong political support and a promoting team with a promotional strategy firmly based on economic activities.

Basic Conditions for Operation

The conclusion we derive from the above observations is that 'community development plans' should continue, but with a different approach, i.e. according to a promotional strategy in which priority is given to economic production, and its corresponding social, organizational and educational components. In practice, community development programmes usually have more limited aims and do not attempt structural transformation. Here we offer some specific recommendations for the operation of such programmes.

Political Support

The projects to be initiated must have identifiable objectives, for which political support can be found. Such objectives should include:

an increase in productivity and production;
an increase in income;
a more egalitarian income distribution;
the extension of programme services to the majority of peasants within the area;
improving the economic organization of peasants at local and regional level;
integrating productive organizations, either horizontally or vertically;
reducing unemployment;
lowering prices of basic consumer goods;
increasing local savings and investment.

The attainment of these objectives should be sought with the maximum participation and control of the peasants.

Because of the competitive relationships that exist between official agencies working in rural areas, the competent political authority should precisely define the competence of each agency and attempt to establish mechanisms for co-operation. This should reduce the degree of obstruction encountered.

Minimum Duration of the Programmes

Whether they be regional or nationwide, it is necessary to assure a basic time for the execution of the promotional work. A minimum of three and a maximum of five years appears to be a realistic figure for Mexico. A shorter time would not allow for consolidation and a longer period might convert the relevant zone to a state of permanent dependence.

Economic Support for Operations

Continuity of financial supplies is often a problem for the programmes. This can affect the payment of the promoters, and the delivery of materials and equipment required for projects. Because of the existing mistrust towards government, it is necessary to be strictly punctual with the supply of funds.

Financial Support for Projects

The demand for credit that will be stimulated by promotion of projects can be estimated from past experience, and must be used in negotiating with the Rural Credit Bank funds for financing specified activities. If sufficient funds do not exist, it is better to limit the number of projects than to raise peasants' expectations and face them with bureaucratic procedures that may end in a blank wall. The total credit needed should be approximately five times the operating costs of the programme (salaries and current expenses).

It is also necessary that, for these programmes, the bank ease application procedures, relax credit conditions and speed up the whole process of approval.

One idea tried and found useful in the programme studied was that of a revolving fund. This could operate as a 'bridging credit' for those groups waiting for bank credit already applied for. The fund could also give small credits to peasants who do not satisfy bank requirements but whose projects are economically feasible. The recommended amount available to this revolving fund would be about twice the operating costs.

These are conditions which must be met before a programme starts, if performance in the field is to be satisfactory.

Planning Process

Below, we present a set of recommendations concerning the planning process for community development programmes.

Regional Focus

First, the country must be divided into operational regions. At present several proposals for such divisions exist, drawn up either by planners or official agencies. However, the important point is not the existence of regional divisions, but the application of regional programmes.

There is a diversity of ecological conditions which must be recognized. And planning on a regional level will, in the end, minimize the cost of the programme and the size of its bureaucratic apparatus. Finally, regional plans are attractive because they allow a degree of autonomy within the national guidelines.

Preparation of Regional Studies and Plans

Each regional programme should begin with technical studies undertaken by an interdisciplinary group of specialists to specify regional conditions, resources and requirements, and suggest appropriate economic projects. The next step would be to analyse the feasibility of each project from the point of view of resources, financing and profitability. Credit requirements should then be estimated, and the promotional stage not started until credit is guaranteed.

Specific Recommendations

Some specific points to be taken into account are the following:

each region must receive individual treatment, geared to local potential;
the programmes must very clearly specify — for operative and evaluation purposes — their objectives, criteria and activities;
the projects must focus more on present productive activities;
in addition to production groups, others such as consumer or savings co-operatives, must be formed;
regional production should be linked with regional consumption, reducing to a minimum dependence on external market mechanisms that extract surplus;
the economic modules proposed should be of most cost, and generate a sizeable number of jobs;
the economic modules should not be vulnerable to variations in the market, and they must respond to basic regional or national consumption needs;
a limited range of actions should be proposed for each region so that support mechanisms and technical assistance can be specialized;
each economic module should be accompanied by an instruction pamphlet similar to those employed in the programme studied;

a permanent evaluation system must be designed and operated throughout the programme. If funds are not available for carrying out evaluation studies, at least there should be studies by institutions such as universities, which may be useful both to the programme and to the institutions.

Promotional Strategy

Once the regional plan is formulated, promotional actions can be started. The outlining of stages is essential.

Formation of the Promotion Team

We propose the team should not be made up of professional promoters, but of people with a high level of formal education and preferably professional studies. They should be young university graduates or experienced amateur promoters. Ideological compatibility with the approach of the programme is also required. This means they should clearly understand the problems of the country and the peasantry, and think in terms of structural change and not only in terms of marginal improvements.

The kind of seminars held to train the promoters in the Guanajuato programme seem adequate: one weekend of seminars every month. Before fieldwork starts a longer preparation is necessary.

Contact with the Communities

The promotional work should be carried out by pairs of promoters, not necessarily a man and a woman. As opposed to the situation of the studied programme, each pair of promoters should be in charge of 15 to 20 villages. This is necessary because of the need for greater efficiency and concentration on economic activities.

The promoters must make contact with local authorities in each village and explain to them the specific projects they are promoting. They should also take note and discuss the feasibility of other projects proposed by the villagers.

At this point a meeting or an assembly may be called for, in which the possible projects are described. It is vital to find out if the people are interested in undertaking these or other proposed activities. If petitions exist for projects related, for example, to public services, they may be submitted to the relevant official agencies, and people should be instructed in how to proceed with a formal request.

If a low level of interest exists in the village, either because of mistrust or ignorance of the activity to be carried out, the promoters should not persist beyond offering sufficient information. If there is still no interest, they should turn to other villages.

Integration of Groups

In those villages where sufficient interest exists, it is important to tailor the form of the groups set up to local patterns of solidarity and participation. These groups may then apply for credit, and start on their projects. Training must also be started to develop or improve the required skills.

Initiation of Operations

We propose two alternative ways to start the operation of productive units. The first is with the entire organization and responsibility for the scheme in the hands of peasants. From the outset, the property administration and distribution of benefits is completely in their hands.

Another pattern is for the managing role to be taken by the promoter, though with the idea of training people to take over within a limited period. The promoter should insist that his role is only temporary and he should encourage increasing participation in the decision-making, administration and work. This pattern should protect the take-off stage and make the project more likely to achieve its economic aims.

Internal Consolidation of Groups

Once the operations have started it is necessary to consolidate the groups from a social and technical point of view. This may be achieved through education of a technical, administrative and social nature. By this we mean the provision of better information about national and rural problems, alternative forms of association and their legal aspects and the need to strengthen solidarity.

The economic nature of our proposal is not intended to diminish the importance of educational or organizational activities but to suggest they be related to, and used to further, definite economic activities.

Relationships among Production Groups

We agree with the proposition that production and consumption units must be integrated to form larger societies, as is proposed in the new Mexican legislation.[1] This integration may follow the logic of products or geographical zones. Larger associative forms may allow a better analysis of market mechanisms and the ways peasants can defend their interests. Integration would also allow increases of scale and complexity in production units such as pasteurizing or meat-packing plants.

Withdrawal of Promoters

This should be the last stage, when the groups have consolidated their productive and administrative activities, and strengthened their internal relations.

As was proposed by the programme we studied, it is advisable to establish a centre for technical assistance and educational purposes. This would be funded by small contributions from the profits of each group. A solidarity fund must also be established against crises groups may suffer, or to sponsor the promotion of new groups.

A final moment should arrive in which the promoters leave the zone. This would mean the achievement of the basic objectives of the programme.

We have listed what we considered to be the most important 'lessons to be learned', hoping they may be of use to people interested in this kind of programme. We accept the limitations of our study, having only arrived at a modest level of interpretation of the complex reality. More penetrating and exhaustive studies are still needed to shed light on some of the issues we have dealt with.

Note

1. Diario Official, *Ley de Sociedades de Solidaridad Social* (Congreso de la Unión, Mexico, 1976). The reference is to Social Solidarity Societies, which allow production groups to affiliate to regional and national federations and benefit from a solidarity fund to which all members contribute.

APPENDIX: RESEARCH AGREEMENT

(The following document was the outcome of the initial planning meeting for the research which was held in Seoul, 26-30 April 1976. All the researchers took part in the meeting with the exception of Dr Mushi who was unfortunately prevented from attending, but had provided a written prospectus for the planning meeting.)

1. The research shall consist of comparative case studies of community development programmes in a small number of villages chosen to highlight features which contribute to the success or failure of such programmes.
2. To make the case studies as intensive as possible, the sample of villages should not be more than six; four might be better, and for the detailed analysis of the process of implementation of the CDP it may be advisable to concentrate on two.
3. No attempt will be made to make the sample of villages representative of the country as a whole.
4. The sample shall consist of 1, 2 or 3 matched pairs of villages, each pair being similar in several basic physical characteristics, but differing in the extent to which the CDP appears to have effected changes in the directions intended. The characteristics for which each pair is to be matched are:
     size
     resource endowments
     distance from towns or main roads.

In size, all villages should be chosen from the 50-300 household range, and in location should be neither suburban satellites of a large town nor exceptionally remote. In choosing successful villages, the obvious showpiece village, constantly being shown off as an example of success, should be avoided. The ideal would be two pairs, each pair drawn from the same administrative unit and subjected to similar administrative approaches. The within-pairs comparison might then concentrate on differential community response, the between-pairs comparison on differences in programme administration.

5. A village for this purpose shall be the smallest unit with a formal

structure for collective action in the context of the CDP — the natural village or small agglomerations of 2 or 3 natural villages.

6. It is worth spending a good deal of time reconnoitring possible villages before deciding on the sample both because the choice will determine the chances of learning something useful from the study, and because the knowledge so gained of the general shape of the programme will prove useful in itself.

7. The proposed plan of each final country report — which also defines the substantive content of the study — is as follows:

Part I. The Top-down View

1. The national setting

Basic information about the country, its level of socioeconomic development and overall development strategy, with special reference to the place of agricultural development in that strategy. Some major points to be covered are:

Proportion of the population engaged in agriculture
Agriculture's contribution to GNP
Relative rates of growth of agricultural and industrial sectors
Relative consumption levels in urban and rural areas
Direction of net resource flows between industry and agriculture
Man/land ratio, general pattern of land distribution, the employment problem in rural areas.

2. Origins and general purposes of the Community Development Programme (hereafter CDP)

A historical account, putting the CDP into its setting as outlined in previous chapter. The main phases through which it has gone: who initiated each, for what reasons; how far generally considered a success or otherwise.

3. The specific objectives of the particular phase/particular regional manifestation of the CDP to be studied. The following is a check-list of objectives frequently embodied in CDPs which might be useful in drafting this chapter:

External

a. Economic transfer
(a) Transfer some of the proceeds of industrialization to rural areas or

(b) Self-sufficient rural development

or

(c) Sufficient rural growth to transfer surplus to industry

b. Political links

Not stressed

To develop national consciousness generally

To evoke commitment to certain national objectives

To evoke support for current regime

Internal

c. Economic change

Primarily agricultural development or

Diversification

Concerned predominantly with aggregate production or

Concerned with distribution of benefits

d. Political change

Evolving leadership which will promote economic and social change

Ensuring stability and dominance of leaders loyal to centre

Maximizing participation and diffusion of political skills

e. Cultural/educational change

Primarily, transmission to village of 'modern' values or

Primarily, development, preservation of indigenous, 'national' culture

f. Social relational change

Emphasis on:

Quality of family life

Quality of community life

Individual dignity/equality/freedom from traditional constraints

g. Consumption change

Emphasis on:

Better health

Nutrition

Elimination of wasteful/immoral expenditure

Family planning

Is an increase desired, or not, in communally provided consumption?

In addition to saying whether the above objectives (a) to (g) appear as declared objectives or not, please also consider:

What weighting was given to the different objectives

Whether there was any clear strategy for pursuing different objectives in a clear sequence.

Whether the weighting of objectives changed over time in the course of the campaign.

What basic strategy (persuasion, animation, offer of financial incentives, etc.) was adopted for implementing the campaign and what assumptions about peasants and rural communities were implicit in that choice of strategy.

4. The instrumentalities of the CDP as planned with reference to the region(s) of the case studies. This should cover:

The administrative structure:

(a) the special administrative structure for the campaign, including recruitment and training plans, and covering also the non-official village leaders, etc.

(b) the routine administration structure and how it was to be mobilized and linked with the special structure.

(c) The control hierarchy, reporting systems, degree of delegation of authority and decentralization of function of both the above.

The financial resources made available.

Part II. The Bottom-up View

5. The villages

Outline of basic information concerning the major features of the sample villages:

Household numbers and household size

Distribution of holdings by size: type of agriculture, possession of equipment, etc.

Facilities such as electricity, water, etc.

Literacy levels and school enrolments

Basic structural features — caste, class, factional divisions, etc.

Physical settlement pattern (maps would be helpful)

6. The programme and its execution

A selective chronological narrative of what happened in the village; what attempts were made to bring about change and what was their outcome. The various projects/ elements of the campaign: who initiated them, how decisions were taken, what organization was created, what benefits or disbenefits derived by whom. A compositive account derived from free interviews with officials, village leaders and other villagers, taking off from documents (e.g. project account books) wherever these available. Special attention to be paid to:

How officials interpreted their roles

The officials' and the villagers' perceptions of CDP activities and possible discrepancies between them

In the analysis of inputs, the relative contributions of the official structure and the villagers

The division of benefits between different strata, groups of villagers

The decision-making process: balance between local initiative and central direction

The way this account is presented will inevitably to some extent prejudge the analysis in Chapter 8 (the description is bound to suggest: this project ended up in a mess because so-and-so failed to do such-and-such). This is inevitable, but don't labour the explanation at this point; try to make it as dry and factual as possible.

7. Overall evaluation of the programme's effects

An accounting exercise, showing the balance of inputs and outputs for physical projects and trying to estimate the efficacy of attempts to change behaviour, social relations, etc.

For physical projects, give distribution of input between government and villages, and don't forget, also, administrative overhead costs; please show their (especially officials' salaries) relation to total costs.

For some items — behaviour/consciousness change, income change, etc. — results of house-to-house surveys may be used, but don't forget that, e.g., answers to questions about attitudes to birth control are less convincing than changes in the birth rate. Try to concentrate on questions which are as concrete as possible.

Throughout the distinction should be borne in mind between changes which involve only changes in individual household action/ living patterns, and those which involve co-operative/collective action/ collective property/collective consumption.

The check list in Chapter 3 will be useful here.

In general this chapter will take up only those items of the check list relevant to the particular local campaign, except that everyone should give whatever information is possible and meaningful on the following even if they were not a concern of the CDP.

438 *Appendix: Research Agreement*

a. Changes in income levels and distribution (in so far as concrete reliable indicators — consumption levels, cash income, possession of household/agricultural equipment, etc. — are available)
b. Changes in school attendance
c. Changes in agricultural production levels and patterns, and major changes in marketing problems

A section should also be included on change — developmental change — which has taken place in the time period studied but which cannot plausibly be explained as a consequence of the CDP.

8. Explanation

Why did the campaign have different outcomes in different villages? A check list of the sort of explanatory factors which one might look for runs as follows:

(i) the nature of the campaign's objectives (their concreteness or diffuseness, their degree of consonance with pre-existing values of the community — or sections of the community — their realism in the light of the structural economic constraints and opportunities which face the community, etc.)

(ii) the modalities of the campaign — the training or operating style of the 'animators', the national class structural framework which sets the pattern of relationships (cultural distances, etc.) between animator and community members, the level of material resources at the animator's disposal, etc.

(iii) the economic environment of the community, in particular the existence or otherwise of underutilized material or human resources which were available to be mobilized.

(iv) the political environment of the community, in particular the nature of its links to central government through party or bureaucracy.

9. Community development and the notion of community

In this chapter we take out one of the fields in which one might seek explanations of the success or failure of CDPs for special treatment. This will be a common core which we agree to explore in special detail. The sort of questions which it will be necessary to ask are:

1. i How far was a high degree of community solidarity (in the target villages) assumed to exist and relied on to facilitate the attainment of CD objectives (as opposed to reliance only on the motives of individual self-interest)?

    ii How far did the *actual* degree of community solidarity affect the success of the CDP?

2. i How far was it an objective of the CDP to strengthen the sense of community solidarity?

    ii And why? As a means to more effective change in other spheres? Or because fraternity and solidarity were seen as desirable ends in themselves?

    iii And how far were such efforts successful (if there were any)?

    iv And why? In particular how far do the variables of solidarity/ CDP success or failure correlate with characteristics of the internal political structure of communities such as: scale of participation in decision-making; degree of social equality (or institutionalization of deference); persistence or otherwise of traditional patterns of ascribed leadership; patterns of leaders' relations with officials of the external CD and routine administrations, and articulation of these patterns with internal authority structures.

For these purposes, some of the indices of community solidarity that one might look for are:

The existence or otherwise of cohesive sub-groups (caste, lineage, class, political/factional) within the community

The extent to which social interactions of community members are confined within, or cross-cut the boundaries of, the community

The way people use the word 'we' in various situations

The extent to which there is willingness to tolerate collective action which involves only a loose, not carefully and exactly calculated, equation of costs and benefits (e.g. willingness to contribute to a village school even if one doesn't have children to go to it)

The frequency of occasions on which the villages' collective interest is engaged *vis-à-vis* other villages (e.g. upstream villages versus downstream villages in a river irrigation system in a drought year) or some outside agency.

10. The lessons to be learned.

11. Appendix

Describing the process of sampling and the reasons for the particular sample chosen, the methods of research, etc. and attaching any questionnaire, etc. schedules were used.

All the above in 30,000 words, though researchers may of course wish to write a more extensive version for distribution in their own country.

INDEX

AID 85

Bangalore 15, 296
Bannikuppe 261, 281, 293, 295, 296
Betangere 284
Bidadi 29, 40, 255, 256, 292
  FSS: actions of 299-302;
      appraisals of 308-12, 325-30;
      performance 302-24
  see also under Ganakal, Seshagiri-
      halli
Bowles, Chester 251
Bwakira Chini 171-4 *passim*

Carbajal
  agriculture 379
  bell tower 418, 419
  Cieneguilla, differences from
      406-11
  collective work, attitudes to
      409-10
  community development
      programme in 382-7;
      participation in 31, 32; results
      of 387-8, 412-25 *passim*
  community feeling in 413-19
  dam 22, 380, 384, 385, 386, 417
  description of 377, 406-11 *passim*
  education in 22, 381, 386, 387,
      417, 418
  electricity 417
  geographical features 377
  government, attitudes to 410-11
  housing 380
  incomes 379, 417
  knitting industry 379-80, 421
  land distribution 378, 409
  leadership of 407-8
  location 364
  needs expressed 417-19
  nutrition 417
  population 406, 408-10
  productivity 378
  social features 21, 22
  water tank 383-4
China 147
Church World Service Organization

85
Cieneguilla
  agriculture 416
  bee-keeping 395, 397-8, 404
  Carbajal, differences from 406-11
  collective work, attitudes to
      409-10
  community action: programme
      executed in 394-403; results
      of 403-5, 412-25 *passim*
  community feeling in 413-19
  description of 289-94, 406-11
      passim
  education in 392, 393, 399, 400,
      403, 415
  electricity 405, 416
  fruit growers' group 395, 401-2
  geographical features 389
  government, attitudes to 410-11
  hat factory 403
  health services in 392, 399, 400,
      415
  housing 391-2, 397, 415
  incomes 390, 391, 416
  knitters' group 400
  knitting industry 391, 421
  land ownership 409
  leadership in 39-40, 41, 407-8
  livestock owners' group 395
  location 364
  needs expressed 414-17
  nutrition 391, 416
  pig farm 38, 396-7, 401, 403-4
  population 390, 408-10
  rabbit rearing 400-1
  Savings and Loans Cooperative
      398-9, 404-5, 416
  social features of 21
  square, rebuilding of 395, 401,
      404, 415
  well 395, 402, 405, 415
  women's group 395, 399-400
Community development
  bureaucracy and 13, 38-45
  community solidarity and 18-23
  environments, constraints of
      13-16, 36-7

441

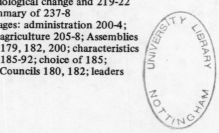